# SERMON STUDIES ON THE GOSPELS

# SERMON STUDIES ON THE GOSPELS

## (ILCW Series B)

### Ernst H. Wendland
*General Editor*

### G. Jerome Albrecht
*Manuscript Editor*

NORTHWESTERN PUBLISHING HOUSE
Milwaukee, Wisconsin

Library of Congress Card 87-61580
Northwestern Publishing House
1250 N. 113th St., P.O. Box 26975, Milwaukee, WI 53226-0975
© 1987 by Northwestern Publishing House.
Published 1987
Printed in the United States of America
ISBN 0-8100-0269-8

# CONTENTS

# PREFACE

This book adds another volume to our presentations of sermon studies on ILCW pericope texts. Previous volumes have taken up the following series:

Series C — Gospels
Series B — Old Testament Selections
Series A — Epistles

The Gospel texts from Series B (with those from Mark and John predominating) are the focus of attention in this volume.

Our contributors, who represent a cross-section of pastors and professors from the Wisconsin Evangelical Lutheran Synod, are listed in alphabetical order: Frederick S. Adrian, Michael J. Albrecht, Daniel N. Balge, Robert O. Balza, William O. Balza, James A. Bare, David J. Beckman, Allen R. Beyersdorf, Marcus R. Bode, Mark E. Braun, John M. Brenner, Dennis L. Broehm, Mark A. Cordes, Charles L. Cortright, Charles F. Degner, Steven C. Degner, Edwin C. Fredrich, Joel D. Fredrich, James A. Fricke, Mark D. Gieschen, Vilas R. Glaeske, Mark S. Grubbs, Karl R. Gurgel, Robert R. Gurgel, Thomas W. Haar, David L. Hein, James R. Huebner, Daniel W. Kelm, David P. Kolander, Roger Kovaciny, David A. Krien, Keith C. Kruck, Arnold J. Kunde, Kieth B. Kuschel, Herbert C. Kuske, Wayne A. Laitinen, H. Curtis Lyon, Gregory P. Lenz, Mark J. Lenz, Bruce A. McKenney, Thomas P. Nass, David A. Nottling, Terry B. Nuckolls, Curtis A. Peterson, Donald J. Pieper, Herbert H. Prahl, Robert Y. Rhyne, W. Keith Roehl, Glen A. Schaumberg, John H. Schmidt, Allen K. Schroeder, Joel B. Schroeder, Mark G. Schroeder, Robert J. Schumann, Glenn L. Schwanke, E. Allen Sorum, Stephen P. Valleskey, David A. Voss, Paul O. Wendland, Ernst H. Wendland, Paul H. Wilde, Michael A. Woldt, Mark G. Zarling, Paul E. Zell, James A. Ziesemer.

Their contributions again reflect a welcome variety of writing styles, methods and points of emphasis. The same law-gospel message predominates throughout, together with a clear intent to let the Holy Scriptures bring the message of salvation.

Our sincere thanks for their conscientious work!

Ernst H. Wendland


NOTE: Previous volumes in this series have included comments on all three readings for a given Sunday, and the authors have briefly

10

pointed out how the readings are related to each other. This feature is not included in this volume, since the ILCW Series B readings were so treated in *Sermon Studies on the Old Testament*, Series B. We refer you to that volume for this information.

# THE GOSPEL OF MARK

Since most of the texts in the ILCW Series B pericope are taken from the Gospel according to Mark, it is appropriate to review some of the chief isagogical points concerning this book.

A straightforward reading of the Gospel itself should put to rest all the "scholarly" theories of the historical critics regarding the book's origin, originality and integrity. To quote B. F. Westcott: "In substance and style and treatment, the Gospel of St. Mark is essentially a transcript from life. The course and the issue of facts are imaged in it with the clearest outline. If all other arguments against the mythic origin of the evangelic narratives were wanting, this vivid and simple record, stamped with the most distinct impress of independence and originality ... would be sufficient to refute a theory subversive of all faith in history" (*Introduction to Study of the Gospels*, p 369).

The opening words of Mark's Gospel can well serve as the theme of his entire work: "The beginning of the gospel about Jesus Christ, the Son of God." The author was concerned about introducing his readers to the "gospel," the "good news" about the Savior. This began with Jesus Christ, who proved himself to be the Son of God. His words and deeds bore mighty witness to this fact (1:14 to 8:26). His self-predicted suffering, death and triumphant resurrection gave mighty testimony to the same (8:27 to 16:20).

Mark, the book's author, was the son of a Mary referred to in Scripture as the owner of a house in Jerusalem where the early Christians assembled (Ac 13:5,13; 12:12). Although not himself an apostle, his close association with Paul and Peter give his writing an apostolic stamp (Ac 13:5,13; Col 4:10; Phm 24; 2 Ti 4:11; 1 Pe 5:13). Peter refers to Mark as his "son," and one can assume that Mark was with Peter in Rome when the latter wrote his First Epistle in the early sixties. Although Mark's early experiences with Paul were not very happy ones, the two became closely associated at the time of Paul's last imprisonment in Rome. Early church tradition refers to Mark as the "interpreter of Peter" while the two were together in Rome, and later as the founder of the church in Alexandria, Egypt, where he is said to have died a martyr's death.

The style and character of Mark's Gospel indicate that it was written for Gentile readers. It is a Gospel of action, emphasizing the mighty deeds of Jesus, yet not neglecting the Savior's authoritative words. Significantly, Peter is highlighted in Mark's Gospel (1:16;

8:29; 16:7), and the expressions, bearing and feelings of Jesus are so vividly portrayed that the source of the account undoubtedly came from an eyewitness. Jewish customs are explained (7:2-4; 15:42), and Hebrew and Aramaic expressions are elucidated (3:17; 5:41; 7:11; 14:12; 15:22). All this adds support to the traditional view that the Gospel was first directed to Gentile Christians in Rome.

Bible critics have debated at length concerning which of the three synoptic Gospels was written first, also concerning the extent to which all three may have relied on an "earlier source" (Logia Collection). Conservative students of Scripture are generally agreed that, although Matthew, Mark and Luke give a common view of the ministry of Christ, each one worked quite independently of the others with a distinctive purpose in mind (cf. above) and that whether Matthew or Mark wrote first is of little consequence. Both of them no doubt wrote sometime in the sixties and before the destruction of Jerusalem.

The contention, supported especially by Th. Zahn, that Mark left his Gospel unfinished and that Mark 16:9-20 was added by some later writer as a "conclusion" has some textual-critical validity. Textual evidence for the genuineness of vv. 9-20, however, is equally strong (cf. *Novum Testamentum Graece*, A. Souter). If a choice has to be made, it would seem logical to agree with R. C. Lenski that Mark completed his work himself, especially since the concluding verses of chapter sixteen fit in so well with the rest of the Gospel (*Interpretation of Mark*, pp 750-755). In any case, the preacher need have no qualms over using these verses as an inspired basis for a sermon.

# FIRST SUNDAY IN ADVENT

## The Scriptures

Old Testament — *Isaiah 63:16b,17; 64:1-8*
Epistle — *1 Corinthians 1:3-9*
Gospel — *Mark 13:33-37*

## The Text — Mark 13:33-37

Jesus spoke the words of our text on the Tuesday of Holy Week, the week in which he suffered and died for the sins of the world. Jesus spent much of this Tuesday in the temple courts at Jerusalem. Here the leaders of the Jews had questioned his authority as a teacher (Mk 11:27-33). Here he spoke to various groups of people and to individuals on a number of topics (M 12:1-40). Here he observed the gift of a widow (Mk 12:41-44). As Jesus was leaving the temple for the last time, he warned his disciples about how this beautiful building would be totally destroyed and how this destruction of the temple at Jerusalem was a picture of the destruction of the whole world on the last day (Mk 13:1-37).

Included in these words of Jesus concerning the end of the world is the warning found in our text:

v. 33 — *"Be on guard! Be alert! You do not know when that time will come."*

The NIV translates the Greek imperative βλέπετε with the words "Be on guard!" The following imperative, ἀγρυπεῖτε, is translated "Be alert!" (A third imperative, προσεύχετε: "pray," is included in some manuscripts.) Any number of synonyms fit the imperatives, which call for Christ's followers to take care, to be awake, to keep their eyes open.

The reason for this watchful attitude is given. The specific time (ὁ καιρός), the end-time which Jesus has been talking about in this entire chapter relating to his second coming, is unknown. The uncertainty connected with this lack of knowledge is no reason for carelessness or indifference. The very opposite is true. Uncertainty calls for increased watchfulness, as Jesus illustrates in the verse which follows:

v. 34 — *"It's like a man going away: He leaves his house and puts his servants in charge, each with his assigned task, and tells the one at the door to keep watch."*

The comparison presented here by Jesus is of a man who is absent from his home for a time (ἀπόδημος), as a man away on business or an absentee landlord. At the time of his departure he gives instructions to his servants to conduct his household and manage his affairs while he is absent. Each of the servants has an assigned task. Especially the doorkeeper is to keep watch, so that he can alert the others when the master makes his return and also admit the master when he arrives.

The application of this picture is found in Scripture itself. The master of the house is Jesus. His servants are his followers. The leave-taking of the master refers to Jesus' ascension into heaven. The task assigned to the servants refers to the many directives given by Jesus to his church prior to his ascension — to use his means of grace wisely, to live as children of a heavenly Father, to spread his gospel at every opportunity. Especially the watchmen of the church are to warn Christians to be ever on the alert and prayerful, ready to receive the Lord at his second coming, whenever that may be.

Worthy of note in this verse is the fact that each servant is given a special assignment (ἑκάστῳ τὸ ἔργον αὐτοῦ) while awaiting the Lord's return. There is no such thing as an inactive follower of Christ, or to use another comparison, a dead member of his body. Christian duties and responsibilities vary. Gifts differ as well. But Scripture repeatedly points out that each member is to function according to his station in life to the glory of God and to the welfare of others —whether that be as a father, mother, son, daughter, child or senior citizen, executive or blue-collar worker, teacher or student.

Even those who are seemingly helpless and dependent on others can by Christian patience and forbearance set a powerful example of faith to others. The application is simple and straightforward, but it offers an important reminder to believers who feel useless, unimportant, lost in the shuffle of humanity, and grow indifferent to their Christian responsibilities.

Those who are to serve as the Lord's watchmen are reminded to keep their people alive, awake, constantly ready for Christ's return. Here lies the special Advent emphasis of this text. Christ Jesus, who once came to save all humanity, who comes to us even now in word and sacrament, is most certainly coming again. We do not know when that will be. It could be at anytime. The sinful world, which goes on its outwardly merry but purposeless way, is totally oblivious to this fact. Christians can so easily be lulled into following a similarly aimless course. If the leaders of the church do not alert their people to this Advent call, who will?

> Watchman, tell us of the night,
> What its signs of promise are. (TLH 71:1)

The watchmen of the church, however, do not only proclaim doom and destruction. Theirs is also a message of promise, of final deliverance from sin and death. The Lord who is coming again is our Savior! The text continues in this tone:

vv. 35,36 — *"Therefore keep watch because you do not know when the owner of the house will come back — whether in the evening, or at midnight, or when the rooster crows, or at dawn. If he comes suddenly, do not let him find you sleeping."*

According to Christ's picture the doorkeeper is to be on the alert so that he can keep the servants of the house watchful. The point is that *all* are to be on the alert, and the watching is to be *continuous* (γρηγορεῖτε, a present imperative).

Of special interest in this illustration are the four nighttime designations: in the evening, at midnight, at cockcrow, at dawn. The master of the house will arrive sometime during the hours of the night, at a time least expected, when people are most likely to be asleep.

Hence the direct, *personal* application: "Do not let him find *you* (ὑμᾶς) sleeping." When preaching on this text, the preacher will want to direct the Lord's exhortation to his hearers in as forceful and intimate a way as possible. This will be done not in a high-handed manner, but out of deep concern for their souls' eternal welfare. "This means you," the Lord wants us to know, "because I am concerned about you!"

Human nature likes to postpone, to put things off until the morrow. Christians, too, have this *mañana* nature very much with them, which tells them: "Maybe tomorrow I'll have more time to think about my Christian responsibilities," or "Perhaps next year I'll be able to devote more thought to spiritual matters." The Advent message puts its emphasis on the "now," the "today." Tomorrow or next year may be too late.

Hence the Lord's closing admonition of this Advent text:

v. 37 — *"What I say to you, I say to everyone: 'Watch!' "*

The present imperative γρηγορεῖτε closes this text with a direct, personal, stirring appeal to every Christian: "Watch! Be awake! Keep on the alert!"

When we understand the situation which confronted the twelve disciples at this moment, we can appreciate the Lord's personal concern that they be especially alert. In short order the Lord was to be anointed by Mary of Bethany for his death and burial; he was to institute his Holy Supper; he was to be arrested, tried, condemned, crucified, and buried; he was to rise triumphantly on the third day; he was to commission his disciples to preach the good news to all creation; he was to ascend into heaven. Each event fit into the master plan for the salvation of the world, and all was to take place in the light of his second coming, when all the pieces would finally fit together for all eternity!

To live in this spirit of anticipation, to see in God's plan of salvation his purpose for all mankind and for oneself — that is to live as an Advent Christian.

### Homiletical Suggestions

This text has great Advent potential. It remains for the preacher to proclaim it "like it is," in all its fulness.

A superficial treatment of the text will emphasize in a general way the Lord's warning to be watchful in the light of his second coming, stressing the usual admonition that the Lord is surely coming again at the end of time, that his coming will be unexpected, and that the sincere follower of Christ will want to be prepared at any time for this event.

While this warning is an important part of the text, there is more to it than that. The master who leaves his servants "each with his assigned task" places a personal responsibility upon them in the light of his second coming. Especially does he place a solemn duty upon the watchman, who is to help the others keep alert as they carry out their assigned tasks (v. 34).

Christ's urgent appeal in the light of the text's entire situation adds a note not only of earnest warning, but of watchful anticipation. By keeping their eyes open to the momentous events which lie immediately ahead, believers can be ready, not merely to avoid eternal doom, but to enjoy eternal salvation (vv. 35-37).

Viewing our text in this way will give a fuller Advent picture. As another church year begins, the Christian will be encouraged to hear:

### Christ's Advent Call: "Watch!"

1. Beware of indifference (v. 33)
2. Take care of your responsibility (v. 34)
3. Await your Lord's return (vv. 35-37)

Emphasizing the personal nature of Christ's Advent exhortation, one can use the same thoughts and divisions of the text under the basic outline:

### Advent Means YOU!

1. Be an alert Christian (v. 33)
2. Be a responsible Christian (v. 34)
3. Be an expectant Christian (vv. 35-37)

Viewing this text from its position at the beginning of another church year suggests the following treatment:

## Another Year Of Grace Lies Ahead

1. A year of watchfulness (v. 33)
2. A year of opportunity (v. 34)
3. A year of expectancy (vv. 35-37)

# SECOND SUNDAY IN ADVENT

## The Scriptures

> Old Testament — *Isaiah 40:1-11*
> Epistle — *2 Peter 3:8-14*
> Gospel — *Mark 1:1-8*

## The Text — Mark 1:1-8

The opening words of Mark's Gospel are the text for the second Sunday in Advent. These words report the fulfillment of Isaiah's prophecy in the Old Testament lesson for the day. God had promised to send a forerunner to prepare the way for the coming of the Lord. John the Baptist was that forerunner, and his message was one of repentance. That is why this text serves well in the Advent season. As we prepare to celebrate the coming of the Savior, we need proper Advent preparations of repentance.

v. 1 — *The beginning of the gospel about Jesus Christ, the Son of God.*

The opening words of Mark's Gospel indicate the theme of his entire work. Mark wrote primarily for Gentile readers. He was concerned with telling the "good news" about the Savior, Jesus Christ, the Son of God. Jesus was mighty in word and deed, thus proving his deity (1:14-8:26). His suffering, death and resurrection substantiated the same (8:27-16:20).

vv. 2,3 — *It is written in Isaiah the prophet: "I will send my messenger ahead of you, who will prepare your way" — "a voice of one calling in the desert, 'Prepare the way for the Lord, make straight paths for him.' "*

Mark tells us that he is quoting from Isaiah. He does this, though not immediately. In verse 2 he first quotes from Malachi 3:1, and then in verse 3 he quotes from Isaiah. This method of quoting, naming only one source when the reference is to two, is not unique to Mark. Matthew does this also (cf. Mt 27:9,10). This, however, should cause no problem for the preacher. The important thing is that Mark shows John's coming to be in fulfillment of God's promise to send a forerunner. It is another evidence that our God keeps his word.

Isaiah's words picture John as God's messenger preparing the way for the coming of the Savior. Just as a messenger was sent ahead of a king or ruler to get people to repair the road on which he was to travel, so John was sent ahead of God's Son to prepare the hearts of the people for Christ's coming.

v. 4 — *And so John came, baptizing in the desert region and preparing a baptism of repentance for the forgiveness of sins.*

"And so" clearly indicates that John's coming and his entire ministry were not by human authority. They were in fulfillment of God's promise. John was sent by God and his mission was divinely ordained. So it is with every messenger of the gospel. Those who serve God as messengers are doing so, not by human authority, but on the basis of the "divine call." The divine call reminds the Lord's messengers of their awesome task and comforts them with the realization that divine authority undergirds their work.

As the forerunner of the Messiah, John's mission was to prepare the hearts of the people through a call to repentance and a baptism for the forgiveness of sins. There is ample reason for us to understand the Greek word μετανοίας in its wider sense. True repentance involves godly sorrow over sin and trust in God's promise of forgiveness. True repentance was John's message, and it is a timely message for the Advent season. As God's people make outward preparations to celebrate Christmas, they also need to prepare their hearts. Godly sorrow over sin and trust in God's forgiveness are proper Advent preparations for God's people.

Some Bible students maintain that the baptisms performed by John were different from and inferior to the baptism later commanded by Christ. A close look at this verse quickly settles the matter for us. Here Mark writes that John's baptism was εἰς ἄφεσιν ἁμαρτιῶν. The Greek preposition εἰς with the accusative expresses purpose. Since John's baptism was "for the remission of sins," it did indeed mediate the forgiveness which Christ accomplished on the cross. Although the preacher may not dwell on this point in his sermon, it is good to point out that John not only denounced sin; he also announced the forgiveness of sins. The Baptist's message of repentance was one of sin and grace, law and gospel.

v. 5 — *The whole Judean countryside and all the people of Jerusalem went out to him. Confessing their sins, they were baptized by him in the Jordan River.*

The preaching of John made a profound impression on the people. Multitudes went out to see and hear this fiery prophet of God. As to the multitudes, they are described in somewhat figurative language. The expression "countryside" may be considered a synedoche, a figure in which one object is called by another closely associated with it. As to "all," this is hyperbole.

The Greek ἐξομολογούμενοι is a present participle of attending circumstances. It shows that many heeded John's call to repentance and were baptized by him "while confessing their sins." We note this because Reformed theology denies the efficacy of baptism. Confession of sins does not give baptism its power; rather baptism brings the blessing of forgiveness because the power of God's word stands behind it. Again, there is the reminder that the proper attitude of the heart is true repentance, which embraces both contrition and faith.

A point that always needs emphasis here is that repentance is not a work of man. The Holy Spirit works repentance in men's hearts as they are crushed through the law and made alive through the gospel.

v. 6 — *John wore clothing made of camel's hair, with a leather belt around his waist, and he ate locusts and wild honey.*

Mark describes John's outward appearance and way of living as being very primitive. John's life and his diet were in direct fulfillment of the angel's announcement to Zechariah that his son was to be a Nazirite ((cf. Lk 1:15). Even John's outward appearance reflected a message of repentance from overemphasis on "material things." As a prophet of God he lived what he preached.

v. 7 — *And this was his message: "After me will come one more powerful than I, the thongs of whose sandals I am not worthy to stoop down and untie."*

As the forerunner, John's calling was to point the people to the Savior. Although Jesus at one time called John "the greatest in the kingdom of God," John knew that his role was not to draw attention to himself. He was only a witness to the greater one to come. In regard to the time of birth and the beginning of his public ministry, Jesus had come after John (cf. Lk 1:26,36; 3:23). But Jesus was greater in that he was and is God and Savior of all. John recognized this, and his humble words in this verse are consistent with what he told his own disciples later on: "He must become greater; I must become less" (cf. Jn 3:27-30).

v. 8 — *"I baptize you with water, but he will baptize you with the Holy Spirit."*

There is some debate concerning this verse also. It has been used to support the idea that John's baptism was different from the baptism which Christ instituted (Mt 28:18-20). But with these words John is simply continuing to highlight the greatness of the Savior. In other words, John is telling the people that he is only the Lord's instrument in applying the waters of baptism, but the coming Messiah gives baptism its power through the Holy Spirit. Jesus also gave visible proof of this through his bestowing of the Holy Spirit on Pentecost Day (cf. Mt 3:11; Ac 1:5; 2:33).

**Homiletical Suggestions**

John the Baptist is an excellent example for every preacher. Whenever a preacher steps into the pulpit, he is to serve as a witness to Christ. He is not to draw attention to himself but to direct his listeners to their Savior. The purpose of every sermon is to show the need for a Savior from sin and the answer to that need in Christ Jesus. Like John the Baptist, we are to impress God's people with their Savior, not with ourselves.

The seasonal message of Advent is that Christ is coming. This text reminds us that Christ has come, as John said, and that he comes to our hearts through the preaching of the word.

The following theme and outline emphasize John the Baptist's and the preacher's role in the kingdom of God:

**On Jordan's Bank The Baptist's Cry**

1. Denounces mankind's sin (vv. 1-6)
2. Announces mankind's Savior from sin (vv. 7,8)

John came by God's authority and brought sinners God's message of sin and grace. God kept his promise and sent a forerunner to prepare the way for the Savior. Now we need to listen to that forerunner's message. That suggests this treatment of the text:

**Listen To God's Advent Preacher**

1. He was sent by God (vv. 1-3)
2. He calls you to repent (vv. 4-6)
3. He announces that the Savior is here (vv. 7,8)

During Advent we often get caught up with worldly and outward preparations for Christmas. This text reminds us of the proper spiritual preparations we should make:

**Make Proper Christmas Preparations**

1. Renounce your sinful ways (vv. 1-6)
2. Look to your Savior in faith (vv. 7,8)

# THE GOSPEL OF JOHN

Twenty-one of sixty-eight readings in the ILCW Series B Gospels are from St. John. It is, therefore, appropriate to review some of the chief isagogical points concerning this Gospel.

The Gospel of John is unique in authorship and purpose. The Apostle John was the son of Zebedee and Salome. Salome is noted in Scripture as one of the devoted followers of Jesus (Mt 27:56; Mk 15:40,41). From Zebedee, John learned the trade of a fisherman, working with his older brother, James, on the Sea of Galilee, (Mt 4:21; Mk 1:19,20). John seems to have been a man of some means, perhaps even owning his own home (Jn 19:27).

The event which changed the life of John was Jesus' call, "Follow me" (Mt 4:21,22). John, his brother James and Peter became the three disciples who enjoyed a rather intimate relationship with our Savior. John was with Jesus at the raising of Jairus' daughter (Lk 8:51) and at the transfiguration (Mt 17:1), and he personally beheld the agony of our Savior in the Garden of Gethsemane (Mt 26:37). It was Jesus who named John and James "Boanerges," which means "Sons of Thunder" (Mk 3:17), reflecting their fiery nature as indicated in Luke 9:51-56. At the institution of the Lord's Supper he reclined at the place of honor next to Jesus (Jn 13:22-25; 21:20). He is frequently referred to as the disciple "whom Jesus loved" (Jn 13:23; 19:26; 20:2; 21:7,20). In humility he refers to himself in his written record as "the other disciple" (Jn 20:2). He was at the foot of Jesus' cross and was entrusted with the care of Jesus' mother (Jn 19:27). He rejoiced with the others at the Easter celebrations and at the mount of ascension.

His fervor for the cause of Christ was by no means dampened by the ascension of our Savior. He was active with Peter (Ac 3:1, 4:13-20; 8:14). Paul refers to John as one of the "pillars" of the church (Ga 2:9). While his brother James was put to death by Herod Agrippa I, King of Judea, about A.D. 44 (Ac 12:2), John seems to have continued his efforts from Ephesus as he helped administer the Asia Minor mission field, which had been founded under the direction of the Apostle Paul. Tradition indicates that he labored in that area for as much as twenty years until his appearance on the island of Patmos in the Aegean Sea (Re 1:9), where he was imprisoned by the Roman Emperor Domitian. There he wrote the book of Revelation. While exact dating is difficult, tradition supports the opinion that John wrote his Gospel while at Ephesus after his release from the isle of Patmos about A.D. 97, thus making it the last of the four Gospels written.

Unique features of the book include its lengthy records of some of Jesus' discourses (ch. 1,3,4,5,6,7-10,11,12,13,14,15-17,21) and a lengthy study of the work of the Holy Spirit (ch. 14-16). John, however, records fewer of the miracles of Jesus than the other three Gospels. Luther writes concerning this point: "Since John records very few of the works of Christ, but very many of His discourses, while the other three evangelists, on the other hand, record many of His works, but few of His words, therefore the Gospel according to St. John is much to be preferred to the other three and to be extolled more highly" (*Introduction to the Books of the Bible*, Christopher Drewes, p 141).

One other unique feature is that John records his message in chronological order, mentioning three Passover celebrations during the ministry of Jesus, while the other Gospel writers do not definitely note more than one. It is, therefore, from John's Gospel that we know that the public ministry of Jesus extended over a three-year period.

Mention also might be made of the unique style of John in regard to terms such as "synoptic" and "autoptic." Matthew, Mark and Luke are labeled synoptic Gospels, for they "see together" the life of Christ. The synoptic Gospels share a common outline, reporting similar details of Christ's life, even to expressing some details with identical words.

The term "autoptic" refers specifically to John's Gospel, emphasizing John's unique eyewitness point of view when writing. His point of view is different from the synoptic writers in regard to content (John deals almost exclusively with Jesus' Jerusalem ministry rather than the Galilean ministry). John does not refer to the many parables of Jesus. He omits some of the unique events of the ministry of Jesus such as the temptation in the wilderness, the Sermon on the Mount, the institution of the Lord's Supper, Gethsemane and the ascension. Yet he adds references to specific events that the others have passed over, such as the Cana miracles, Jesus' discussion with the woman of Samaria, the raising of Lazarus, and Jesus' high-priestly prayer.

One must, however, be constantly mindful of the working of the Holy Spirit in the lives of the Gospel-writers as he inspired each of them to record in his own unique manner the message which is before us in Scripture.

One other point should be considered. John writes at length concerning the divinity of Christ. While that in itself is not unique, it might suggest to us God's special reason for moving John to select his material and write his Gospel as he did. John stresses by God's guidance, "Jesus did many other miraculous signs in the presence of his disciples, which are not recorded in this book. But these are written that you may believe that Jesus is the Christ, the Son of God, and that by believing you may have life in his name" (20:30,31). This fact is also emphasized in the opening words of the Gospel. Without a detailed presentation concerning the birth of Jesus, John clearly sets forth in chapter one the fundamental truths to which the rest of his Gospel will bear witness. John proclaims that Jesus is indeed the life and the light of the world, the promised Savior, who fulfilled all that the Old Testament Scriptures foretold about the coming Redeemer. His opening message concerning the Word and John the Baptist's witness of Christ emphasize that central truth of the Gospel of John.

Even though he makes no direct reference to the emerging heresy that we call Gnosticism, he refutes Gnostic errors by his clear proclamation of the truth concerning Christ. Gnosticism denied the divinity of Jesus Christ and rejected the basic gospel truth that Jesus' death and resurrection accomplished our salvation.

May our witness to Jesus Christ clearly express the faith of the Apostle John as we boldly and joyfully proclaim the glory of our Savior-God.

# THIRD SUNDAY IN ADVENT

## The Scriptures

> Old Testament — *Isaiah 61:1-3,10,11*
> Epistle — *1 Thessalonians 5:16-24*
> Gospel — *John 1:6-8,19-28*

## The Text — John 1:6-8,19-28

John the Baptist, the forerunner of our Savior, is introduced in these opening verses of the Gospel of John. The inspired writer introduces the Baptist's God-given mission (vv. 6-8) and then proceeds with the personal witness of John the Baptist (vv. 19-28).

These verses describe the "coming out party" for Jesus which God the Father wondrously planned through the witness of John. They go on to mention the personal qualities which marked the forerunner of Jesus. John's clear and bold witnessing for Christ serves as an example for all Christians.

v. 6 — *There came a man who was sent from God; his name was John.*

John's simple style in basic Greek, unmarred by any significant textual variant, is clearly seen in these words of introduction.

John the Baptist was a man like any other in his person and in his spiritual need. He was unique in that he was an important part of God's special plan and purpose. Luke offers us the details of his early life. John highlights the special mission assigned to him by the Lord, that of the forerunner of Christ. The significance of that is revealed in verses nineteen and following.

Not only did God pick the man and assign the mission, but Luke reminds us that God also chose his name. John, "Merciful is Jehovah," was the name by which he was to be known (Lk 1:13).

v. 7 — *He came as a witness to testify concerning that light.*

John was a μαρτύριος, a witness, one sent to proclaim to the world that the promised Savior was beginning his work. His calling was to bear witness to the work of another. God had caused his light to appear in the midst of a sin-darkened world in the person of Jesus, the Savior. John's message was simply, "Don't miss him!"

v. 8 — *He himself was not the light; he came only as a witness to the light.*

John clearly understood that his purpose was not bearing witness to himself and his own greatness, but glorifying the Savior. The spiritual gifts of faith, humility, selflessness and faithfulness to the great privilege of his calling were expressed in the life of John, for he was true to his conviction. "He must become greater; I must become less" (Jn 3:30).

Verses six through eight have introduced John. The remaining verses of our text demonstrate in John's words the purpose of his call.

v. 19 — *Now this was John's testimony when the Jews of Jerusalem sent priests and Levites to ask him who he was.*

John's appearance on the scene, his manner of life and other features of his ministry were extraordinary. His work had provoked sensational comment and had attracted unusual attention. Curiosity and concern for their own welfare as subjects of Rome prompted the sending of an official fact-finding delegation from Jerusalem. Their question was simple, "Who do you claim to be, and what place do you aspire to?" The emphasis of their question, as the Greek text indicates, is on the word *you!*

v. 20 — *He did not fail to confess, but confessed freely, "I am not the Christ."*

Without hesitation, John rejected any notion that he might be the promised Messiah. He had no right or claim to the honor which belonged to the Christ alone.

v. 21 — *They asked him, "Then who are you? Are you Elijah?" He said, "I am not." "Are you the Prophet?" He answered, "No."*

The Jews had a false understanding of the prophecy of Malachi (4:5). Malachi describes the forerunner of Christ as one who would possess the spirit of the Old Testament prophet Elijah. John the Baptist was not the prophet Elijah resurrected for a renewed ministry, but Jesus declared that Malachi's words of prophecy find their fulfillment in the spirit and preaching of John (cf. Mt 17:10-13). John the Baptist preached with the spirit and power of Elijah.

John was not in doubt concerning his God-appointed mission. His words were simply a rejection of any false conclusions. So also was his response to their question concerning "that prophet." Deuteronomy 18:15 speaks of a special prophet, Christ the Savior. The Jews also misunderstood this prophecy, considering "that prophet" to be some other special prophet yet to come.

v. 22 — *Finally they said, "Who are you? Give us an answer to take back to those who sent us. What do you say about yourself?"*

Impatience and persistence marked the delegation's demand for an immediate and clear answer. They were under obligation to bring back an answer.

v. 23 — *John replied in the words of Isaiah the prophet, "I am the voice of one calling in the desert, 'Make straight the way for the Lord.' "*

Quoting the word of the Old Testament prophet (Isa 40:3), John the Baptist describes himself as one crying out urgently and loudly, "Make straight (εὐθύνω) the way for the Lord." Give heed to the message of God's word that the Lord might touch your hearts with his call to repentance, preparing you for the coming of Christ. In the simplest of terms the purpose of John's ministry is proclaimed, namely, calling people to repentance.

Special physical preparations would be made for the coming of a king. John, however, was concerned with a "straightening out" of man spiritually, from the inside out, reminding us of Christ's words that "the kingdom of God is within you" (Lk 17:21). The kind of internal demolition and reconstruction of which John is speaking comes about only by the Holy Spirit's working through the means of grace.

Now the delegation had a message for those who sent them, but they still had a question about the authority by which he was baptizing.

vv. 24-27 — *Now some Pharisees who had been sent questioned him, "Why then do you baptize if you are not the Christ, nor Elijah, nor the Prophet?" "I baptize with water," John replied, "but among you stands one you do not know. He is the one who comes after me, the thongs of whose sandals I am not worthy to untie."*

Concern for their own man-made rules and regulations on the part of the priests and Levites is evident throughout the Gospels. Hence their concern voiced in the question, "Who gave you the authority to baptize? Did someone in Jerusalem authorize or sanction your ministry?" Their question was a clear challenge to the ministry of John.

John's baptism, a true means of grace, proclaimed his purpose in calling Israel to repentance. Israel needed to confess its sin and turn in faith to the only source of forgiveness, Christ, the Savior from sin. That Savior was already in the world, but he was yet unknown to them. John further proclaimed the glory of that Savior. Although he would appear after John in time, that Savior would far surpass John in his person, his power, and his office. John, the humble servant of

28

that Savior, proclaimed that truth by declaring his own unworthiness to even untie the sandals of his Savior's feet. John clearly understood his purpose and person compared to that of his Savior, Jesus Christ.

The clarity and humility of John's witness is a meaningful example for every Christian as we too let our light shine to the glory of God.

v. 28 — *This all happened at Bethany on the other side of the Jordan, where John was baptizing.*

This testimony was given by John on the eastern side of the Jordan River in the village of Bethany. Textual debate questions the reading Βηθανία. Some have preferred the reading Βηθαβαρά, because we know no city called Bethany "on the other side of the Jordan." Bethany is the preferred reading, however, but this Bethany must not be confused with the hometown of Lazarus located on the Mount of Olives a few miles from Jerusalem.

### Homiletical Suggestions

Advent is a time of repentance, a time to prepare one's heart for the coming of Christ. Since that was the purpose of John's preaching in the wilderness near the Jordan River, the message of our text is most fitting.

Several aspects of the text stand out as one considers present-day applications. John the Baptist's reference to the Prophet Isaiah and "the voice of one calling in the desert" catches one's attention. An outline capturing the significance of that prophecy might be constructed like this:

### A Voice Still Cries In The Wilderness

1. A faithful voice (vv. 19-22)
2. A humble voice (vv. 23-27)
3. A voice with a mission (vv. 6-8)

The introduction might present in passing the unique appearance and life-style of this man of God (Jn 3:1-7). Yet in the spite of the external uniqueness of John, this special messenger of God was a man with whom we have much in common. While his voice has been silenced here in time, the sound of his message is still being heard as Christians proclaim the message of repentance and grace through Christ. The wilderness in which the voice of the gospel still rings is our sin-darkened world.

The unfolding of the text proclaims the qualities of the messenger. Part one speaks of John's faithfulness amidst much discouragement and hardship. Faithfulness to Christ "for better or for worse" is still a mark of discipleship. Part two reminds us that the Christian's strength and glory is not found in man, but rather in the God who claims, calls and equips us to be his own. Part three reminds us of our mission before God. Man is not here merely to pass time. As Christians we are to be ever aware of whose we are and where we are going. God's agenda, God's purpose for our life, is to be our agenda. The challenge of Christianity is keeping that purpose before our mind's eye as we faithfully use his message to prepare our hearts and the hearts of others for the coming of the Lord. That mission then has an impact on our personal living.

Focusing our attention on the witness of John, the following outlines might be considered:

## Witness To The Light

1. Do not witness to your personal glory (vv. 19-22)
2. Rather witness to the glory of Christ (vv. 6-8,23-27)

Or another,

## Witness Effectively To The Coming Of Christ

1. Understand your calling (vv. 6-8)
2. Speak with humility and clarity (vv. 19-27)

The spirit of the Advent season might be noted more effectively with this outline:

## Celebrate Advent With John The Baptist

1. With rejoicing — as we behold the fulfillment of prophecy (vv. 19-23)
2. With humility — as we confess our need for Jesus' coming (vv. 6-8)
3. With faithfulness — as we daily proclaim his glory (vv. 24-27)

May the character and message of John the Baptist inspire us daily in our worship as we prepare for the coming of Christ.

# FOURTH SUNDAY IN ADVENT

**The Scriptures**

> Old Testament — *2 Samuel 7:8-11,16*
> Epistle — *Romans 16:25-27*
> Gospel — *Luke 1:26-38*

**The Text — Luke 1:26-38**

In his introduction to the Gospel of Luke, Dr. Martin H. Franzmann remarked, "If Matthew's Gospel is at once the most austere and the most compelling of the Gospels, if Mark's is the most vivid and dramatic recital of the deeds of Christ, Luke's is the warmest and most winning story of them all. . . . It is Luke's Nativity story that has most decisively shaped the church's Christmas celebration" (*Concordia Self-Study Commentary*, N.T., p 58). In the text before us, Luke transports us to a humble home in the town of Nazareth and introduces us to a virgin named Mary. Gabriel's message heightens our anticipation as we prepare our hearts and homes to celebrate the birth of the Savior.

First Luke sets the scene for the announcement of the Lord's birth:

> v. 26 — *In the sixth month, God sent the angel Gabriel to Nazareth, a town in Galilee,*

With his opening words Luke ties this account directly to the preceding section, where John the Baptist's birth was announced. It was Elizabeth who was "in the sixth month" of her pregnancy. Just as Gabriel had been sent to proclaim the "good news" of the forerunner's birth, so now he was sent from God to bring Mary a message that would change her life. Gabriel was serving in his role of messenger (ἄγγελος), a role which he also filled in Old Testament times (Da 8:16).

The setting for this majestic announcement of Jesus' birth would come as a shock to many. Nazareth in Galilee hardly had a first-rate reputation (Jn 1:46). It was three days' journey from the religious and cultural center of Jerusalem, in the heart of the despised province of Galilee. Yet it was here that God chose to reveal his grace to a humble virgin:

> v. 27 — *to a virgin pledged to be married to a man named Joseph, a descendant of David. The virgin's name was Mary."*

Luke repeats "virgin" (παρθένος) as if to emphasize the miraculous nature of the Savior's birth. The perfect passive participle (ἐμνηστευμένην) indicates that Mary "had already been pledged" in a public ceremony to a man named Joseph, and so could rightfully be considered his wife (cf. Dt 22:23,24).

The Greek phrase ἐξ οἴκου Δαυείδ fits grammatically with Joseph. The descent of Mary "from the house of David" is certainly implied, if not directly stated, in passages like 1:32, 1:69, 2:4; Ro 1:3; 2 Ti 2:8; He 7:14.

Now that the scene has been set, we are told:

v. 28 — *The angel went to her and said, "Greetings, you who are highly favored! The Lord is with you."*

The greeting (Χαῖρε) was common for the day, but the message which followed and the messenger who delivered it certainly were not. The perfect participle κεχαριτωμένη describes Mary as "one to whom the Lord has been and continues to be gracious." The text certainly does not contain any hint of the virgin as a dispenser of grace, as Roman Catholicism teaches. The greeting is gospel. The focus is on what God has done and is now doing for Mary. As a member of the sin-burdened human race, Mary was completely dependent on her Lord. What a comforting assurance it must have been for her to hear, "The Lord is with you"! The God of free and faithful grace never forgets his people. The words of the Prophet Isaiah come to mind (41:10).

The phrase "You who are highly favored among women" (ἐυλογημένη σὺ ἐν γυναιξίν) has wide textual support but is generally regarded as a later insertion from Luke 1:42. It has not been included in the UBS text.

As well we might expect, the greeting from Gabriel came as a shock to Mary:

v. 29 — *Mary was greatly troubled at his words and wondered what kind of greeting this might be.*

Certainly the mere presence of one of God's holy angels would have been enough to cause the sinner, Mary, to be greatly troubled (διεταράχθη). This kind of reaction was shared by Zechariah and later by the shepherds in the hills of Bethlehem. But we are also told that Mary was perplexed by the message which the angel brought. The imperfect form διελογίζετο indicates that Mary kept debating with herself over the nature of the greeting. "What's going on here? Why is this angel in my house? What is God trying to tell me?"

With these questions racing through Mary's mind, the angel Gabriel once again brings comforting words of grace and peace:

v. 30 — *But the angel said to her, "Do not be afraid, Mary, you have found favor with God."*

Not only does Gabriel tell Mary to "stop fearing" (μὴ φοβοῦ), he also gives her the best reason of all for putting aside her fear completely. She has found "favor" (χάριν) with God. We recognize χάρις as God's undeserved love which reaches out to the unworthy and is given as a free gift. It is God's grace that removes the fear of eternal death from our lives and replaces that trembling with the assurance of sins forgiven and a place in the family of God. Mary did not "earn" God's favor any more than we have. The words of Paul in Ephesians 2:8,9 speak clearly.

Gabriel now goes on to explain the reason for this special visit:

v. 31 — *"You will be with child and give birth to a son, and you are to give him the name Jesus."*

Attention is drawn to the marvelous message which the angel presents by the introductory word ἰδού, "Behold!" The birth of any child is a gift from the Lord, as the psalmist reminds us (Ps 127:3), but the birth of this child would be especially noteworthy. First of all, this child (a son) would be conceived in the womb of a virgin. There had been other miraculous births (Isaac, John the Baptist), but never before was there a virgin birth. The words of Isaiah 7:14 are being fulfilled. Secondly, this birth is noteworthy because of the name which Mary is to give her son. The name Jesus means "the Lord is salvation."

The name Jesus (or the Jewish equivalent "Joshua") was common. Not so Mary's Son. The full significance of his birth and his name becomes apparent as the message continues to unfold:

v. 32 — *"He will be great and will be called the Son of the Most High. The Lord God will give him the throne of his father David,"*

The adjective "great" (μέγας) had been used by the angel to describe John the Baptist (1:15), but the "greatness" of Mary's child would far surpass that of the Baptist (Mt 3:11; Mt 12:42; Php 2:9-11). This child would rightfully be called "Son of the Most High" (υἱὸς ὑψίστου). Apart from its topographical use, ὕψιστος always designates "God" in the Septuagint. Jesus is the "Son" of Psalm 2 and would be acknowledged as the Son of God by disciple and demon alike (Mk 5:7; Jn 6:69). He is Immanuel — "God with us." God's plan of salvation continues to unfold. "God sent his Son, born of a woman" (Ga 4:4).

The Lord God (Κύριος ὁ θεός) was about to fulfill his gracious Messianic promises by giving this holy child "the throne of his father David." The Lord had promised on oath that he would place one of David's descendants on an enduring throne (2 Sm 7:12,13,16). See also Jeremiah 23:5.

This thought is expanded as the angelic announcement continues:

v. 33 — *"and he will reign over the house of Jacob forever; his kingdom will never end."*

With the words "over the house of Jacob" (ἐπὶ τὸν οἶκον᾽Ιακὼβ), the sphere of the Savior's ruling activity is described. His kingdom has no earthly boundaries. He will rule in the hearts of the true, spiritual Israel — those who are sons and daughters of Abraham through faith (Ro 9:6-8; Ga 3:29; Php 3:3). Jesus certainly has fulfilled the words of the angel by defending and proteting God's people from all evil. And this kindom will last "forever" (εἰς τοὺς αἰῶνας). Death itself will not separate the child of God from this king's loving rule (2 Tm 4:18).

This stunning announcement of the Savior's birth leaves Mary perplexed, as we shall see:

v. 34 — *"How will this be," Mary asked the angel, "since I am a virgin?"*

Zechariah wanted a sign as assurance that the angel's words were true (1:18). Mary does not ask for a sign. She displays no doubt at this glorious message, but she does ask for an explanation. Her confusion is understandable. She was still a virgin (ἄνδρα οὐ γινώσκω).

Mary's question received an immediate reply:

v. 35 — *The angel answered, "The Holy Spirit will come upon you, and the power of the Most High will overshadow you. So the holy one to be born will be called the Son of God."*

Mary's child would have no human father. The Holy Spirit would begin a life in her through supernatural means. The words describing the conception are carefully chosen and befit the majesty of this blessed event. The first verb, "come upon" (ἐπέρχομαι), is also used by Luke to depict the activity of the Holy Spirit at Pentecost. The verb "overshadow" (ἐπισκιάζω) was used in the Septuagint to describe the activity of the Shekinah in Exodus 40:35.

Ever since the fall into sin people have been conceived and born in sin (Job 14:4; Ps 51:5). By nature they are the objects of God's wrath (Eph 2:3). But Mary's child would be "the holy one" (ἅγιον). By virtue of his virgin birth Jesus shared in our humanity, but not our sinfulness. Such a perfect, holy Savior was necessary. It was this Savior who kept the law perfectly in our place and offered himself as the atoning sacrifice for our sins.

The proper title "Son of God" (υἱὸς θεοῦ) belongs only to Jesus. We are reminded of John 3:16, 1 John 4:9 and other passages that refer to the saving work of this one and only Son of God.

Mary had not asked for a sign that the angel's words were true, but now she receives one:

v. 36 — *"Even Elizabeth your relative is going to have a child in her old age, and she who was said to be barren is in her sixth month."*

The degree of relationship between Mary and Elizabeth is not determined by the word "relative" (ἡ συγγενίς). Elizabeth was a descendant of Aaron (1:5) and Mary a descendant of David (2:34; Ac 2:30; Ro 1:3). It would appear that their family trees had become entwined through intertribal marriage at some point.

The pregnancy of Elizabeth was miraculous. She had come to be known as "barren" (στεῖρα), but now in her old age God was blessing her with a special son. The joy which Mary and Elizabeth share when they review God's almighty power and amazing grace is recorded by Luke in the section following our text (1:39-56). One is reminded of the privilege we have to gather with fellow Christians and review God's blessings and love in our lives (He 10:25).

The angel concludes his response to Mary's question with these words:

v. 37 — *"For nothing is impossible with God."*

The almighty God operates over the laws of nature as we know them. This same thought was phrased as a question at the time Isaac's birth was promised (Ge 18:14). Jesus also applied this principle when speaking about entrance into the kingdom of God in Matthew 19:26. Jesus' disciples rightly deduced that it would be impossible for anyone to enter the kingdom of God, but Jesus reminded them that God can make the impossible a reality. It was God who accomplished the impossible when he forgave the unforgiveable through the death and resurrection of Jesus.

What was Mary's reaction to the angelic announcement?

v. 38 — *"I am the Lord's servant," Mary answered. "May it be to me as you have said." Then the angel left her.*

Mary's faithful response is clear evidence of God's grace in her life. Her God-given faith allows her to accept the angel's message without question and humbly place herself in the Lord's service. Notice the similar response of David in 2 Samuel 7:25-29. We would do well to imitate Mary's response in our lives; to place ourselves totally at the Lord's disposal as his "servant" (δούλη) and cling to his gracious promises expressed in his saving Word.

The angel's work was now done. The glorious message had been delivered. The next time we shall meet angels in Luke's Gospel is on the night of our Savior's birth when this marvelous announcement finds its fulfillment in the coming of the Christchild.

## Homiletical Suggestions

This Advent text exudes God's grace and favor. Why was the angel Gabriel sent to a virgin named Mary in the insignificant town of Nazareth? The answer lies in God's grace. Why was God making good a promise he had given to people who had so often turned their backs on him? The answer is grace. What caused Mary to accept as truth the unbelievable message which the angel brought? Again we come back to the grace which God had given to her.

As we approach the celebration of our Lord's birth we, too, need to be reminded that it was God's love for us that moved him to send his Son into the world, conceived by the Holy Spirit, born of the virgin Mary, to be our Savior. The following outline attempts to capture the emphasis on God's grace and favor:

## The Angelic Announcement Demonstrates God's Grace

1. In grace God chose Mary to be the mother of his Son (vv. 26-30)
2. In grace God fulfilled his promise to send a Savior and King (vv. 31-33)
3. In grace God led Mary to believe his promise (vv. 34-38)

The preacher will want to lead his hearers to recognize God's grace in their lives. God came into our lives and chose us to be his own by grace. By grace we have been led to acknowledge Jesus as our Savior and King. By grace God has caused us to accept the "foolishness" of the gospel as wisdom from God (cf. 1 Co 1:26-31).

An alternative outline emphasizes the miracle of the incarnation:

## A Miracle Is About to Happen!

1. A miracle announced by an angel (vv. 26-31)
2. A miracle promised by God (vv. 32-37)
3. A miracle accepted by faith (v. 38)

The hearers need to be reminded that God continues to announce his miraculous plan of salvation to us through the gospel. What a comfort to know that the God who made good on his promise to send a Savior is our God. We can cast *all* our cares on him, for with God *all* things are possible. While we may not be able to comprehend the miracle of the virgin birth, we accept it by faith, just as Mary did. What a beautiful introduction to Christmas Day, when we see the miracle of God's love lying in the manger.

This text may also be pared down in order to focus on a particular aspect of the angel's announcement. For example:

## What Kind Of Child Will He Be?

1. A human child, born of Mary (vv. 30,31)
2. A divine child, conceived by the Holy Spirit (vv. 32-35)

This division allows the preacher to concentrate on the person of Christ and the necessity of both the human nature and the divine nature to accomplish the great work Jesus was sent to do.

# CHRISTMAS DAY —
# NATIVITY OF OUR LORD

## The Scriptures

Old Testament — *Isaiah 62:10-12*
Epistle — *Titus 3:4-7*
Gospel — *Luke 2:1-20*

## The Text — Luke 2:1-20

Many of the people in the pews on Christmas Day know these twenty verses from memory. The words are written indelibly on their minds from repeated recitations in children's Christmas services. While the familiarity of these verses pleases the parishioners on the festival of Christ's birth, that same familiarity may intimidate the preacher. How can I say anything new about this text?

Lest apprehensions like that rob the preacher of the joy connected with delivering a Christmas Day sermon, let him remember that the Lord of the church hasn't called his servants to proclaim anything new. He has called them to preach the gospel of Jesus Christ. And these twenty verses relate that good news so clearly, so sweetly, so wonderfully. Instead of considering Luke 2:1-20 as a routine account of the birth of Jesus, the preacher should view it as a scriptural treasure-chest full of rich preaching gems.

The Holy Spirit could have inspired Luke to write nothing more than, "A son was born of Mary in Bethlehem." But in his wisdom the Holy Spirit told Luke to record other facts as well: the census that brought Joseph and Mary to Bethlehem, the lowly birth of the Savior of the world in the stable, Jesus' first crude clothes, the angelic announcement to the shepherds, the shepherds' enthusiastic response to the gospel message, Mary's meditation on the birth of her Savior, and the natural evangelism method of the shepherds as they returned to the fields.

The preacher will have to decide which of those items from the sacred record he wants to include as application and/or appropriation. The central thought of any sermon on any portion of these verses will be, "Today in the town of David a Savior has been born to you; he is Christ the Lord" (v. 11). It is vital to keep the sermon that is based on Luke 2:1-20 centered where it should be and not on a Christmas sidelight. The latter approach may be tempting to the preacher who thinks he has run out of fresh Christmas material in Luke 2:1-20. Read the verses again. See where the attention is focused? Focus the listeners' attention on the same person: the God-man, Jesus Christ.

vv. 1-4 — *In those days Caesar Augustus issued a decree that a census should be taken of the entire Roman world. (This was the first census that took place while Quirinius was governor of Syria.) And everyone went to his own town to register. So Joseph also went up from the town of Nazareth in Galilee to Judea, to Bethlehem the town of David, because he belonged to the house and line of David.*

The Roman emperor was an unwitting participant in God's plan for having the Savior born in Bethlehem. God used the pride of Caesar Augustus to fulfill his heavenly plan to the last detail. "The time had fully come" (Ga 4:4). Not man's time, but God's time, 4,000 years after the first Messianic promise. History truly is his story.

vv. 5-7 — *He went there to register with Mary, who was pledged to be married to him and was expecting a child. While they were there, the time came for the baby to be born, and she gave birth to her firstborn, a son. She wrapped him in cloths and placed him in a manger, because there was no room for them in the inn.*

Joseph and Mary's marriage was "pledged" but not yet consummated by sexual relations. The baby is described as Mary's πρωτό-τοκον, her "firstborn," not as her μονογενῆ, her "only-born." Mary was not required by law to accompany her fiancé on the census trip, but she went at the guidance of the Holy Spirit, who was intent on fulfilling the prophecy mentioned earlier.

The fact that the Savior planned to be born in such humble surroundings and of such an unassuming mother was not meant to make us feel sorry for him. The manner of his birth was in keeping with his mission. "The Son of Man did not come to be served, but to serve, and to give his life as a ransom for many" (Mt 20:28). There would be no posh palace on earth for this king. His reign on earth would be marked by humility.

vv. 8-14 — *And there were shepherds living out in the fields nearby, keeping watch over their flocks at night. An angel of the Lord appeared to them, and the glory of the Lord shone around them, and they were terrified. But the angel said, to them, "Do not be afraid. I bring you good news of great joy that will be for all the people. Today in the town of David a Savior has been born to you; he is Christ the Lord. This will be a sign to you: You will find a baby wrapped in cloths and lying in a manger." Suddenly a great company of the heavenly host appeared with the angel, praising God and saying, "Glory to God in the highest, and on earth peace to men on whom his favor rests."*

Though the Savior's birth was humble, its significance for sinners is life-changing — eternally so. Such an event was worth a heavenly announcement that would make the most pretentious press conference on earth look like child's play. The Lord chose angels and his glory (δόξα, corresponding to כָּבוֹד, the Old Testament term for the presence of the Lord) as the vehicles to make that blessed birth announcement.

Look at that birth announcement and note the Greek names listed for the newborn King: σωτήρ, the "Savior" who rescues sinners from eternal disaster; χριστός, the "one anointed" and appointed by God himself for history's most important mission; κύριος, the true "Lord" of free and faithful grace, come to do what only he can do.

And because he would be completely successful in living up to all those names, heavenly angels could already shout, "Glory to God!" Even though Christ was only a tiny infant at that time, the angels were quite correct to proclaim that his arrival already meant peace on earth — not political peace between super powers, but spiritual peace between God, who demands perfection, and sinners, who render damning disobedience, a spiritual peace made possible by the baby's perfect obedience and sacrificial death to come.

vv. 15-18 — *"When the angels had left them and gone into heaven, the shepherds said to one another, "Let's go to Bethlehem and see this thing that has happened, which the Lord has told us about." So they hurried off and found Mary and Joseph, and the baby, who was lying in the manger. When they had seen him, they spread the word concerning what had been told them about this child, and all who heard it were amazed at what the shepherds said to them.*

If only we could celebrate Christmas the way the shepherds did! No Santa Clauses to clutter the view of the Christchild. No idea that it has to be white outside for us to be in the Christmas spirit. No hustle or holiday hucksters. No bustle to buy the right gifts. Oh, to hear the Lord speak to us about the birth of the Savior without media celebrities singing about jingling bells! The shepherds heard about him who would become known as the Good Shepherd and went to worship him. They asked no questions. They simply took the Lord at his word. And then they spread that word, spread it in their own simple, natural way. "How beautiful on the mountains are the feet of those who bring good news, who proclaim peace, who bring good tidings, who proclaim salvation" (Isa 52:7)

vv. 19,20 — *But Mary treasured up all these things and pondered them in her heart. The shepherds returned, glorifying and praising God for all the things they had heard and seen, which were just as they had been told.*

Mary not only wondered about all the things that had happened, she also "treasured" them. She valued the birth of her son and her Savior so highly that she kept this miracle guarded in her heart. It was not guarded to prevent anyone from seeing it, but guarded like a priceless jewel in a museum: available for all to see, but impossible for any to steal from her.

And those shepherds were changed forever by what "they had heard and seen." They didn't trade in their shepherd's staves for clerical collars. They returned to their livelihood: shepherding. But they were new men. They couldn't stay quiet about what God had done for them and all sinners.

Does our Christmas celebration move us the same way it moved Mary and the shepherds? If not, why not? Could it be because our celebration is focused on the wrong gift?

## Homiletical Suggestions

If this is being read in mid-December, the following advice is too late. Try it next year. Put your Christmas outline together in summer. That is not suggested here primarily as a time-saving device for one of the pastor's busiest weeks of the year. It is mentioned here to allow the preacher to study the Christmas gospel apart from the holiday hoopla of December. Meditating on the birth of Christ when the grass is green, the colored lights are still safe in the attic, and there are no gift lists in sight is spiritually refreshing and awakening.

The preacher will have to decide whether he wants to treat all twenty verses in the sermon or only portions of the Christmas Day Gospel. As has been mentioned, regardless of which verses are highlighted, the spotlight must shine on the baby in Bethlehem, Jesus Christ.

If the Advent sermon texts were Old Testament prophecies of the Savior, the following treatment of the Christmas Gospel will be a natural crowning point for the celebration the parishioners have spent a month preparing for:

## Jesus, The Savior, Is Born!

1. Born just as foretold (vv. 1-7)
2. Born to redeem all sinners (vv. 8-14)

If the preacher wants to cover the whole text in one sermon, he might choose to go at this way:

## Let's Go To Bethlehem!
1. Where the promises of old are fulfilled (vv. 1-4)
2. Where the eternal Word is made flesh (vv. 5-7)
3. Where the gate of heaven is opened for sinners (vv. 8-20)

To impress on the believer that the birth of Christ is a gift that lasts a lifetime, that never wears out, and is a celebration that never ends, the concluding verses of the text work well. A caution here —don't speak too much about the shepherds at the expense of treating the gift, Jesus Christ.

## Celebrate Christmas All Year Long
1. By welcoming God's gift as the shepherds did (v. 15)
2. By worshiping God's gift as the shepherds did (vv. 16,17)
3. By talking about God's gift as the shepherds did (vv. 17,18,20)

Although this suggestion focuses on the shepherds, the entire text can be referred to as the parts unfold.

# FIRST SUNDAY AFTER CHRISTMAS

**The Scriptures**

> Old Testament — *Isaiah 45:22-25*
> Epistle — *Colossians 3:12-21*
> Gospel — *Luke 2:25-40*

**The Text — Luke 2:25-40**

For many the Christmas "hype and hoopla" are over. Now comes the time to unwind and just watch the bills come in. How different for Joseph and Mary. Their "Christmas" was over, but within eight days they were at the Jerusalem temple for the required purification of the mother and presentation of her first-born son. How different also for God-fearing, Spirit-filled Simeon and Anna, who didn't even realize the first Christmas had come and gone. They were still waiting — fervently, longingly, hungrily.

But the fulness of the time had come, and Simeon and Anna would finally see with their very own eyes what they and countless other believers in the Lord had been yearning for since the Edenic protevangel. Christmas Day was over, but the glow of Christmas had just begun to shine with peaceful glory.

> vv. 25-27a — *Now there was a man in Jerusalem called Simeon, who was righteous and devout. He was waiting for the consolation of Israel, and the Holy Spirit was upon him. It had been revealed to him by the Holy Spirit that he would not die before he had seen the Lord's Christ. Moved by the Spirit, he went into the temple courts.*

Even a quick reading of the words brings out the obvious emphasis on the Holy Spirit. For it was the Holy Spirit who made Simeon different from the others in Jerusalem who weren't longing for the "consolation" (παράκλησιν — "comfort") of Israel. It was the Holy Spirit who converted Simeon into a "righteous" (δίκαιος) and "devout" (εὐλαβής) man. The Holy Spirit had even personally revealed to Simeon in some way that he would not die until he had seen "the Lord's Christ" (τὸν Χριστὸν κυρίου). In this connection it is good to note that, although Simeon is often pictured as an old man, we have no real evidence to claim that for certain.

But imagine! The one promised by God to Adam and reaffirmed by all the prophets through Malachi was going to come during this man's lifetime! Each morning must have brought new anticipation!

Eight days after Jesus' birth the anticipation ended. The Holy Spirit, the companion of Simeon and all believers, moved Simeon (he "came in the Spirit") to enter the temple courts, where the Christmas gift of salvation was about to be revealed in personal form.

vv. 27b-28 — *When the parents brought in the child Jesus to do for him what the custom of the Law required, Simeon took him in his arms and praised God, saying:*

Simeon is not the only person of the Spirit in this text. Humble Mary and godly Joseph also followed the will of the Spirit by obediently fulfilling the requirements of the Mosaic law, which demanded that a mother be purified (Lev 12:1-8) and that a firstborn son be redeemed (Ex 13:1,2,11-16).

We don't know exactly how the Holy Spirit identified Jesus of Nazareth as the one for Simeon to take into his arms, but take him into his arms he did. And, judging from the words which follow, we can almost imagine the reverent awe with which he held the holy babe.

vv. 29-32 — *"Sovereign Lord, as you have promised, you now dismiss your servant in peace. For my eyes have seen your salvation, which you have prepared in the sight of all people, a light for revelation to the Gentiles and for glory to your people Israel."*

Simeon's reverence exploded into a song of praise as he gave honor to his Lord and Savior. As he is in all of Scripture, the Lord is the central figure of this text — not Simeon, not Mary and Joseph, not Anna the prophetess — but our Lord and God, God the Father who sent his Son and who gave his Spirit. That attitude is shown by Simeon's choice of words: "Lord, Master" (δέσποτα), "servant, slave" (δοῦλον). The Lord, of course, is the one who should be acknowledged and praised — a good reminder for us as we decide how best to divide and treat this text.

The Greek verb ἀπολύεις ("dismiss") may be either indicative or imperative. The point is that Simeon can now live in total peace of mind and soul because he has seen the reason why he can die in peace — his Lord and Savior. He, in fact, calls Jesus "salvation" (σωτήριον). Jesus is the embodiment of salvation, the one who has set Simeon free (the root meaning of ἀπολύω) for the rest of his life.

The details of this salvation were not worked out in some dark corner. They were not kept hidden from the nations of the world, reserved only for the inhabitants of Palestine. God's dealings with the ancestors of the Savior and the Savior's actual birth were accomplished in full view of all (κατὰ πρόσωπον πάντων τῶν λαῶν).

What a beautiful Spirit-wrought faith which realized the missiological nature of the Messiah's coming! Simeon knew his Scriptures. He knew Jesus was Savior of both Jew and Gentile. His choice of expressions in this beautiful *Nunc Dimittis* reflects the thoughts of the prophet Isaiah in 40:5; 52:10; 42:6; 49:6,9; 25:7; and 46:13. A serious student of this section will want to familiarize himself with these allusions so that in his preaching he can better breathe the spirit of Simeon.

The Savior truly is a light for "revelation" (ἀποκάλυψιν) to the Gentiles and the "glory" (δόξαν) of God's chosen Israel. The sin-darkened eyes of the godless can now openly see the salvation of the Lord, salvation in the person of Jesus, the splendor and crowning delight of the faithful in Israel.

vv. 33-35 — *The child's father and mother marveled at what was said about him. Then Simeon blessed them and said to Mary, his mother: "This child is destined to cause the falling and rising of many in Israel, and to be a sign that will be spoken against, so that the thoughts of many hearts will be revealed. And a sword will pierce your own soul too."*

Little wonder Joseph and Mary marvelled (θαυμάζοντες) at what Simeon said. We, too, can only wonder with amazement as we realize and appreciate the feeling of peace which is ours when facing frustrations in life and fears at death. How appropriate it is to sing these words after receiving the blessing and assurance of our Lord in his Supper: "Depart in peace."

But there is another side to spiritual "peace" and "consolation" in Israel. Not all people belong to God's family of believers. Not all desire or care about the salvation which the Lord offers them. This Simeon also predicted. Turning to Mary, he pointed out that the little baby in his arms would also be a stumbling block for many in the land of Israel. Jews, we are told, looked for signs (cf. Lk 11:29; 1 Cor 1:22), but the "sign" of Jesus they would not accept. They saw the Lord of their salvation only as an agent of the devil, his gospel only as foolishness. The Prince of peace, it is clear, would also be the Christ of conflict.

The pain unbelievers would later inflict on Jesus would make its way into Mary's soul as well. But the sinful "thoughts" and human reasonings (διαλογισμοί) would be "revealed" (ἀποκαλυφθῶσιν). Tragically, the spiritual blindness of all who reject the Savior will be brought to light in the flashing brilliance of judgment day. Part of the preacher's task, obviously, is to remind his hearers that the Christmas Savior was not treated as a lovingly gift-wrapped present. He bore the pain of hell itself — for us. God help us to view the Savior's passion in humble repentance and with honest examination so that we can properly answer the Savior's probing question, "What do *you* think of Christ?"

vv. 36-38 — *There was also a prophetess, Anna, the daughter of Phanuel, of the tribe of Asher. She was very old; she had lived with her husband seven years after her marriage, and then was a widow until she was eighty-four. She never left the temple but worshiped night and day, fasting and praying. Coming up to them at that very moment, she gave thanks to God and spoke about the child to all who were looking forward to the redemption of Jerusalem.*

Another beautiful child of God comes to our attention. Anna, designated as a "prophetess" (προφῆτις), one who understands and explains the Word for mutual upbuilding, was "very old" (προβεβηκυῖα ἐν ἡμέραις πολλαῖς). Whether she was eighty-four or about one hundred and five is an exegetical question. Either way, she was an elderly, Spirit-filled woman who is characterized as one who could constantly be found at the temple fasting and praying. (Note the imperfect tense of ἀφίστατο — she regularly made it her habit not to leave the temple court for extended periods of time.) In a very real way the temple was her home.

When she saw Jesus, she realized the significance of the moment. As one who longed for the "redemption" (λύτρωσιν) of Jerusalem, Anna just had to tell her fellow believers what the Lord had allowed her to see. The ransom price needed to free God's people from their iniquity would be paid by the one who himself had just been redeemed by a pair of little doves.

Both Simeon and Anna had expressed what was overflowing in their hearts — the thankful feelings of peace and joy brought about by the fact that their God had ended their lonely exile by causing his Son to appear. They had to share what they had seen and heard.

vv. 39-40 — *When Joseph and Mary had done everything required by the Law of the Lord, they returned to Galilee to their own town of Nazareth. And the child grew and became strong; he was filled with wisdom, and the grace of God was upon him.*

Now Mary and Joseph could finally go back to Nazareth and begin to "settle down" after celebrating the world's first Christmas. But they didn't leave until the Mosaic rites had been fully carried out. Their son, though above the law in his Godhood, was born under the law in his humanity. And that was one of the reasons God's favor (χάρις) was upon him. Jesus was God's Son, who pleased the Father highly. He lived as one of us and he died for all of us, a death that was necessary, ironically, because we who should have died under the law could in no other way live eternally before our holy God.

That kind of Christmas gift can only cause us to marvel like Joseph and Mary. It can only cause us to live and confess like Simeon and Anna. It can only cause us to look at all the days after Christmas as special days to give God praise.

## Homiletical Suggestions

This text allows us to step back and take a meditative look at the Savior whose birth we just celebrated. We have the opportunity to look through the eyes of spiritually alive Simeon and Anna, people of God who were led by the Spirit in their lives of faith. As we reflect on the work of the Holy Spirit in their lives, we must take note of the far different spirit that has permeated so much of the pre-Christmas build-up, the spirit of artificial love, peace and good will, the spirit of hucksterism and outright greed. Through this section of God's word we have a precious opportunity to think about:

### The True Spirit Of Christmas

1. Leads to a life in Christ (vv. 25-28,36,37,39)
2. Leads to a confession of Christ (vv. 29-35,38)

As we read the words of verse 40, we are humbled by our inability to comprehend the mystery of how Jesus could grow up as a normal child and yet could at all times remain the Son of God. In addition, as we listen to Simeon's song and observe Anna's response upon seeing their Savior from sin, we can only marvel with the Christmas song writer:

### What Child Is This?

1. The Christ who was predicted and expected (vv. 25-28,36-38)
2. The Christ who brings peace and the sword (vv. 29-35)

To capture the earnest yearning of the faithful in Israel as they awaited the day of the Messiah's birth, we can take off on the Advent hymn which prayed for the Savior's coming. Part one speaks of the general purpose of the Savior's mission, while part two speaks to us as specific individuals who need and who have the Savior Simeon sang about:

### He Came! He Came! Emmanuel

1. To ransom captive Israel (vv. 29-35)
2. To bring peace to thirsting souls (vv. 25-28,36-38)

# NEW YEAR'S DAY

**The Scriptures**

> Old Testament — *Numbers 6:22-27*
> Epistle — *Romans 1:1-7*
> Gospel — *Luke 2:21*

**The Text — Luke 2:21**

vv. 21 — *On the eighth day, when it was time to circumcise him, he was named Jesus, the name the angel had given him before he had been conceived.*

This twenty-first verse of the second chapter of the Gospel according to St. Luke lives in the shadow of the glorious Christmas Gospel reading of Luke 2:1-20. The familiarity of the Christmas story and the glory of its wondrous revelation with its supernatural wonders and signs may at first cause this lone verse to become not only overshadowed, but almost lost. In fact, the magnetic charm of the account of Christ's birth compared to the stark record of his circumcision may at first glance make the latter seem not only insignificant, but almost a repulsive appendage to the verses of Luke 2:1-20.

The circumcision and naming of Jesus is the scriptural subject for the festival of New Year's Day, a festival which has increasingly become more secular than sacred. Just as the festival has lost its religious importance, so some might prefer that this twenty-first verse of Luke 2 had also been lost so that the glistening pristine whiteness of Christmas might be unstained by the red blood of Christ's circumcision.

The full meaning of Christmas is not found in the fact that the Word was made flesh, but also in the purpose for which he entered our flesh and blood. Already on the eighth day of his earthly existence his blood flowed. As it flowed, it was both portent and promise of the redemptive blood of Calvary, which was the goal and purpose of Bethlehem. Lily-white purity contrasted with blood-red guilt! What a poignant sequence of stories from verse 20 to verse 21! What an apt perspective of the full meaning of Christmas it provides! What an appropriate observance on the octave of Christmas! How wonderfully meaningful becomes the name Jesus in its light!

The Child whose birth was recorded in the opening verses of the chapter had come to fulfill the law. "When the time had fully come, God sent his Son, born of a woman, born under law, to redeem those under law, that we might receive the full rights of sons" (Ga 4:4,5). He fulfilled the law to establish the gospel.

This fulfillment was to be perfect. Therefore, meticulous attention to the Lord's command is revealed with the words, "On the eighth day, when it was time to circumcise him.... " God had said circumcision should be performed on the eighth day (Ge 17:12), so the eighth day it was. He who had come to do his Father's work did his Father's will with delight (Ps 40:6-8). This circumcision rite was a part of Christ's state of humiliation, of which Paul speaks in Philippians 2:5-8.

The rite of circumcision was given to Abram as "the sign of the covenant between me and you" (Ge 17:11). In witness of the unilateral gospel covenant God graciously had made with Abram, this sign was instituted. That gospel promise had awakened faith in Abram's heart to receive its blessings of forgiveness and eternal life. "Abram believed the LORD, and he credited it to him as righteousness" (Ge 15:6). Now the outward seal whereby God attested Abram as his child and heir was established. "And he received the sign of circumcision, a seal of the righteousness that he had by faith while he was still uncircumcised" (Ro 4:11).

This covenant of circumcision for Abram served to strengthen the faith he already had. His offspring became God's children through the faith-creating power of this gracious Old Testament seal. Circumcision did not save apart from faith but through faith. The presence of that genuine faith by which one became God's child became evident in the "heart circumcision" of their lives, as Jeremiah said: "Circumcise yourselves to the LORD, circumcise your hearts" (Jer 4:4).

Circumcision was a God-ordained sign of the promise of the Savior. When that promise was fulfilled, the sign passed away. It was a gospel element of the old order which passed away with the new. The unbelieving Jews had made it into a law for man to perform in order to become righteous through the doing of it. They then based their assurance on their work of the flesh, not on God's promise received by faith. In this same way people today wrongfully seek to turn baptism into a grace-destroying work of man.

Circumcision was an outward sign signifying one's membership in God's convenant family. Submitting to circumcision would be an outward confession of faith that one believed God's promise and wanted to be included among his people. Parents having a child circumcised were likewise confessing their faith in and obedience to God in the same way that Christian parents do when they bring their children to baptism today. In the same way the Old Testament parents were to train their children to know the Lord whose gracious covenant had been received. They were also to watch that their children reflected their covenant relationship with God by circumcising their lives from sin. Without that inward disposition of the heart the outward mutilation of the flesh was nothing (Ro 2:25-29).

Jesus' circumcision was not only an act of obedience and a picture of redemption to come through his blood; it was also a declaration of his membership — yes leadership among the people of God as the Seed of Abraham (with a capital S). As his baptism put the power in our own, so his circumcision validated and empowered that Old Testament rite.

This initiatory rite obeyed by Christ, fulfilled and rendered obsolete by him, is a good picture of our own baptism, especially infant baptism: outwardly foolish and apparently impotent, yet possessing the saving strength and wisdom of God's word, command and promise. It humbles us and our flesh and mind while exalting and honoring the word and will of God.

The crowning touch of this particular event was not the rite of circumcision, but the royal Name bestowed upon him who received it. That name was Jesus — 'Iησοῦς in the Greek and יֵשׁוּעַ in the Hebrew.

The name comes from the Hebrew root יָשַׁע to set free or deliver, to bestow salvation. The prophecy of Zechariah 9:9, describing the Messiah in his work, makes this meaning clear: "Thy King cometh unto thee: he is just, and having salvation" (KJV). The name Jesus doesn't merely mean Savior, but "the Lord Saves."

This name Jesus was not an uncommon name. It it used of other men in the Bible, most notably and prophetically of the leader of Israel who led the people of God into the promised land of Canaan. Here this common name is used for an uncommon person, who is himself the Lord who saves!

The uniqueness and miraculous nature of this person was revealed to his mother and step-father by the angel who announced his conception and birth. Mary was told he "will be called the Son of the Most High" (Lk 1:32). Also, "the holy one to be born will be called the Son of God" (Lk 1:35). Matthew says that this birth was in fulfillment of Isaiah's prophecy: "The virgin will be with child and will give birth to a son, and they will call him Immanuel" — which means, "God with us" (Mt 1:23). God with us, not merely God on our side, but God physically present among us in the person of this child! Both Mary and Joseph thus were told that his name was to be Jesus

— literally the Lord saves — because this child is himself the Lord who saves his people from their sins.

This revelation was not restricted to Mary and Joseph but also announced to the shepherds in the fields of Bethlehem who were told: "Today in the town of David a Savior has been born to you; he is Christ the Lord" (Lk 2:11).

The name of this child and the name God or Lord are not just sounds, but sounds filled with meaning. The name of the Lord is his reputation. He made that name known to Moses when he preached a sermon on it in Exodus 34:6,7: "The LORD, the LORD, the compassionate and gracious God, slow to anger, abounding in love and faithfulness, maintaining love to thousands, and forgiving wickedness, rebellion and sin. Yet he does not leave the guilty unpunished; he punishes the children and their children for the sin of the fathers to the third and fourth generation."

Through the prophet Isaiah he refined that sermon to one word — "Savior": "For I am the LORD, your God, the Holy One of Israel, your Savior . . . " (Isa 43:3). "I, even I, am the LORD, and apart from me there is no savior" (Isa 43:11). " . . . there is no God apart from me, a righteous God and a Savior" (Isa 46:21).

Savior is the Lord's name and right alone! This child is called Jesus by divine right since he himself is "the Lord Who Saves"! As the angel said to Joseph: "He will save his people from their sins" (Mt 1:21). As Joshua led the Old Testament people of God into the promised land of Canaan, this Jesus blazed the trail that opened everlasting paradise for all, paradise which is received and enjoyed through faith in him as the Lord who saves!

## Homiletical Suggestions

Sermons built upon this verse will go to the heart of the Second Article of the Apostles' Creed, with emphasis upon the person and work of Christ. The blood of Christ, which he assumed in his incarnation, first flowed here as a promise of things to come, leading us into the heart of the gospel, the blood-atonement of Christ. All sermons from this text will of course expound on the meaning of his name, the wondrous name of love, Jesus. The active and passive obedience of Christ might also well be considered from this starting point. Our outlines are suggested along these lines:

### What's In A Name?
1. This name tells us who Jesus is
2. This name tells us what Jesus does

**The Lord Who Saves** (literal meaning of the name)
1. This child is the Lord!
2. This child saves!

**"He Was Named Jesus"**
1. Named by God for who he is
2. Named by God for what he does

**We Are Purchased By Precious Blood**
1. This blood is the precious blood of God
2. This blood flowed to purchase us

Combining the thought of the beginning of another secular year with this religious festival, we could also suggest:

**Begin The New Year In Jesus' Name**
1. Mindful of his love for us
2. Mindful of our love for him

Using the same theme we can word the parts:
1. A name of fulfillment of things past
2. A name of assurance for things ahead

# SECOND SUNDAY AFTER CHRISTMAS

## The Scriptures

> Old Testament — *Isaiah 61:10-62:3*
> Epistle — *Ephesians 1:3-6,15-18*
> Gospel — *John 1:1-18*

## The Text — John 1:1-18

That John's Gospel account of our Lord Jesus is different from the synoptics is immediately apparent. He takes the reader back to eternity, before there was time or matter. John wrote his account some thirty years after the synoptics were completed. New challenges to the truth of Jesus the Christ had arisen. The Holy Spirit led John to write in answer to these challenges. So this Gospel emphasizes who Jesus *is* to a far greater degree than the synoptics. In the process he establishes and underscores the full deity of Jesus and his co-equality with the Father.

vv. 1,2 — *In the beginning was the Word, and the Word was with God, and the Word was God. He was with God in the beginning.*

The term "the Word" (ὁ λόγος) is peculiar to John. Note the way it ties in with the opening words of Genesis and also with the final word of this section ("made him known" — v. 18). God is not a silent being. His desire to communicate about himself is inherent in his being.

The Greek preposition πρός indicates a sense of relationship, that is, to be "in company with" someone. Julian Anderson translates this phrase nicely: "He was living with God." John is instructing us to think of the Word as a distinct person within the Godhead.

But we should not think of the Word as inferior in some way to the Father, for *the Word was God.* (The article with λόγος identifies it as the subject; the lack of article with θεός marks it as the predicate.) The nature and essence of the Word is the nature and essence of God. The Word is not some "form" of God or semi-deity. He is God. Note how this is expressed in the Athanasian Creed.

With these eloquent phrases John is setting the stage in our minds for his observation in verse 14: "The Word became flesh and made his dwelling among us". To think that this Jesus, who was seen by men and lived among us, is actually the eternal Word of creation boggles our minds! It makes us marvel at his interest in us! Can we be *that* important to him?

Luther comments: "Again the evangelist reminds the reader that the Father and the Son are two distinct Persons, equally eternal. But he does this in a manner which at the same time apprises him of the fact that the eternal Father sprang from no one, was not made, created, or born, while the Son, the image of the eternal Father, was born of the Father alone and was not made or created. Before Jesus Christ was Mary's Son and became flesh, he was with God and was true and eternal God of one divine essence with the Father, although a Person distinct from the Father.... No evangelist other than John was able to stress and describe this article of faith in such a masterly manner."

v. 3 — *Through him all things were made; without him nothing was made that has been made.*

Not only did the Word *exist* in the beginning, but he was a functional and active being. Through a positive and a negative statement John carefully points out that the Word was the absolute agent in the creation of everything. There is no other means of creation than God himself through the Word.

These words also establish a link between God and the world we live in. John was faced with the errors of Gnosticism when he was inspired to write his Gospel. The Gnostics taught that only spirit was good, and that matter was essentially evil. But because God through the Word created matter and because the Word became human, the link between the two is inseparable. Matter is not essentially evil. Sin is not native to nature. We live in the hope that sin's corrupting influence will soon be removed (Ro 8:18-25).

v. 4 — *In him was life, and that life was the light of men.*

The life that was in the Word was not mere biological functioning (βιός), but spiritual activity and consciousness (ζωή). The preposition ἔν conveys the idea of a sphere of influence. The place to find life is in the living Word. This is brought out later when Jesus declares, "I have come that they may have life ... to the full" (10:10), and again, "I am ... the life" (11:25).

On "that life was the light of men" Anderson comments: "Life, or 'energy', exists in many different forms — as light, heat, motion, electrical energy, atomic energy, etc., all of which are interchangeable. When God created light, therefore (Ge 1:3), he created all forms of energy from the Life existing in Himself. Here, then, the word 'light' really includes all other forms of energy."

The Word is not merely a maker, but a life-creator. Note the reference to it, for example in Hymn 70 (TLH):

Hosanna to the living Lord!
Hosanna to th' Incarnate Word!
To Christ, **Creator**, Savior, King,
Let earth, let heav'n, hosanna sing.

He does not merely call into existence, but he himself continues to live on endlessly to control and direct the affairs of that which he creates.

Just as a flame does not exist simply to burn, but to give light and other forms of energy to its surroundings, so the life does not exist in the abstract or in a void, but serves as the light of men. Once again we note Anderson's translation: *and His Life was the source of the light men need.*

"*Appears*" (φαίνει) is the first verb in the present tense (all previous verbs were aorists). This light continues to shine so that men of even the latest age are to see by it and find life.

v. 5 — *The light shines in the darkness, but the darkness has not understood it.*

The concept of darkness is a metaphor for the spiritual condition of natural man. It is the very opposite of the light. Since the light is also the life, the darkness is death with its separation from the light, the life, the Word, God!

The verb καταλαμβάνω can mean, "win, attain, make one's own," and so it would convey the idea that although the light of God was shining in the world of sin-darkened mankind, still they did not grasp or comprehend it (so the NIV here). The verb also can mean "suppress, overcome," and so it would imply that darkness attempts to extinguish ("put out" — Goodspeed) the light but is not able because the light is eternal and unextinguishable. It might well be that John had both concepts in mind.

The similarities between verses 1-5 and Genesis 1 are both striking and intentional. With breathtaking majesty and awe we note that the Son being called the Word, his pre-existence in the beginning, his divine nature, his involvement in creation, his being the source of light and life — all have their counterparts in the opening book of Scripture. Even the simple, powerful use of words is the same. When later we realize that the Word is Jesus Christ, these opening verses not only underscore his deity and equality with the Father, but they also explain how he has such a command of natural forces (calming the winds and waves, multiplying the loaves, walking on water, etc.) You may wish to compare these verses in Paul's inspired commentary on this concept in Colossians 1:15-17.

v. 6 — *There came a man who was sent from God; his name was John.*

The opening words strike us with their abruptness. They arrest our attention. Like the witness at a trial saying, "All of a sudden, seemingly out of nowhere, this person appeared along the highway!" so now John the Baptist makes an abrupt entrance into our world. By using ἄνθρωπος instead of ἀνήρ John emphasizes God's involvement in humanity as a whole rather than the gender of that involvement.

The use of the participle (ἀπεσταλμένος) emphasizes the verbal action, that is, "the sending." The passive form of the verb indicates that this man's coming was initiated by God. So has it ever been with God's prophets. We think of Moses, Amos, Jeremiah, Isaiah, Jonah. God assigned to them their specific ministry and sent them to it. The choice and the mission were of God's design and doing. Even today we understand the divine call to come from God, not man.

"His name was John" — John the Baptist was an imposing figure in his century. He was the first prophet from God to appear since Malachi almost 400 years before him. That he is named for us removes any doubt as to the identity of this man in history. That he is named also shows God's use of an individual to accomplish his will. John was just one man, but he did a yeoman's task in history because he was "sent from God."

This entire verse, eight words in the Greek, could simply have been written as "God sent John." Its length emphasizes John's role in God's salvation history.

v. 7 — *He came as a witness to testify concerning that light, so that through him all men might believe.*

John's purpose in life was to draw attention to someone else. It takes a rare person — one whom God gives the gift of humility — to be himself so gifted and yet at the same time be truly self-effacing.

The Greek demonstrative ὅυτος links this verse unmistakably with John, the one God sent. The aorist verb indicates simply that John came. The sense is punctiliar. He was here; he did his job. He's gone. It's done.

Ἐις μαρτυρίαν is literally "for testimony" and conveys the picture of a courtroom witness giving his account of what he saw and heard. The emphasis, however, is on the testimony, not the person or personality of the witness.

The ἵνα clause with the subjunctive of μαρτυρέω is a purpose clause. John's role is obvious to us who have the advantage of hindsight, but to his contemporaries there was a distinct need to draw attention to Jesus.

The role of a witness makes good sense. Jesus went about his business of teaching, preaching and healing. His words and works were to lead people to their own conclusions. But God, who does all things in a decent and orderly way, sent John to serve as Jesus' "PR man." For the same reason that a local politician up for re-election welcomes the endorsement of a popular, respected and already-established political figure, so Jesus' own ministry would be enhanced and appear more credible to the Jews if a man of such stature as John lent him his full support.

John carried out his role eloquently. His testimony reached its zenith when he pointed to Jesus and declared, "Look, the Lamb of God, who takes away the sin of the world!" (29). If darkness is a metaphor for sin, then Jesus must be the light, for he erased the darkness through his redemptive work.

While John's witness was carried out locally along the Jordan, its impact was to reach far beyond the region. His witness was intended that all, not just Jews, might believe. The Jews are not excluded from God's grace with these words, but the word "all" (πάντες) indicates that they do not have exclusive rights to it. This is further supported with the word "might believe" (πιστεύσωσιν), for no one belongs to God's kingdom by genetic right but only through faith in the Christ. On this Luther says: "John the Baptist initiates the kingdom of Christ; he ushers in a new era. He bears witness to the Light, so that all, Jew and Gentile, may believe through him. Now the boast of the Jews, with their claim that they alone are God's people, is nullified... . Now a kingdom is being founded in which nothing at all avails — whether it bears the stamp of Abraham's seed, his flesh, his lineage, his pants, or his jerkin — nothing else than belief in the Son of God."

God's call to faith is through people. The gospel is the effective power (Ro 1:16), but it is still through people that the message is preached and taught (Ro 10:14). What a privilege for John to give testimony concerning the true light of the world! Is ours any less a privilege?

v. 8 — *He himself was not the light; he came only as a witness to the light.*

John the Baptist's power and influence lead our inspired writer to make his identity clear. Literally we read: Not was that one (John) the Light, but on the contrary (he was) to testify concerning the Light.

The first clause in Greek is powerful in its simple words. The position of οὐκ at the beginning of the sentence marks John for who he is not — *not* the light! The second clause is a word-for-word repetition of v. 7a. John's preparatory role must be crystal clear.

All preachers of the word need to take this clause to heart. They are not the Christ. Who is more capable, more gifted, more effective than John the Baptist? Yet he knew his place. He was simply Christ's witness. He was to decrease, the Christ must increase. John the Baptist was clear on this matter. We need always to perceive and live our role as well. No pastor or teacher of God's word dare leave the impression that he is "God's gift" to the flock. The Jonestown massacre in 1978 is still a vivid if extreme example of this truth.

v. 9 — *The true light that gives light to every man was coming into the world.*

The Word provided genuine, true and dependable light. He was not a mirage or a reflection that would throw a person off course in life or give false hopes. He is the light that guides through the storms of earthly life to eternal life.

This light shines for *every person*. He came for all, not just one race. John grasped the global reach of Christ's saving mission. Compare verse 29: "who takes away the sin of the world." The use of the singular (ἄνθρωπον) makes this saving mission of the Word very personal. He is the light for every person, but also each person. We hear this echoed later in 3:16: "that whoever believes in him . . . "

Hendriksen translates the participle ἐρχόμενον with "the act of coming." As a result of John's stunning testimony all people were to know that the long-expected Savior was at hand!

vv. 10,11 — *He was in the world, and though the world was made through him, the world did not recognize him. He came to that which was his own, but his own did not receive him.*

What stunning news John relates! Any father who has ever returned home from work only to find his whole family ignoring him has a feel for the "cold shoulder" God's world gave him at his coming. The disgusting nature of this is that "the world was made through him" and these people were "his own." God's ownership doesn't faze the world. The world isn't interested in him. Its inhabitants are only interested in themselves. Compare this with Isaiah 1:2-4. John uses "world" (κόσμος) in a specialized way to designate mankind alienated from God by sin and in need of deliverance.

vv. 12,13 — *Yet to all who received him, to those who believed in his name, he gave the right to become children of God — children born not of natural descent, nor of human decision or a husband's will, but born of God.*

By God's grace there are exceptions to the pathetic truth of the previous two verses. The word ὅσοι ("as many as" — KJV) stresses the inclusiveness of everyone within this concept of "receiving him." The NIV inserts the relative clause "to those who believe in his name" immediately after the opening words to clarify what "receiving him" means. "His name" is the revelation of himself to man as the Word, the life, the true light, and (later) God's Lamb.

The right to become God's children is God's gift. It is a right he "gives." No one takes it on his own initiative. Nobody born into the darkness of sin has a natural claim to this. Only Christ gives this power (ἐξουσίαν) to men through his Spirit (cf. 1 Co 12:3 and Eph 2:8,9). "Children" (τέκνα) is a term of endearment; "sons" (υἱοί) designates legal standing. "Child" expresses relation from; "son" expresses relation to. Lenski notes, "As regards our relation to God, the Scriptures have no sweeter name than this that we are 'God's children' and belong to his household, Eph 2:19."

Just as none of us chose our natural birth, neither can we choose our spiritual birth in God's family of believers. It is not a matter of breeding or family bloodlines (ἐξ αἱμάτων). Human decision or a man's desire for a son has nothing to do with it. The aorist passive verb ἐγεννήθησαν ("born of") shows the desire and decision are God's!

v. 14 — *The Word became flesh and made his dwelling among us. We have seen his glory, the glory of the One and Only, who came from the Father, full of grace and truth.*

At last the identity of the Word is revealed. He became Jesus, the one John and others lived with, and in whom they perceived (ἐθεασά- μεα) the glory of God's one and only Son. Certainly the transfiguration experience comes to mind, but that was not the only time Jesus' glory was evident. Grace and truth permeated Jesus' daily life. What a revelation! God becomes flesh! The Nicene Creed's "and was made man" reflects this profound event. So do a number of fine Christmas hymns (for example: "veiled in flesh the Godhead see, Hail the incarnate Deity!" TLH 94:2).

There is no hint here that the Word became a person. This he already was from eternity. He became "flesh" (σάρξ). He entered the human realm. Yet he did not give up his deity. He retained the glory of being God's one and only Son in all its fullness (cf. Php 2:6,7; Col 2:9). He made his dwelling among us. The Greek verb (ἐσκήνωσεν) means literally "he tented" among us, alluding to his temporary stay, which ended with his ascension.

He was the human embodiment of God's initiating and saving love (χάριτος) as well as the final and authoritative revelation of God to man (ἀληθείας). Luther makes these observations: "The dear church fathers took particular delight in these words, they set great store by them, and they praised God ... for the great honor conferred on us when he humbled himself and assumed our flesh and blood.... He became our flesh and blood. Who can express this adequately? The angels are much holier than we poor sinners, and yet he adopted our nature and became incarnate from the flesh and blood of the Virgin Mary." The more we ponder this great event the more we agree with Paul: "Beyond all question, the mystery of godliness is great: He appeared in a body ... " (1 Ti 3:16).

v. 15 — *John testifies concerning him. He cries out, saying, "This was he of whom I said, 'He who comes after me has surpassed me because he was before me.' "*

John the Baptist's witness is still effective (present tense verb). His witness was bold (κέκραγεν = "cry out, shout"). John's witness is a riddle to anyone who does not believe the pre-existence of the Son of God from eternity. The superlative (πρῶτος) could convey the idea of rank, but more significantly points back in time ("in the beginning" in v. 1).

Of interest is the way Julian Anderson adjusts the verse order. He makes this verse follow verse 18. The "we/us" thoughts then flow smoothly together as well as the account of John's ministry. The use of ὅτι instead of κάι gives license to this action.

v. 16 — *From the fullness of his grace we have all received one blessing after another.*

He who is full of grace and truth and is fully God-in-man is an overflowing well from whom we all have drunk of love we don't deserve. The verb is the aorist indicative. This "receiving" is something that happened. It's not only a possibility. It has occurred. We have been justified by his blood. While ἐλάβομεν can mean "take," it is not used with that connotation regarding grace. We receive what God gives. The "all" (πάντες) of this verse compares with the "all who" (ὅσοι) of verse 12.

"One blessing after another" conveys nicely the meaning of the Greek preposition ἀντί. The basic thought is that one thing is replaced by another. As one wave after another washes the beach with unending regularity, so the grace of Christ flows to us (cf. La 3:22,23; Ps 23:5). Christ is "the gift that keeps on giving."

v. 17 — *For the law was given through Moses; grace and truth came through Jesus Christ.*

John introduces still another contrast for our minds to digest, a contrast he will develop in succeeding portions of his book. The Jews were glued to the law of Moses so tightly that their hearts could not open to the grace and truth of salvation that was in Jesus Christ. See this, for example, in his bread of life discourse (chapter 6) or his claim to be the light of the world (chapter 8).

The Jews accepted and revered Moses. Through him the law had been given. The unbelieving hearts of the Jews did not want to leave the security of rigid rules and formulas for the suppleness of grace or the possibility that they were in error. They refused to abandon their pride and give all honor and praise to a carpenter's son. Yet grace and truth — those gifts sinners need in order to have eternal life —came not by Moses but by Jesus Christ.

There are three contrasts. The law — grace and truth; Moses —Jesus Christ; was given — came. The one common element is agency (διά — "through, by means of"). Moses was God's agent to bring the law. Jesus was the agent through whom God himself appeared in the fullness of grace and truth. The Old Testament ceremonial law was necessary, but only until Christ came (Ga 3:24). How important that we always see Jesus as the fulfillment of the law and that our ministry and preaching convey grace and truth, not sets of New Testament ceremonial laws.

v. 18 — *No one has ever seen God, but God the One and Only, who is at the Father's side, has made him known.*

The Greek text lays its emphasis on God. Throughout these eighteen verses we have been exposed to God in his fullness. But no one "has ever seen" him (ἑώρακεν — perfect indicative of ὁράω) in that fullness. Even Moses saw only God's back (Ex 33:18-23). There is, however, a better way of knowing God (John uses ἐξηγήσατο, which means "interpret, explain, describe"). He sent his Son to be his exegete. Compare this with Jesus' claims, "I and the Father are one" (10:30) and "Anyone who has seen me has seen the Father" (14:9).

The manuscript's divergence between "one and only Son" and "one and only God" shows the difficulty our finite minds have in comprehending the incarnation.

That this Son is at the Father's side tells us he has done more than see the Father. His knowledge of the Father is full and complete. He is not a reporter making a two-week tour of a foreign country and culture who then claims to be an expert. He is the ruler's son, who has grown up with the inner workings of the kingdom, who at the appropriate point in time enters our world to make known to us God's will and plans for us.

With this concluding word, "made (him) known" (ἐξηγήσατο), John ties these opening verses into a neat package, for to make someone known is the purpose of words. The Word came from heaven to make the Savior-God known to us, his creatures.

## Homiletical Suggestions

The grand sweep of these verses, covering the key themes which John develops in the rest of his Gospel, causes some difficulty for the preacher. There is so much to preach on! Usually we find ourselves breaking the verses down into sections. John's overriding interest is that we believe Jesus Christ is very God who has become flesh so that we might share in his life and light.

One suggestion might be:

### The Word Became Flesh

1. The Word in eternity (vv. 1-9)
2. The Word among us (vv. 10-18)

The first part would point out the eternal nature of the Word as creator, life and light. The second part would bring in the fact of the incarnation, the reason for it, and what value it has for those who believe.

A play on words might develop around the theme:

### Here's A Real Human Interest Story For You

1. God had every good reason not to care (vv. 4,5,10,11)
2. God's nature is to call us to himself (vv. 1-3,6-9,12-18)

Our society concentrates on Christmas during Advent and makes the holy season into a holiday that comes and goes all too quickly. If we pick up on the thoughts expressed in one of our favorite Christmas hymns, it would allow us to draw out some of the depth in the short season of the church year. A theme might develop such as this:

### Veiled In Flesh The Godhead See

1. John the Baptist's testimony points to it (vv. 1-9,15))
2. John the evangelist lived with it (v. 14)
3. Faith accepts this mystery and the blessings it brings (vv. 10-13,16-18)

The above thoughts for outlines can be woven into a use of this text as a homily, developing the themes by means of a running exposition of the text. This method, however, is not recommended for use unless one has had some experience with this kind of treatment!

# EPIPHANY OF OUR LORD

**The Scriptures**

> Old Testament — *Isaiah 60:1-6*
> Epistle — *Ephesians 3:2-12*
> Gospel — *Matthew 2:1-12*

**The Text — Matthew 2:1-12**

Since this is the first of only three texts from Matthew in ILCW Series B, a few comments about Matthew's Gospel are in order. Matthew wrote his Gospel about A.D. 60, perhaps earlier than the other Gospel writers. Writing primarily to Jews, Matthew shows the clashes between Jesus and the Jewish leaders who lived, not according to the Scriptures, but according to the traditions of their unbelieving fathers. Rejection by the Jews and acceptance by the Gentiles is foreshadowed in our text for the Epiphany of Our Lord.

Matthew's purpose is to present Jesus as the Messiah, "the Anointed One," the King of the Jews. He is the fulfillment of every prophecy about the Savior who would "save his people from their sins" (Mt 1:21).

Already in his second chapter Matthew introduces the Gentile Magi, indicating that Jesus' people whom he would save included more than the Jews. This, too, is in fulfillment of a prophecy by Hosea (2:23): "I will say to those called 'Not my people,' 'You are my people'; and they will say, 'You are my God.' " At the first epiphany of Jesus' star, we see how the future holds rejection by Jesus' physical people, but intense, sacrificial devotion by his spiritual people who feel their need for him, seek him out, and worship him with their gifts and obedience.

vv. 1,2 — *After Jesus was born in Bethlehem in Judea, during the time of King Herod, Magi from the east came to Jerusalem and asked, "Where is the one who has been born king of the Jews? We saw his star in the east and have come to worship him."*

Within months of Jesus' birth, while he was still living with his mother and stepfather Joseph in Bethlehem, the first Gentile worshipers of the newborn King arrived. These were the Magi, traditionally called Wise Men, the university professors and scientists of their day, who studied the wisdom of the ancients and especially the stars. Recently they had seen a special star which they somehow knew was an announcement of the birth of the "king of the Jews." They wanted to worship him as their Savior.

How they made the connection between this special star and the special birth is not stated in our text. But we do know that centuries earlier a Jew named Daniel had lived in exile in Babylon. Because of his God-given wisdom Daniel was "placed...in charge of all [Babylon's] wisemen" (Da 2:48). Daniel and other Jews like him in the *diaspora* witnessed fearlessly about the true God who had promised a Savior for all people. Perhaps through Daniel's witness passed down over the centuries, or through the testimony of other believing Jews, the Holy Spirit had led these Magi to see this star in Balaam's Messianic prophecy of Numbers 24:17: "A star will come out of Jacob; a scepter will rise out of Israel." Imagine their delight when at last they saw the star shining brilliantly in the heavens, beckoning them toward their promised king!

The Magi's eagerness to worship their Savior made distance and time insignificant for them. They may have had to journey over 500 miles from Babylon, although the oldest opinion places the journey of these Magi almost triple that distance to present-day Yemen, which is the ancient "Sheba" mentioned in Isaiah 60:6: "And all from Sheba will come, bearing gold and incense and proclaiming the praise of the LORD." (Note: This is part of the Old Testament lesson for the day.) Wherever they came from, these Magi still present a shining example of sincere devotion for modern Christians who sometimes must overcome obstacles of travel and time to worship their Savior and King.

Once they had reached the land of the Savior, the star apparently disappeared. Needing further information, the Magi naturally went to the ruler of the country, no doubt expecting to find the Jews already rejoicing about this momentous event.

v. 3 — *When King Herod heard this he was disturbed, and all Jerusalem with him.*

This is the King Herod known as "Herod the Great" because of his magnificent building projects, such as Herod's temple in Jerusalem and the Roman capital at Caesarea. From a Christian point of view, however, this Herod was "great" only in his wicked lust for power. There would be other Herods, but none more bloodthirsty and ruthless than Herod the Great.

The unsuspecting Magi arrived at the close of Herod's life after he had murdered one of his ten successive wives and three of his own sons, all of whom seemed to be plotting against him. No wonder Herod was so "disturbed" to hear the Magi ask, "Where is the one who has been born king of the Jews?" Herod's Jewish subjects in Jerusalem were "disturbed ... with him," not because of any loyalty for this non-Jewish puppet of the hated Romans, but because they had seen Herod's violent reaction to other "competitors." All their bottled-up hopes of a king to free them from Roman oppression mixed with their fear of Herod, the great murderer, causing genuine stir in the capital city.

v. 4 — *When he had called together all the people's chief priests and teachers of the law, he asked them where the Christ was to be born.*

Herod directed the Magi's question to members of the most prominent priestly families and the men who copied and taught the Old Testament Scriptures, the "scribes" (KJV). Matthew's Greek records Herod's question indirectly, using the same tense and mood that Herod used, the present indicative γεννᾶται. By using the present tense, Herod simply asked about a theological problem without stating it as a fact as the Magi had done. After all, Herod considered himself to be the king of the Jews, and he intended to keep it that way.

vv. 5,6 — *"In Bethlehem in Judea," they replied, "for this is what the prophet has written: 'But you, Bethlehem, in the land of Judah, are by no means least among the rulers of Judah; for out of you will come a ruler who will be the shepherd of my people Israel.' "*

The Jewish scholars were quick with their answer. They quoted the prophet Micah (737-690 B.C.), who was a contemporary of Isaiah, Hosea and Amos. Interspersed among Micah's messages about the destruction of unfaithful Jerusalem and Samaria are beautiful gospel promises of deliverance for the faithful remnant in Israel. The answer to the Magi's question came from one of these promises in Micah 5:2: "But you, Bethlehem Ephrathah, though you are small among the clans of Judah, out of you will come for me one who will be ruler over Israel, whose origins are from of old, from ancient times."

It is interesting as well as enlightening to compare Micah's original prophecy in the Hebrew Old Testament with the Greek version of the priests and teachers in Matthew 2:6. The New Testament Greek may at first seem to contradict the Hebrew. Whereas the Hebrew says Bethlehem "is small" in comparison to the rest of Judah, the Greeks says she is "by no means small" (οὐδαμῶς ἐλαχίστη εἰ). Since the Holy Ghost inspired both, both are correct. The Hebrew means Bethlehem is small in size. The Greek speaks not of size, but importance, as the NIV indicates with "by no means least." The thoughts combine quite naturally: Although you are small in size, Bethlehem, you are by no means small in significance, because the ruler of my people will come from you.

One must look to the third verse of Micah 5 to find the thought which corresponds to the "shepherding" (ποιμανεῖ) of Matthew 2:6. In Micah 5:4 the prophet foretells: "He will stand and shepherd his flock in the strength of the LORD. . . . " Specific examples of how Jesus protects, rules, governs, and tends his flock will be comforting here.

The priests and scribes skipped part of Micah's prophecy: "whose origins are from of old, from ancient times." This omission proved to be part of a national tragedy for the Jewish leaders and their people. If they had made the connection between Jesus Christ and his eternal origins, they could have seen him for what he is, true God and true man, their Savior from sin.

Alfred Edersheim in *The Life And Times Of Jesus The Messiah* (Vol. I, p. 206) explains these differences between the Greek and the Hebrew as "Targuming of the Old Testament . . . neither literal versions, nor yet paraphrases, but something between them, a sort of interpreting translation." The apostles themselves often gave such interpretive translations, rather than verbatim quotations (e.g. Acts 1:20; 2:17-21; 13:41). The Holy Spirit can inspire a paraphrased interpretation as easily as the original prophecy, even in the mouths of unbelieving priests and teachers of the law.

vv. 7,8 — *Then Herod called the Magi secretly and found out from them the exact time the star had appeared. He sent them to Bethlehem and said, "Go and make a careful search for the child. As soon as you find him, report to me, so that I too may go and worship him."*

Herod needed precise information to eliminate this "threat" to his throne. He secretly called the Magi, since any Jews present would easily have seen through his duplicity. He "ascertained exactly" (ἠκρίβωσεν) the time when the star first appeared, assuming this appearance corresponded with the time of Jesus' birth. Herod had so much at stake here! His kingdom, or so he thought. It is a sad fact of history that so many rulers have seen Christianity as a threat to their power rather than the stabilizing influence that it really is, a way in which citizens are taught to honor the government as God's arm of justice, law and order (Ro 13:1-7). Herod's fear robbed him of a precious opportunity to take care of a far more urgent need — his soul.

Herod wanted the Magi to inquire just as diligently (ἀκριβῶς), to leave no stone unturned in their search for the child. (Παιδίον is "a very young child" or "an infant.") To remove every trace of suspicion and to hurry the Magi back to him, Herod used the reason they gave in verse 2 as his reason for wanting to know about Jesus: "so that I too may go and worship him."

vv. 9,10 — *After they had heard the king, they went on their way and the star they had seen in the east went ahead of them until it stopped over the place where the child was. When they saw the star, they were overjoyed.*

The covert meeting ended; the Magi were on the road again. But there was nothing sinister about the wonderful sight overhead. Most translations lose the sense of surprise depicted in ἰδού, "Behold!" The devout travelers may not have expected to see it again, but there it was. We can almost hear them exclaim, "Look! The star!"

There is some question about whether Matthew describes this as "the star they had seen in the east," or "the star they had seen when it rose" (NIV footnote), both possible translations for ἐν τῇ ἀνατολῇ. Whether they first saw the star "when it rose" toward the west over Palestine, or whether it was more local, rising in the east and moving ahead of them toward the west, matters little. This was a special star provided by God for a very special purpose. Perhaps the simplest translation, "in the east," is preferred for lack of a compelling argument for the other.

There is no question about whether this was a star, a constellation or a meteor. These were learned astronomers, who certainly knew the difference. Besides, when the Holy Spirit calls it a "star," all argument or question should end.

The precise information Herod demanded and the Magi desired was provided by God through this special star. With it God led the Magi right to the house (v. 11) where Joseph had, by this time, moved his wife and divine stepson. The Magi's reaction to the reappearance of the star was indescribable joy, which must have kept mounting until the star finally showed them the blessed end of their arduous journey.

Pause and look back over the situation. The star could have led the Magi directly to Jesus at Bethlehem. But after the Magi had come so close to their goal, the star disappeared, forcing them to seek help. Help came from the Word of God. Even the Jewish leaders would not have known the answer to the Magi's question without the Scriptures in Micah 5:2. Thus the Holy Ghost once again underscores the importance of the Word. The Lord wants us to "search the Scriptures" (Jn 5:39 KJV), not look for special signs and revelations. On our own we cannot find the Savior or the answers for life's questions, no matter how wise we may be. For us too the Lord may sometimes increase our eagerness to find our Savior and his answers by "removing the star," so to speak. Then he lovingly fills the need he himself created.

v. 11 — *On coming to the house, they saw the child with his mother Mary, and they bowed down and worshiped him. Then they opened their treasures and presented him with gifts of gold and of incense and of myrrh.*

No distracting details are given about the house. Matthew focuses our attention where the eyes of the Magi were fastened with a devotion that wouldn't look anywhere else. Jesus! O dear Jesus! They saw not a child, but their King and their God. Standing was out of the question. On their knees in reverence reserved for high-ranking persons or divine beings, they did what they had come so many, many miles to do, what is rightly done only for God himself. They "worshiped him," praying to him and praising him, as they respectfully welcomed the Son of God who "made his dwelling among us" (Jn 1:14).

Treasure-filled hearts were matched by treasure-filled hands. The Magi show us Christian giving at its best. They gave "treasures," very valuable gifts, precious to the giver. They gave freely and so intently that neither distance nor difficulty could stop them from giving. They wanted to give.

There is praise from God in the Greek word δῶρα. It is God's mercy that calls the things we give back to him who first gave them, not taxes or dues or payments, but "gifts." He looks upon our thankful returns as "gifts."

The gold the Magi gave was not as precious as the faith that presented it (1 Pe 1:7). The incense, valuable as it was, did not compare to the value of their prayers which ascended as incense (Ps 141:2), carried to God's throne by their newborn mediator. Myrrh would be used only a few years later to embalm Jesus' corpse (Jn 19:39). This Christchild was born to die.

Though much as been made of these gifts of gold, incense and myrrh, the preacher needs to be careful not to make more of them than the text does and thereby blur the focus on the Savior. Luther says it well: "They simply follow the verse of the prophet and the testimony of the star and believe Him to be King, fall down, worship Him, and give presents to Him" (Luther, 11, 355.2113). Thus the Magi became the first fulfillments of Psalm 72:10,11: "The kings of Tarshish and of distant shores will bring tribute to him; the kings of Sheba and Seba will present him gifts. All kings will bow down to him and all nations will serve him."

As with joyful steps they sped, Savior, to thy lowly bed,
There to bend the knee before thee whom heaven and earth
adore,
So may we with willing feet ever seek thy mercy seat! (TLH
127:2)

v. 12 — *And having been warned in a dream not to go back to
Herod, they returned to their country by another route.*

The simple trust of the Magi would have led Herod, the great
murderer, to slaughter the Savior they loved if God had not directly
intervened. When a miracle was needed to protect God's plan to
redeem all people, the Lord provided a dream, unmasking Herod's
evil intent and sending the Gentile worshipers home by another
route.

This may have added many more miles to their long and difficult
journey. Yet the Magi didn't consider this command a burden, because their hearts were so in tune with the God of truth. When he told
them the truth about Herod, they were glad to go another direction to
avoid hurting Jesus. If only we could see all of God's commands in
this light and gladly obey them, if for no other reason than to avoid
hurting Jesus.

## Homiletical Suggestions

Epiphany comes from the Greek word ἐπιφαίνω which means "to
show, to bring to light, to appear," or "to become visible" when
referring to a celestial body such as a star. When referring to a
person, ἐπιφαίνω means "to become clearly known, to show oneself."

How appropriate it is, then, to begin the Epiphany season of the
church year with the star which became visible to make Jesus clearly known. During Epiphany Jesus shines forth as the "star out of
Jacob" (Nu 24:17). Jesus' glorious childhood, his baptism, and the
miracles of his early ministry all show him to be the true God in the
flesh, the fulfillment of Old Testament prophecies. Epiphany reminds us that "when the kindness and love of God our Savior appeared (ἐπεφάνη), he saved us, not because of the righteous things we
had done, but because of his mercy" (Tit 3:4,5).

This rich Epiphany text holds several challenges for the gospel
preacher. One look at a few commentaries shows how easy it is to be
distracted by details about the star, the Magi, Herod, the treasures,
etc. While some of these things need to be mentioned to give the
picture depth and color, Matthew's focus is ultimately the goal of the
Magi's quest: Jesus. We need to lead God's people to feel their need

for this child as acutely as did the Wise Men, so that they may kneel with us and the Magi in humble worship.

Since this text shows mostly the response to the gospel, the preacher must also do some digging to find the specific gospel in it. Here a careful study of the names for the child will be helpful: "Jesus" (Mt 1:21), "king of the Jews" (Ge 49:10; 2 Sm 7:12,13; Isa 9:7), "Christ" = "Messiah" = "Anointed One," "shepherd" (Jn 10, especially verses 27,28). Skillfully weave these names into the fabric of the sermon and God's people will thrill with the gospel joy of the Gentiles who first followed the star to Bethlehem.

The faithfulness of God to his prophetic promises, and thus to his promises for modern Christians, comes clear in the first outline below. The fact that ten verses speak of worship and only two of joy can be used to show how worship should be our primary goal. Joy is a blessed byproduct. Just as God used the star to light the way to the Savior, the preacher can also utilize this object in this way:

**Follow The Light Of The Epiphany Star**

1. To worship your promised King (vv. 1-8,11,12)
2. To be filled with joy (vv. 9,10)

To show the wonder of the gospel to the Gentiles and indicate that true spiritual "Jews" include believing Gentiles, the preacher can call God's people by that name. He can also focus the sermon on the gospel names of our Savior with this theme and parts:

**Come, Gentiles, To Your Light**

1. Jesus is your saving Shepherd (vv. 1,6)
2. Christ is your King (vv. 2-8)
3. This child is your God (vv. 9-12)

Genuine Christian worship doesn't come naturally for any of us. This text can help God's people learn how to worship him by using the Wise Men as a shining example. The following outline also shows how God protects his plan of salvation by giving special emphasis to the twelfth verse:

**Copy The Wise Men's Worship**

1. It overcomes obstacles (vv. 1-8)
2. It gives generously (vv. 9-11)
3. It lives lovingly (v. 12)

# FIRST SUNDAY AFTER EPIPHANY

## The Scriptures

> Old Testament — *Isaiah 42:1-7*
> Epistle — *Acts 10:34-38*
> Gospel — *Mark 1:4-11*

## The Text — Mark 1:4-11

This text is a straightforward message of sin and grace, law and gospel. Since the Epiphany season seeks to honor Christ as "the light of the Gentiles" as well as the "glory of his people Israel," the text is well chosen. It reminds the sinner of his need for repentance and faith in Christ. It also reminds the believer that he, as a member of Christ's church, has been charged by the Lord to make disciples of all nations by proclaiming this gospel to them and by baptizing them in the name of the triune God.

> vv. 4-6 — *And so John came, baptizing in the desert region and preaching a baptism of repentance for the forgiveness of sins. The whole Judean countryside and all the people of Jerusalem went out to him. Confessing their sins, they were baptized by him in the Jordan River. John wore clothing made of camel's hair, with a leather belt around his waist, and he ate locusts and wild honey.*

John the Baptist occupies a singular position in God's economy of salvation. He is the prophet whose coming and message were themselves prophesied in the Scripture. His importance lies in the fact that he was to prepare the way for the immediate arrival of the Messiah; he was to introduce the Messiah who was already at hand.

The preacher can make the point that John's message was authentic, for John came as the fulfillment of those Old Testament passages concerning the second Elijah, the immediate forerunner of the Christ (e.g., Mal 4:5). He can also point out that John's manner of life and his place of activity, the harsh, unpeopled Judean desert (ἔρημος), symbolized his stern message of repentance and judgment (Lk 3:9). No doubt the rugged place of John's activity and his austere appearance served to reinforce and give "impressive power" to his words, for despite the terrain multitudes of people left the comfort of their cities and homes and flocked to hear him.

All this, however, is merely a prelude to the main thrust of John's testimony — Jesus as the promised Messiah. He focuses on the necessity of repentance for receiving Christ aright, on the person of Christ as both God and Savior, and on baptism for those who sincerely repented and believed in the Messiah. John also alludes to the baptism with the Spirit and with fire that Christ will give to his people to carry out his saving mission in the world.

John's call for repentance still speaks to us today. The Greek word μετάνοια signifies a change of heart and mind. Sincere repentance is a necessary preparation of the heart for receiving the Christ. The heart turns away from sin, loathes it, and wishes to be rid of it. Repentance also involves the desire to make amends wherever possible for wrongs that have been committed against a fellow human being. John the Baptist told his hearers, "Produce fruit in keeping with repentance" (Lk 3:8). And when they asked how this could be done, he answered with specific directions for each person according to his station in life (Lk 3:11-14).

In other words, true repentance means not only sorrow over sin and dread of God's punishment, but a turning of mind and heart away from sin that expresses itself in outward ways wherever possible. True repentance will not allow the penitent soul to continue to live in sin. In view of the rampant worldliness that constantly entices God's people, John's stern call to repentance needs to occupy a prominent place in the message of the modern preacher, too.

Then John points the penitent sinner to faith in Jesus as "the Son of God" (Jn 1:34), the one who is so far above him that he, John, is not worthy to stoop down and untie his shoes; and also as the "Lamb of God, who takes away the sin of the world" (Jn 1:29). These words of John concerning the person of Jesus constitute a remarkably full testimony to the glory of the Savior. They embrace the core of the gospel. Jesus Christ is man, yes. But he is also the mighty God. Jesus is the promised Redeemer, who came to offer himself as the divine Lamb in payment for the sins of the whole world. Calvary is in view. The cross is foreshadowed. The fulfillment of God's age-old plan of salvation is at hand. And they who wish to claim this salvation for themselves are invited to be baptized, confessing their sin and acknowledging their need for and faith in the Savior.

The preacher may or may not want to discuss the question as to whether John's baptism was the equivalent of ours. Our fathers in the old Synodical Conference maintained that it was identical in every important way. (Cf. Adolph Hoenecke, *Ev. lutherische Dogmatik*, vol. 4, pp. 82ff., and Francis Pieper, *Christian Dogmatics*, vol. 3, pp. 288ff.) John's baptism, too, worked forgiveness of sins, delivered from death and the devil, and gave eternal salvation to all who

72

believed. To those who choose to see in John's baptism merely a promise of future forgiveness, Pieper answers: "You either have forgiveness, or you have it not" (*op. cit.*, p. 289). There is no scriptural warrant for a tentative or incomplete forgiveness.

v. 8 — *"I baptize you with water, but he will baptize you with the Holy Spirit."*

When John said these words, he was no doubt speaking to men who would, at his own urging, very shortly leave him to become disciples of Jesus (Jn 1:35). In due time they were to experience this baptism of the Holy Spirit and fire on the day of Pentecost. When the Spirit came upon them on that day "they saw what seemed to be tongues of fire that separated and came to rest on each of them," and they declared in many languages the "wonders of God" (Acts 2:3,11).

Earlier, on Easter Sunday evening, the Lord appeared to the Ten and told them, "Receive the Holy Spirit. If you forgive anyone his sins, they are forgiven; if you do not forgive them, they are not forgiven" (Jn 20:22,23). So the Lord brought his church into being and gave it the power of his Spirit to forgive or to retain sins.

vv. 9-11 — *At that time Jesus came from Nazareth in Galilee and was baptized by John in the Jordan. As Jesus was coming up out of the water, he saw heaven being torn open and the Spirit descending on him like a dove. And a voice came from heaven: "You are my Son, whom I love; with you I am well pleased."*

Having given his selfless testimony to the infinitely greater one who was to come after him, John is now privileged to have a most special role in inaugurating the Messiah into his own ministry. We know from the other Gospels that John protested when Jesus came to him to be baptized. After all, Jesus was the Messiah, the Son of God. He had no sins to confess! Why did he need to be baptized for the remission of sins that didn't exist? Jesus simply answers: "Let it be so now; it is proper for us to do this to fulfill all righteousness" (Mt 3:15).

In allowing himself to be baptized, Jesus was showing his solidarity with sinners. Though himself sinless, he was identifying himself with sinners by giving himself to the work of bearing their sins. Moreover, as Luther points out, Jesus was here rightly beginning to be Christ, the anointed one, and "was thus inaugurated into his entire Messianic office as our Prophet, High Priest, and King" (quoted in Lenski, *Matthew*, p. 133). The voice of the Father from heaven and the abiding of the Holy Spirit on Jesus (in the form of a dove) demonstrated the concurrence of all the persons of the Godhead in what was taking place.

Thus the one true God, the holy Trinity, Father, Son and Holy Spirit, is now launching the climax to his great plan of salvation. The long period of expectation and preparation is now over. The most momentous days the world will ever know, the three years of Christ's public ministry, culminating in his crucifixion, resurrection and ascension, are about to begin. Satan's power and dominion are doomed. The world's redemption is at hand.

## Homiletical Suggestions

A major problem with this text will be to keep it distinctive. The Gospels for both the Second and Third Sundays in Advent deal with John the Baptist's ministry. Moreover, the text for the Second Sunday in Advent shares five verses with this one (Mk 1:4-8) — which means that the preacher who uses the Series B Gospels consecutively will cover much of the same territory three times within a month or so.

Nevertheless, the text provides opportunity to preach a basic law-gospel message, which can be linked with the Epiphany theme of showing forth Christ as the divine Savior of the world. The possibility of a mission emphasis here is self-evident.

A simple outline that divides the text into its logical parts is the following:

## Jesus Of Nazareth Attested As Savior Of The World

1. By the forerunner John the Baptist (vv. 4-8)
2. By the holy Trinity (vv. 9-11)

Another outline that could be used as an Epiphany/mission approach or, for that matter, at a pastoral conference or at the installation of a pastor, is this one:

## Proclaim The Gospel In All The World

1. Call people to repentance (vv. 4-6)
2. Point people to Christ (vv. 7,8)
3. Baptize people into the family of God (vv. 9-11)

Another approach can highlight the matter of baptism:

## Our Baptism In The Light Of Christ's Baptism

1. Ours acknowledges sin; his fulfilled all righteousness (vv. 4-5)
2. Ours confesses faith; his proves he is the Savior (vv. 9-11)
3. Ours makes us God's children; he is God's Son (vv. 10,11)

74

## SECOND SUNDAY AFTER EPIPHANY

### The Scriptures

> Old Testament — *1 Samuel 3:1-10*
> Epistle — *1 Corinthians 6:12-30*
> Gospel — *John 1:43-51*

### The Text — John 1:43-51

Two other texts in this series have been selected thus far from the first chapter of John's Gospel. The selection for the Third Sunday in Advent, 1:6-8,19-28, drew our attention to the preparatory work of John the Baptist. The selection for the Second Sunday after Christmas, 1:1-18, presented the Christchild as the Word who became flesh. The text we are considering for this Sunday is the only selection from John for the Series B Epiphany season. It is a most appropriate selection, for it ties together the theme of John's Gospel and the theme of the Epiphany.

Epiphany means "showing forth," "making known." The Epiphany message is that Jesus of Nazareth, by his words and deeds, showed himself to be the Christ, the true and eternal Son of God, the Savior of the world. That is also John's purpose, for he writes concerning his Gospel, "These are written that you may believe that Jesus is the Christ, the Son of God, and that by believing you may have life in his name" (John 20:31).

John, then, has an Epiphany message, and that message is brought out beautifully in our text. It presents Jeus of Nazareth as the Son of God, and it shows that his believers are on an Epiphany mission — making known that most important truth.

*vv. 43,44 — The next day Jesus decided to leave for Galilee. Finding Philip, he said to him, "Follow me." Philip, like Andrew and Peter, was from the town of Bethsaida.*

This was the fourth day since the beginning of John the Apostle's description of John the Baptist's ministry in the Judean desert. During that time the Baptizer had testified that Jesus of Nazareth was the Christ (vv. 25,26), the Lamb of God sent to take away the world's sin (v. 29) and the very Son of God (v. 34). John's preaching had attracted the attention of men who had become his disciples, some of whom were from Galilee. The two disciples whom John the Baptist directed from himself to Jesus on the third day were Andrew and John, the latter being the unnamed disciple and author. Andrew acted as the first missionary for Christ and brought his brother Simon Peter to Jesus that very day.

"The next day," when our text begins, Jesus heads for Galilee, presumably to arrive at Cana in time for the wedding to which he and his family had been invited. Another Galilean, Philip, would join the Teacher and his new disciples. John's mention of the fact that Philip was also from the hometown of the other disciples leads us to believe that Philip would have had some knowledge about Jesus prior to his encounter with him in verse 43. This may also indicate that Philip was somewhat cautious about following Jesus at first but with his friends' encouragement accepted Jesus' invitation, "Follow me."

There is more in Jesus' words to Philip than an invitation to join the party on the way back to Galilee. These words express to Philip the same invitation that Jesus had extended to Andrew and John: "Come, and you will see" (v. 39).

Jesus expressed that invitation to committed faith using similar terms when he said, "If anyone would come after me, he must deny himself and take up his cross and follow me" (Mk 8:34). The Lord also described the life of faith when he said, "I am the light of the world. Whoever follows me will never walk in darkness, but will have the light of life" (Jn 8:12).

Jesus' words to Philip, then, are an invitation to faith. The Greek verb form is a present imperative, implying a continuing action. Jesus' invitation calls for a continuing response. Philip is to begin and keep on trusting in Jesus as the Savior, the sin-bearer, the Son of God, who leads his believers to eternal life. The words are also an invitation to grow in faith as Philip continues to learn from the divine Teacher in his traveling school of discipleship.

Jesus' invitation to follow him is still found in the Word. It is an invitation for sinners to keep trusting in Jesus as the Savior and to keep growing in faith as they follow the instruction of Christ's holy Word.

v. 45 — *Philip found Nathanael and told him, "We have found the one Moses wrote about in the Law, and about whom the prophets also wrote — Jesus of Nazareth, the son of Joseph."*

Philip's action shows us that disciples of Jesus are eager to understand and to share the good news of the Savior.

Philip begins in the most natural of all mission fields. He finds his close friend, Nathanael, who is from Cana in Galilee (Jn 21:2). In the lists of the apostles, the one closely connected with Philip is Bartholomew (Mt 10:3). It is therefore assumed that Nathanael ("gift of God") and Bartholomew are the same person.

Philip speaks for the disciples whom Jesus has already called when he says, "We have found." This is subjective faith confessing Jesus as Savior and Lord. But that faith is present only because the Holy Spirit did his work in their hearts by the powerful gospel invitation of Jesus (Ro 1:16; Jn 6:63). It is not Philip's own fanciful imagination, but it is a conviction shared with the others whom Jesus has called to faith. The Holy Spirit can use the compelling nature of a gospel encouragement coming from a number of people who share a common conviction.

Philip says that Jesus of Nazareth, the son of Joseph, is the one about whom Moses and the prophets wrote. Philip and his companions were Jewish disciples familiar with the threefold division of their Holy Scriptures — the Law of Moses, the Prophets and the Psalms or Writings (Lk 24:44). Jesus, then, is not only the fulfillment of Moses' promise of a greater mediator-prophet (Dt 18:15), but he also fulfills perfectly all of God's promises throughout the Scriptures.

Philip's knowledge of this fulfillment, of course, was not yet as complete as it would become, but it was sufficient to see that in Jesus God's promises were coming true. This, then, is a confession that Jesus, the legal son of Joseph raised in Nazareth, is the promised Messiah. Philip would also learn more fully that Jesus is the one and only Son of the Father from eternity.

Disciples of Jesus not only witness to their faith but delight in the fact that they, by the work of the Holy Spirit, have found the one from whom the entire message of God's word to man gets its meaning and significance. Disciples of Jesus will constantly look into the Word to find with ever-increasing clarity a description of Jesus and his saving work.

v. 46 — *"Nazareth! Can anything good come from there?"*
*Nathanael asked. "Come and see," said Philip.*

Nathanael does not immediately catch Philip's enthusiasm for this new-found Messiah. Nathanael hears one word with which he can find fault in Philip's confession of faith. He hears the word "Nazareth," and in that geographical reference he finds reason enough to doubt Philip's faith. There is little evidence that Nazareth had a worse reputation than any of the other small towns in Galilee. Galilee was the land of "half-breeds" despised by the "pure-bred" Judeans, but Nathanael himself was a Galilean. His objection, then, lies in the fact that he was familiar with this village and, as a Jew familiar with Messianic prophecies of the Scriptures, he knew no prophecy that said the Savior should come from Nazareth. His question asks if anything good can come from that familiar, humble little town, and it reveals his doubt that Philip had found the one who is perfectly good.

Philip hears the objection, but he does not counterattack with a cleverly designed argument. The Spirit has worked faith in his heart through the power of Christ's word. He loves his friend, he knows he has a genuine interest in spiritual matters, and he wants him to come under the influence of that same gracious word. Philip's response to Nathanael's objection is simple but effective. "Come and see" places his friend's doubting soul into the hands of the loving Savior.

People still pick at words and find many reason for doubting the truthfulness of the Christian faith. Each believer has his doubting friends. The counterattack must remain the same. Clever arguments do not work saving faith. For those tempted to "argue religion," Paul's words have timeless significance: "My message and my preaching were not with wise and persuasive words, but with a demonstration of the Spirit's power, so that your faith might not rest on men's wisdom, but on God's power" (1 Co 2:4,5).

The doubter who, like Nathanael, is nevertheless interested in spiritual things can only be brought to a right relationship with Jesus through that Savior's word. How appropriate to invite the doubter to "come and see" that the words of Jesus "are spirit and they are life" (Jn 6:63). When the Spirit works faith through the word of Christ, then seeing is believing. We find that in the case of Nathanael.

vv. 47,48 — *When Jesus saw Nathanael approaching, he said of him, "Here is a true Israelite, in whom there is nothing false." "How do you know me?" Nathanael asked. Jesus answered, "I saw you while you were still under the fig tree before Philip called you."*

Having accepted Philip's invitation to "come and see," Nathanael is exposed to the saving and powerful word of Jesus before there is even time for a formal introduction. With Nathanael still approaching, Jesus characterizes him in a voice loud enough so that Nathanael and all present can hear.

Since the Greek word ἀληθῶς is an adverb, a better translation might be, "*Truly* here is an Israelite in whom there is nothing false." This was a true statement about Nathanael worth everyone's attention. Most surprised of all is Nathanael, for from his question we know that he and Jesus had never met. Jesus is saying that Nathanael was a true believer in the Messianic promise and was looking for the Savior's spiritual kingdom. He was not a "false" Israelite, that is, a Jew by physical descent only. Jesus' statement peers into Nathanael's heart and soul and puts on display his saving faith.

Nathanael's question reveals that his heart had been read. The Greek word for "know" is γινώσκεις, to know from personal experience or insight. Jesus' statement has called Nathanael's attention to the Savior's omniscience.

Jesus answers "How do you know?" with "I saw." Nathanael had been alone, possibly off in a secluded place for prayer and meditation, a custom of pious Jews in that day. Jesus uses his divine attributes of knowing and seeing all to prove to Nathanael who he really is. The powerful word of Jesus convinces Nathanael of this important truth.

v. 49 — *Then Nathanael declared, "Rabbi, you are the Son of God; you are the King of Israel."*

After this brief encounter, Nathanael is already convinced of who Jesus of Nazareth really is. He addresses him, "Rabbi" or "Teacher," as did Andrew and John the day before (v. 38). Jesus is already a respected teacher of spiritual truth, and they looked to him for increased understanding. Nathanael's spiritual learning, however, led him beyond comprehension to faith, and that faith became evident in a clear confession.

Nathanael, who was looking for the right kind of Savior, now confesses that the spiritual Messianic kingdom is to be realized in Jesus of Nazareth. Jesus is the Son of God. That is a correct understanding of his person, and it shows his relationship to God the Father. Jesus is the King of Israel. That is a correct understanding of his office and his work, and it shows his relationship to his people, spiritual Israel, the church. Perhaps Nathanael's familiarity with biblical prophecy brought to mind such passages as Psalm 2:6,7; Isaiah 7:14; 9:6,7; Micah 5:2. The Son of God's kingdom would be a kingdom of grace in which sinners are called to repentance and faith.

Nathanael's confession of Jesus as the Son of God is a bold and compelling statement, especially in view of the fact that the idea of deifying human beings was appalling to the Jews. This strong confession would continue — Peter in Matthew 16:16, all the disciples in Matthew 14:33, Thomas in John 20:28. So strongly would Jesus' disciples continue to believe this central truth that they would lose their lives for it rather than recant. To present Jesus as the saving

Son of God is the very purpose of God's revelation to sinners (Jn 20:31). Belief in Jesus of Nazareth as the true Son of God in human flesh is and always will be the very heart of the Christian faith.

vv. 50,51 — *Jesus said, "You believe because I told you I saw you under the fig tree. You shall see greater things than that." He then added, "I tell you the truth, you shall see heaven open, and the angels of God ascending and descending on the Son of Man."*

To Nathanael's confession of faith Jesus adds some words of encouragement. He is not reprimanding Nathanael because it took miracles to get him to believe. He is accepting Nathanael's confession as evidence of faith worked in him by the power of the word, and he is encouraging Nathanael to grow in faith through the "greater things" that he would witness. True faith is never satisfied to rest on what one has already discovered, but it continues to grow through new discoveries in one's life with Christ. That would be true in respect to the things Nathanael would experience. It is still true of Bible students today. As Jesus continues, he points out what the "greater things" are which Nathanael would see.

Jesus and the inspired author both send up flags to draw our attention to the importance of what Jesus is about to say. John writes, "He then added." Jesus introduces his explanatory and authoritative statement with, "I tell you the truth."

Three passages of Scripture come to mind in Jesus' closing words to Nathanael.

In Isaiah 64:1 the prophet prays, "Oh, that you would rend the heavens and come down." In Jesus Christ God has come down to earth.

"The angels of God ascending and descending on the Son of Man" brings to mind Jacob's dream (Ge 28:10-22), in which the angels going up and down the stairway assured Jacob of the truthfulness of God's promise and the sureness of his communion with the true God. In Jesus the gap between heaven and earth has been bridged perfectly and completely. Through Jesus' intimate communion with the Father, which Nathanael and the other disciples would witness, the Mediator's work of redemption would be completed. In Jesus heavenly truth is brought to earth and sinners are assured of being taken to eternal glory where there will be perfect, endless communion with God.

The phrase "the Son of Man" is the phrase Jesus frequently uses to describe himself in the four Gospels. The phrase fulfills the prophecy of Daniel 7:13,14, where "one like a son of man, coming with the clouds of heaven" is "given authority, glory and sovereign power" and is one whom "all peoples, nations and men of every language" worship. Since Jesus readily accepted Nathanael's confession of him as "the Son of God," use of the phrase "Son of Man" does not diminish Jesus' deity. It rather emphasizes in a humble way that he was the promised Savior who was to be born of a woman, and that he came to serve all humanity as a spiritual Savior rather than to become a political messiah for the Jewish nation.

John therefore ends this opening section of his Gospel by underscoring the Epiphany theme. Jesus is the true Son of God who came to earth to save the world. It is a message that calls believers to a faithful response, just it called these early disciples to a life of faith, growth and witnessing.

## Homiletical Suggestions

The challenge for the preacher in this text is to try to condense the wealth of applicable material into one sermon. Obviously a choice will have to be made as to what is going to receive the major emphasis.

First choice during Epiphany may be to follow the seasonal theme and simply let the text present Jesus as the Son of God. An analytical approach would invite the believer to:

### Come And See The Son of God

1. He's the one who fulfills the Scriptures (vv. 43-45)
2. He's the one who reads our hearts (vv. 46-49)
3. He's the one who brings us heaven (vv. 50,51)

If the preacher wishes to stress the mission aspect of Epiphany, this text is an excellent basis for an evangelism sermon. Encourage Christians to:

### Invite People To Come And See Jesus

1. Jesus' word draws people to him (vv. 43-49)
2. Jesus' promise keeps people with him (vv. 50,51)

The imagery present in the closing verses may suggest another approach. Using Jesus' obvious reference to Jacob's dream, assure God's people that:

### Jesus Is The Stairway To Heaven

1. In Jesus our God descends to us (vv. 43-48)
2. In Jesus we ascend to our God (vv. 49-51)

Part one of the above outline could emphasize the incarnation, the fulfillment of prophecy and the Lord's gracious call in his word. Part two could emphasize coming to faith, confessing one's faith, spiritual growth and the ultimate glory of eternal life.

# THIRD SUNDAY AFTER EPIPHANY

## The Scriptures

Old Testament — *Jonah 3:1-5,10*
Epistle — *1 Corinthians 7:29-31*
Gospel — *Mark 1:16-20*

## The Text — Mark 1:16-20

Mark begins his account of Jesus' Galilean ministry with verse fourteen of chapter one. In verse sixteen, Jesus is already gathering his first disciples, Simon and Andrew. We know from John 1:35-42 that Simon and Andrew had met Jesus before. Simon and Andrew were once John the Baptist's disciples but left him to follow Jesus. Shortly after their first encounter with the Lord, Jesus withdrew for one of his periods of seclusion. Simon and Andrew returned home to their fishing business. Our text indicates that Jesus has now returned to Galilee (from a feast in Jerusalem) to call Simon and Andrew to be his full-time disciples.

Luke's account of the calling of Simon and Andrew (Lk 5:1-11) adds some interesting details to Mark's version. Mark tells only of the events which occurred early in the day: Jesus was walking alone; Simon and Andrew were still casting their nets; Jesus interrupted their labors by promising to make them fishers of men. Luke tells us what happened later that day: A crowd gathered; Jesus used Simon's boat for a pulpit; after the sermon Jesus instructed Simon to let down his nets for one last pull; Simon was less than eager because of his total lack of success the night before. But when Simon saw the miraculous haul, he fell to his knees and cried, "Go away from me, Lord; I am a sinful man!" At this point Jesus repeated his promise spoken earlier in the day, "Don't be afraid; from now on you will catch men."

The Epiphany theme is that Jesus is God as well as man. One might think that Luke bears this out more clearly than Mark since Luke includes the miraculous catch. But the miraculous catch of fish was no more a miracle than Jesus' wonderful catch of disciples as recorded in Mark. Jesus revealed his Messiahship and the power of his word by persuading these men to forsake all to follow him. Every time any sinner is moved by the Spirit to hand his heart to the Lord, the power of Christ is manifest. This is exactly the emphasis Mark gives us in the verses of his account:

vv. 16-18 — *As Jesus walked beside the Sea of Galilee, he saw Simon and his brother Andrew casting a net into the lake, for they were fishermen. "Come, follow me," Jesus said, "and I will make you fishers of men." At once they left their nets and followed him.*

There was no need for introductions, explanations or small talk. Jesus simply confronted Simon and Andrew with an invitation to train for a new, although related, occupation. Jesus called them to follow him in order to *become* fishers of men. The Greek clearly indicates that this was to be the beginning of their internship under the chief Fisher of Men: "I will make you to become . . . " (ποιήσω ὑμᾶς γενέσθαι).

How long would it be until Simon and Andrew fully understood the rich metaphor "fishers of men"? In time they would discover that their "catch" would not be snagged and sold; rather, it would be rescued and set free! The disciples' new net would not be of twine and weights, but of the words of Christ, the gospel, the power unto salvation to all who believe. Think of everything these disciples would see and experience before they were finally sent out on their own with the words, "You will be my witnesses in Jerusalem, and in all Judea and Samaria, and to the ends of the earth" (Ac 1:8).

Immediately Simon and Andrew dropped their fishing gear and followed Jesus. The Greek adverb εὐθύς ("at once") gives testimony to the power of the Epiphany Lord's word. Do not marvel at Simon and Andrew's obedience or at their readiness to follow Christ. We know better. They obeyed Christ's call not because of their righteousness or daring but because of Christ's mercy. They were chosen, called and convinced by the power of Jesus' word. Discipleship is a gift of grace. Marvel at Christ's mercy and the power of his word!

The Holy Spirit had persuaded Simon and Andrew to follow Jesus. Little did they realize what it would cost them to carry a net for Christ. To follow Jesus would mean much more than tagging behind the Master on his trips to Jerusalem and back. Following Christ would involve much more than learning how to catch men for Christ. What an opportunity these verses give us to tell our people what it really means to follow Jesus!

To follow the Lord means first of all to *subordinate* everything to the Lord. Give yourself — heart, mind and soul — to Jesus. Subordinate yourself and you may follow. Hand over all your boats and nets, your business and your wealth. Those who will follow the Lord pursue riches of a totally different nature, which rust and moth cannot destroy. To follow the Lord requires that one subordinate, perhaps even sever, other earthly relationships. Whoever loves father or mother, husband or wife, parent or child more than Jesus is not worthy to follow Jesus.

To follow the Lord also means that one will strive to *simulate* the Savior in all his ways. Be holy! "But just as he who called you is holy, so be holy in all you do" (1 Pe 1:15). Be humble! "Your attitude should be the same as that of Christ Jesus . . . " (Php 2:5-11). Love and forgive unconditionally! "Be kind and compassionate to one another, forgiving each other, just as in Christ God forgave you" (Eph 4:32).

To follow Christ is to *share the cross* of Christ. Perhaps this is the greatest expense which faces the one who will carry a net for Christ. A person might just challenge us, "Did Jesus really say all this was necessary to follow him?" Check Jesus' own recruitment motto in Matthew 10:38: "Anyone who does not take his cross and follow me is not worthy of me" (cf. 1 Pe 2:21). It was on the cross that Jesus achieved atonement with God for the world. Our cross is a sign of our discipleship. Will we lift it, or let it lie?

Finally, to follow Christ means to *share the work* of Christ. This point receives a mighty emphasis in Jesus' statement, "I will make you fishers of men." The preaching of the gospel was Jesus' highest priority. His gospel was more important than eating and drinking, than healing and miracles, than any personal comfort. The gospel is: Believe in Jesus, who suffered your hell in your place, and you will be saved. Jesus was determined to fulfill that gospel and to proclaim that gospel to sinners. His followers will share that commitment throughout their lives.

There is an old favorite gospel song entitled "Where He Leads Me." The chorus goes like this:

> Where he leads me I will follow,
> Where he leads me I will follow,
> Where he leads me I will follow,
> I'll go with him, with him all the way.

Our human nature would like to change this chorus to sing like this:

> I'll go with him till the summer,
> I'll tag along until I'm tempted,
> I'll follow if the cost is cheap.
> If not, I'll say so long, so long all the way.

This portion of God's Word confronts us with some very important questions. Will we take up our cross daily? Will we follow no matter what the cost? Can we afford to carry a net for Christ? Which chorus are we singing?

Our text continues:

vv. 19,20 — *When he had gone a little farther, he saw James son of Zebedee and his brother John in a boat, preparing their nets. Without delay he called them, and they left their father Zebedee in the boat with the hired men and followed him.*

The call James and John received was the same call Simon and Andrew received. Their discipleship would be no less expensive. Yet Jesus was as successful in calling James and John as he was with Simon and Andrew. But at this point let's remember that their call was not to poverty, isolation or relentless misery. The call to be a follower of Jesus Christ was and still is a call to fullness of life (Jn 10:10), the freedom of faith and the future of eternal glory.

By the grace of God's Holy Spirit, these four fishermen never forgot who called them. The Lord of the universe had invited them to become his closest, dearest companions for an exciting and unforgettable three years. Above all, they never forgot in whom they had placed all their confidence for the salvation of their souls.

Jesus wants to share with all mankind his glory, his resurrection, his home and his life, so he calls disciples to carry this message to the world. He is still calling disciples who will carry a net for him regardless of the cost. People still need to hear the gospel before they can believe it. If it is left up to us, and it is, will those people ever hear the good news?

This is the message, and this is the question of this powerful text.

## Homiletical Suggestions

There are two important truths that demand special attention in this portion of God's Word. First, we must declare the full implications of following Christ. Secondly, let us carefully emphasize the grace, the unmerited privilege, we have been shown by receiving the call through the gospel to be Jesus' disciples.

There is no denying that the price of discipleship runs steep. Jesus never hesitated to let people know up front what it would cost to follow him. But Jesus was also quick to assure his first followers, even as he assures us, that if we remain faithful unto death we shall receive a crown of life.

With these two points forming the principle parts, encourage the flock entrusted to your care to:

## Carry A Net For Christ

1. It requires unconditional commitment (vv. 16-18)
   A. Subordinate everything to the Savior
   B. Simulate the Savior's ways

C. Share the cross of the Savior
D. Share the work of the Savior

2. It guarantees unimaginable compensation (vv. 19,20)
   A. By grace, enjoy a life of service on earth
   B. By grace, enjoy the Savior's glory in the life to come

Following the same lines of thought we can add a seasonal flavor to the above:

**The Epiphany Lord Calls You**

1. To a life of total commitment
2. To a life of glorious service

# FOURTH SUNDAY AFTER EPIPHANY

**The Scriptures**

> Old Testament — *Deuteronomy 18:15-20*
> Epistle — *1 Corinthians 8:1-13*
> Gospel — *Mark 1:21-28*

**The Text — Mark 1:21-28**

"Blessed . . . are those who hear the word of God and obey it," Jesus told his disciples (Lk 11:28). The Scripture readings emphasize this. Moses had advised the people to listen to the prophet that God would raise up among his people. Paul in the Epistle reminds us that "there is but one Lord, Jesus Christ, through whom all things came and through whom we live" (1 Co 8:6). In today's Gospel we see Jesus the prophet at work. The text follows immediately upon last week's Gospel, Mark 1:16-20. There Jesus called his first four disciples to follow him. Here we see the disciples strengthened through the word and work of God's Savior.

vv. 21,22 — *They went to Capernaum, and when the Sabbath came, Jesus went into the synagogue and began to teach. The people were amazed at his teaching, because he taught them as one who had authority, not as the teachers of the law.*

The Gospel relates a common occurrence in the ministry of Jesus. He went to the synagogue on the Sabbath. This was his custom and practice. He often used this as an opportunity to teach.

Mark doesn't record the message he delivered, but he does record the reaction. The people were amazed at his teaching. There was a marked diffeerence between Jesus and the other rabbis the people were accustomed to hearing. Jesus is the Son of God. What he delivered he received from the Father. John said, "In the beginning was the Word, and the Word was with God, and the Word was God" (Jn 1:1). He could speak as someone with authority because all authority had been given him. So a noticeable difference could be expected. He knew the whole will of God from eternity. He knew how the promises of the Old Testament would be fulfilled.

The Old Testament believers did not have the benefit of the 20/20 hindsight that we have. They trusted the promises of God, but they did not know exactly how and when God would fulfill his promises. Look at some of the prophecies concerning Christ. Some speak of him as a suffering servant, while others call him a king who would rule victorious forever. Moses described him as a prophet (Dt 18:15), but he would also be a priest. Furthermore, the Messiah would be a descendant of David. An Old Testament priest could not come from the tribe of Judah. All priests had to be descendants of Levi. How the Messiah could be all three, prophet, priest and king, is much easier for us in the New Testament to see, especially after we have had the benefit of studying the book of Hebrews.

A problem with the rabbis in Jesus' day was their emphasis on teaching the people the traditions of the elders. They were so concerned about teaching their many man-made precepts and the opinions of other rabbis, that they had difficulty coming to a final conclusion about anything. They were so busy explaining things *about* the Scriptures that many times they missed Scripture's message.

That is also a danger for us. We tend to treat the Bible like any other book. It suffers from neglect. We may read the newspaper each day, because it's important to keep up to date on what is going on. Right beside our papers and periodicals can lie the Bible, but we don't bother to read it. We can come up with all kinds of excuses, but we know that there really is no excuse for such indifference. The Bible is God speaking to us with his authority.

vv. 23,24 — *Just then a man in their synagogue who was possessed by an evil spirit cried out, "What do you want with us, Jesus of Nazareth? Have you come to destroy us? I know who you are — the Holy One of God!"*

Here is the first instance of demon-possession in the Gospel of Mark. We are not told how this man was affected by the evil spirit that possessed him. Sometimes demon-possession involved physical ailments (e.g., a bent-over woman, Lk 13:11; convulsions, Lk 9:39). The demon-possessed man in the region of the Gerasenes had superhuman strength, and Satan was using that man's body as his own personal instrument (Lk 8:26-29). To the slave girl at Philippi he granted supernatural powers (Ac 16:16-18).

One thing all the demons had in common. They all recognized Jesus for who he was. Satan realized that Jesus had come to take away his death-hold on creation. His position as the "prince of this world" was under attack. Jesus had already defeated him at his temptation in the wilderness. He continued to defeat Satan on every turn. We read:

vv. 25,26 — *"Be quiet!" said Jesus sternly. "Come out of him!" The evil spirit shook the man violently and came out of him with a shriek.*

The evil spirit had to obey Jesus' command. Jesus would have many more encounters with Satan. Each time Jesus would end up the victor. Satan's final desperate attack would be directed at Jesus on the cross. There Satan's power in connection with sin and death would be put to an end. Jesus would meet death and defeat it.

Jesus told the demon to be quiet, even though he had correctly identified Jesus as the "Holy One of God." Jesus did not need or want the testimony of devils. His words and his deeds would speak for themselves. In due time he selected apostles to speak for him, and he calls upon all believers to be his witnesses. That unclean spirit has to be quiet and depart. The incident shows the strength of Satan, but it also shows how his power has been curtailed by him who has all authority in heaven and on earth.

vv. 27,28 — *The people were all so amazed that they asked each other, "What is this? A new teaching — and with authority! He even gives orders to evil spirits and they obey him." News about him spread quickly over the whole region of Galilee.*

Something wonderful happened that day at Capernaum. Those people had heard the word of God before, probably all their lives, but here they were confronted with the Word personified. They were amazed at the authority of his words and his work. News about him spread quickly.

The "special services" are over for a while in the church year. Now that it is about a month after Christmas and Epiphany, have things quieted down into the same old routine? Don't let this routine rob you of the ongoing blessings offered to you in Jesus' word. That word brings life, a life which never ends. As we proclaim that to our congregations this week, may God's message also find a place in our hearts and continue to bless us. May it not only cheer our hearts with the assurance of an open heaven, but also be our motivation to spread the news of Jesus near and far. No matter where God has placed you, he will give you many opportunities to share that news. Through the missions of our synod God gives us opportunities to spread the news of Jesus in many areas of the world.

### Homiletical Suggestions

This Gospel proclaims Jesus and his work as prophet. It offers encouragement to be about our Lord's work. It also warns us not to proclaim the word of life in a dull and uninteresting way, as the teachers of the law of Jesus' day did.

Looking at our text in this Epiphany season, we can be encouraged to:

### Spread The News Of Jesus

1. Speak his marvelous word (vv. 21,22,27,28)
2. Tell of his wonderful works (vv. 23-26,27,28)

Part one reminds us of the divine authority that goes with everything Jesus says. The second part reminds us of what Jesus has accomplished for us. His defeat of Satan in the miracle recorded in this text was a foreshadowing of what he would accomplish on Golgatha's cross. Let us encourage each other to continue to spread the news of Jesus.

On the two preceeding Sundays the call to discipleship and the task of discipleship were stressed. In John 1:43-51 we were invited to "come and see." In Mark 1:11-20 Jesus said, "Come, follow me, and I will make you fishers of men." This Sunday could follow up on that theme of discipleship with a look at:

**The Blessings of Discipleship**

1. Security in our Savior's power (vv. 23-26,27)
2. Strength from his word (vv. 21,22,27,28)

Another possibility is to stress the church-attendance aspect in the theme:

**In Church With Jesus, Our Epiphany Lord**

1. To receive his miracle (vv. 23,26)
   (This part would apply the miracle of Jesus over Satan to his victory for us on the cross, which also was a defeat of Satan.)
2. To share his word
   A. Strengthened in faith (vv. 21,22,27)
   B. Strengthened in witnessing (v. 28)

# FIFTH SUNDAY AFTER EPIPHANY

## The Scriptures

Old Testament — *Job 7:1-7*
Epistle — *1 Corinthians 9:16-23*
Gospel — *Mark 1:29-39*

## The Text — Mark 1:29-39

The events described in this text take place in Capernaum on the Sabbath day. As Mark points out in the preceding verses, Jesus had spent the earlier part of the Sabbath in the synagogue, teaching and healing a man possessed by an evil spirit.

Now Jesus leaves the synagogue to go to the home of Peter and Andrew.

v. 29 — *As soon as they left the synagogue, they went with James and John to the home of Simon and Andrew.*

Jesus, in company with Peter, Andrew, James and John, the four men he had called as his first disciples (vv. 14-20), made his way to the home of the two brothers, Peter and Andrew. Since no mention is made at this point of the serious illness of Peter's mother-in-law, it is likely that Jesus was going to his followers' house simply to share their evening meal with them.

v. 30 — *Simon's mother-in-law was in bed with a fever, and they told Jesus about her.*

In this simple manner Mark informs us of the illness of Peter's mother-in-law. No detail is given beyond the fact that her fever was serious enough to keep her in bed. Yet we can be sure that her illness was serious, since Luke describes it as "a high fever" (4:38).

We don't know about the rest of the apostles, but Peter was a married man. This is interesting in view of the Roman church's claim that Peter was the first pope and their general requirement of celibacy for their clergy.

v. 31 — *So he went to her, took her hand and helped her up. The fever left her and she began to wait on them.*

In his loving manner Jesus goes to this suffering woman. Mark does not directly call this healing a miracle, but the miraculous nature of her recovery is evident. The inverted word order of the Greek gives emphasis to the amazing, sudden end of the woman's illness (καὶ ἀφῆκεν αὐτὴν ὁ πυρετός).

Under normal circumstances, a person who has been seriously ill with a fever is weak and tired when the fever breaks. Yet Peter's mother-in-law had the strength to get up immediately and serve not just her family members, but their guests as well. Her healing was complete, and she was eager to show her thankfulness to the man who had healed her.

v. 32 — *That evening after sunset the people brought to Jesus all the sick and demon-possessed.*

The Sabbath had come to an end with the setting of the sun. Only then did the Jews feel free to do the work of leading and carrying all the sick and possessed to Jesus. The news of Jesus' earlier miracle of healing in the synagogue had by now spread throughout the whole city.

Mark clearly distinguishes here between two groups of people who were brought to Jesus that evening. The first is made up of those who are described as sick (κακῶς ἔχειν — the idiomatic expression is standard usage in the Greek). The second group is composed of those who are demon-possessed.

This verse reminds us of the reality of demon-possession. These people were not just suffering from emotional imbalance or organic disease. They had become the dwelling-places of unclean spirits.

We can speculate about the frequency of demon-possessions in our own day. Could it be that many illnesses which give the impression of being purely medical or emotional problems actually are the result of possession? The text clearly allows for that possibility. And yet it does not leave us as Christians cowering before the manifest power of Satan's forces. Every reason for being struck with terror by the devil's ability to possess people is removed because Jesus proved his superiority over these powers when he cast all of them out. Neither regular disease nor demon-possession is beyond the control of God's Son.

It seems there is an unhealthy concern — almost a preoccupation — with the subject of the occult, possession, Satan worship, etc., in our day — even among some Christians. Our text shows the Lord's power over all forces and forms of evil. Scripture speaks of Jesus' overthrow of Satan, his victorious descent into hell, etc. We Christians share in the Lord's victory and, therefore, need not fear the devil's power over us. Surely, God's appointed weapon against Satan — his powerful word — cannot fail us or lose its power. As Luther said in "A Mighty Fortress": "One little word can fell him."

The scene could not be more dramatic as this group begins to grow larger before the house of Peter the fisherman:

vv. 33,34 — *The whole town gathered at the door, and Jesus healed many who had various diseases. He also drove out many demons, but he would not let the demons speak because they knew who he was.*

The "many" (πολλούς) here does not indicate that some people were healed and some left unhealed, but rather that the numbers of those whom Jesus healed were great.

Mark tells us here that Jesus would not allow the demons to speak "because they knew who he was." Here, as in many other parts of Scripture, we see the devils' recognition of Jesus Christ as the Savior — indeed, as God incarnate. But why should this knowledge lead Jesus to prevent their speaking? There are at least two possibilities. One is that their blurting out of Jesus' identity would have necessitated a change in Jesus' usual way of reaching others. Jesus consistently preached his message, frequently underscoring its authority with miracles. It was in this way that he elicited confessions of faith, rather than by beginning with a direct proclamation of his identity. Obviously, if the devils had loudly proclaimed his identity, this normal procedure would have been circumvented.

A second, and more likely, explanation for Jesus' forbidding the demons to speak is that any demonic proclamation of his identity would have been inappropriate. The holy message of Jesus' identity did not need to come from demons.

v. 35 — *Very early in the morning, while it was still dark, Jesus got up, left the house, and went off to a solitary place, where he prayed.*

Jesus got going early that morning because he knew it wouldn't be long before people would show up to see him, to hear him, perhaps to be healed by him. So he sought a solitary place where he could be alone as he prayed to his heavenly Father.

v. 36 — *Simon and his companions went to look for him,*

Even though Jesus felt the need to be alone in order to pray to his Father, still his followers did not leave him alone for long.

v. 37 — *and when they found him, they exclaimed: "Everyone is looking for you!"*

The NIV does well when it renders the Greek λέγουσιν . . . ὅτι with "exclaimed" to show emotion in the disciples' voices when they located the Lord. The Greek verb ζητέω also shows the intensity of their searching. It means "to look for diligently."

v. 38 — *Jesus replied, "Let us go somewhere else — to the nearby villages — so I can preach there too. That is why I have come."*

Jesus does not want to linger in Capernaum. Even though the preceding verses spoke at length of the healing Jesus had done following his preaching that morning in the synagogue, here Jesus puts the emphasis not on the miracles, but on the preaching. He wants to go on so that he can preach in other places. And he makes that most important work stand out when he says, "That is why I have come."

This is a clear reminder that the miracles of Jesus were viewed by the Savior primarily as ways to emphasize and substantiate his preaching. It was the preaching — the message of forgiveness through his work as the Messiah — that was always most important. Better than anyone else, he knew that the miracle of bringing a sinner to faith was infinitely more important than even the most dramatic healing or exorcism.

Truly, we can say that, although Jesus performed many great miracles, he did not come primarily as a miracle worker. Although he healed many sick people, he was not primarily a healer. Although he cast out many demons, he did not come primarily as an exorcist. No, Jesus' mission was to redeem the world, to seek and to save what was lost. No wonder he felt such a need to go on and to share that message with more people. After all, his message was nothing less than the message of eternal life through him.

v. 39 — *So he traveled throughout Galilee, preaching in their synagogues and driving out demons.*

It is hard to say why Mark does not mention more physical healings in this verse. But the basic idea is clear: Jesus was fulfilling his desire to preach throughout Galilee. And as he went, those ancillary miracles, so often used to show his authority and point to the truth of his message, followed after him.

## Homiletical Suggestions

This text puts emphasis on the Epiphany Lord's ability to heal, not just those suffering from various physical maladies, but also those suffering from demon-possession. Our Epiphany Lord is a Lord of power.

In any sermon dealing with this text we want to remind our people that, even though nearly two thousand years have passed since Jesus healed those people in Capernaum, he still has the same almighty power to heal physical diseases and keep us safe from the power of Satan's forces. Since demon-possession seems a remote and strange thing to many people in our modern and sophisticated world, it would be good to remind them of the reality of both Satan and his power. And yet, even when we allow the possibility of possession in our own day, we need to emphasize above all else the surpassing power of our God to guard and keep us Christians safe. Together with our powerful Savior, we are already victors over the devil!

As mentioned above, physical healings and the casting out of devils do get a lot of attention in this pericope. Yet we miss the overall point and message of this section if we make those the only emphases of the text as a whole. The miracles were wonderful, but they had a purpose behind them — a greater purpose. Indeed, they pointed to the authority, power and identity of the one who performed them. They underscored what Jesus had come to do — his primary purpose — namely, to preach the gospel.

Jesus himself establishes the vital connection between the miracles and his preaching of the good news. In v. 38 he speaks of moving on in order to preach in other places and then adds, "That is why I have come." That statement is the key to understanding this pericope and preaching effectively on it. To do justice to the text we need to incorporate both the miracles and their purpose in underscoring Jesus' preaching in our theme and parts:

**The Epiphany Lord Reveals His Authority ...**

1. Over sickness (vv. 29-31)
2. Over Satan (vv. 32-34)
3. Over sin (vv. 35-39)

The first part may emphasize Jesus' healing activity today — both direct healing and healing through the use of medicine and the healing arts. Part two could emphasize Jesus' authority as crucified and risen Savior to protect and defend his people from even the most virulent attacks of the devil. And part three would explain how Jesus' most important work during his ministry was preaching the forgiveness of sins through his blood. It is the preaching of that gospel message which heals our most serious disease — the disease of sin.

Another possibility is the following wording, using the same text divisions:

**Epiphany Miracles With A Purpose**

1. They showed Jesus' power over disease
2. They proved his authority over the devil
3. They pointed to his message of salvation

# SIXTH SUNDAY AFTER EPIPHANY

**The Scriptures**

> Old Testament — *2 Kings 5:1-14*
> Epistle — *1 Corinthians 9:24-27*
> Gospel — *Mark 1:40-45*

**The Text — Mark 1:40-45**

The event in this text took place sometime during Jesus' Galilean ministry. Jesus was reaching the high point of his popularity. Opposition by church authorities was mounting at the same time. Both of these trends were due to Jesus' miraculous signs and the authoritative way in which he preached. The cleansing of the leper in this text is a good example of how Jesus' popularity increased and the message of his saving power was spread abroad.

More importantly, this text reveals the divine Rabbi who can cure the ravages of sin and cleanse the soul of the sinner.

*v. 40 — A man with leprosy came to him and begged him on his knees, "If you are willing, you can make me clean."*

The Greek word here translated as "leprosy" includes a wide range of skin disorders — from psoriasis to a terminal disease which disfigures limbs and face. The degree or extent of this man's leprosy is not important. What is important is that he fell under the restrictions of Leviticus 13. There Moses shows us that leprosy was a disease which was dreaded not so much for its hygienic implications as for its spiritual implications. Leprosy was an object lesson of what sin does to God's people. The leper had to live separated from God's people (Lev 13:46). The corresponding Hebrew word for λεπρός has as its root a word which means to "strike down" or to "scourge." Leprosy was considered God's scourge upon the sinner.

So closely was leprosy associated with sin that the leprous man asked Jesus to "cleanse" (καθαρίσαι) him. We might have expected him to ask Jesus for "a cure" or for "healing."

The leprous man expressed his faith by falling to his knees in worship of Jesus. It is true that the apostles also performed miracles, but they made it clear that their power came from Jesus, not themselves. The apostles refused worship such as Jesus accepts in this account (Ac 10:25,26).

The act of "falling to his knees" (γονυπετῶν) coupled with the confession of his lips, " . . . you can make me clean," was a strong testimony by the leprous man that Jesus is the almighty Son of God. He knew Jesus was able to cleanse him. He did not as yet know whether Jesus was willing to do so. So he humbly resigned himself to the will of the one who is infinitely wiser than himself.

v. 41 — *Filled with compassion, Jesus reached out his hand and touched the man. "I am willing," he said. "Be clean!"*

The pitiful condition of the leprous man filled Jesus with compassion. In fact, the Greek word σπλαγχνισθείς indicates that this was a "gut-wrenching" experience for our Lord.

Jesus' compassion moved him to do something which was totally unacceptable in Jewish society. "Jesus reached out his hand and touched the man." If a rabbi touched a leper, it would make bigger headlines than if a rabbi cleansed a leper. It was unheard of. In Jewish society leprosy was one of the "fathers of uncleanness." Touching a leper stood second only to defilement from touching the dead. Alfred Edersheim wrote in his book *The Life and Times of Jesus the Messiah,* "No one was even to salute (the leper); ... No less a distance than four cubits (six feet) must be kept from a leper; or, if the wind came from that direction, a hundred were scarcely sufficient. Rabbi Meir would not eat an egg purchased in a street where there was a leper. Another Rabbi boasted that he always threw stones at them to keep them far off, while others hid themselves or ran away. To such an extent did Rabbinism carry its inhuman logic in considering the leper as a mourner, that it even forbade him to wash his face" (Book III, chapter 15, page 495). Elisha did not even approach Naaman prior to his healing. Had Jesus cleansed him with his word first and then touched him, it would have been acceptable. But that is not how it happened. The Almighty did not recoil from touching the lowest of the low in order to cleanse him and bring him back into fellowship with God's peole. The touch was accompanied by the omnipotent word, "I am willing. . . . Be clean!"

v. 42 — *Immediately the leprosy left him and he was cured.*

The cleansing process was not gradual. The disease fled as the words left Jesus' lips. The NIV says, "and he was cured." It would be more consistent to say, "and he was cleansed" (ἐκαθερίσθη). This also puts the emphasis on the leper's restoration to the Old Testament church, which was by far more important than a cure for an infection.

vv. 43,44 — *Jesus sent him away at once with a strong warning: "See that you don't tell this to anyone. But go, show yourself to the priest and offer the sacrifices that Moses commanded for your cleansing, as a testimony to them."*

Jesus was not using reverse psychology when he admonished this man not to tell anyone about the miracle. Jesus dismissed him "with a strong warning" (ἐμβριμησάμενος from βριμάομαι: "to be moved with anger"). Increased popularity would result in escalated opposition. There may also have been the concern that too much of his time would be taken by those who would besiege him with medical requests, but who had no interest in him as their Savior from sin.

But there was something the cleansed leper could do to further the kingdom of God. Jesus told him to "go, show yourself to the priest and offer the sacrifices that Moses commanded for your cleansing, as a testimony to them" (to the preists). It was God's will that the people of Israel be clean. Jesus had cleansed one such person. By doing this Jesus fulfilled God's law. As he said in the Sermon on the Mount, "Do not think that I have come to abolish the Law or the Prophets; I have not come to abolish them but to fulfill them" (Mt 5:17). The sacrifices which Moses prescribed are found in Leviticus 14:2-32.

v. 45 — *Instead he went out and began to talk freely, spreading the news. As a result, Jesus could no longer enter a town openly but stayed outside in lonely places. Yet the people still came to him from everywhere.*

The cleansed leper proclaimed Jesus' miracle "freely" (κηρύσσειν: "to proclaim openly") and widely (διαφημίζειν: "to spread abroad"). The unfortunate result of this man's well-intentioned disobedience was that Jesus' kingdom work had to be put on hold for the time being. He could no longer enter a town conspicuously (φανερῶς), probably for fear that his divine agenda would be shouted down by the din of the mob's requests. Jesus was forced to seek refuge in "lonely" (ἐρήμοις: "forsaken") places. Even there people came to him "from everywhere."

Jesus knew that if he cleansed this leper there would be a risk involved. The man's sanctification might not be up to the test of keeping silent. Jesus' ministry might be stalled or thrown off course temporarily. Nevertheless, his compassion for this man moved him to set aside personal risk and social stigma to reach out and touch an untouchable. Jesus' touch and word made the most foul clean.

## Homiletical Suggestions

This text fits comfortably into the Epiphany season. The obvious thrust is that Jesus' deity is made manifest in the cleansing of the leper. The power of Jesus' word brought all things into existence in the beginning. When sin took its toll, Jesus came to help restore his creation to its original health and innocence. This restoration is clearly seen in the healing of a disease which carried with it the stigma of moral uncleanness.

By birth we share a common moral uncleanness. We were helpless to avoid the sin which separated us from the saved people of God. Daily we rebel against our Maker. Our sins are as real as the shiny white spots on the leper's skin. We must cry out to God and the world that we are unclean, as did the lepers of old. The gracious mystery of the Christ is that he did not use his omnipotence to condemn us. He touched us. And with his word (found also in the sacraments) he healed us and brought us back into communion with the Father and God's people.

Someone might say that Jesus did not contract leprosy or become morally unclean when he touched the leper in this text. Strictly speaking, he did not. Yet, in touching the man an exchange took place which was seen here and on Calvary's cross. The sin and its consequent disease touched Jesus. At the same time Jesus' holiness and health flowed to the leper. This same exchange took place in us at our baptism.

Holy living is the response of the converted, joyful soul. In the case of lepers, a testimony was given to the priests by bringing the sacrifices which Moses prescribed. This suggests an evangelism directive in our new life under Christ. We, too, are to give a testimony to all people through Christian living and witnessing. The preacher is usually loathe to say things which may give the flesh excuse not to speak the good news boldly. It is sometimes difficult enough to speak the gospel at all. However, this text reminds us that there is a right time and a wrong time to spread the news. Much depends on the attitude of the listeners and the immediate situation. The gospel is a precious pearl worthy of mounting in an appropriate setting.

The leper's words to Christ suggest this basic outline:

## "If You Are Willing, You Can Make Me Clean"

1. Jesus is willing (v. 41)
2. Jesus cleansed you (vv. 41,42)
3. Testify about it (v. 44)

Although some homileticians warn against "allegorizing "when associating the physical cleansing of leprosy with the spiritual cleansing of sin, a comparison between the two is not out of line with the thoughts suggested by Scripture itself, referred to also in our text study.

Another approach brings in the season of the church year as follows:

**Behold Our Epiphany Lord**

1. In his compassion (vv. 40,41)
2. In his power (vv. 41,42)
3. In his testimony (vv. 43,44)

# SEVENTH SUNDAY AFTER EPIPHANY

**The Scriptures**

Old Testament — *Isaiah 43:18-25*
Epistle — *2 Corinthians 1:18-22*
Gospel — *Mark 2:1-12*

**The Text — Mark 2:1-12**

Jesus had just returned from a trip throughout Galilee. He had also visited the region of the Gadarenes and had healed two demon-possessed men. And all the thanks he got for it from the majority of the people was to be asked to leave! So Jesus went home to Capernaum, his adopted hometown, since the people of Nazareth had turned him away in their attempt to kill him.

vv. 1,2 — *A few days later, when Jesus again entered Capernaum, the people heard that he had come home. So many gathered that there was no room left, not even outside the door, and he preached the word to them.*

While some had shown great eagerness to get rid of Jesus, others were just as eagerly awaiting his return home. And now, once he had arrived, they crammed themselves into every nook and cranny of the house where he was staying, filling it to the limit with no standing room available even outside the door. And to this packed house Jesus spoke the word of God. Jesus, we well might say, preached a "house sermon" that day. He never missed an opportunity to preach the word!

vv. 3,4 — *Some men came, bringing to him a paralytic, carried by four of them. Since they could not get him to Jesus because of the crowd, they made an opening in the roof above Jesus and, after digging through it, lowered the mat the paralyzed man was lying on.*

What was in the process of happening was going to take the dedicated efforts and consent of five people: four men to carry the man and the paralytic who allowed himself to be carried. And when they were forced by the press of the people to take an alternate route to Jesus through the ceiling, what they did there on the housetop could hardly have escaped the notice of those below. When they finally succeeded in getting the roof tile removed and the man on the stretcher lowered right in front of Jesus, it must have been clear to all what was desired. This man, who had been let down, wanted to be lifted up, allowed to walk again.

v. 5 — *When Jesus saw their faith, he said to the paralytic,* *"Son, your sins are forgiven".*

If there was so much urgency in getting this man to Jesus that this could not wait until a more convenient time then it may have seemed that Jesus missed the whole point of this man's being brought to him. They heard Jesus forgive the man while doing nothing for his body. Merely forgiving him still left him a helpless paralytic. And wouldn't it appear that the reason this man was brought to Jesus was so that Jesus might heal him?

We're told, however, that Jesus saw their faith, the faith of all five of them. Obviously there was faith, confidence in Jesus, on the part of the four men who had gone to so much trouble to get their sick friend down in front of Jesus. They would never have gone to so much trouble if they had thought their labor would be in vain.

But the man lying on the mat also had faith. If he had not trusted in what Jesus could do for him, would he ever have permitted himself to be carried to the roof of a house and then lowered down through the ceiling?

But as urgent as his physical need was, don't we see what must have been an even greater burden for him? It was a need only Jesus could see, the press and weight of his sins which kept him from standing upright in God's presence. And so, tenderly, like a father to his son, Jesus spoke kindly to him. "Son, your sins are forgiven. I'm lifting the weight of guilt from your shoulders so that, pardoned by me, you can stand upright before God, even though you are still lying flat on your back."

vv. 6,7 — *Now some teachers of the law were sitting there,* *thinking to themselves, "Why does this fellow talk like that?* *He's blaspheming! Who can forgive sins but God alone?"*

They were sitting there while many others were standing even outside the door. Had they gotten there so much earlier than all the rest? Or was this the position of honor given them by the common people who, unlike Jesus, could not see through their very thin religious veneer?

While they were sitting there, "thinking to themselves," it was their reason which stood in the way, blocking the door to faith in Jesus. And so they continued to reason, deep down within themselves, while the answer they were seeking was visible on the surface to seeing eyes and easily audible to hearing ears.

"This man," they were thinking, "does not have the right to forgive sins."

Their one premise was correct: only God, ultimately, can forgive sins. However, their second premise was wrong. Because they did

not believe Jesus was God, their conclusion was a fallacy: Jesus did
not have the divine authority to forgive sins.

vv. 8-11 — *Immediately Jesus knew in his spirit that this was
what they were thinking in their hearts, and he said to them,
"Why are you thinking these things? Which is easier: to say to
the paralytic, 'Your sins are forgiven,' or to say, 'Get up, take
your mat and walk'? But that you may know that the Son of
Man has authority on earth to forgive sins. . . . " He said to the
paralytic, "I tell you, get up, take your mat and go home."*

Talk about instant communications! Jesus knew immediately
what these men were thinking! Even though they did not know he
knew it, he did and told them so. This should have demonstrated to
them why he had claimed the authority to forgive sins. For here in
Jesus' knowledge of their thoughts was the omniscience which God
alone possesses! And Jesus had it, showing himself to be God.

The question Jesus asked them, "Which is easier?", seems to have
such a simple answer. Of course, humanly speaking, it seems much
more difficult to heal than just to forgive sins. But isn't Jesus really
asking for more of an answer than just that?

By their own admission, given reluctantly a number of times
before, they could not deny Jesus' miracles. There were too many
witnesses, too many people who had been helped by them. And so
may Jesus not have been asking here, "If you do not question my
ability to do what seems harder to you, performing miracles, why
would you question my authority when I do what seems easier to
you, forgiving sins?"

They would not willingly concede him anything. But now, if he
would perform before their watching eyes the act of healing which
they thought to be more difficult, would they not be forced to admit
that he also must have the authority to forgive?

Jesus, showing his divine authority, did no more outwardly now
than when he had earlier forgiven this man his sins. Jesus simply
spoke to him, telling him what to do and, in the power of that word,
giving him the strength to do it.

v. 12 — *He got up, took his mat and walked out in full view of
them all. This amazed everyone and they praised God, saying,
"We have never seen anything like this!"*

The results were in; it was time to count the votes. The man got up,
picked up his mat and, before the startled eyes of all, walked out of the
room. "The bed had borne the man; now the man bore the bed" (Bengel). Overwhelmed by what they had seen, they praised God, who had
permitted someone to do the like of which they had never seen before.

## Homiletical Suggestions

It is Mark's theme to display Jesus as the Christ by his words and works. Since that is so obviously what Jesus is doing here, judging from his own words, "But that you may know that the Son of Man has authority on earth to forgive sins" (v. 10), and because this emphasis fits so nicely into the Epiphany season, that surely is the place to begin with this text. So the first suggested treatment of this text would be:

### Jesus, The Great Physician

1. Since he knows the cause, (vv. 1-8)
2. He can treat the effects (vv. 9-12)

Because people today are so conscious of the needs of the body, there is danger that the church might promote the social gospel. To re-emphasize the saving gospel and, at the same time, show a proper, God-pleasing concern for the needs of the body, we might suggest two themes:

### Body And Soul In Need Of Jesus

1. First the soul (vv. 1-5)
2. Then the body (vv. 6-12)

### Total Care With Jesus

1. He gets to the heart of the matter, (vv. 1-8)
2. So that the whole body feels better (vv. 9-12)

Finally, this could also be an excellent mission festival text, as so many Epiphany texts are. The following theme might fit well on such an occasion:

### Bring Others To Jesus

1. Don't let anything stop you (vv. 1-4)
2. His message fits them all (vv. 5-8)
3. Bodily needs are not ignored (vv. 9-12)

# EIGHTH SUNDAY AFTER EPIPHANY

**The Scriptures**

> Old Testament — *Hosea 2:14-16,19,20*
> Epistle — *2 Corinthians 3:1b-6*
> Gospel — *Mark 2:18-22*

## The Text — Mark 2:18-22

It is early in Jesus' ministry. The opposition of the teachers of the law and the Pharisees has been mounting. They had questioned his authority to forgive the paralyzed man brought to him (2:6,7). They had asked the disciples why Jesus was eating at Levi's home with "sinners" and tax collectors. Now, no doubt prompted by the Pharisees, some asked why Jesus and his disciples were not fasting.

v. 8 — *Now John's disciples and the Pharisees were fasting. Some people came and asked Jesus, "How is it that John's disciples and the disciples of the Pharisees are fasting, but yours are not?"*

John's disciples may well have been offended at Jesus' informal manner of life, especially since John had been thrown into prison for his preaching.

Fasting in the Old Testament was commanded by Moses during the annual Day of Atonement (Lv 16:29; 23:27). Other days of fasting were added over the years, especially to commemorate the destruction of Jerusalem and the temple (Jer 52; Zech 8:19). It was to be a time of repentance and sorrow in view of God's judgment. The Pharisees made it a tradition to fast on the second and fifth days of every week (cf. Lk 18:12) in commemoration of Moses' ascent on Mt. Sinai on a Thursday and his descent on a Monday. They were offended that Jesus' disciples were eating and drinking and having a good time on those days.

vv. 19,20 — *Jesus answered, "How can the guests of the bridegroom fast while he is with them? They cannot, so long as they have him with them. But the time will come when the bridegroom will be taken from them, and on that day they will fast."*

Jesus' compassionate presence among the people was to be a time of rejoicing for them. He is the "bridegroom" making preparations for the wedding feast with his guests. (Οἱ υἱοὶ τοῦ νυμφῶνος are the bridegroom's attendants, who as guests were closest to the groom and played an essential part in the wedding ceremony.) Therefore fasting and sorrow are not fitting, but rather feasting and joy.

The term "bridegroom" is used often by the Lord in the Old Testament to describe his faithful, patient and forgiving love for the believers, his bride (Isa 54:5,7,8, e.g.). But the bridegroom is also Isaiah's suffering servant. The joy of the disciples will turn to sorrow when he is violently taken away "by oppression and judgment" (Isa 53:8). In the meantime, however, they are to know that his coming makes everything new and wonderful.

v. 21 — *"No one sews a patch of unshrunk cloth on an old garment. If he does, the new piece will pull away from the old, making the tear worse."*

The old Mosaic covenant with its rituals and ceremonies fit well for immature Israel as a preview of the coming Savior. But now that Christ and the promised Messianic covenant have come, the old has passed away. The new is not just to be added to or mixed with the old. It is not merely an improvement or enlargement of the old. These are two distinct covenants, as two garments are distinct from one another.

When other Christians would have us believe that faith in Christ is not enough, but rather that we must do something — pray, give up a certain food or drink, do penance or have a pentecostal experience — then they also are trying to add a piece of new cloth to the old, which will end up destroying both.

St. Paul makes this a major point in his letter to the Galatians. "The law was put in charge to lead us to Christ that we might be justified by faith. Now that faith has come, we are no longer under the supervision of the law" (3:24,25). Because the Judaizers in Galatia were trying to mislead the Christians into thinking they still had to follow Moses as well as believe in Christ, he wrote, "In Christ Jesus neither circumcision nor uncircumcision has any value. The only thing that counts is faith expressing itself through love" (5:6). And to the Colossian congregation he also wrote, "Do not let anyone judge you by what you eat or drink, or with regard to a religious festival, a New Moon celebration or a Sabbath day. These are a shadow of the things that were to come; the reality, however, is found in Christ" (2:16,17).

Jesus is not just a new prophet whose teachings can simply be added to those of Moses and the prophets. His words are as different as feasting is from fasting. He's not a patch to be sown on to Jewish piety, not a mellow wine to be added to the old wineskins of Jewish tradition.

v. 22 — *"And no one pours new wine into old wineskins. If he does, the wine will burst the skins, and both the wine and the wineskins will be ruined. No, he pours new wine into new wineskins."*

New wineskins are easily stretched and thus necessary for new wine, since it expands from fermentation for a while after being preserved. Old wineskins become stiff and brittle. New wine in old skins would spell sure disaster.

Jesus is here stressing the necessity of getting rid of the old life of the Mosaic law. It is too rigid, too restrictive and too cramped for the Christian's new life of the Spirit. Having seen the fullness and abundance of God's grace for sinners in Jesus Christ, especially in his death and resurrection, we are compelled by such love to live for him who died for us and rose again. Because he loved us first, we love. We want to do good to all people, to carry each other's burdens, not to rest until we share the gospel with our fellow citizens, all the while overflowing with thankfulness. Therefore, whatever we do, whether in word or deed, even eating or drinking, we do it in the name of the Lord Jesus for the glory of God.

This free expression of love and joy toward God and our neighbors in our everyday lives is all the result of the new life Christ has worked in us by faith through his gospel.

### Homiletical Suggestions

Christ has had an epiphany in the heart and life of every believer. By faith alone in his completed work we are moved to serve God and our neighbor with a life of love. And we do so willingly and cheerfully as our song of praise to our gracious and merciful Savior. This marvelous relationship between the believer and Christ is reflected in Christian marriage. It will find complete fulfillment at the marriage feast in heaven.

The following outlines are offered in view of the above comments:

### Christ Means Feasting, Not Fasting

1. Let us feast on his great love for us (vv. 18-20)
2. Let us show this love in our lives (vv. 21,22)

### Rejoice, The Bridegroom's Here!

1. Forget the sad rigidity of Moses (vv. 18,21,22a)
2. Enjoy the freedom of Christ (vv. 19,20,22b)

Realizing that by nature we all have a work-righteous Pharisee in our heart (*opinio legis*) which makes us legalists, we need the gospel daily in the war within us.

**Christ Reveals New Life For Old**

1. The old life under Moses is past (vv. 18,21,22a)
2. The new life under Christ has come (vv. 19,20,22b)

**New Hearts For Old**

1. Old hearts of works must go (vv. 18,21,22a)
2. New hearts of grace are here (vv. 19,20,22b)

# TRANSFIGURATION OF OUR LORD — LAST SUNDAY AFTER EPIPHANY

**The Scriptures**

> Old Testament — *2 Kings 2:1-12*
> Epistle — *2 Corinthians 3:12-4:2*
> Gospel — *Mark 9:2-9*

**The Text — Mark 9:2-9**

vv. 2-4 — *After six days Jesus took Peter, James and John with him and led them up a high mountain, where they were all alone. There he was transfigured before them. His clothes became dazzling white, whiter than anyone in the world could bleach them. And there appeared before them Elijah and Moses, who were talking with Jesus.*

This major event in the Savior's ministry took place "after six days" — six days after Jesus made the first prediction of his approaching passion and death. Matthew also reports that the transfiguration occurred "after six days" (Mt 17:1), while Luke says it happened "about eight days after Jesus said this" (Lk 9:28). Attempts to draw a parallel between these six days and the six days of creation in Genesis are both incorrect and ill-advised. Such incidental references to time assure us that the record of the life of Christ is grounded in history and fixed in the memory of eyewitnesses.

The synoptic Gospels are careful to indicate the sequence of events. Jesus asked the disciples, "Who do people say I am?" and received the answer, "You are the Christ." He then began to teach them that "the Son of Man must suffer many things and be rejected . . . . , and that he must be killed and after three days rise again." Peter vehemently disagreed with the Savior's prediction, and Jesus replied that not only he but also his disciples must deny themselves and take up the cross (Mk 8:27-38; cf. also Mt 16:13-28; Lk 9:18-27).

Mark switches to the historical present to describe the action: "Jesus *takes* (παραλαμβάνει) Peter, James and John and *leads* (ἀναφέρει) them up a high mountain, where they (are) all alone." The traditional site of the transfiguration is Mt. Tabor; for some this is too far south. Later exegetes have suggested Mt. Hermon; for many this is too far north. Jesus and the disciples had been traveling through the villages around Caesarea Philippi (Mk 8:27). The Gospel writers offer no additional geographical clues. *What* happened is more important than *where* it happened.

Why Peter, James and John? When Jesus raised Jairus' daughter from death, "he did not let anyone follow him except Peter, James and John the brother of James" (Mk 5:37). Jesus "took Peter and the two sons of Zebedee along with him" when he prayed in the Garden of Gethsemane (Mt 26:37). It has been suggested that these three had shown themselves "especially spiritually responsive" to Jesus' message. Peter in particular had boldly confessed, "You are the Christ" (Mk 8:29).

An equally valid case could be made, however, that these three had hardly distinguished themselves above the rest. Peter was often impetuous and outspoken. James and John, in a strange brew of holy wrath and unholy revenge against an unfriendly Samaritan village, asked Jesus, "Lord, do you want us to call fire down from heaven to destroy them?" (Lk 9:54). Even if these three had displayed a greater "spiritual responsiveness," such responsiveness was itself a gift of grace. Ylvisaker says, "They were to witness his greatest glory on earth, but also his deepest degradation. Both required the fuller faith."

"There," Mark says, "he was transfigured before them." The Greek μεταμορφόω means "to transform" or "to change in form." The verb is an aorist passive. Jesus didn't request this display of glory; he received it from the Father. Mark adds, "His clothes became dazzling white, whiter than anyone in the world could bleach them." Matthew describes it: "His face shone like the sun, and his clothes became as white as the light" (Mt 17:2). Luke reports, "The appearance of his face was changed, and his clothes became as bright as a flash of lightning" (Lk 9:29).

Attempts have been made to offer a rational explanation of the transfiguration. Perhaps the disciples were dreaming or hallucinating. Maybe the reflection of the morning sun off snowcapped mountains made him look bright. Such explanations demean God's unlimited power and insult his unerring word. Thirty years later Peter insisted that the event on this mountain was neither illusion nor myth: "We were eyewitnesses of his majesty. . . . We ourselves heard this voice that came from heaven when we were with him on the sacred mountain" (2 Pe 1:16,18). John also wrote, "We have seen his glory, the glory of the One and Only, who came from the Father" (Jn 1:14). "That which was from the beginning, which we have heard, which we have seen with our eyes, which we have looked at and our hands have touched — this we proclaim" (1 Jn 1:1).

Lenski mentions that the Greek noun μορφή "always denotes the essential form, not a mask or transient appearance, but the form that goes with the very nature." As the Son of God, Jesus from eternity possessed divine glory. By virtue of the communication of attributes this divine glory was communicated to the human nature of Christ. For most of the 33 years Jesus lived visibly in our world, he emptied himself of the use of that divine glory (Php 2:6-8). He masked his divine nature behind his human nature. Luther once said that just as the worm covers the fishing hook and hides the hook from the fish's eye, so the humanity of Christ covered his deity and hid it from people's eyes. Yet "in Christ all the fullness of the Deity lives in bodily form" (Col 2:9). On this occasion the Father permitted his Son's divine nature to shine through the human shell. The Son of God was manifest in the son of the virgin. The form of God shown through the form of the servant.

Mark says, "And there appeared before them Elijah and Moses, who were talking (συλλαλοῦντες) with Jesus." Luke adds the significant detail: "They spoke about his departure (ἔξοδον), which he was about to bring to fulfillment (ἤμελλεν πληροῦν) at Jerusalem." The original exodus had been God's way of rescuing his Old Testament people from slavery in Egypt. This exodus would lead Jesus to the cross to rescue people from slavery to the guilt and power and punishment of sin.

Why Elijah and Moses? Moses had received the law from God's hand. Elijah had been zealous to defend that law in an age of widespread unbelief in Israel. These two stood as testimony that the Law and the Prophets agreed with the plan that Jesus would go to his death at Jerusalem. Both had lived under Sinai law, yet both gave evidence that they and the world needed someone who would make the exodus to the cross to pay for the people's sins.

vv. 5,6 — *Peter said to Jesus, "Rabbi, it is good for us to be here. Let us put up three shelters — one for you, one for Moses and one for Elijah." (He did not know what to say, they were so frightened.)*

All three evangelists record Peter's response (καὶ ἀποκριθεὶς ὁ Πέτρος) to this remarkable sight. He wanted to freeze the scene as it was. He wished to put such majesty on hold. He wanted to preserve this glorious moment. "Teacher, noble (καλόν) it is for us to be here. We will make three tents (ποιήσωμεν τρεῖς σκηνάς)," Peter suggested, so that these famous guests could remain where they were and so that Jesus could remain as he was.

It was "good" for those three disciples to be there, and it is good for us to witness this amazing display of the Savior's glory. In a short time Jesus would endure the brutal agony and indignity of the cross.

This glimpse of Jesus' glory was meant to remind the three disciples — and it reminds us — that Jesus was and ever is the eternal Son of God.

Remember, however, that Peter expressed vehement disapproval with the Savior's prediction that he would "suffer many things and be rejected, . . . [and] be killed." Undoubtedly Peter at first believed first-century Jewish opinion that the Christ would come to be a political ruler. Many Jews looked for a Messiah who would crush the Gentiles, expel the Romans from their land, and restore to Israel the political glory she had enjoyed in David's days. Peter was anxious for the *glorious* Christ to be unveiled; he was offended at the suggestion of a *suffering* Christ. His desire to hold on to this glory was for Jesus a temptation to avoid his impending cross. This temptation was just as great as Satan's temptation at the beginning of Jesus' ministry: "All this I will give you if you will bow down and worship me" (Mt 4:9).

This impetuous, ill-advised comment was entirely in character for Peter. "He did not know what to say, they were so frightened." It wasn't the first time Peter spoke when he should have been listening; and it wouldn't be the last.

Luke mentions that "Peter and his companions were very sleepy, but when they became fully awake, they saw his glory" (Lk 9:32). Did the transfiguration occur at night? If so, Jesus' glorified appearance was all the more majestic against the dark sky. Peter's mixture of exuberance and fear is all the more understandable if he had been dozing on the hillside.

v. 7 — *Then a cloud appeared and enveloped them, and a voice came from the cloud: "This is my Son, whom I love. Listen to him!"*

The cloud which then enveloped them (ἐπισκιάζουσα) links this dramatic event with a chain of important occurrences in the Old Testament. When the LORD appeared to Abram to give him a visible assurance that his descendants would inherit the land of Canaan, he appeared in "a smoking fire pot with a blazing torch" (Ge 15:17). When the LORD called Moses to lead Israel, "the angel of the LORD appeared to him in flames of fire from within a bush" (Ex 3:2). The LORD led Israel through the wilderness "in a pillar of cloud to guide them on their way and by night in a pillar of fire to give them light" (Ex 13:21). At Sinai the LORD confirmed his covenant with Israel in the presence of the seventy elders. "When Moses went up on the mountain, the cloud covered it, and the glory of the LORD settled on Mt. Sinai. For six days the cloud covered the mountain. . . . To the

Israelites the glory of the LORD looked like a consuming fire on top of the mountain" (Ex 24:15-17).

The book of Exodus makes the summary statement, "In all the travels of the Israelites, whenever the cloud lifted from above the tabernacle, they would set out; but if the cloud did not lift, they did not set out.... The cloud of the LORD was over the tabernacle by day, and fire was in the cloud by night, in the sight of all the house of Israel during all their travels" (Ex 40:36-38). Much later, when Solomon dedicated Israel's permanent temple in Jerusalem, "the cloud filled the temple of the LORD. And the priests could not perform their service because of the cloud, for the glory of the LORD filled his temple" (1 Ki 8:10,11).

August Pieper wrote, "Its simple form was a flare of fire enveloped in smoke or a cloud, supernaturally produced by God at any given place.... Where this manifestation appears, it constitutes a proclamation through an act — not only that the Lord God is there present in a special manner, but also that He is about to go into action in a supernatural way, that He will do something special, something that is otherwise not revealed but very momentous. And that which is thus unannounced invariably pertains to the plan of salvation" (*The Glory of the Lord*, pp. 3,4). The appearance of the cloud at Jesus' transfiguration indicates that the Savior God is moving his plan of salvation another significant step forward — one step closer to the cross.

The voice from the cloud was the voice of the Father. He repeated two words he had spoken at Jesus' baptism: "You are my Son" was a reference to Psalm 2, while "whom I love" was a reflection of Isaiah 42. Those two words spoken at his baptism indicated that Jesus was a king who would assume the role of a servant. Now the Father added, "Listen to him!" This word was a quotation of Deuteronomy 18:15. The Father thereby acknowledged that Jesus was the prophet Moses had looked forward to: "The LORD your God will raise up for you a prophet like me from among your own brothers. You must listen to him."

vv. 8,9 — *Suddenly, when they looked around, they no longer saw anyone with them except Jesus. As they were coming down the mountain, Jesus gave them orders not to tell anyone what they had seen until the Son of Man had risen from the dead.*

In the excitement of the appearance of Elijah and Moses and the cloud and the voice from heaven, the disciples likely had hidden their faces from this remarkable yet terrifying sight. When they looked up again, and looked around, everything had returned to normal. The cloud was gone. Elijah and Moses had departed. Jesus was no longer "transfigured before them." "They no longer saw anyone with them except Jesus."

In the first announcement of his suffering, Jesus predicted, "after three days [the Son of Man will] rise again" (Mk 9:31). Here Jesus also referred to his coming resurrection. He "gave them orders (διεσ-τείλατο) not tell anyone what they had seen until the Son of Man had risen from the dead." It is clear that the disciples did not fully grasp what "rising from the dead" meant (v. 10). On other occasions the disciples misunderstood Jesus because they took his figurative speech too literally (e.g., Mk 8:14-21). Here they were unable to understand Jesus' predictions about his resurrection because they didn't take his words literally enough. Like Martha (Jn 11:24), the disciples expected a resurrection "at the last day." Here, however, Jesus was clearly talking about some other event.

Why did Jesus forbid them to tell anyone about the transfiguration? Many in Israel did not understand Jesus or his reason for coming into the world. News was spreading that he was a miracle worker. His healings and his control over nature could be misinterpreted. It was only after the resurrection, and the ascension, and the sending of the Holy Spirit on Pentecost, that his purpose would become clear. Then it would be appropriate that the disciples "go into all the world and preach the good news to all creation" (Mk 16:15). The time was not yet right.

### Homiletical Suggestions

One approach to this text is to see it *from the viewpoint of the Savior*. The transfiguration occurred first of all to benefit Jesus. It gave him comfort and strength for his approaching agony.

### Jesus Was Transfigured To Prepare Him For His Passion

1. He received the confirmation of Old Testament witnesses (vv. 2-4)
2. He endured the misunderstanding of earthly disciples (vv. 5,6)
3. He welcomed the approval of his heavenly Father (vv. 7-9)

A second approach treats the text *from the viewpoint of the disciples*:

### The Disciples Got A Glimpse Of The Savior's Glory

1. It exposed them to the Savior's deity
2. It prepared them for the Savior's death

In a similar vein, the text may be treated *from the viewpoint of twentieth century disciples*:

## The Transfiguration Helps Us Understand Our Savior

1. It discloses his heavenly nature
2. It anticipates his agonizing death
3. It foreshadows his glorious resurrection

# ASH WEDNESDAY

**The Scriptures**

> Old Testament — *Joel 2:12-19*
> Epistle — *2 Corinthians 5:20b-6:2*
> Gospel — *Matthew 6:1-6,16-21*

**The Text — Matthew 6:1-6,16-21**

The words of our text come from Jesus' Sermon on the Mount (Matthew 5-7). The main theme of this sermon is: "Don't use outward appearances as the yardstick for your spiritual health." The Beatitudes tell us that even though our outward circumstances may not look very impressive, yet we are truly blessed if we follow God's path. The rest of the sermon warns us against using the outward examples of the Pharisees as a guide for Christian living. In fact, Jesus says, "I tell you that unless your righteousness surpasses that of the Pharisees and the teachers of the law, you will certainly not enter the kingdom of heaven" (Mt 5:20). Instead of imitating the outward example of the Pharisees, Jesus gives his disciples practical examples of what God wants from his followers. Our text is part of these practical examples.

v. 1 — *"Be careful not to do your 'acts of righteousness' before men to be seen by them. If you do, you will have no reward from your Father in Heaven."*

This verse sets the theme for the sixth chapter. It gives the general command and the general threat. The rest of the chapter gives practical examples of this general theme.

The term "righteousness" (δικαιοσύνη) in Pauline thought is a quality of justification declared by God to sinful man, appropriated by faith. In this context, however, it has a slightly different meaning. It refers to our response to our justification, the upright things we do because of our being justified, the good works that come from a heart filled with God's grace.

Jesus warns against doing our good deeds "before men, to be seen by them." In Matthew 5:16 Jesus said, "In the same way, let your light shine before men, that they may see your good deeds and praise your Father in heaven." Far from being contradictory, these two verses say the same thing, one from a positive aspect and the other from the negative. The positive reason for doing good deeds before men is that they "may praise your Father in heaven." In our text

Jesus gives us a negative warning regarding doing our good deeds "before men." He warns us against doing our good deeds "to be seen by them." Jesus doesn't forbid doing good deeds before men. What he forbids is doing our good deeds just so others will see what we do and glorify us, not God.

If we do not heed Jesus' warning, if we have the wrong attitude, if we do things just so people will be impressed with us, then Jesus says, "you will have no reward from your Father in heaven." The word "reward" (μισθός) means "the fruit naturally resulting from toil and endeavors." Jesus is talking about receiving a reward or literally "wages" from God for the good things we do.

Of course, it is unscriptural to even think that we can earn eternal life in heaven by the good deeds we do. Isaiah 64:6 and Romans 7:15-25 are but two passages that show us how impossible that is. Ephesians 2:1-10 shows us that the only way to heaven is by God's free gift apart from our actions. Consequently, the reward Jesus talks of is not eternal life. That is ours already by God's grace.

But there are passages that do talk about good works receiving a reward from God (cf. Mt 25; Jn 5:9; 1 Co 3:10-15). God keeps track of the good deeds we do. They never go unnoticed. God remembers them and will reward us for them on the last day.

In these verses Jesus reminds us of this fact, but he also adds the warning that we dare not do our good deeds to be seen by men, or to be remembered by people, or in the hope of gaining some reward. If we do them for personal glory or recognition, we receive nothing from God. But even the smallest deed we do with the proper attitude will be remembered and rewarded by God.

v. 2 — *"So when you give to the needy, do not announce it with trumpets, as the hypocrites do in the synagogues and on the streets, to be honored by men. I tell you the truth, they have received their reward in full."*

The Greek construction that begins each of these sections (vv. 2,5,16) is ὅταν with the present subjunctive, an indefinite relative clause. This construction says nothing about commanding us to do these things. Jesus is not setting up a new law that we have to give alms, or that we have to pray, or that we have to fast. He is simply saying here, Whenever you do any one of these things, make sure your attitude is right.

The phrase translated "giving to the needy" literally says, "Whenever you do mercy." The phrase is general; it includes not just giving money to people, but any way of having pity and mercy on someone. The New English Bible does a good job of translating this verse:

"Thus, when you do some act of charity, do not announce it with a flourish of trumpets, as the hypocrites do." Whether or not rich people actually sounded the trumpets to call people over to show them their charitable acts can't be determined from the text. Either Jesus is here criticizing a particular practice that some people followed, or he is using an example of how far self-righteous pride can go. Either way, the point is clear. Christians are not to call attention to themselves when they do their deeds of charity.

Those who call attention to their deeds of charity because they want to be honored by men Jesus calls hypocrites. It wasn't the sounding of the trumpets that made these people hypocrites. It was their attitude, their reason for sounding the trumpets, namely, "to be honored by men." The purpose for their charity was not to have men give glory to God, not to help the needy, but to gain for themselves the honor of men. They wanted the applause, the recognition, and the admiration of the people for their generous acts of charity.

But Jesus says, "I tell you the truth, they have received their reward in full," or literally, "they are receiving their reward in full." Whatever acknowledgment they receive, that is the full extent of their reward. When the echo of the applause ends, so does their reward.

v. 3 — *"But when you give to the needy, do not let your left hand know what your right hand is doing."*

The pronoun "you" is emphasized by being in the first position in the clause. It could be translated: "But as for you, when you do your mercy. . . . " Jesus is making a contrast between the hypocrites and "you" in this verse and in verses 6 and 17. Hypocrites may do this, but not you. You do it differently.

When Jesus says, "Do not let your left hand know what your right hand is doing," he is speaking figuratively. He speaks as though each part of the body has a mind of its own. The right hand does an act of charity so secretly that even the left hand doesn't know about it. The meaning is clear. Jesus wants us to do our good deeds so secretly that no one, not even our closest friends, knows what we've done, so that we ourselves are hardly aware of our own good deeds.

Whenever you do something creditable, try to forget what you did. Don't pat yourself on the back and think, "My, what a good fellow I am!" If you do that, you have your reward in full. An interesting parallel situation can be found in the dividing of the sheep and the goats (Mt 25:31-46), when God mentions the good things the sheep have done. They don't remember doing them, but the Lord remembers and graciously rewards their good deeds.

v. 4 — " . . . *so that your giving may be done in secret. Then your Father, who sees what is done in secret, will reward you.*"

No one likes to be taken for granted or to do something and have it go unnoticed. We want to be appreciated. That's why we are all tempted to be like the hypocrites. Oh, we don't sound the trumpet when we do a good deed; we do it humbly and secretly. But then we hope that people find out what we've done and show their appreciation. If we don't get the apprecation we think we deserve, we feel hurt and disappointed.

Jesus reminds us that our Father "sees in secret." Nothing escapes his attention. Whether anybody else notices what we've done or acknowledges what we've done or even cares what we've done doesn't matter. God notices and God keeps a record.

God not only sees in secret, and keeps a record, but he also "will reward you." The thrust of this Greek word (ἀποδώσει) is "to give back, to restore, to give what is due." God sees all of our secret deeds, keeps a record of them, and will give us a proper reward for them. So, don't be upset when your best works go unnoticed, for they are noticed by God, will be remembered by God, and one day will be rewarded by God.

v. 5 — "*And when you pray, do not be like the hypocrites, for they love to pray standing in the synagogues and on the street corners to be seen by men. I tell you the truth, they have received their reward in full.*"

Jesus turns his attention from the general, "doing good deeds," to the specific, "prayer." The hypocrites "love to pray standing in the synagogues and on the stree corners." There's nothing wrong with loving to pray. There's nothing wrong with standing up as you pray. There's nothing wrong with standing in the synagogue or on the street corner as you pray. In fact, these actions can be excellent demonstrations of faith. As is always the case with hypocrites, it's not their outward actions that are wrong; it's their attitude.

The hypocrites' purpose in praying in the synagogues and on the streets was not to praise and glorify God but to be seen by men, so they would be commended and applauded.

The question is sometimes raised, "Should we pray at a restaurant as we sit down to enjoy our meal?" The answer is: "It all depends on what your purpose is." Do you want to ask God's blessing, confess your faith, and teach your children to pray, no matter where they are? Or do you want to have people think that you're an exceptionally God-fearing person? You must answer those questions for yourself.

Hypocrites don't want to bring glory to God; they want to be seen and applauded by men. But Jesus' verdict is the same for them as it was for those who sounded the trumpets: "I tell you the truth, they have received their reward in full."

v. 6 — *"But when you pray, go into your room, close the door and pray to your Father, who is unseen. Then your Father, who sees what is done in secret, will reward you."*

It's not the prayers in public that Jesus condemns, just those that are prayed "to be seen by men." Jesus tells us to pray in secret, to get out of the public eye, to get off where we can be alone with God. This can done, even in a crowded restaurant. Forget the other people who are there, and pray to God as if it were only you and God in the entire room. Pray to God in the humble spirit of Hannah (1 Sm 1:12-16) and the publican (Lk 18:13-14).

Pray in secret because your Father "sees what is done in secret." We can pray in our hearts so no one even knows we're praying. But our Father will know, for he sees in secret and will give us a reward.

v. 16 — *"When you fast, do not look somber as the hypocrites do, for they disfigure their faces to show men they are fasting. I tell you the truth, they have received their reward in full."*

God commanded his Old Testament people to fast only one day each year, the great Day of Atonement (Lev 16:29). Throughout Israel's history fasting became more and more the accepted way to show one's faith. In Jesus' time the Pharisees had raised fasting to a grand demonstration of faith as they fasted twice a week (Lk 18:12).

Jesus doesn't command fasting as a duty for all Christians, nor does he forbid fasting altogether. He simply states that if you fast, have the proper attitude.

Jesus rejected the fasting of the hypocrites because they were always "somber." The Greek word comes from σκυθρός ("angry, gloomy") and ὤψ ("face"). The word then means "with a sad or gloomy face." When the hypocrites fasted, everyone could tell, for their faces were sad, gloomy, and forlorn, as though they were suffering terribly from this sacrifice to God. But Jesus says, "Don't be like the sad-faced hypocrites."

"For they disfigure their faces." The word translated "disfigure" comes from the Greek ἀφαίνω ("not to shine, give light, appear, be visible"). It develops the meaning, then, to "make something invisible, or unrecognizable, or to render unsightly."

The Pharisees would never liturally disfigure their faces, for that was contrary to God's law (Lev 19:28). They would make their faces so misshapen with expressions of pain and misery that one could hardly recognize them.

The reason they did this was "to show men they are fasting." Once again, Jesus isn't condemning the fasting, or the sad face, but the desire to have everyone know that they were fasting.

Again, Jesus' judgment of the situation is the same: "I tell you the truth, they have received their reward in full." The brief applause, the acknowledgment of how pious they were — that was the extent of their reward.

v. 17 — *"But when you fast, put oil on your head and wash your face."*

Instead of looking sad and gloomy when they fast, Jesus advises the people to anoint themselves with oil, which was customary for festive occasions, and to wash their faces, which was a sign of joy. Instead of looking as though they were fasting, Jesus wanted them to look as though they were feasting. Instead of drawing attention to the positive things we do, we are to appear as if nothing out of the ordinary is taking place.

And the reason for this action is this:

v. 18 — *"So that it will not be obvious to men that you are fasting, but only to your Father, who is unseen; and your Father, who sees what is done in secret, will reward you."*

Fasting is to be a matter between the individual and God. No one else has to know. God knows, and he will reward you.

We tend to judge a person's faith on the basis of his outward good deeds. We may even look at our own lives and question whether we are really believers, because we don't seem to be doing the spectacular good deeds that other people do. But Jesus warns us never to judge faith by outward circumstances alone. True good works are often those we don't see, or don't remember.

v. 19 — *"Do not store up for yourselves treasures on earth, where moth and rust destroy, and where thieves break in and steal."*

Jesus turns from positive commands to a negative command, literally, "Do not treasure for yourselves treasures upon the earth." Treasures are those things we consider most valuable. Jesus warns against having as our top priority things that are "on earth" because these things can easily be lost.

The Lord mentions three things that can destroy our wealth. The first is the moth whose larvae eat clothing. In the Mideast clothing was very important to people. It demonstrated a man's wealth. But

Jesus points our how easily such wealth can be destroyed. All it takes is one moth and a little time.

The second enemy of earthly treasures is expressed by the Greek word βρῶσις, translated "rust." The word literally means "eating." It can refer either to the rust and corrosion that can quickly eat away the precious metals that make up a person's wealth, or it can refer to the "eating and drinking" and other expenses that can eat away a person's wealth.

Whichever meaning you choose, these two enemies can "destroy" a person's wealth. The Greek word translated "destroy" (ἀφανίζει) means "to make invisible." Jesus says, "Don't place too high a priority on these earthly treasures, because they can quickly and easily disappear."

Then comes the third enemy to wealth, namely, "thieves," who "break in and steal." No matter how sturdy you make the safe, no matter how impregnable you make the house, no matter what precautions you take to protect your valuables, some thief can devise a plan to break in and steal it, or to get it away from you by some scheme.

Any one of these three enemies can destroy a man's wealth overnight. Jesus isn't forbidding saving money or enjoying wealth. He is forbidding making these your most valued treasures, your number one priority, your god.

v. 20 — *"But store up for yourselves treasures in heaven, where moth and rust do not destroy, and where thieves do not break in and steal."*

Earthly treasures are transient. They are here one minute and gone the next. Jesus says, "Don't treasure up for yourselves earthly treasures, but rather heavenly treasures." Do not concentrate on the things that will make your physical life easier. Rather emphasize those that will help your spiritual life: peace with God, forgiveness of sins, faith, perseverance, hope, love. These will sustain your spiritual life as you look forward to eternal life in heaven. So store up these types of treasures for yourself.

One of the greatest things about these spiritual treasures is that absolutely nothing can take them from us — no calamity, no pest, no inflation, no thief. (Ro 8:35-39).

v. 21 — *"For where your treasure is, there your heart will be also."*

Your treasure is that which means the most to you. So, wherever you put your treasure, that is where you will put your heart, your energy, your hope, your work, your love.

Jesus doesn't forbid savings accounts, IRAs, insurance policies, or attempts to make our lives more comfortable. What he forbids is making these our gods. God wants us to plan and work for financial security, always remembering that material possessions can easily be taken from us. Our real treasure is God and his saving grace. This treasure moth and rust can never destroy and thieves cannot break in and steal.

## Homiletical Suggestions

Ash Wednesday is a time for repentance, a time for each of us humbly and reverently to bow before God, confessing our sins, recognizing what we deserve from God and begging for his mercy. Ash Wednesday is a time to emphasize, not just outward forms of worship, but the humble spirit of worship. Come to worship in body and spirit. This point is brought out in the Old Testament lesson, which tells us to "rend your hearts, not your garments." God doesn't want just outward adherence to some religious ceremony. He wants heartfelt worship. And this is the point of the words of our text. Don't just do it for show, do it for the love of God.

Using our text as three examples of this principle, we could emphasize this point and encourage our people to make sure their worship is done not for show, especially during Lent when they are confronted with the necessity of Christ's cross, but for giving glory to God. Our theme could be:

## Don't Observe Lent Just For Show

1. Don't worship like the hypocrites, to be seen by men (vv. 1,2,5,16)
2. But worship sincerely, to bring glory to God (vv. 3,4,6,17,18)

One is reminded, of course, of the hypocritical ways in which so many "Christians" blow off collective steam in unbridled fashion immediately before Lent, so that their practice of extreme piety during the lenten season can give evidence of true remorse by way of contrast. We also have those "Lenten Christians" who manage to become seasonally religious, and then disappear from church after Easter.

Along this line, following Christ's sequence of warnings analytically, we also suggest:

## Let Your Life Of Repentance Ring True

1. In your doing (v. 1)
2. In your giving (vv. 2-4)
3. In your praying (vv. 5,6)
4. In your fasting (vv. 16-18)
5. In your evaluating (vv. 19-21)

# FIRST SUNDAY IN LENT

## The Scriptures

Old Testament — *Genesis 22:1-14*
Epistle — *Romans 8:31-39*
Gospel — *Mark 1:12-15*

## The Text — Mark 1:12-15

Mark's summary of Jesus' baptism immediately precedes this text and offers an important perspective on it. A year or so of Messianic activity, as recorded in John 1:19-5:47, occurred between the baptism and temptation of Jesus and the calling of his first disciples. Split down the middle, this text brackets the first third of Jesus' public ministry. Nevertheless, each text half is illuminated by light shed from the baptism account. Jesus' baptism was a public, obvious way whereby he formally took his place alongside the sinful human race. The sinless second Adam did not need baptism's forgiveness, yet he willingly identified himself as our brother, the man who would "fulfill all righteousness" (Mt 3:15) in our place. God the Father's pronouncement upon his Son in Mark 1:11 is the authority for and substance of the message he preached in word and deed throughout his earthly ministry. This text succinctly highlights Jesus, our Substitute, and his message, our salvation.

vv. 12,13 — *At once the Spirit sent him out into the desert, and he was in the desert forty days, being tempted by Satan. He was with the wild animals, and angels attended him.*

Alongside the more detailed accounts in Matthew 4:1-11 and Luke 4:1-13, Mark's record of Jesus' temptations is but a brief summary. Matthew and Luke recount three key temptations — to change stones into bread, to leap from the temple pinnacle, and to bow to Satan — with their attending conversations and circumstances. Highlighted is Jesus' skillful wielding of the word in defense against the "father of lies." In contrast, Mark's account is terse and stark. Yet his inspired conciseness conveys a mood for the deadly one-on-one struggle between the King of light and the prince of darkness. There is a sense of aloneness and desolation in Mark's compact report, heightened by the only detail not mentioned by the other synoptists — the wild animals. In lean prose Mark spells out the essence of Jesus' forty days in the desert, really of his thirty-three years on earth, a fierce fight with the devil, a one-man war only he could wage and win.

"At once" (εὐθύς) indicates the close connection between Jesus' baptism, which just preceded, and the temptation. Immediately after publicly affirming his membership in the human race, the Son of God and Man "goes forth to war" as the sinners' Substitute. He went according to God's will, plan and direction ("the Spirit sent him"), not carelessly or recklessly exposing himself to danger. This sending does not connote an unwillingness on Jesus' part, though the Greek does use a strong word (ἐκβάλλει), often employed for the casting out of demons (Mk 1:34,39). This forceful verb here describes the Holy Spirit impelling Jesus to go, and neatly dovetails with Luke's (4:1) description of the Savior as "full of the Holy Spirit" (πλήρης πνεύματος ἁγίου), who had so recently descended upon him in the form of a dove. Jesus' will mirrored the Spirit's perfectly. According to God's good purpose (1 Jn 3:8) Jesus engaged Satan in the desert, a deserted place probably in eastern Judea toward the Dead Sea. Jesus was cut off from all human contact and support, a circumstance underscored by the nearness of the wild beasts of this wilderness.

In isolation amidst desolation Jesus was tempted by Satan. The temptation, continuous and ongoing (πειραζόμενος is a present participle) during the forty days, put Jesus to a great test. Matthew and Luke state that he fasted for the forty days as he wrestled with the devil. That most powerful of evil angels attacked in full strength. Certainly the deceiver, who could so glibly quote Psalm 91 to tempt (Mt 4:6), fully understood the import and impact of Genesis 3:15 and fought with the frenzied fierceness of a cornered animal. If Jesus had sinned even one time, hell's ruler would have won for all time. Each of the synoptists uses a genitive of personal agent (ὑπὸ τοῦ Σατανᾶ in Mark; ὑπὸ τοῦ διαβόλου in Matthew and Luke), pointing to the intensity and personalness of the struggle. This is hand-to-hand combat. This is a close-quarters duel with Satan, whose very name in Aramaic means "adversary," "opponent."

Jesus won. His victory is implicit in the angels' ministering to him, explicit in the Gospels of Matthew and Luke. The angels brought him the nourishment and companionship he had forgone for forty days. They were a reminder of the Father's love for him and of his concern for the Messiah's mission.

This victory did not mark the end of Satan's effort to trip or trap the Savior. Luke 4:13 records that the devil left Jesus "until an opportune time." While there was never again a graphic head-to-head encounter such as this, Satan put Jesus to the test in subtler ways. Crowds tried variously to kill Christ (Lk 4;29) or to crown him (Jn 6:15). The deceiver used Peter to try to distract the Savior from going to the cross (Mt 16:23). Satan, seen here at the beginning of Jesus' public ministry, was there at the end in Pilate's sneers (Jn 18:38) and in the Jewish hierarchy's taunts (Mt 27:42).

Through it all Jesus remained sinless and perfect though "tempted in every way, just as we are" (Heb 4:15). He did what Adam and Eve and you and I and everyone else couldn't, and he did it for Adam and Eve and you and me and all the rest. This text proclaims our Substitute's victory over Satan's power and is a prelude to the final, eternal triumph trumpeted by Easter's empty tomb.

vv. 14,15 — *After John was put in prison, Jesus went into Galilee, proclaiming the good news of God. "The time has come," he said. "The kingdom of God is near. Repent and believe the good news!"*

In these verses Mark directs our attention to the message and core of Jesus' preaching. Together with the first half of our text these verses capture the essence of Jesus' mission on earth, the defeat of Satan and the preaching of the gospel. Between the temptation of Jesus and the beginning of his work in Galilee many events occurred — the calling of the first disciples, the Cana wedding, the first temple cleansing, the instruction of Nicodemus, the mission work among the Samaritans begun at Sychar's well, the healing of the Capernaum official's son, the healing of the invalid at Bethesda's pool, as well as preaching in Judea.

Sometime toward the end of this better part of a year John the Baptist was imprisoned by Herod Antipas. It had been the life and work of John the Baptist to be the prophesied and prophesying forerunner. Now that work was ended and that life was nearly over. Matthew (4:12), as well as Mark, reports John's imprisonment as the beginning of Jesus' Galilean ministry, a great light dawning among people living in darkness (Isa 9:1,2; Mt 4:14-16).

Mark looks back to the details of John's jailing and execution in 6:17-29. Into the land of the shadow of death Jesus came heralding (κηρύσσων) boldly the gospel of life, the good news whose Author and Source is God (τὸ εὐαγγέλιον τοῦ θεοῦ). Present participles (κηρύσσων, λέγων) point to the ongoing activity of preaching the message summed up in verse 15.

"*Fulfilled* has been (πεπλήρωται) the time"; the perfect tense of the Greek verb and its position at the beginning of the sentence pack an emphasizing punch and underline the immediacy of the message for Jesus' hearers. God's own good, right time (καιρός), history's (his story's) proper, golden moment, had been realized, and now, even as the words entered their ears, centuries of looking and longing were ended. Time had filled the period of waiting to brim-high fullness and now was spilling into the present reality of the Messiah's arrival.

The closeness of God's time is matched by the nearness of God's kingdom. "Near has come (ἤγγικεν) the kingdom of God"; again Greek verb tense and position stress the message's immediacy. This spatial expression corresponds to the preceding temporal expression, though God's kingdom is not of space, not of this world. What Jesus speaks of here as near and close at hand is God's gracious rule of love in the hearts and lives of his believing children. Standing before those Galileans was the King of that kingdom, speaking the word through which that kingdom is established.

That word is put into a nutshell by Jesus' next sentence, which empitomizes law and gospel. "Repent" (μετανοεῖτε), look into the mirror of God's standards of perfection and know that you don't and can't measure up. Feel the sorrow and sadness which flow from a broken and contrite heart. Know the grief of having offended your holy God. "And believe [in] the good news!" Nowhere else in the New Testament is the verb "believe" (πιστεύετε) followed by "in" (ἐν) and a neuter object. Again there is an emphasis of nearness, of closeness, of immediacy. The believer is not merely aware of or acknowledging the gospel; he believes and lives in the sphere of the good news. His thoughts and his trust are enveloped and developed by the fact that Jesus Christ lived and died and rose for him. Both imperatives (μετανοεῖτε, πιστεύετε) are present and direct the hearer to a lifelong awareness of his own sin and God's grace. This summary of Jesus' preaching serves well as the background, indeed the backbone, of every sermon faithful to God's word.

**Homiletical Suggestions**

Every human being is responsible in his own struggle with the devil. He needs to defeat Satan and obey God. On our own we lose the fight. Jesus fought and won the battle for us. This text gives us a picture of Jesus' purpose and role as our holy Substitute. He lived for us and died instead of us. His innocent death on the cross paid the law's penalty and crushed the serpent's head for eternity. His victory means our forgiveness. Tempted in every way just as we are, Jesus understands the loneliness of our struggle with Satan and is our strength through faith to resist the devil's temptations.

Jesus' life and words spell out clearly his mission and message. Yet too often modern thought and even modern Christianity assess him merely as a good man, a kind healer, an insightful prophet, or a splendid example, nothing more and sometimes less. They have nothing left but a hollow, false Christ, whose image only serves to endorse political causes and excuse work-righteous religions. Such thinking utterly misses the Messianic point. Jesus spoke, and still speaks, law and gospel. We need to hear him again and again.

These thoughts suggest the following outline:

## Understand The Point Of Jesus' Life

1. He defeated Satan for us (vv. 12,13)
2. He preaches salvation to us (vv. 14,15)

Important to the application of the above outline is the consideration that it can also serve as a framework for understanding the point of a Christian's life on earth — to resist Satan and thus gratefully praise God by keeping his law and to tell others God's good news.

Brought to bear more directly on this Sunday in the church year, this text may serve well as:

## A Lenten Invitation To You:

1. Relive the Warrior's battle (vv. 12,13)
2. Believe the Victor's message (vv. 14,15)

Here is ample opportunity to introduce the new church year season and to preview Lent's events and significance as an encouragement to midweek service attendance.

Along the same lines the following may help to set the tone and ingrain the thought of the season:

## Lent In A Nutshell

1. Satan defeated (vv. 12,13)
2. Salvation completed (vv. 14,15)

# SECOND SUNDAY IN LENT

**The Scriptures**

> Old Testament — *Genesis 28:10-17*
> Epistle — *Romans 5:1-11*
> Gospel — *Mark 8:31-38*

**The Text — Mark 8:34-38**

The Galilean ministry of our Savior is the setting for this text. This has been called his retirement ministry, a period characterized by more private, repeated instruction of his disciples. At Caesarea Philippi, the setting for our text, our Lord asked the disciples what the crowds were saying about him, then proceeded to ask, "But what about you? . . . Who do you say I am?" (Mk 8:29). Peter's dramatic confession of faith (Mk 8:29) signals a significant transition point in Jesus' ministry. While the first part of the Savior's ministry had emphasized, by words and deeds of affirmation, that Jesus is truly the Son of God, now his emphasis is directed to his upcoming suffering, death and triumphant resurrection.

Previous to our text are the words: "He then began to teach them that the Son of Man must suffer many things and be rejected by the elders, chief priests and teachers of the law, and that he must be killed and after three days rise again" (Mk 8:31). The disciples were no longer shielded from the painful realities of the sacrifice which Jesus had to make. Peter balked at the words, but Jesus rebuked him and carried the message a step further by detailing the involvement of all who would call themselves disciples:

v. 34 — *Then he called the crowd to him along with his disciples and said: "If anyone would come after me, he must deny himself and take up his cross and follow me."*

The call of the gospel is voluntary; the Greek (εἴ θέλει) is a simple conditional clause. The KJV translates: "Whosoever will come after me. . . . " To the person who wants to be his disciple or follower Jesus gives three specific commands. First, "deny yourself." The Greek aorist imperative of ἀπαρνέομαι signifies a once-for-all action. This is not a legalistic demand, but a command of love. What could be better than losing the sinful self and "being found in Christ"?

The second command, "take up your cross," is also a Greek aorist imperative, of the verb ἀράτω. The disciple of Jesus should be willing, once and for all, to bear the burden which being a Christian implies in a world of sin. Whether "taking up one's cross" was a common or uncommon phrase before this statement is uncertain. But our Savior knew what its eternal significance would be. However large the cross we bear might seem to be, we must remember that *his* cross has removed the eternal, unbearable burden for us. The cross was an instrument of shame; the cross Jesus refers to should not be confused with the hardships we face in life as a consequence of sin. It refers, rather, to our willingness to bear shame for being a Christian. The preacher dare not use this passage to make the Christian life of sanctification appear burdensome. He will point out that the apostles rejoiced "because they had been counted worthy of suffering disgrace for the Name" (Ac 5:41). The Luke account adds the word "daily" to the command to bear the cross.

The third command, "follow" (ἀκολουθέω), is a present imperative, indicating a continuous action: "Keep on following." The disciple of Christ, whose heart has been set free from sin, willingly denies self, takes up his Christian cross and keeps on following Jesus.

v. 35 — *"For whoever wants to save his life will lose it, but whoever loses his life for me and for the gospel will save it."*

Our Lord explains the importance of willingness to be a disciple. In a future more vivid clause, he points out the blessed result of discipleship. One who is willing to suffer the loss of his life for Jesus will find that he has lost nothing, but gained everything.

Sweet loss! The Greek word φυχή can mean either "life" or "soul," but in this context must certainly convey "life." The clause construction adds certainty to the results of following self or Jesus. Life will be lost or saved

While "for me and for the gospel" could be understood as one and the same, it is important to note that Jesus specifically emphasizes the gospel. All of the words which he gives us are to be treasured and protected and defended by his followers, even if that faithfulness results in shame or cries of sectarianism.

v. 36 — *"What good is it for a man to gain the whole world, yet forfeit his soul?"*

No rational man could fail to see the proper choice indicated by the Savior's question. Granting the impossible for a moment and accepting it as real, would the entire accumulated wealth of the world be worth the loss of the soul? We recall the story of the rich fool and his bigger barns, whose life was ended by God. But to be declared innocent through Jesus makes one rich for an eternity in heaven.

In the realm of heaven, how true! But in the realm of santification on this earth, it is equally true. The gaining of things perishable, no matter how many or how much, can never be worth the loss of anything imperishable, even for a moment. Justified souls need to be reminded that the way of life is still Christ. Those avenues chosen in Christ receive his blessing and bring joy. Those chosen apart from Christ cause harm and, if allowed to predominate, can destroy.

v. 37 — *"Or what can a man give in exchange for his soul?"*

Our Lord drives the point home further with a rhetorical question. We are to recall that "the ransom for a life is costly, no payment is ever enough" (Ps 49:7). No accumulation of meritorious "deeds" can be offered in exchange (ἀντάλλαγμα, literally "price") for the salvation of the soul. The deliberative subjunctive (δοῖ) is in the aorist, indicating a one-time action. Our repeated attempts to earn God's favor can only come up short, but his once-for-all sacrifice was the payment which satisfied God's demand. "He sacrificed for their sins once for all when he offered himself" (Heb 7:27)

A contemplation of the value of the soul, our inability to earn its freedom, and the tremendous sacrifice the Savior made to win it for eternity should lead the disciple to a joyful willingness to sacrifice all for Jesus. Satan's offers attempt to erode the rock-solid grasp of reality which Jesus presents here. Those offers may sound attractive if we do not count their cost and see the relationship between perishable and imperishable. The disciple of Christ will ponder this question frequently.

v. 38 — *"If anyone is ashamed of me and my words in this adulterous and sinful generation, the Son of Man will be ashamed of him when he comes in his Father's glory with the holy angels."*

In another future more vivid clause, Christ shows us the eternal destiny of those who deny Christ: eternal condemnation. The very thought of being ashamed of Jesus was totally foreign to God's perfect creatures. But the advent of sin changed all that, and Jesus explains how such thinking can be possible: the age is "adulterous and sinful." We think of God's Old Testament indictments of his bride, the people of Israel, who prostituted themselves to a world of other gods. Adulterers here are lovers of the world, as typified by the religious rulers who "loved praise from men more than praise from God." (Jn 12:43).

The act of adultery discovered brings shame. Being ashamed of Jesus is the very worst sort of adultery. Christians need to focus on the blessings of their marriage to Christ, the Bridegroom, and not let a sinful, vice-versa world of logic make us see beauty in shame.

> "Ashamed of Jesus, that dear Friend
> On whom my hopes of heav'n depend?
> No; when I blush, be this my shame,
> That I no more revere his name." (TLH 346:4)

The indefinite temporal "when he comes" carries the reminder that Jesus' return could be at any time. That final appearance will display the glory of the Father, which causes praise and joy, not shame. The holy angels, God's special creation in heaven, will silence the tongues of proud men. What believer could fail to rejoice at the thought of this coming and confess with the apostle Paul: "I am not ashamed of the gospel, because it is the power of God for the salvation of everyone who believes" (Ro 1:16)!

## Homiletical Suggestions

The historic introit for Reminiscere, the second Sunday in Lent, contains the words: "Do not let me be put to shame" (Ps 25:2b). While the season of Lent focuses on the sufferings of our Savior to gain salvation for us, our text goes a step beyond to describe the suffering which Christians should expect as a result of being the Lord's followers. The Father put his own Son to shame so that we need never be ashamed.

Tongue-wagging and finger-shaking may evoke a response of fear, but a faithful exposition of the text will lead the preacher to point first to the suffering of Jesus as the joyful motivation for the Christian's cross-bearing. Failure to proclaim the gospel of grace faithfully may lead the hearer to view this text as a work-righteous command, but a Christ-centered sermon will lead its listeners to a joyful comprehension of the voluntary nature of discipleship. The rhetorical questions posed by our Savior should lead to praise, not fear, as we recall that we have been saved for eternity in Jesus.

Yet the text is a challenge to all followers of Christ. Deny self! Take up your Christian cross! Keep on following! Lose yourself for Jesus! Keep counting the cost of your soul! Never be ashamed of Jesus! With these challenges in mind, the text might follow this outline:

### Ashamed of Jesus?

1. The shame of the cross (v. 34)
2. The shame of indifference (v. 35)
3. The shame removed (vv. 36-38)

Focusing first on the suffering of Jesus and his sweet victory on the cross might lead to this emphasis:

**The Christian And The Cross**

1. Consider Christ's cross
2. Take up your cross (vv. 34-37)
3. The cross becomes a crown (vv. 35-38)

An outline which begins, as Jesus does, with a command, then focuses Christians on the joyful alternative of discipleship and salvation, might look like this:

**Remain A Disciple**

1. Follow Jesus' commands (vv. 34,35)
2. Consider the alternatives (vv. 36-38)

# THIRD SUNDAY IN LENT

## The Scriptures

Old Testament — *Exodus 20:1-17*
Epistle — *1 Corinthians 1:22-25*
Gospel — *John 2:13-22*

## The Text — John 2:13-22

Luke 2:41-50 records Jesus' appearance at the temple when he was twelve years old. Matthew 21, Mark 11 and Luke 19 record his attendance at the Passover at the end of his ministry. The incident in our text takes place at the beginning of his ministry, when he was in Jerusalem for the Passover.

These three Passover celebrations have one common theme. Jesus was always about his Father's business. Jesus' disciples had been given an indication at the Cana wedding that Jesus had a glory that exceeded his obvious human nature. The time had now come for them and others to witness also his authority. As he began his ministry, he showed friends and enemies alike what it meant to be about his Father's business.

v. 13 — *When it was almost time for the Jewish Passover, Jesus went up to Jerusalem.*

The feast that commemorated God's deliverance of his people from Egypt was the occasion for the manifestation of Jesus' authority. Multitudes of people were present for the most frequently attended convocation of the Jewish year. As they recalled the details of the first Passover, they were directed to Jesus Christ. The death of the lamb, the blood that saved God's believers from death, the deliverance from the oppression of Egypt, the bitter herbs that recalled the suffering of the people, the meal of haste and finality in Egypt were all called to mind. These were reminders that gave a clear picture of the Savior and his work. In the midst of that symbolism Jesus revealed his authority for being about his Father's business as he demonstrated what his Father's business really was. It did not appear, however, that there were many who understood God's business.

v. 14 — *In the temple courts he found men selling cattle, sheep and doves, and others sitting at tables exchanging money.*

To be sure, there was activity at the temple, but only in the most shallow sense could it be called God's work. The outward forms and rituals demanded provisions. Animals needed to be available for those coming from a distance. Their quality had to be checked by a qualified inspector. Change had to be made for foreign currency and to provide exact change for residents for the temple tax. These services were usually provided in the outlying country some two months in advance of the feast, and then also provided at the temple about two weeks before the celebration. Though necessary, they were also subject to abuse.

The money-changing and animal sales were carried on in the Court of the Gentiles, the first portion of the temple grounds that celebrants would enter. The appearance of the Court of the Gentiles under these circumstances could not lead anyone to think of a spiritual relationship with the God of Israel. Instead of prompting the singing of psalms of joyful expectation, visitors would more likely be inclined to hold their purses and their noses. The stench of so many animals gathered in one place along with bargaining and bickering over the cost of animals, the rates of exchange and so forth also made it a spiritual stench. This was not God's business, but man's. Humanly speaking, it was good business.

Along with the dealings that went on in the Court of the Gentiles there was the added shame of dishonesty. No one objected when Jesus said that he was standing in a "den of robbers" (Mt 21:13). According to Josephus, the thieves were none other than the sons of Annas, the high priest. Jesus might as well have been walking into the temple grounds in the days of Eli and his sons.

The time had come for Jesus' lesson as to what the Father's business was meant to be:

vv. 15,16 — *So he made a whip out of cords, and drove all from the temple area, both sheep and cattle; he scattered the coins of the money changers and overturned their tables. To those who sold doves he said, "Get these out of here! How dare you turn my Father's house into a market!"*

No one introduced Jesus, and very few even knew who he was. The Son of God and the Son of Man introduced himself. He made a whip of cords. There must have been plenty of cords with all the animals there. With his whip he cleansed the court of the filth that had accumulated from animals and people alike. He overturned tables and scattered money. He forced cages for birds into their sellers' hands and drove them all out. All this was done without any recorded objection from the objects of his righteous wrath.

Could it be that he had actually pricked the consciences of hardened and perhaps dishonest businessmen? Was it that the whole episode took place so fast and with so little warning? The answer we need is recorded for us. This was his Father's house. Jesus went to work with the same indignation a faithful son in a household would have when seeing his father's house being used for uninvited revelry. There was no question which Father Jesus was talking about. This was God's house and God's Son was talking. People may have thought this was their temple and their place of business, but they were in God's house. Jesus gave them a forceful reminder of that.

This is not the way most people think of Jesus. He is the gentle Shepherd who loves the sheep enough to give up his life for them. But he is also the Son of God with divine righteousness and holiness. He did not lose control and explode in anger. He demonstrated the righteous wrath of God against people who dared to abuse the holy place.

If there was bewilderment and amazement among those who watched and those who were being driven out, it must have reached its height in the minds of the disciples who watched.

v. 17 — *His disciples remembered that it is written: "Zeal for your house will consume me."*

The disciples recalled the words of David in Psalm 69:9. David had righteous zeal for the house of God and the service of the tabernacle, but now the righteous zeal of God himself was being revealed by David's Son and David's Lord. The disciples had never seen anything like it.

All the evidence was there. The temple was not a place of business, but the house of God. God will not tolerate the abuse of worship that belongs to him alone. Rituals and ceremonial provisions serve only as an aid to worship that comes from hearts that belong to God. God the Son was in the house that belonged to God the Father.

There was no question about the propriety of what Jesus had done, even from the Jewish authorities; they just wanted to know what authority he had for doing it.

v. 18 — *Then the Jews demanded of him, "What miraculous sign can you show us to prove your authority to do all this?"*

This verse gives the impression that these Jewish leaders were willing to give Jesus a chance to prove himself. They wanted to appear to be fair in their judgment of Jesus. From time to time self-appointed prophets had challenged the authority of the Sanhedrin, but all of them had failed in their purpose. These Jewish leaders wanted to expose Jesus as just another false prophet, who would also be a failure — but they were the ones who failed.

The request for a sign is interesting and familiar. Since the time of Abraham the nation had been taught to live by faith (see the Epistle for the day). The sign that the Jews asked for was really an indication that they had not learned the lesson. They requested a sign because of unbelief, not because of faith.

This deep spiritual problem still presents itself repeatedly, particularly among those who have a charismatic bent. Without a sign of God's power and love, these people lack faith in God's power and love. That is not living by faith, but by sight (see Jesus' words to Thomas in John 20:29).

v. 19 — *Jesus answered them, "Destroy this temple, and I will raise it again in three days."*

Jesus answered these leaders with an imperative that was also a prediction and judgment. In the Greek word Λύσατε ("destroy") we have an imperative. Jesus was saying, "Go ahead and destroy this temple if that's what you're determined to do." While they asked for a sign about him and his authority, Jesus gave his opponents a sign about themselves and their unbelief.

Outwardly, Jesus looked like the one destroying the temple. The fact was that those buying and selling and the leaders who allowed, encouraged and participated in it were the destructive ones. Under their leadership the temple had gone from being a house of prayer to being a marketplace and stockyard where thieves worked.

Jesus' response also had a very personal significance. Here at the beginning of his ministry Jesus told these leaders what would identify them as opponents all the way through his ministry. As they heartlessly destroyed the true worship of Israel, they would destroy the temple of his body by crucifixion. When they carried out that act, they would have the undeniable sign that they had been the temple-destroyers. Only God could rebuild it.

vv. 20,21 — *The Jews replied, "It has taken forty-six years to build this temple, and you are going to raise it in three days?" But the temple he had spoken of was his body.*

In typical shallowness the Jews thought only of the temple Jesus had just cleansed. There is no indication that they recognized the perversions they had allowed and fostered in it. They saw nothing to be learned from Jesus' accusation that they were temple-destroyers. Much less could they think in terms of Jesus as the one who was really about his Father's business, the one whom they would destroy, the one who would rise again.

138

The building of the temple that took 46 years was actually a rebuilding and refurbishing project that was ongoing. Rather than being a 46-year construction project, it was a continuing improvement of the existing building under Herod. The fact of the matter was, however, that Israel's temple and Israel's worship were continuing to decline. It would continue to decline because it had been robbed of real purpose for most of Israel. The proof would be in its ultimate destruction in A.D. 70.

Only when Jesus was put to death by his own people, and only after he had risen again, did the real destruction become evident. These people were guilty of destroying the true worship of God. They would also become guilty of "destroying" the Messiah by putting him to death on the cross. Only God could make Israel's worship what he intended it to be, a worship of faith in the Savior who was pierced for our transgressions and crushed for our iniquities (Isa 53:5). "He was delivered over to death for our sins and was raised to life for our justification" (Ro 4:25).

v. 22 — *After he was raised from the dead, his disciples recalled what he had said. Then they believed the Scripture and the words that Jesus had spoken.*

The Jewish leaders were not the only ones who were slow to understand what Jesus was talking about. In some ways they were ahead of Jesus' own disciples. The Jews recalled this prediction early enough to want to post a guard at Jesus' tomb to prevent a deception about Jesus' resurrection. Our text tells us that the disciples didn't think of that until after Jesus rose. It was then that the facts of his ministry began to come together for them. In some ways the opposition appears to have been better organized than the allies.

Jesus had already outlined the course of his entire ministry. Everything he said was in perfect harmony with promises and prophecies that went back as far as the fall into sin. Everyone still had a great deal to learn, but the entire framework was there in this encounter on the first Passover visit of Jesus' ministry. There could be no doubt about who Jesus claimed to be, whose house the temple was, how God's people should act in it, what the characteristics of the Jewish leaders were, who the opposition was, what the opposition was determined to do, how the risen Savior would prove his superiority over the temple of Herod and how the world would know that God's words and ways will be done.

**Homiletical Suggestions**

This text can easily be used in at least three different ways. Verses 13-17 would be appropriate for a sermon on the dangers of a superficial religiosity. The forms of religion, though beneficial, are also subject to the same abuses found by Jesus in the temple in Jerusalem. From this point of view verses 13-17 could be treated as follows:

**Let Jesus Show You How To Worship**

1. In the form (v. 13)
2. With your heart (vv. 14-16)
3. To communicate with God (v. 17)

Considering verses 18-21 alone, we are brought into a direct Lenten application as the suggested Sunday implies. Treating this portion from that point of view we might consider that:

**The Lord Reveals His Mission**

1. In the face of opposition (vv. 19,20)
2. With the promise of victory (vv. 19,21)
3. To strengthen his believers (v. 22)

The text is, however, suggested as a unit for the Third Sunday in Lent. The entire text lends itself to a unit treatment with a Lenten and resurrection emphasis. A possible presentation might be:

**Jesus Was About His Father's Business:**

1. Cleansing his house (vv. 13-17)
2. Warning his opponents (vv. 18-21)
3. Giving hope to his church (v. 22)

Emphasizing the authority of the Savior as he entered upon his ministry and set the stage for all that followed, we might suggest that:

**Jesus Is In Charge Here**

1. He rules our worship (vv. 13-17)
2. He is our hope (vv. 18-22)

# FOURTH SUNDAY IN LENT

## The Scriptures

> Old Testament — *Numbers 21:4-9*
> Epistle — *Ephesians 2:4-10*
> Gospel — *John 3:14-21*

## The Text — John 3:14-21

Word is getting around. Jesus of Nazareth is not the ordinary, run-of-the-mill rabbi. He does things no other rabbi would think of attempting. John 2 relates how Jesus mystified people with his first miracle, changing water into fine wine at Cana. The same chapter has Jesus shocking the people of Jerusalem with his authoritative purging of the temple. It is becoming obvious that Jesus possesses divine power and authority.

Nicodemus wants to know more. Either from a desire to satisfy religious curiosity, or to fulfill some inner spiritual emptiness, Nicodemus finds himself knocking on Jesus' door late one evening. This member of an elitist religious sect, a prominent religious and political leader among his people, one who we would think would have it all together, is now sitting in the presence of Jesus, the carpenter's Son. Could this Jesus be the Messiah? It is obvious that he has a special connection with God. Nicodemus wants to be in on the ground floor if the Messianic kingdom is about to unfold.

Jesus gets right to the issue. There is no need to dabble in the peripheral. The overriding question of the moment is whether Nicodemus is in the kingdom of God. If not, then he needs to know how to get there. Most masterfully Jesus leads the earth-bound mind of Nicodemus from thoughts of natural birth to thoughts of spiritual rebirth, from the cool breeze of the evening to the warm wind of the Spirit.

Once Nicodemus sees the necessity of being born by the Spirit and is confident that Jesus knows something about the subject, he is ready to hear the good news which Jesus has to share. Jesus begins by directing Nicodemus' attention to an Old Testament event well known to every proud Jew.

vv. 14,15 — *"Just as Moses lifted up the snake in the desert, so the Son of Man must be lifted up, that everyone who believes in him may have eternal life."*

Jesus draws a comparison. The point of the comparison is that both the serpent and the Son of Man are lifted up so that people may look at them and be saved from dying. When the snake-bitten people simply laid their eyes on the bronze snake, they were healed. How could a simple look at a lifeless, metal replica of a snake provide deliverance? The answer is that God caused it to be so. By comparison, the simple act of a dying sinner looking at the Son of Man with faith will bring a greater blessing, a new life that never ends.

Both the Old Testament type and the New Testament antitype defy human reason. But that is the point. Jesus wanted Nicodemus and us to despair of what human intelligence can grasp and to rely confidently and only on what God says and does. How strikingly different these words must have been to a Pharisee with a work-righteous, merit-oriented mindset.

In one short sentence the Master Teacher has shifted the focus to the Son of Man and the life available in him. (Some interpreters attach the variant ἐν αὐτῷ to "life," rather than εἰς αὐτὸν to "believing.") Jesus again uses the exclusive self-designation of "Son of Man," implying that he is the epitome of a true human being. Yet he is much more, for the title is packed with Messianic overtones (Da 7:13,14). The emphasis is that there is new life in connection with **the** Son of Man. By so teaching, Jesus is inviting Nicodemus to faith so that he may be born again and enter the kingdom of God. Life and faith go together. Life, real life with God, unending life, begins the moment one places full confidence in the Son of Man.

v. 16 — *"For God so loved the world that he gave his one and only Son, that whoever believes in him shall not perish but have eternal life."*

Jesus said in v. 15 that "the Son of Man **must** be lifted up." He now goes on to explain the basis for that necessity. It is God's love for a world of sinners. Jesus' words formulate the most succinct, the simplest yet most profound expression of the good news his Father sent him to bring to a perishing world.

Unlike the often shallow, sentimental, sensuous, and inherently selfish love between people, God's love (ἀγάπη) is intelligent and intentional. It moves beyond sentimental feeling to purposeful action. How can God love a world of rotten, rebellious sinners? His action of love toward the unlovely, and seemingly unlovable, is prompted by nothing other than the pure loving nature of his own being (1 Jn 4:16; Ro 5:8).

This incomprehensible and incomparable love of God extends to the entire inhabited world, including every single human being of generations gone by, generations now living, and all generations yet to be born. His universal love is perfect in its quantity. It is also perfect in its quality. There is nothing that God would hold back in order to procure deliverance for a world enslaved in sin. There is no effort too great, no price too high to provide salvation for lost sinners. Hence, in love God gave his dearest and best. He gave "his one and only Son." That giving includes all that is entailed in the incarnation and the atonement.

The NIV translation of μονογενῆ as "one and only" seems to indicate the fact that God had only one Son to give, rather than the fact that God has a special intimate relationship with the Son within the Godhead. Many dogmaticians have wrestled with the latter, trying to unfold the "eternal generation" of the Son. Let us be content to leave the mystery unexplained, but let us not overlook it. That is why this writer prefers to retain the translation "only begotten." It is richer in meaning and has adequate linguistic support.

God's love is universal, extending to the entire world of people, yet at the same time it is distinctly personal and must be received on an individual basis. The "whoever" in our text has both universal and individual implications. Support for both objective and subjective justification is found in this verse.

As indicated also in v. 15, only the believer will benefit from the gift of God's love. Again, the gospel-powered call is going out to Nicodemus that he should believe in the Son and have eternal life. The need for such a gift of life should become all the more obvious as Jesus makes his student aware of the only alternative, perishing in hell with no hope of reprieve.

vv. 17,18 — *"For God did not send his Son into the world to condemn the world, but to save the world through him. Whoever believes in him is not condemned, but whoever does not believe stands condemned already because he has not believed in the name of God's one and only Son."*

With another explanatory γάρ Jesus expands on the meaning of "gave" in v. 16. God gave by sending his Son into the world. His mission was exclusively one of rescuing and deliverance, rather than judging and condemnation. The judgment is being reserved for the second coming of Christ at the last day. Then there will be no further rescue-mission for the lost.

God had plenty of reason and every right to summon the world into court and have his Son "judge" (κρίνω) it, distinguishing between the acceptable and the unacceptable. The verdict would have been condemnation, eternal banishment from the loving presence of God. God's love intervened and changed judgment to salvation.

Such salvation was to be accomplished "through him" (δι αὐτοῦ), through the mediating and meritorious work of God's Son.

The believer in God's Son no longer stands in the arena of judgment with the possibility of condemnation. His faith in the Savior has removed all cause for an adverse decision. He is not, and never will be, condemned. The unbeliever, on the other hand, remains under the condemnation, the only verdict possible in his unregenerate state. He stands condemned because he has not looked in faith to God's only begotten Son. The greatest of his sins is that he has refused to place his trust in God's "name" (ὄνομα), his revelation of himself and his love in the person of his Son.

As Jesus speaks, Nicodemus must be cringing at the preaching of the condemnation of the law. Where did he stand in the eyes of God? But was he hearing the sweet assurances of the gospel? Jesus' words are drawing Nicodemus to find out about the Son, who alone can rescue perishing sinners.

vv. 19-21 — *"This is the verdict: Light has come into the world, but men loved darkness instead of light because their deeds were evil. Everyone who does evil hates the light, and will not come into the light for fear that his deeds will be exposed. But whoever lives by the truth comes into the light so that it may be seen plainly that what he has done has been done through God."*

Having established the necessity of believing and having declared how faith in Christ averts every kind of judgment, Jesus now draws a clear distinction between the believer and the unbeliever. Before he is finished with his lesson, Jesus wants Nicodemus to realize his own condition and great need to follow the truth. Jesus not only teaches basic doctrine here, but he seeks to win a lost soul for the kingdom.

The clear difference between believer and unbeliever is readily recognizable in their attitude toward Jesus. He came as the light of men to shine in the darknes (1:4,5). Unbelievers reject that light and prefer the darkness instead. They love (ἀγαπάω) the darkness with the kind of love God has for the world. They deliberately and intelligently, although foolishly, choose to remain under the control of the prince of darkness. When the saving light comes to them and tries to free them from their enslavement, they fight back and insist on remaining in their evil deeds. The light is objectionable to them and they actually despise it. They do not want their worthless lives of evil exposed for what they are. Unbelief is more than blindness to the light. It is the refusal to accept the light that can remove the blindness.

Believers, on the other hand, are completely the opposite. They are willing to live with the reality of their own unworthiness, relying on the love of God which covers their shame. They readily seek out the light so that they can live the truth. They are not afraid of any exposure because God is at work in their lives and is using them to his glory. They gladly reflect the light that he has shined into their hearts.

Christians need to be reminded of the clear distinction between the believer and the unbeliever, between the uncondemned and the condemned. That distinction is not as obvious today as it ought to be. It is being clouded over by materialism and immorality, and former believers are fighting for the right to live that way. As with Nicodemus, Jesus would teach us that being in his kingdom means having new life now, tomorrow, and forever.

## Homiletical Suggestions

As the preacher approaches this text, he may wonder how he is going to edify hearers, most of whom know John 3:16 very well. In order to stimulate the listener, he may fall into the temptation of trying to dress the almost tritely familiar in new garb of profound insights and catchy ideas. We can take our key from Jesus. After he focuses Nicodemus' attention on the need for new life, he immediately proceeds to give a straightforward presentation of the gospel. Our people today need to hear the same clear proclamation, and they yearn to be comforted by it. They are searching for strength and something secure on which to build their lives. The good news of God's love is the answer. It is God's power to convert and to change what is wrong in their lives.

This text also gives a good opportunity to clarify the role that faith plays in a person's salvation. Most people are aware of the facts of God's love, but many know them only with their minds. They do not possess the deep inner convictions of the heart that make the tremendous difference in their lives. Devout Christians recognize the great need for growth in their faith.

Since the text is being used during the Lenten season, emphasis will quite naturally fall on how God gave his Son into suffering and death, how Jesus fulfilled the mission for which he was sent, how he averted the sinner's condemnation, how he is the light and truth by which believers live.

The following outline may help to develop a gospel-centered, faith-building approach to this premiere text:

**There Is Good News For You**
1. God sent his Son for your salvation (vv. 14-16)
2. Through faith in his name you will never be condemned (vv. 17,18)
3. Your life counts in the kingdom of God (vv. 19-21)

Or using the same text-division with different wordings:

**God's Love Is For All Sinners**
1. It is revealed in His only begotten Son
2. It is received by every believer
3. It results in new life now and forever

**Believers Are A Breed Apart**
1. They look to God's uplifted Son
2. They lean on God's unlimited love
3. They live according to God's unveiled truth

# FIFTH SUNDAY IN LENT

## The Scriptures

Old Testament — *Jeremiah 31:31-34*
Epistle — *Hebrews 5:7-9*
Gospel — *John 12:20-33*

## The Text — John 12:20-33

The events recorded in our text took place on the Tuesday of Holy Week. Jesus spent much of this Tuesday in the temple courts at Jerusalem. Here the leaders of the Jews had questioned his authority as a teacher (Mk 11:27-33). This Tuesday was to be the last day Jesus taught publicly before he died. Many pilgrims from all over the empire were in Jerusalem because it was the feast of the Passover.

One group of these pilgrims consisted of the proselytes mentioned in our text:

v. 20 — *Now there were some Greeks among those who went up to worship at the Feast.*

Undoubtedly the Greeks were proselytes, Gentiles who had converted to the Jewish religion, because they came up to Jerusalem to worship. Perhaps when they got to Jerusalem, but even more likely before they arrived, they were interested in seeing Jesus, whose reputation had been spread abroad.

v. 21 — *They came to Philip, who was from Bethsaida in Galilee, with a request. "Sir," they said, "we would like to see Jesus."*

Those Greeks sought out Philip, one of the disciples with a Greek name. It is unlikely that they knew Philip before, because they addressed him with κύριε ("sir": lit. "lord, master"). And it is even more unlikely that they had ever met Jesus before, because of the way they phrased their request — they wished to see (ἰδεῖν) Jesus. Apparently they would not recognize him at first sight. Their request was merely to get a glimpse of the one they had heard so much about.

v. 22 — *Philip went to tell Andrew; Andrew and Philip in turn told Jesus.*

Why did Philip have to consult with Andrew? One would think that he was not so timid after this much time with Jesus to be afraid of granting the Greeks' request. A possible explanation is that Philip was ignorant of the Old Testament concern for the salvation of the Gentiles. Perhaps Philip felt uneasy about introducing these Greeks to the one who was "sent only to the lost sheep of Israel" (Mt 15:24).

There is no mention in the text that Jesus actually met with the Greeks. Instead of the details for arranging a meeting, the question of the Greeks evokes a sober answer from Jesus:

v. 23 — *Jesus replied, "The hour has come for the Son of Man to be glorified."*

When Jesus hears of this request, he is reminded that his work is quickly to come to its completion so that the good news could be shared with many more the world over. He has glorified the Father and will now be glorified himself (Jn 17:4,5). Now the time has come for the glory of the Lord to rise over Israel and for nations to come to that light and kings to the brightness of its rising (Isa 60:1-7). The Greeks, representative of all Gentile nations, are knocking at the door. That knocking reminds Jesus of the work he is about to do:

v. 24 — *"I tell you the truth, unless a kernel of wheat falls to the ground and dies, it remains only a single seed. But if it dies, it produces many seeds."*

Jesus must now be the seed that dies in order for the abundance of fruit to be harvested. He has fulfilled the Father's will; a few final, but most important, acts remain.

What is meant by the "many seeds" which are produced? These "seeds" include all people who receive life as a result of Jesus' death, all who are made spiritually alive in this world and who become heirs of eternal life in heaven. While the humbled Christ focused on Israel, the soon-to-be-exalted Christ would focus on the whole world (Ps 2:8). Because of the question of these Greeks the Gentile "seeds" are foremost in Jesus' mind at this time.

By his own death Jesus will glorify himself, but he will also be glorified when others "die."

v. 25 — *"The man who loves his life will lose it, while the man who hates his life in this world will keep it for eternal life."*

Following Jesus as a disciple is a matter of self-denial; that the Scripture makes clear (Mt 16:24,25). When a follower of Jesus dies in respect to his sinful flesh, he is glorifying the Son with that death. In fact, he shares in the death of the Son by baptism (Ro 6:4) and really no longer lives — Christ lives in him (Ga 2:20). Christ living in us is a guarantee of eternal life.

v. 26 — *"Whoever serves me must follow me; and where I am, my servant also will be. My Father will honor the one who serves me."*

The same principle of self-denial and service applies to Jesus' disciples in their lives of ministry. Wherever that service to God takes a person, no matter what it demands, that we must do. But a heavenly goal motivates us, a crown already won. Each faithful servant of the dear Lord looks ahead to the promise in Revelation 2:10: "Be faithful, even to the point of death, and I will give you the crown of life."

v. 27 — *"Now my heart is troubled, and what shall I say? 'Father, save me from this hour'? No, it was for this very reason I came to this hour."*

The reality of being the sin-bearer is closing in on Jesus. The question of the Greeks has reminded him how close the hour of his final suffering is. Jesus' question in this verse looks forward to Gethsemane and indicates that the suffering of that hour has already begun.

The suffering is glorifying the Father's name:

v. 28 — *"Father, glorify your name!" Then a voice came from heaven, "I have glorified it, and will glorify it again."*

The Father's name has been glorified by Jesus' word and work. In the future Jesus' death will glorify the Father's name, and his resurrection will become a trademark of that glory. By glorifying the Son, the Father is glorifying his own name.

v. 29 — *The crowd that was there and heard it said it had thundered; others said an angel had spoken to him.*

Jesus heard the words, but the assembled crowd heard the sound and recognized it as something supernatural. Was it intended that they should hear it? The next verse answers that conclusively:

v. 30 — *Jesus said, "This voice was for your benefit, not mine."*

The miraculous manifestation of the Father had the same purpose as all of the other miracles that took place while Jesus was on the earth: the undergirding of the truth of the gospel.

v. 31 — *"Now is the time for judgment on this world; now the prince of this world will be driven out."*

The defeat of Satan by Jesus' word and work, and his ultimate defeat at the cross, meant the redemption of the world. The eternal destiny of mankind is about to be determined at the cross, and at that point the devil loses his power. The head of the serpent is crushed. What is the judgment of God on the world? With the powerless devil looking on, God declares all men righteous through the merits of the Son.

v. 32 — *"But I, when I am lifted up from the earth, will draw all men to myself."*

With either variant reading, the sense is the same. The work on the cross is done for all people. It was always planned that way. Jeremiah 31:3 says, "I have loved you with an everlasting love; I have drawn you with loving-kindness." That drawing to himself in glory is for all. It was always planned that way. Psalm 2:8 says, "I will make the nations your inheritance, the ends of the earth your possession." The Father draws all men to the Son (Jn 6:4), and the Son also draws all men to himself.

v. 33 — *He said this to show the kind of death he was going to die.*

Jesus' death was to be an atoning death for the sins of the world. The world includes all people, Jew and Greek. His death was to glorify the Father as well as the Son, and for that matter, also the Holy Spirit.

## Homiletical Suggestions

Viewing the approaching death on the cross in this way leads the Lenten heart to appreciate:

### The Magnetism Of The Cross

1. It draws people to Jesus
2. It draws people through Jesus

Emphasizing an individual's involvement in and response to the text, one can use the same thought divisions:

### Faith's Lenten Plea

1. Show us Jesus
2. Glorify your name

Another option is to emphasize the word-picture that Jesus uses as soon as he is reminded of his approaching death:

### The Lesson Of The Seed

It teaches us:

1. The benefit of Christ's death
2. The purpose of the Christian life

A way of presenting the text that would lend itself well to describing the fulfilling of Old Testament prophecy is:

### Christ's Hour Has Come

1. To crush the serpent's head
2. To draw all men to himself

Other homiletical suggestions:

## The Cross — The Path To Glory

1. Jesus' great hour of glory
2. The believer's only hope for glory

## Jesus Glorified Through The Cross

1. The cross is Christ's great victory
2. The cross is our great motivation

(The thoughts suggested in these outlines run through the entire text rather than following analytically from one part of the text to the other.)

# PALM SUNDAY

**The Scriptures**

> Old Testament — *Zechariah 9:9,10*
> Epistle — *Philippians 2:5-11*
> Gospel — *Mark 11:1-10*

**The Text — Mark 11:1-10**

We have before us Mark's description of the triumphal entry of Christ into Jerusalem on that first Palm Sunday. Mark begins by setting the scene:

> v. 1a — *As they approached Jerusalem and came to Bethphage and Bethany at the Mount of Olives . . .*

Jesus is coming from Jericho on his final journey. It might be useful for the preacher to describe the scene so that his listeners can "see" it in their minds. The road from Jericho makes a steep ascent of over 3,500 feet in the course of the seventeen miles it takes to reach Jerusalem. As a person approaches Jerusalem from the east, the city is not visible, since it is hidden behind the Mount of Olives. Upon reaching the crest of the mount, however, the traveler suddenly finds the whole city spread out before him. As Alfred Edersheim describes it, "A turn in the road, and the city, hitherto entirely hid from view, would burst upon him suddenly, closely and to most marked advantage" (*The Temple*, p. 29). It is not hard to imagine bands of weary pilgrims joining in a psalm of joyful thanksgiving at this point.

The villages of Bethany (home of Lazarus, Mary and Martha) and Bethphage lie on the eastern slope of the Mount of Olives, the side away from Jerusalem. Jesus has to pass through them on his way to the city. The two villages would be a clear sign to travelers that they are nearing the goal of their journey. Recognizing this, Jesus does the following:

> vv. 1b-3 — *Jesus sent two of his disciples, saying to them, "Go to the village ahead of you, and just as you enter it, you will find a colt tied there, which no one has ever ridden. Untie it and bring it here. If anyone asks, 'Why are you doing this?' tell him, 'The Lord needs it and will send it back here shortly.' "*

In complete charge of the events of his life, Jesus has decided to declare by his actions that he is the Messiah. He directs two of his followers to go the village ahead of them (probably Bethphage) and bring back a colt for him to ride into the city. In this way he will demonstrate to anyone who knows Scripture that he is the Messianic King. Zechariah the prophet had said, "Rejoice, ... Daughter of Zion! ... See, your king comes to you ... riding ... on a colt, the foal of a donkey" (Zec 9:9).

Jesus shows himself as the Lord in several other ways as well. First, he gives the two disciples an exact description of what they will find on the road ahead. A clear demonstration that our King knows all things! And if Jesus knows what his disciples will encounter in the village of Bethphage, he most certainly knows what lies ahead for him in the city of Jerusalem. Jesus knows where he is going and what he will find there. As God's true King, he deliberately sets into motion the final act of his Father's saving will, though it will mean the cross for him. Secondly, Jesus gives directions to his followers which he expects them to carry out. As the one who will redeem them by becoming their slave, he has the right to claim their willing obedience. Thirdly, Jesus tells the two disciples to refer to him simply as "the Lord," should anyone ask any questions. Martin Franzmann makes the interesting comment here, "This is the first time in Mark that Jesus calls himself Lord; this act is a royal requisitioning" (*The Concordia Self-Study Commentary*, New Testament, p. 51).

At one and the same time we notice how completely different this King is from the kings this world produces and admires. He does not ride a war-horse or in a chariot but on a donkey's colt, a humble beast of burden. The prophet Zechariah makes special mention of this point as a sign of the Messiah's gentleness. We shall be taking note later on of other ways in which Jesus, God's ideal King, shows himself to be completely different from the kings and authorities of this present evil age. It is enough to say here that even today people expect rulers and men of authority to arrive in limousines and Mercedes Benzes. So much is this the normal way that the people of Kenya, for example, refer to their influential people as "Wa*Benz*i," naming them after the cars they drive. If this is what people expect, will they turn away from a King who comes riding "in lowly pomp" on a donkey's colt?

Jesus tells his disciples that the colt was unbroken — never before ridden. God in the Old Testament Scriptures had given directions that when animals were going to be used for spiritual reasons, they should not have been previously used for any other purpose (see Nu 19:2; Dt 21:3; 1 Sm 6:7). It's only right that when God's King comes riding into Jerusalem to establish his spiritual kingdom, he comes on an animal never before ridden.

*vv. 4-8 — They went and found a colt outside in the street, tied at a doorway. As they untied it, some people standing there asked, "What are you doing, untying the colt?" They answered as Jesus had told them to, and the people let them go. When they brought the colt to Jesus and threw their cloaks over it, he sat on it. Many people spread their cloaks on the road, while others spread branches they had cut in the fields.*

It is worth noting here that many of the Greek verbs Mark uses to describe what happened on that day are in the present tense. It's as if someone is actually "replaying" the events of the day in his mind and describing it as it unfolds: "They are drawing near Jerusalem... Jesus is sending... he is saying to them... they are untying the colt ... bringing it to Jesus ... putting their cloaks on it." From ancient church tradition we learn that Mark was a disciple of the apostle Peter. No doubt Mark is here transcribing Peter's eyewitness account of what happened on that day.

We also see in these verses more evidence of our Lord's power. This unbroken colt, never before ridden, calmly proceeds to Jerusalem with Jesus on its back. This in the face of crowds singing and waving branches! Under normal circumstances, with any other rider, this colt would have bolted, bucked or balked. Lenski's cavalier statement, "The colt was gentle enough — any man could have ridden it" (St. Mark's Gospel, p 482), only goes to show he never attempted to ride an unbroken colt. This colt "knows" it is carrying its Creator, its Lord. So it is calm.

We now turn our attention to the way the disciples and people respond to the Lord. The two disciples take Jesus at his word, obeying it in simple thrust, and find things to be just as Jesus said they would be. The words Jesus gave them, "The Lord needs it," are enough to establish their right to take the colt. God's words are always true. When we follow them, they will not send us in the wrong direction. Through his Word our Lord also lays claim to us and all we have. Since he is our King we will gladly give him what he tells us he needs.

The disciples and others show their respect for Jesus by taking off their outer clothing and putting it on the colt and in the road. Since these are poor people for the most part, this is truly a sign of how much they love their Lord and wish to honor him (see Ex 22:26,27). By this action they are clearly saying, "This man is our King" (see 2 Ki 9:13). Some of the people go into the fields and cut off leafy branches from the trees. They place them in the path so that their Lord's donkey will not have to touch the dust of the common road.

In addition to honoring him with their actions, they also honor the Lord with their voices:

vv. 9,10 — *Those who went ahead and those who followed shouted, "Hosanna!" "Blessed is he who comes in the name of the Lord!" "Blessed is the coming kingdom of our father David!" "Hosanna in the highest!"*

Combining the accounts of Mark and John, we get a full picture of the crowds on that memorable day. There were really three groups: one which came out from Jerusalem to meet the Lord (Jn 12:12,13), another which walked ahead of the Lord and a final one following him. That there should be so many people in the area willing to greet the Lord is really no surprise. This was Passover time, one of the three great festivals at which God called his people to appear before him in Jerusalem (Ex 23:14-17). Many pilgrims were there from all parts of Palestine to celebrate the feast. Over the past three years they had seen Jesus' miracles and heard his gracious words. Now they were fully prepared in heart and mind to hail him as their King.

"Hosanna" is a Hebrew word which originally meant "Save, now!" But here it probably is no more than a way of saying, "Hail!" or "Praise be to you!" The happy people are singing words from Psalm 118:25,26: "Hosanna, blessed is he who comes in the name of the Lord." It is helpful to look at the entire psalm to see what these words mean in context. In this way we can better understand what the pilgrims are saying by them.

In Psalm 118 the Messiah-King urges God's people to give thanks to the LORD for his unfailing love. He describes how he had won a great victory with the LORD's help. The King's life had been under great threat: he had been in anguish (v. 5) . . . surrounded by his enemies on every side (v. 11) . . . pushed back and about to fall (v. 13) . . . severely chastened by the LORD to the point of death (vv. 17,18). Yet the King did not base his hope of being rescued on the size of his army, the strength of his warriors or any alliances he might make with other princes (vv. 8,9). He won the victory "in the name of the LORD," that is, relying on the LORD to help him according to his gracious promise (v. 12). Now he is coming to the temple to praise God for giving him the victory, and the people hail him as the one who comes "in the name of the LORD."

By singing these words to Jesus as he rides into Jerusalem the people are declaring their belief that Jesus is the King who will give the words of Psalm 118 their full meaning. They are acclaiming him as the Messiah who will win the victory over the dark spiritual forces that threaten mankind. He will win the victory, not through armies and earthly might, but "in the name of the LORD." He will win by simply relying on the promised help of the LORD God.

In so doing, Jesus is acting as a true son of David, God's ideal king in the Old Testament. Here we think particularly of David's great battle with Goliath. Everybody else in the army of Israel was afraid to fight the giant. They were afraid because they saw the battle only in earthly, physical terms. This was a battle — as they perceived it — which a person could win only with earthly power, physical weapons. Goliath was huge, over nine feet tall. His armor alone was enough to cause a normal warrior to stagger under the sheer weight of it. "His spear shaft was like a weaver's rod, and its iron point weighed six hundred shekels " (1 Sa 17:7). Who in Israel had power to match him? Every warrior in Israel looked at Goliath, shook his head and said, "Not me!"

All except for David. David knew the battle was spiritual. His enemy was not simply to be viewed in earthly terms, but in spiritual ones. Goliath had defied the only true God. He had shouted insults at the army of God's people. Because David perceived the battle in spiritual terms, he knew that victory could only be won with spiritual strength. He didn't need bigger muscles, better hardware. He needed the spiritual strength the LORD had promised to supply those who put their trust in him. Listen to what he said to Goliath, "I come against you in the name of the LORD Almighty . . . whom you have defied. This day the LORD will hand you over to me . . . and all those gathered here will know that it is not by sword or spear that the LORD saves; for the battle is the LORD's" (1 Sa 17:45-47).

The next phrase in our text simply underscores the same idea, "Blessed is the coming kingdom of our father David." The LORD had promised David long ago that one of his descendants would be the ruler of an everlasting kingdom (2 Sa 7:12,13). David's earthly kingdom, ruled over by his descendants, had crumbled long before this. But the faithful in Israel were certain that another Son of David would one day come along to establish this everlasting kingdom, the kingdom of God. He would rule as a worthy successor to David and be a man after the Lord's own heart. The people now see the dawn of that new kingdom in the arrival of Jesus at the gates of Jerusalem.

"Hosanna in the highest" closes out the pilgrim's song. Since the people recognize Jesus as the King sent by God, they expect their shouts of joy to find an answering echo also "in the highest (heavenly) places." Just as at the birth of Jesus, so now as he enters the final and most crucial phase of his work, voices in heaven and earth must join together in one matchless song of praise to the God who saves.

We complete our text study with a reflection on the difference between spiritual power and earthly power, and what each can achieve. What if Jesus had not come "in the name of the LORD"? What if he had come in some other way? He could have. As he himself said to Peter, he had the angel armies of heaven at his beck and call (Mt 26:53). According to his divine power, he could have forced the world to obey him, to proclaim him King. It would have been no problem for him the first time he came to demand the obedience of all — the Pharisee, the scribe and the Roman alike. But could he have won our hearts? Would the Scripture — God's inscribed plan for saving the world — have reached fulfillment in his life? The first time he came, the Lord Jesus could have virtually wiped out all disease and created a kingdom where bread was free. He had that power. But man's real problem would have remained. The spiritual battle would have been conceded to Satan. People would still be dying in their sin. People would still be condemned to spend the length of eternity away from God and his joy.

So he came looking powerless, a slave. He came not as a "WaBenzi," but riding on a donkey's colt. He came to fight and conquer our real problems. He came to wage war on our behalf against the spiritual enemies which threatened us. He came — just like David his forefather — armed with the only weapons that would work. He came in the name of the LORD, relying on the spiritual strength God had promised in his word to supply. Jesus laid aside the full use of his divine power. He kept it hidden, in obedience to the Father. The result? Death is abolished, the victory is won.

This leads us to sing, "Blessed is he who comes in the name of the LORD!" It teaches us to see our earthly trials and struggles as more than physical: they are spiritual. We do not fight against flesh and blood (Eph 6:12). We fight against Satan. We fight against the spiritual evil in ourselves and all around us. The only way we can achieve victory is "in the name of the LORD."

## Homiletical Suggestions

The focus in this text is naturally on Christ, our King. The prophetic Scripture declares him King. His actions proclaim him King. His followers acclaim him King. His divine nature and omniscience are seen in the precise directions he gives to the two disciples. He clearly knows what lies in the road ahead, in more ways than one. We also see his power in the miraculous way the colt proceeds so calmly to Jerusalem.

To a world which has been a witness to the rise and fall of so many kings, this one is clearly different. He rides a donkey's colt. He comes armed with "the name of the LORD" and nothing more. He is not interested in increasing his own power, but in securing our eternal freedom. He uses none of his authority to serve himself. As God's ideal King he puts himself at his subjects' disposal and becomes their slave. In this way he wins our hearts and inspires our joyful obedience, compelled by no force aside from his compelling love for us.

These are the basic thoughts from the text which the preacher will want to bring out in his sermon. Toward this end, the following outlines are offered:

**Blessed Is He Who Comes In The Name Of The Lord**

1. A song for one who is truly a King (vv. 1-8)
2. A song for a King like no other on earth (vv. 7-10)

The verses overlap, but each part emphasizes different aspects. In the first part, we want to make clear that Jesus is truly the Messiah, predicted by the Old Testament Scriptures. His divine power and majesty are clearly seen also in this account — by those who have believing hearts. In the second part, we proclaim Christ's uniqueness. He is a spiritual King engaged in spiritual warfare with spiritual weapons: "in the name of the LORD." He does not seek to glorify himself. He comes humbly riding a donkey's colt in order to secure our salvation. For both of these reasons we want to offer our praise to him, as did the pilgrim band on the first Palm Sunday.

The same basic division, stated differently:

**Not Just Another King!**

(He is)

1. Greater than all
2. Yet gentle and meek

For a three part division we might use:

**Sing Hosanna To Our King**

(by noting)

1. Who he is (vv. 1-8,10)
2. How he comes (vv. 7,9)
3. How we ought to meet him (vv. 4-10)

Again, some verses are used more than once in different parts of the sermon. Yet again we are emphasizing different things in each part. The first examines the nature of Christ. In the second we speak of how he comes with his power hidden under the form of a servant, in the name of the LORD. In the third we emphasize our proper response: because he is our Redeemer, we obey him without question. We gladly give him what he says he needs. Finally we give him praises fit for a King.

# MAUNDY THURSDAY

**The Scriptures**

Old Testament — *Exodus 24:3-11*
Epistle — *1 Corinthians 10:16,17*
Gospel — *Mark 14:12-26*

**The Text — Mark 14:12-26**

A comparison of the parallel and supplementary accounts (Mt 26:17-30; Lk 22:7-30; Jn 13:1-30; 1 Co 11:23-26) with the present text will help the preacher avoid jumping to shaky conclusions about the sequence of events, the exactness of quotations, and similar matters.

Little beyond that needs to be said to introduce so familiar a text. It is worth remembering that Jesus' mode of living during the first part of Holy Week was to go to the temple in the daytime and to spend the night outside the city walls on that part of the Mount of Olives (Lk 21:37,38) where the village of Bethany was situated (Mt 21:17; Mk 11:11,12,19,27; 14:1-3). The references in Mark make it clear that this description of Jesus' movements applies to Palm Sunday, Monday and Tuesday. Concerning Wednesday we know nothing certain. The events of the text took place on Thursday, and verse 13 shows that the initial setting is somewhere outside of Jerusalem.

v. 12 — *On the first day of the Feast of Unleavened Bread, when it was customary to sacrifice the Passover lamb, Jesus' disciples asked him, "Where do you want us to go and make preparations for you to eat the Passover?"*

The Greek word πάσχα, "Passover," can mean the festival, or the lamb, or the entire meal, depending on the context.

According to the Jewish calendar, Passover lambs were to be slaughtered on the afternoon of Nisan 14 and eaten on the evening of Nisan 14/15. Then came the week-long Feast of Unleavened Bread, starting on Nisan 15. But in loose usage the rabbis sometimes included Nisan 14 as the first day of the Feast of Unleavened Bread. In the text the clause "when it was customary to sacrifice the Passover lamb" shows decisively that Mark is employing that loose usage. Accordingly it was sometime (probably morning) on Nisan 14, the day we call Maundy Thursday, that the disciples asked Jesus about the Passover meal which was only hours away.

Does it seem strange that they waited so long before asking about arrangements? After all, Jerusalem was swarming with Passover pilgrims and available accommodations would quickly become scarce. The disciples also knew that their special bond to Jesus transcended ordinary ties; he and they would feast together instead of with their families, and so they recognized it as their duty to prepare the meal for the Master. But with such a knowing and authoritative Master they hesitated to take the initiative, especially at a time when he had reason to avoid spending nights in Jerusalem. And though he had not yet mentioned the subject of Passover accommodations, they saw no need to panic. He was still in control, and his devoted followers in the city could be counted on to make room for him. Or would he under the circumstances prefer to observe the feast outside the city walls within the boundaries of greater Jerusalem, as was considered lawful? (See. J. Jeremias, *Jerusalem in the Time of Jesus*, Section III.A.1.b.) All these factors may have caused them to wait in silence. Luke 22:8,9 seems to indicate that finally Jesus did indeed take the initiative and broach the subject.

vv. 13-16 — *So he sent two of his disciples, telling them, "Go into the city, and a man carrying a jar of water will meet you. Follow him. Say to the owner of the house he enters, 'The Teacher asks: Where is my guest room, where I may eat the Passover with my disciples?' He will show you a large upper room, furnished and ready. Make preparations for us there." The disciples left, went into the city and found things just as Jesus had told them. So they prepared the Passover.*

The two disciples were Peter and John (Lk 22:8). The reason for choosing "a man carrying a jar of water" as an unmistakable sign may have been that it was ordinarily the task of women to carry water jars. The suggestion that the house was the home of John Mark, the author of this Gospel, is interesting (Mk 14:51; Ac 1:13; 12:12) but unprovable. In any case the owner of the house was evidently a Christian.

The unusual nature of the errand was not intended to be an arbitrary display of foreknowledge. The secrecy obtained by this manner of proceeding was designed to thwart Jesus' enemies, Judas in particular, from planning his arrest before he was ready. The special measures Jesus took show how important it was in his judgment to have an opportunity for prolonged, private and undisturbed fellowship with his closest followers. Even the setting plays a part: an upper room would be less susceptible to interruptions and distractions due to traffic on the main floor.

Jesus provides similar opportunities for congregations to have sustained, undistracted fellowship with him in divine services, and he attaches the same importance to such opportunities in our day. A Maundy Thursday evening communion service is an especially appropriate time to elicit among Christians that sense of continuity with the fellowship ideals Christ strove for during his ministry.

There is no need to rule out the possibility of prior arrangements between Jesus and the owner of the house. They may well be reflected in the phrase "Where is *my* guest room?" and in the circumstances that the room was ready for occupancy even before Peter and John inquired. It is just conceivable that the arrangements included instructions for the servant to carry a water jar home when he saw Peter and John enter the city, but Mark does not give us the least encouragement to draw that inference. His account seems rather to place emphasis on the confident authority and special knowledge of Jesus, as in Mark 11:1-6. This is evident already in the fact that Jesus perceived Judas's hidden treachery (Mk 14:10,11) and took these special measures to thwart him.

vv. 17-19 — *When evening came, Jesus arrived with the Twelve. While they were reclining at the table eating, he said, "I tell you the truth, one of you will betray me — one who is eating with me." They were saddened, and one by one they said to him, "Surely not I?"*

According to John 13:18 Jesus plainly referred to Psalm 41:9 as a Scripture fulfilled by the sin of Judas. Mark's "one who is eating with me" (ὁ ἐσθίων μετ ἐμοῦ) contains an echo of that psalm verse, but the purpose here is not so much to emphasize the fulfillment of prophecy (that theme is saved for Mark 14:21) as to show the heinousness of the deed. Table fellowship conveyed deeply felt obligations. At the same time we see in these shocking words an indication of the Savior's grief and distress over Judas (Jn 13:21). Every individual is dear to him.

Jesus deliberately frames his words indefinitely — "one of you will betray me" — so as to move each listener to self-examination. The intended effect was achieved (v. 19). "Surely not I?" (μήτι ἐγώ;) expects a negative answer but expresses uncertainty all the same. Every Christian who hears the Savior's words is being called upon to search his heart and to recognize the potential for treachery lurking there. The admonition is especially fitting at a Maundy Thursday service in view of the obligation to examine oneself before communing (1 Co 11:28).

"They were saddened" (ἤρξαντο λυπεῖσθαι). The NIV, like the Evangelist Mark, understands how to convey weighty emotion by brevity and understatement. The preacher who pulls all the stops of pulpit oratory and dwells on the emotional intensity of the occasion will not electrify his listeners so much as weary them.

vv. 20,21 — *"It is one of the Twelve," he replied, "one who dips bread into the bowl with me. The Son of Man will go just as it is written about him. But woe to that man who betrays the Son of Man! It would be better for him if he had not been born."*

It is difficult to see verse 20 as a more specific identification of the traitor than verse 18. "One of the Twelve" restates "one of you" (unless we assume that besides the Twelve other disciples were present), and "one who dips bread into the bowl with me" may mean nothing more than "one who is eating with me" (unless there were several sauce bowls and Jesus meant to narrow the circle of suspicion to those who were situated closest to him and were using the same bowl he was).

Since Mark shows no interest in reporting the unmasking of Judas in the next verses, it seems best to understand Jesus' words here as once again deliberately indefinite, an emphatic repetition summoning all the disciples to self-examination. This repeated, open declaration in Mark would then set the stage for the *sotto voce* conversations in John 13:23-26 and Matthew 26:25. Did Judas leave before the institution of the sacrament? Mark gives no answer. A comparison of all accounts yields nothing certain on this point.

In verse 21 Jesus confronts us with the mystery of divine foreknowledge and human responsibility. Application could be made along these lines. We have a way of turning God's grace and omniscience into a fail-safe system that makes us feel comfortable when we see ourselves backsliding. "It is unthinkable that God would succeed in bringing us to a state of grace and then let us slide back so far that we would actually lose our salvation! A gracious God, foreseeing that outcome, would sooner take us from this life than let that happen." That kind of thinking is one of the wretched props of "once saved, always saved" theology; it is not far from blaming God for sin and damnation. By the same standards it ought to be unthinkable that God would let Judas even be born if his being born will result in a fate worse than non-existence. But that is precisely the shattering law-preachment our Lord impresses on us here. God did *not* stop Judas from destroying himself.

What about you? Is it conceivable that you could become a traitor to Christ and bring yourself to a state worse than never having been born?

vv. 22-24 — *While they were eating, Jesus took bread, gave thanks and broke it and gave it to his disciples, saying, "Take it; this is my body." Then he took the cup, gave thanks and offered it to them, and they all drank from it. "This is my blood of the covenant, which is poured out for many," he said to them.*

Scholarly attempts to locate the institution of the Lord's Supper within the details of a traditional Passover observance involve a considerable number of assumptions and speculations. The results can be interesting, but they have little to do with the matters the evangelists are intent on reporting. Mark, for example, merely lets us know that it was a Passover meal and that the institution took place "while they were eating." Apart from that vague connection, his interest is entirely occupied by the new meal Jesus created as a sacrament in its own right, not as a mere variation whose features need to be traced back to the details of the Passover observance if they are to be understood correctly.

It is therefore unwarranted by the New Testament texts and disastrous in results when scholars try to legitimize a figurative interpretation by speculating that Jesus' words "This is my body.... This is my blood" would be heard as parallels to the words of interpretation spoken at a traditional Passover: "This is the bread of affliction which our fathers ate in the land of Egypt."

The degree of influence on the meaning could be contested even if the parallel were to be accepted, but there is a more fundamental objection. We do not know what Jesus said with reference to the ordinary Passover meal, apart from one comment without any bearing here (Lk 22:15,16). Whatever else he may have said the apostles have left unreported as being irrelevant to the meaning of the new sacrament.

Theodore Zahn in his commentary on Matthew scrutinizes the oft-proposed figurative interpretation with careful attention to linguistic matters and to the demands of the immediate context. He refutes it thus: "Even apart from the fact that, understood figuratively, the words would depart from every pattern of figurative speech used by Jesus, the action itself, the eating and drinking commanded by Jesus, would then become incomprehensible. Symbols as such are meant to be contemplated and understood, not eaten and drunk. If, however, the action itself, the eating and drinking, is to be a symbol of the appropriation of Jesus' body and blood, then it would be impossible to discover how the appropriation of Jesus' physical nature is to be mediated and effected, since the symbolical imitation of an action is no guarantee that the represented action itself is taking place." Illustration: a poor man can imitate the actions of a rich one by symbolically entering huge sums in his bankbook, but that imitative action will not make him one bit richer.

In the case of John 13:2-17 we have an example of a genuinely symbolical action which shows how different the Lord's Supper is. The footwashing was intended primarily as a symbol of humble, loving service, and so it was not Christ's intention that the apostles perpetuate a ritual of literal footwashing; rather, the symbol was to be contemplated and understood — and since in this case the meaning of the symbol is a call to service, Christians show that they have understood the symbolism by engaging in humble service in every sphere of life. Many Christians use that symbol well without even once in a lifetime literally washing another person's feet.

Now if the Lord's Supper were a comparable symbolical action, then the proper use of this Supper would be to read about it in the Gospels and 1 Corinthians, to contemplate the symbolism and grasp its meaning, and then to put that meaning into practice elsewhere. Suppose we decided that the meaning is this: Christ in his sacrificial death is the "food" that keeps our faith alive. Then it would be proper to respond to the lesson of the Lord's Supper by letting faith feed upon Christ in private devotions and at public services of the word. There would be just as little reason ever to go through the motions of actually communing as there would be to perform a literal footwashing. It is plain that the New Testament church saw the difference between these two actions of Christ. The New Testament gives no evidence that there ever was a ritual of footwashing, but it does show that the repeated eating and drinking of the Lord's body and blood were vital to the church's existence.

Concerning the words "This is my body" Werner Elert writes: "There may be no disputing about these words. . . . They are not words *about* the Sacrament. . . . They are creative words of Christ himself. They are about analogy and are therefore not to be explained by means of other examples. They do not describe the Sacrament; they constitute it. They speak personally to each communicant. They claim faith, and yet unbelief cannot frustrate them" (*Eucharist and Church Fellowship in the First Four Centuries*, p. 38).

There is no way of knowing whether the thanksgivings spoken by Jesus before distributing the bread (εὐλογήσας) and the wine (εὐχαριστήσας) were ordinary table prayers, or consecrations for sacramental use. It has been claimed that they must have indicated the special nature of the sacrament or else the disciples would have received the wine without knowing it was the Lord's blood, but such a claim unnecessarily assumes that Mark means verses 23 and 24 to be strictly chronological — as though they all drank and only then did Jesus say, "This is my blood. . . . " Matthew's wording suggests strongly that the sacramental words preceded or at least accompanied the distribution of the wine.

Mark gives no additional words following "This is my body" because the sacrament's purpose of benefiting the recipient by conveying pardon is expressed clearly enough in the words he records in connection with the cup: "This is my blood *of the covenant, which is poured out for many.*" The Old Testament reading from Exodus 24 shows the use of blood to ratify a covenant and to seal the covenant blessings for the people. If real blood was used in the Old Testament shadow, how much more in the New Testament reality (Col 2:17)!

Just as significant in Exodus 24 is the fellowship meal with God in which the food from the sacrifice serves as a pledge assuring those who eat it of their participation in the blessings of covenant and sacrifice. This background helps a great deal to clarify why Jesus did not say, "I am giving you myself" (which is true enough), but rather, "This is my body. . . .This is my blood." He gives to us and focuses our attention on the elements that are left when the Victim is slain, for it is these elements that communicate the blessing of the sacrifice to those who receive them. That in turn clarifies the time-relationships. The act of sacrifice is by its very nature a once-for-all act, finished, fixed in history and unrepeatable. The sacrificial meal, however, can be prolonged indefinitely, and so again and again the church returns to the Lord's Table. We may speak of repeated observances of the sacrament provided that we recognize it is really the same meal: Christ is still the Host inviting us to his table, and the food does not change.

The "covenant" Christ refers to is plainly the new covenant of forgiveness (Jr 31:31-34), as the other accounts indicate even more plainly. There may also be an echo of Zechariah 9:11.

The "many" for whom Jesus' blood is poured out (ἐκχυννόμενον — a present participle in form, but probably to be understood as "timeless," like Hebrew participles) are all people, as in Mark 10:45. Secular Greek generally uses (οἱ) πολλοί exclusively ("many, but not all"), whereas biblical Greek, under Semitic influence, frequently uses it inclusively (J. Jeremias paraphrases it: "The many who cannot be counted," "the great multitude," "all." For details see TDNT VI, 536-545). Roman 5:12-19 affords clear instances of the use of "many" as a synonym for "all."

v. 25 — *"I tell you the truth, I will not drink again of the fruit of the vine until that day when I drink it anew in the kingdom of God."*

Much is mysterious here. We cannot adequately picture or understand the new mode of existence waiting for us in heaven, and so we cannot grasp the details of this hint of future glory. Jesus will then drink wine "anew." The word καινόν does not designate a new batch of the kind of wine we are familiar with (in Mark 2:22 and parallels, wine fresh from the winepress is not καινός but νέος). Here it indicates something new in kind. Another mystery: why does Jesus make this avowal of abstinence at all? Perhaps he wishes to show that though we shall enjoy intimate fellowship with him during these last days of history, as we do in the sacrament, our present joy is like austere abstinence compared with the supreme joy yet to come.

v. 26 — *When they had sung a hymn, they went out to the Mount of Olives.*

Here we find two aspects of Christian life prefigured. From the quiet, refreshing intimacy of the Lord's table we go out to wrestle with enemies and temptations; so it will ever be in the church militant. Nevertheless we sing praises and express confidence in the Lord who delivers us. Those are two recurring features of the psalms traditionally sung at a Passover observance (Psalms 113-118). We sing *to* the Lord, and we sing *with* him also, as at the Last Supper. He has promised to pray both for us (Ro 8:34) and with us (Mt 18:19,20). It is fitting for Christ's people to remember that as they sing on Maundy Thursday in anticipation of and thanksgiving for their communion.

## Homiletical Suggestions

When the occasion is Maundy Thursday and this text is chosen for preaching, without a doubt the sacrament will be prominent in the sermon. Hermann Sasse's *This Is My Body: Luther's Contention for the Real Presence in the Sacrament of the Altar* is a rich sourcebook on the sacrament in general and Luther's exegesis in particular.

The main homiletical question is whether to preach on the entire text or only on the institution of the Lord's Supper. The chief thoughts of the entire text can be covered with this outline:

### Christ Wants To Come Closer

1. Closer to the wanderers (vv. 18-21)
2. Closer to his friends (vv. 12-17,22-26)

Part 1 would show that the intention behind the Savior's grievous words concerning Judas was to reclaim him for the fellowship and to protect the other disciples in their fellowship with Christ by putting a searchlight on their capacity for wandering. Part 2 would show that no matter how long and how well we have known him, the Savior wants to draw even closer to us and takes pains to provide the opportunity for us to do so. He sees to both the outward circumstances of quiet intimacy (vv. 12-17,26; application: the character of the divine services he provides for us) and the inner means of drawing closer to him (vv. 22-25; in speaking of the gospel in word and sacrament, emphasis will naturally fall on the special closeness effected in the Lord's Supper by virtue of the Real Presence). Appropriate concluding thoughts would be either a reference to verse 25: "a still closer and more joyful fellowship with Jesus awaits us" — or a summary: "God make us, like the Eleven, receptive to both of Jesus' concerns — ready to ask, 'Is it I?' and eager for a closer bond, no matter how long and how well we have known him."

If the preacher prefers to follow the sequence of verses in the text, the same basic outline could be used with one modification: verses 12-17 could furnish material for an introduction drawing attention to the "upper room" character of our divine services as something Jesus regards as important and still provides for us today. Then the body of the sermon would concentrate on the more pointed features of law (vv. 18-21) and gospel (vv. 22-25).

A shorter selection featuring the heart of the text (vv. 22-25) lends itself to treatment in this fashion:

**The Supper That Spans The Ages**
1. Pointing to the past (v. 24)
2. Bringing blessing in the present (vv. 22-24)
3. Foreshadowing a still brighter future (v. 25)

Part 1 would explain the meaning of the phrase "blood of the covenant" against the background of Exodus 24:3-11 (the Old Testament reading) and Jeremiah 31:31-34. It would naturally also include those things which are past for us though not for the disciples at the institution of the sacrament, particularly the death we proclaim as we commune.

In Part 2 the preacher would speak of the presence of the whole Christ as the Host to whose table we are invited, the Real Presence of the Victim's body and blood together with the wonderful blessings they bring into the present for us, and also the relationship between the ongoing sacrificial meal and the finished, unrepeatable sacrificial act.

Part 3 could be expanded to include verse 26 if the preacher wishes to call attention to eschatological emphases in the hymns chosen for the service. Ancient Israel certainly sang the Passover psalms with a keen sense of longing for the consummation of bliss. Conclusion: the Supper does indeed bring the saving power of past deeds of salvation and an anticipatory taste of future bliss into our present. Thank God for it!

# GOOD FRIDAY

## The Scriptures

Old Testament — *Isaiah 52:13-53:12*
Epistle — *Hebrews 4:14-5:10*
Gospel — *John 19:17-30*

## The Text — John 19:17-30

In this text lies the heart of Christianity. Without a crucified Savior there is no salvation. The Son of God dies on the cross so that the sins of mankind are forgiven. John was an eyewitness of the Good Friday event. The other Gospels flesh out his report.

v. 17 — *Carrying his own cross, he went to the place of the Skull (which in Aramaic is called Golgotha).*

Christ carried his own cross. That is akin to digging your own grave or building your own gallows. The humble one who stooped to wash his disciples' feet is also willing to stoop under the load of the cross. While the sight of Christ walking on the Via Dolorosa may be incomprehensible to us, yet we know that he came for just this purpose.

A similar event had occurred when Isaac trudged up the mountain carrying the wood for the altar on which he was to be sacrificed. Isaac, too, was an only son unworthy of such a death. For Isaac a ram was provided as a substitute. There could be no substitute for Christ because he was already the Substitute for all of us.

The place of Jesus' crucifixion is called Golgotha in Aramaic, Calvary in Latin and the Place of the Skull in English. Some have conjectured that there were skulls lying around the place of crucifixion. It is most unlikely that the Jewish leaders would have tolerated such a thing. They requested that the legs of the crucified ones be broken in order to hasten their deaths, so that their bodies could be removed for burial before sundown. They wanted no unburied bodies to defile their Sabbath. It is more likely that the hill had the appearance of a skull, perhaps from the vantage point of Jerusalem. Indentations may have given the hill a ghoulish look. The fact that executions took place there may have reinforced the idea.

v. 18 — *Here they crucified him, and with him two others — one on each side and Jesus in the middle.*

The temptation is great to dwell on the horrible details of death by crucifixion, the nails, the spear, the blood, the thirst, the wrenching pain as limbs are almost pulled out of their sockets, the exposure, torturous breathing, the pressure on lungs and heart. The agony is real. But resist the temptation to weep for Jesus. The point of Good Friday is not to draw sympathy from the hearts of people. Direct people rather to the cause of the suffering — sin. Let the Good Friday worshiper reflect on the fact that it was also because of his sins that Christ had to suffer so.

The two thieves serve as reminders that such a fate is what every person deserves. Not all people deserve to be executed for crimes against the state, but all deserve death from the hand of God. The beauty of the scene is found in the sinless one who dies with sinners and for sinners.

vv. 19-22 — *Pilate had a notice prepared and fastened to the cross. It read: JESUS OF NAZARETH, THE KING OF THE JEWS. Many of the Jews read this sign, for the place where Jesus was crucified was near the city, and the sign was written in Aramaic, Latin and Greek. The chief priests of the Jews protested to Pilate, "Do not write 'The King of the Jews,' but that this man claimed to be the king of the Jews." Pilate answered, "What I have written, I have written."*

Plaques listing the crimes of the crucified were customarily affixed to crosses. Pilate is not being innovative when he writes the words that appear over Christ's head. There is a stark truth to the words. Christ's offense was that he was the "King of the Jews." He was born as such and died as such. The fact that the charge was written in three languages may have been mere formality, or it may have been done deliberately so that all seeing him would know why he died. God's finger may also have been guiding the pen of Pilate so that the message would get out to the whole world: The King of the Jews has given his life in love.

It would be in order to note that the title is often abbreviated with the letters I.N.R.I. Those are the first letters of the Latin words for "Jesus of Nazareth, King of the Jews."

The complaint of the Jewish authorities about the wording of this superscription falls on deaf ears. Pilate may be a bit miffed at how he has been maneuvered into doing their dirty work. At the same mime he is being used by God to proclaim the truth. Jesus is the King of the Jews, and that is the reason for his crucifixion. Nothing can change that.

vv. 23,24 — *When the soldiers crucified Jesus, they took his clothes, dividing them into four shares, one for each of them,*

*with the undergarment remaining. This garment was seam-
less, woven in one piece from top to bottom. "Let's not tear it,"
they said to one another. "Let's decide by lot who will get it."
This happened that the Scripture might be fulfilled which said,
"They divided my garments among them and cast lots for my
clothing." So this is what the soldiers did*

Jesus' clothes became a little bit of pocket change for the soldiers
as they carried out their morbid duty. As far as we know, those items
may have been the extent of Jesus' earthly possessions. No relatives,
no friend, no antique dealer, no charity would receive his property.
Soldiers disposed of it in quick efficiency. There is no need to dwell on
what articles could have made up four parts that were divided first.
The remaining article was a seamless undergarment, or tunic, that
would lose its value if torn up. It became the prize in a gambling
contest with the winner taking all. Those details lead one to ask
what was left for Christ to wear? Was his dignity totally stripped
away so that he hung there naked? Our love for him provides some
essential clothes, at least mentally.

None of this happens outside of scriptural prophecy. Even the
disposal of his clothing was detailed by David in Psalm 22:18. The
soldiers, like so many others, fulfilled Scriptures without knowing or
willing it.

vv. 25-27 — *Near the cross of Jesus stood his mother, his mother's sister, Mary the wife of Clopas, and Mary Magdalene.
When Jesus saw his mother there, and the disciple whom he
loved standing nearby, he said to his mother, "Dear woman,
here is your son," and to the disciple, "Here is your mother."
From that time on, this disciple took her into his home.*

One could spend a great deal of time discussing whether there were
three or four women near the cross. A Good Friday sermon has too
much else to pursue. We don't want to bog down in a search that may
prove interesting, but hardly as edifying as the meaning of the cross.

At first glance, the words, "Dear woman, here is your son," (γύναι,
ἴδε ὁ υἱός σου) might appear cold and impersonal. But they were
chosen carefully. He used the same form of address at the wedding of
Cana (cf. Jn 2:4) when he also had to draw a distinction between his
sonship with her and his sonship with the Father. The form of
address is polite but intended to indicate that he dies here as more
than her son. He dies here as her Savior too.

These words show how totally human this dying one was. It was
not beneath him at this hour to concern himself with the welfare of

his earthly mother. No mention is made about Joseph. We assume that he had died. If there were other children of Mary, Jesus still chose to pass her ongoing care to his disciple John. Even while enduring the most intense pain, Christ still looked to the needs of others. How much more should we be able to concern ourselves with the welfare of others when we bask in the bounty of God's love.

One should not fail to note that Jesus helped his mother more by the cross than from the cross. Her earthly care would extend to a handful of years. Her heavenly care would extend to all eternity. Mary's Son died for her and for all humanity.

vv. 28-30 — *Later, knowing that all was now completed, and so that the Scripture would be fulfilled, Jesus said, "I am thirsty." A jar of wine vinegar was there, so they soaked a sponge in it, put the sponge on a stalk of the hyssop plant, and lifted it to Jesus' lips. When he had received the drink, Jesus said, "It is finished." With that, he bowed his head and gave up his spirit.*

John is the only one who records Jesus' words, "I am thirsty." Perhaps he is the only one who was close enough to hear them since they were probably barely audible. Jesus' request for something to drink is not precipitated by a desire to quench the raging thirst that often accompanied crucifixion. He had earlier rejected the wine mixed with gall since that could have deadened the pain and dulled the senses. Christ came to taste all the bitterness of God's anger over sin. He was willing to drink the cup of suffering to the last bitter dregs. He requested a drink so that he might speak his final words with a loud voice. He did it in fulfillment of the Scripture which said, "They put gall in my food and gave me vinegar for my thirst" (Ps 69:21). One might have expected water instead of wine vinegar, but God's word cannot be broken even in such a detail.

With this throat moistened Christ spoke the final words recorded by John: "It is finished." The other three Gospels note that his final words were spoken with a loud voice. He died not with a whimper of weakness, but a cry of victory. Jesus did not fade into death, he gave up his spirit into his Father's hands. He chose to die and chose the moment for his death (cf. Jn 10:18).

Jesus knew "that all was now completed" (perfect passive of τελ-έω). Then he declared, "It is finished" (same word — τετέλεσται). When Jesus declared, "It is finished," he meant far more than merely that his earthly life was about to end. This was not a cry of resignation. It was an announcement of a completed life, a life that had accomplished its purpose. He had succeeded in his task of redeeming the world. He had succeeded in living a sinless life. He had succeeded in conquering sin, death, and hell. The victory was complete.

## Homiletical Suggestions

The greatest danger in Good Friday preaching is to get bogged down in the details of the crucifixion and to hurry past the meaning of it. Let the Good Friday worshiper know that it is his Savior from sin who died on the cross. Let the sadness of Good Friday be punctuated with the comforting note that Christ chose to die and that his sacrificial death brings life. The glimmer of the Easter hope should not be avoided in the gloom of Good Friday.

Sin and grace should sound through the sermon. The sin is not just on the part of the Jews, Pilate and the soldiers. It was also our sins that caused the pain and death. Our disgust at sin should not be directed only at evil men near the cross. The fingers must point homeward and inward. The oft-told story about Rembrandt illustrates the point. In a painting of the crucifixion by the Dutch artist one's attention is first drawn to the cross and the one who hangs there. Then the attention is drawn to the crowd around the cross. Different attitudes and actions can be detected. As one's eyes drift to the edge of the picture, another figure stands in the shadow. It is Rembrandt himself. He includes himself among those helping to crucify the Lord. We also are among those responsible for Jesus' death, for he died for the sins of the whole world.

Our eyes must focus on the dying Savior on Good Friday, so we say:

## Look At Jesus

1. As the suffering Savior (vv. 17,18)
2. As the King of the Jews (vv. 19-22)
3. As the fulfiller of Scripture (vv. 23,24)
4. As the dutiful Son (vv. 25-30) — Note: He cared for his mother and obeyed his Father (cf. Philippians 2:8)

The three roles of Jesus on the cross could be captured under the theme:

## The Dying Son

1. As the Son of Man he died as our substitute (vv. 17-24)
2. As the Son of Mary he cared for her needs (vv. 25-27)
3. As the Son of God he obeyed his Father to the end (vv. 28-30)

Those who wish to accent the day of Good Friday might use the theme:

**Why We Celebrate Good Friday**

1. To reflect on Christ's sacrificial death (vv. 17,18)
2. To marvel at his humble kingship (vv. 19-24)
3. To see his love extended (vv. 25-30)

To capture the wide range of the text the homiletician might like to work through the text with this theme:

**Pictures of the Prince of Peace**

1. A partner for thieves (vv. 17,18)
2. A pawn for Pilate (vv. 19-22)
3. A pay-off for soldiers (vv. 23,24)
4. A protector for Mary (vv. 25-27)
5. A pardon for sinners (vv. 28-30)

# EASTER — RESURRECTION OF OUR LORD

## The Scriptures

> Old Testament — *Isaiah 25:6-9*
> Epistle — *1 Corinthians 15:19-28*
> Gospel — *Mark 16:1-8*

## The Text — Mark 16:1-8

"He has risen! He is not here!" The angel's message to the faithful women has become the triumphant cry of the church. Nowhere is the faith of the church more vividly expressed than in this core proclamation of the living Christ, who has burst the confines of the grave and has become the indwelling Lord of the church. The Easter message directs believers in two diretions, one, to *come* again and again to the empty tomb to ponder its centrality to Christian faith and life, and the other, to *go* and by our words and actions tell others of the living power of the crucified and risen Savior.

v. 1 — *When the Sabbath was over, Mary Magdalene, Mary the mother of James, and Salome bought spices so that they might go to anoint Jesus' body.*

"The Sabbath was over" sometime after sunset on Saturday. Merchants made use of the brief twilight period to open up shop, and the women hurriedly went about their business. They had observed the burial of Jesus Friday evening, done in haste to avoid violating the Sabbath (15:47) — though not in such a rush as to neglect the wrapping of the body in the linens and the binding of the face about with a napkin (Jn 20:5,7). Now they took advantage of the opportunity to buy what was necessary to complete the task in the morning.

The two Marys and Salome may have been accompanied by other women (Lk 24:10) as they went out to make their purchases. "Mary of James" is the mother and not the wife of James (cf. 15:40). We know nothing of her before meeting her at the cross except that she and her husband were disciples and at least one of her sons, James the Less, was an apostle. Her husband presumably was Alphaeus (Mt 10:3), who is probably to be identified with the Clopas of John 19:25, but less likely with the Emmaus disciple with a similar name (Lk 24:18). There is little doubt that Salome is the wife of Zebedee whose sons were James and John. She also was at the cross of Jesus (15:40).

Mary Magdalene stands at the head of the list of the faithful women at the cross and at the tomb and holds the honor of being the first to whom Jesus appeared after his resurrection. Often miscast as a woman of ill repute from the misidentification of her with the sinful woman who anointed Jesus' feet (Lk 7:36-50) — the account of which precedes immediately the unrelated mention of Mary as one from whom Jesus drove out devils — Mary is known to us only as one of the women who gave of their substance to support Jesus and his little band of followers (Lk 8:3) and who became prominent as a fiercely loyal devotee of Jesus at the end of his life.

Despite the meager information available on the lives of these women, they provide the homiletician with a fertile field for the exercise of his imagination. Let the preacher who desires to touch hearts enter the thoughts and feelings of the women with all the curiosity and wonder of a Luther to explore their fears, their hopes, their determination, their dedication to duty, their spiritual *Angst*, as they made their preparations, then approached the tomb and heard the angel's words and hurried back to the city to tell the good news.

The women went out Saturday evening and bought spices to anoint Jesus' body for proper burial. Biblical belief in the resurrection of the body has led God's people through the centuries to a careful and respectful handling of the lifeless remains of their dead. The dead will rise! The ἀρώματα were a mixture of myrrh and aloes. Joseph of Arimathea's lavishing of about seventy-five pounds of myrrh and aloes on Jesus in the winding of the linen clothes (Jn 19:39,40) was done in a hurry and did not constitute proper burial in the eyes of the faithful women who saw it done (Lk 23:55). The ἀρώματα comprised a salve or ointment that was to be worked into the body. This meant the body had to be unwrapped, anointed, and then rewound with the linen cloth. None of this, of course, was to happen. Mary of Bethany had it right when she anointed Jesus beforehand for his burial (Jn 12:7).

> vv. 2-4 — *Very early on the first day of the week, just after sunrise, they were on their way to the tomb and they asked each other, "Who will roll the stone away from the entrance of the tomb?" But when they looked up, they saw that the stone, which was very large, had been rolled away.*

Mark double-emphasizes the earliness of the hour ("very early," "just after sunrise"; cf. Mt 28:1: "at dawn on the first day of the week") to impress on us the sense of urgency that compelled the women to their task. It was not proper for them to be about in the dark, particularly at a gravesite, but at the crack of dawn "they were on their way to the tomb." We err if we attribute their haste to no more than a desire to outrace the process of decay that sets in so quickly in the tropical heat. Theirs was the haste of lovers to the side of their beloved as they hurried in the early moments of the dawn to the tomb.

The preacher will do well to emphasize that, although the women believed in Jesus as their Savior, they did not as yet possess resurrection-faith. "They still did not understand from Scripture that Jesus had to rise from the dead" (Jn 20:9). Thus with a great complexity of emotion, of faith mingled with fear and bewilderment, they made their way to the tomb. What was clear to them was their duty to their crucified Lord. They had learned the lesson of discipleship that in moments of confusion and uncertainty one must simply do what is right in the eyes of God for the immediate situation and trust God for the outcome.

In their intensity to do the thing, the women overlooked the obvious until they were already "on their way to the tomb": "Who will roll the stone away from the entrance to the tomb?" But when they "looked up" (ἀναβλέψασαι) or "looked again," the stone was gone. In the first-century Palestine a discarded millstone often was used for this purpose. The stone was rolled into a cavity carved into the stone base at the entrance to the tomb, seating the stone so securely that two or three men could be required to dislodge it.

v. 5 — *As they entered the tomb, they saw a young man dressed in a white robe sitting on the right side, and they were alarmed.*

They were not alarmed at the empty tomb, because they had not yet progressed far enough into the tomb to see the empty place where Jesus had been laid. They were still in the entryway when they were startled (ἐκθαμβέω = "thoroughly amazed"; only in Mark in New Testament literature) at the sight of the young man sitting there dressed in the white robe. Matthew tells us that the νεανίσκος was an angel (Mt 28:2). Luke supplies the additional information that there were two angels. Matthew and Mark focus on the one who spoke to the women.

vv. 6,7 — *"Don't be alarmed," he said. "You are looking for Jesus of Nazareth, who was crucified. He has risen! He is not here. See the place where they laid him. But go, tell his disciples and Peter, 'He is going ahead of you into Galilee. There you will see him, just as he told you.' "*

"He has risen!," the single word ἠγέρθη in each of the Synoptics, is the substance of the angel's message. That single word was to become the theme of the Easter liturgy and hymns and the foundation of New Testament faith. Ἠγέρθη! For this reason you have no need to be alarmed. You have no need to look farther. The tomb is empty. But "go, tell!" The world must hear.

The invitation indeed belongs to the world: "Come and see the place where they laid him." The grave is empty. Christ is risen indeed!

The women are told to inform the disciples that Jesus will appear to them in Galilee. Peter is specially singled out to hear this. The promise of the Galilean appearance is found in Mark 14:28. In the disciples' failure to attain to resurrection-faith (Jn 20:9) this promise may have been misunderstood initially by them as an allusion to the final parousia. Why, we might ask, the pointing to a Galilean appearance when Jesus was to appear to the disciples that very day in the locked room in Jerusalem? One conjecture is that Jesus was here giving an instruction as to how the disciples were to spend their time in the forty days until the ascension — to return to their homes and occupy themselves in their former trades until they were commissioned and received the promise of the Spirit.

v. 8 — *Trembling and bewildered, the women went out and fled from the tomb. They said nothing to anyone, because they were afraid.*

A strange way indeed for the Easter gospel to end — on a note of *trembling, bewilderment, flight* and *fear!* There is no mistaking these words or softening their impact. The women's exit from the tomb was a flight (ἔφυγον), and the emotions they registered were fear (ἐφοβοῦντο) and bewilderment (ἔκστασις = lit. "standing beside oneself," a trance-like state) that showed itself in the physical manifestation of tremors (τρόμος). Matthew tells us that great joy (χαρᾶς μεγάλης) was also part of their makeup (Mt 28:8).

The preacher will not want to pass too lightly over this curious phenomenon. Even those who have attained to resurrection-faith —might we say especially those? — are not by this made aliens to holy fear. "The fear of the Lord is the beginning of knowledge" (Pr 1:7) applies not only to the passage of the unregenerate from darkness into light at conversion but is the characterization of all Christian life. We miss the keen insight of Luther if we reduce the holy fear of his commandment explanations to just another form of the love of God when in fact Luther pointedly sets the two side by side: "We should fear *and* love God. . . . " The preacher is called on to preach also holy fear into the hearts of his hearers in proclaiming to them the message of the Easter angel. In faith and fear and love we hold the risen Christ.

In their holy fear the women said nothig to anyone along the way but went straight to the fulfillment of the mission given them by the angel: "Go, tell his disciples and Peter."

## Homiletical Suggestions

The Easter Gospel suggests reflection on the power of the resurrection as we see it at work in the faithful women on the first Easter. The resurrection remains no less a compelling power in the world today. What is it that fills Christian churches throughout the world each year on Easter Sunday morning but the same angelic proclamation that drew the faithful women into the empty tomb: "He has risen! He is not here!"

The angel's invitation to "see the *place* where they laid him" rightly may lead us to reflect on the place. Thoughts that the preacher might wish to develop in this connection include *the security of the place* that is enclosed within the tomb (the securing of Christ's tomb with the stone and seal may be taken as emblematic of the security of every tomb); that it is *a place of weeping* (is there any place where more tears have been shed than at the gravesides of loved ones?); *the solitariness of the place* (though we be buried with a multitude in a cemetery, Christ's being placed into a tomb where no one was previously laid (Lk 23:53) is a more accurate picture of what it means to lie in the grave: we lie alone); and *the utter finality of the place* (we may speak of business reversals which in fact are perfectly reversible in turn, but the grave is flatly irreversible).

But drawn by the power of the resurrection to the empty tomb, how can we help but see the place where Christ was laid as *the place of the greatest manifestation of the power of God*, greater by far than the divine works of creation or providence, for by Christ's resurrection almighty God has brought life and immortality to light, has sealed the redemption and forgiveness of mankind, has proclaimed victory over the devil, has transformed death into victory, and has given to all believers in Christ the hope of eternal life.

The same power that draws us to the tomb still works in believers today as it worked in the faithful women to send them out to go and tell others of the empty tomb and the risen Christ. Textual thoughts that the preacher might wish to dwell on here might well include: the *fear and bewilderment* that the faithful women overcame as they went out to proclaim the message committed to them, the *promise* that underlies the command, and the *coming* that supplies urgency to the mission.

With these thoughts in mind one might structure one's Easter message in this way:

## The Power Of The Resurrection

1. It compels the world to look at the empty tomb
   (v. 6: "See the place where they laid him.")
2. It compels believers to proclaim God's victory
   (v. 7: "Go, tell his disciples and Peter.")

Or one might center the message on the angel's words:

## He Has Risen! He Is Not Here!

1. The circumstances under which the angelic preachment was made
   1) the seeming finality of the grave
   2) the dashed hopes of those who loved Christ
   3) The unfounded confidence of the enemies of Christ
2. The effect of the preachment on those who believed
   1) filled with holy fear and joy
   2) impelled to tell others the good news
3. The far-reaching consequences of the preachment for every age and generation
   1) sin forgiven
   2) death's power broken
   3) eternal life to all who believe

Or another possible approach:

## The Triumph Of Faith

1. God will vindicate the faith of his people
   (The faithful waiting at the cross, the diligent attendance upon the lifeless remains of our Lord, and the early hastening to the tomb are not without reward, as likewise all acts of faith in God through Jesus Christ.)
2. The prophetic word is sure
   (Christ has risen "just as he told you" (v. 8). Believers' confidence in the faithful Scriptures will not be betrayed. Every word of God is true.)
3. The grave has lost its terror for those who believe
   (The resurrection of Christ is God's pronouncement of justification or forgiveness for the world. Thus the sting of death has been removed, and the grave has become the portal of eternal life. Spread the good news!)

# SECOND SUNDAY OF EASTER

## The Scriptures

Lesson — *Acts 3:13-15,17-26*
Epistle — *1 John 5:1-6*
Gospel — *John 20:19-31*

## The Text — John 20:19-31

Why is this text in the Bible? Its purpose is to proclaim the identity and the resurrection of Jesus as a basis for his power to save us.

v. 19 — *On the evening of that first day of the week, when the disciples were together, with the doors locked for fear of the Jews, Jesus came and stood among them and said, "Peace be with you!"*

We have in this text the first two Sunday evening "services" of the New Testament church. Though Jesus had risen from the dead, the Spirit of Pentecost had not yet emboldened the apostles. Thus they met behind locked doors. To strengthen their faith, Jesus appeared to all who were present and filled the old Jewish greeting, "Peace be with you!", with new meaning.

Of this appearance in a locked room Calvin says, "I am far from admitting that what the Papists say is true, that Christ's body passed through the shut door. . . . The Evangelist does not say that He entered through the shut doors" (Commentary on St. John, *in loc.*). In other words, Calvin's rationalistic presuppositions led him to believe that Jesus unlocked the door. How? Miraculously, perhaps? But why then are some miracles possible to Jesus, and others not? Seeing how human reason can lead even so great a scholar as Calvin to deny the obvious, let us be all the more cautious as we examine this text. Traditional or reasonable understandings may blind us to its proper interpretation, and we may lose some important truth in that way.

First, we must remember that there had been some doubt about the identity of the resurrected Jesus. In the garden, Mary Magdalene thought Jesus might be the gardener (v. 15). Of course, the woman was nearly hysterical with grief, and she saw him not only "by the dawn's early light," but through a haze of tears.

But it was broad daylight when the Emmaus disciples failed to recognize him, though he walked with them for miles and preached a mighty sermon about himself on the way. In fact, they did not recognize him until he broke the bread and gave it to them — and they saw the holes in his hands.

And finally, here he appeared to all the disciples — but it was late in the evening, in a lamplit room with the doors, and perhaps the windows, shut for fear of the Jewish leadership. In other words, the scene was emotional and the light was dim.

v. 20 — *After he said this, he showed them his hands and side. The disciples were overjoyed when they saw the Lord.*

Jesus showed them the proofs of his identity, crucifixion and resurrection, and the disciples were filled with the greatest joy they had ever known.

This joy was not to be kept to themselves. Once before, on the Mount of Transfiguration, Peter had suggested that they were with the exalted Savior and should get comfortable around him even though that meant staying away from the world. Such turning inward is a temptation for all ages of the church, including our own. Anticipating this error, Jesus told them not to settle down with the Word, but to take it to others:

vv. 21,22 — *Again Jesus said, "Peace be with you! As the Father has sent me, I am sending you." And with that he breathed on them and said, "Receive the Holy Spirit."*

Since there is a natural play on words between "breath" and "Spirit," both words being the same in both Greek and Hebrew, Jesus symbolized one with the other. This is the Spirit that "proceedeth from the Father *and the Son*" (Nicene Creed).

Be careful with verse 23! It concerns the ministry of the keys, which is almost universally misunderstood:

v. 23 — *"If you forgive anyone his sins, they are forgiven; if you do not forgive them, they are not forgiven."*

The point is easy to miss, but it is an important one. Does our text give authority to the church to legislate forgiveness and condemnation on earth, thus compelling God's ratification in heaven? Or does it rather give us a commission to ratify on earth what God has already decreed in heaven?

If the former is true, then Luther is in hell, bellowing in pain; God had to send him there because of the pope's excommunication. If the latter is true, your sins are indeed forgiven, as you have heard the liturgist say so often.

The latter is true, for our text is merely a clarification of the Lord's statement in Matthew 18:18: "I tell you the truth, whatever you bind on earth will be bound in heaven, and whatever you loose on earth will be loosed in heaven." It is a familiar passage, but almost invariably mistranslated. In fact, the King James, the NIV, Beck's AAT and almost all the versions quoted in *The New Testament from 26 Translations* have it wrong. Only a few, such as Luther, the Amplified, the NASB, J.B. Philips, and an obscure New Testament translator named Charles B. Williams translate Matthew 18:18 correctly. Williams, the clearest, renders Matthew 18:18 as "Whatever you forbid on earth must be what is already forbidden in heaven, and whatever you permit on earth must be what is already permitted in heaven."

How did such mistranslation develop?

The future passive Greek verbs ἔσται δεδεμένα and ἔσται λελυμένα are odd forms to English-speaking people. We so often use the future passive ("shall be forgiven"), and so rarely use the future *perfect* passive ("shall [already] have been forgiven"), that dozens of the most faithful and scholarly translators missed it. And with that incorrect translation we lose the true scriptural basis for the ministry of the keys. No wonder proper church discipline is so seldom practiced, when so many English translations remove the basis for it. But we need to have Matthew 18:18 translated properly not only as a basis for excommunication, but also for confession and absolution.

v. 24 — *Now Thomas (called Didymus), one of the Twelve, was not with the disciples when Jesus came.*

Thomas Didymus (the word means "twin," not "doubter") was absent at that time. We do not know the reason, but without blaming him we can take the week of doubt he suffered as an implied admonition not to "forsake the assembling of yourselves together" (He 10:25, KJV).

v. 25 — *So the other disciples told him, "We have seen the Lord!" But he said to them, "Unless I see the nail marks in his hands and put my fingers where the nails were, and put my hand into his side, I will not believe it."*

Perhaps we can understand Thomas' being a doubter. After all, we've all had doubts ourselves. But how could he be such a "blockhead" as to insist that his two eyes were more reliable than their twenty?

We are mistaken if we think that Thomas was by nature more faithless than the others; after all, his dedication was so great that he believed death with Jesus would be better than life without him, as John reports, "Then Thomas (called Didymus) said to the rest of the disciples, 'Let us also go, that we may die with him' " (Jn 11:16).

All the remaining apostles had their doubts when they heard the first reports of Jesus' resurrection. When they saw the risen Christ in the flesh, they believed. Thomas also had to see the risen Christ with his own eyes before he would believe. So Jesus came to the apostles again when Thomas was with them, and immediately he did what was necessary to remove the doubts of Thomas.

vv. 26,27 — *A week later his disciples were in the house again, and Thomas was with them. Though the doors were locked, Jesus came and stood among them and said, "Peace be with you!" Then he said to Thomas, "Put your fingers here; see my hands. Reach out your hand and put it into my side. Stop doubting and believe."*

We thank you, Thomas. Doubter you may have been, but blockhead never. By your understandable doubts you obtained evidence to help preserve also our faith. Thus the Savior says to us also, "Peace be with you!" (vv. 19,21,26).

But those doubts must not continue once the evidence has been given, so Jesus says, "Stop doubting and believe."

Is this last a rebuke? Was Thomas supposed to believe before the evidence he needed turned up? The Greek does not seem to say so. It is neither an aorist imperative ("stop your doubting") nor a present imperative ("do not continue these doubts"). If either form had been used, it would have implied that Thomas never should have doubted in the first place; but "Be not without faith," (μὴ γίνου ἄπιστος) is a more neutral command without an implied reproach. It implies that the command of verse 27 was given in the light of new evidence or a whole new situation.

Jesus says in our text that every rational doubt has been overturned by the evidence. Only stubbornness is left as a reason for doubt. We are now to crucify the faithless Old Adam, which refuses to believe anything it doesn't want to believe, evidence or no. It is not the Christians who must believe without evidence. It is only the pagans who must believe such nonsense as the idea that Mohammed can save them when they can view his bones and see that he couldn't even save himself. Our faith is built upon evidence — the evidence of an empty tomb and a resurrected Lord.

v. 29 — *Then Jesus told him, "Because you have seen me, you have believed; blessed are those who have not seen and yet have believed."*

Is the first part of verse 29 a question or a statement? Should the semicolon be replaced with a question mark? Scholars are divided on this question. The writer is inclined to go with the question mark, which makes the statement of Christ seem less like a reproof. In any case, the fact remains that Thomas did believe and was blessed by believing.

v. 28 — *"Thomas said to him, 'My Lord and my God!'"*

If only everyone who calls himself Christian had such faith! But though there are many who believe Jesus is the Son of God, all too few call him God the Son.

Tradition asserts that after Pentecost Thomas went to India and preached the gospel. Those who have never crossed the street to speak of Jesus with someone who already believes in God and speaks English have little room to stigmatize this faithful missionary as "Doubting Thomas." (We don't talk about "Denying Peter," do we?) Thomas's title should be "Saint."

The authors of false gospels and traditions about Jesus used the next verse as *carte blanche* for their imaginations, especially after comparing it with John 21:25.

vv. 30,31 — *Jesus did many other miraculous signs in the presence of his disciples, which are not recorded in this book. But these are written that you may believe that Jesus is the Christ, the Son of God, and that by believing you may have life in his name.*

Only those Gospels that create faith instead of attacking it are authentic, and none but the four inspired by the Holy Ghost create true faith.

Still, Jesus did many other unrecorded deeds and spoke many unrecorded words. Have we lost part of God's truth, then? Not at all. The Spirit guided the memories of the evangelists, as Jesus Himself said, John 14:26: "But the Counselor, the Holy Spirit, whom the Father will send in my name, will teach you all things and will remind you of everything I have said to you." We can be confident that we have all we need. We may moon over the words God has not given us only after we have fully mastered those he has.

### Homiletical Suggestions

This post-Easter text declares loudly that Jesus Christ is risen indeed, true God and true man, and that on the basis of this truth the church of Jesus Christ is to proclaim his gospel of forgiveness and eternal life to all the world.

Christ's two appearances related in this text are his first recorded words to all his followers after his resurrection. The first appearance (vv. 19-23) contains the Lord's commission to go forth in the power of his Spirit with the authority of the ministry of the keys — which is really the power of the gospel in word and sacraments. In the second appearance (vv. 24-29) the risen Lord assures one of his followers personally and individually that faith in this momentous miracle can rest upon irrefutable evidence, so that even our doubting nature can be moved to bold confession.

The text closes with a brief summary of John's entire Gospel (vv. 30,31), which has the purpose to serve as the Spirit's instrument in creating faith in Jesus Christ as the Son of God and by such faith to give assurance of life in his name.

But how is the preacher to include all these important truths in one sermon? Simply by letting the text itself do the proclaiming, carefully expounding it and emphasizing its chief points under the following headings:

**The Risen Christ Gives Power To His Church**

1. Power to proclaim his gospel (vv. 19-23)
2. Power to confess his true person (vv. 24-29)
3. Power to have life in his name (vv. 30,31)

We also are reminded of C.F.W. Walther's treatment of the portion of the text dealing with Thomas:

**Does Christianity Demand Blind Faith?**

1. Often this seems to be true (v. 29)
2. This was not true in the case of Thomas (vv. 24-28)
3. This is not expected of us (vv. 30,31)

John's emphasis upon the word of the gospel as found in the closing verses can in this way be closely connected with the fact of Christ's resurrection, upon which our entire Christian faith must rest, and with the Thomas incident which immediately preceded these verses.

A final suggestion for the entire text:

**Peace Be With You!**

1. To the Ten on that first Sunday
2. To the Doubter a week later
3. To all who need it today

# THIRD SUNDAY OF EASTER

**The Scriptures**

> Lesson — *Acts 4:8-12*
> Epistle — *2 John 1:1-2:2*
> Gospel — *Luke 24:36-49*

**The Text — Luke 24:36-43**

The majority of the Gospel texts in the ILCW Series B pericope are taken from Mark's Gospel. Most of the texts for the Easter season are from the Gospel of John. This week's text from Saint Luke's Gospel presents the preacher with an opportunity to concentrate on the distinctive viewpoint of the beloved physician/historian.

It is particularly interesting to compare and contrast our text with John 20:19-23 (the first half of the text for last Sunday). Two different authors describe the same incident: John was an eyewitness, and it seems most likely that Luke's knowledge of this event was gained from interviews that he conducted when he "carefully investigated everything from the beginning" (Luke 1:3) before he sat down to write his Gospel. Since Luke wrote first, John was able to assume that Luke's version was already widely known. So John was able to draw on his own personal experience and concentrate on filling in some of the gaps that were inevitably left by Luke.

Thus there are sufficient similarities to show that both men are writing about the same incident, and yet it is also very interesting and very helpful to take note of the specific details that are peculiar to each account. It need not be unduly repetitious to preach on these two parallel texts on consecutive Sundays. Whereas John emphasizes the missionary responsibility Jesus laid upon the apostles and their overwhelming joy at seeing him, Luke again concentrates especially on the incontestable proof that the resurrected Lord was the same person who had died on the cross and had been laid in Joseph's tomb. The glorified Son of Man who suddenly came and stood in the midst of his disciples was the same flesh-and-blood-and-bones human being who had been born of the Virgin Mary, the same Jesus they had known and loved.

v. 36 — *While they were still talking about this, Jesus himself stood among them and said to them, "Peace be with you."*

That first Easter Sunday had been a busy day for Jesus. His resurrection had been followed by appearances to Mary Magdalene and the other women who had gone to the tomb at daybreak. He had walked to Emmaus with Cleopas and his companion (Luke 24:13-32), and he had appeared to Simon Peter (Luke 24;34; 1 Corinthians 15:5). All of these events were no doubt being discussed in that locked room in Jerusalem where the disciples had gathered. (The NIV says they were talking about "this," but the Greek ταῦτα is plural.)

Suddenly Jesus' glorified body, which was no longer bound by the limitations of time and space (Luke 24:31), materialized before them. It is tempting to speculate how he did it. We know that a solid can pass through a liquid because that is what happens when you dive into a swimming pool. We also know that a liquid can pass through a solid because we have felt the water pass through our clothing when we got caught out in the rain. But it is not a normal everyday occurrence for a solid to pass through a solid (at least not without damaging or destroying one or both).

Before we let ourselves get sidetracked by such questions, however, we do well to remind ourselves that one of the divine attributes of the glorified Jesus is omnipresence. It is not quite right to think of Jesus as being absent from that room until the moment when he somehow passed through the doors or the walls. Forty days later he would command his disciples to go into all the world and preach the gospel to every creature. And together with that great commission he would also give them the promise, "I will be with you always."

It would be a mistake to presume (as Godet does) that during the 40 days between Easter Sunday and Ascension Day Jesus was somehow "in transition" from his state of humiliation to his state of exaltation. Already on that first Easter evening our glorified Savior was present everywhere simultaneously. We cannot possibly comprehend that, but let us not forget it either. Rather than striving to grasp or explain a mystery which surpasses our understanding, we ought simply to comfort ourselves with Saint Paul's assurance that Jesus "will transform our lowly bodies so that they will be like his glorious body" (Php 3:21).

The words with which Jesus greeted his disciples were the ordinary Jewish salutation, "Peace be with you." But coming from his lips they conveyed more than a pious wish. Jesus' words create and convey peace (Eph 2:17). As he had promised before his death, "Peace I leave with you; my peace I give you. I do not give to you as the world gives" (Jn 14:27). This he accomplished "by making peace through his blood, shed on the cross" (Col 1:20). And that is why we can join with Saint Paul in asserting that "since we have been justified through faith, we have peace with God through our Lord Jesus Christ" (Ro 5:1).

v. 37 — *They were startled and frightened, thinking they saw a ghost.*

The two Greek words which Luke uses to describe the reaction of the disciples are very much his own. Luke is the only New Testament writer to use the Greek word πτοηθέντες (tr. "startled"), and he uses it only two or three times (depending on what you decide about the variant reading at Luke 12:4). In his discourse on the signs of the times Jesus encourages his disciples, "When you hear of wars and revolutions, do not be frightened" (μὴ πτοηθῆτε, Lk 21:9). And here in our text they experienced that kind of fear.

The Greek word ἔμφοβοι ("frightened") is only slightly more common in New Testament usage. Luke employs it four or five times (this time the textual uncertainty is in Acts 22:9), and John uses it once in the book of Revelation. When we read of a severe earthquake which destroyed a tenth of the city and killed 7,000 people, we can understand that "the survivors were terrified" (ἔμφοβοι, Rev 11:13). And that helps us to appreciate the emotion that arose in the hearts of the disciples at the sudden sight of the risen Lord.

These two peculiarly Lucan words suggest a sermon on "Easter fear." While we normally think of "Easter joy" as the dominant emotion of the day, perhaps there is some value in seeing that the atmosphere in Jerusalem on that first Easter Sunday seems to have been charged with various kinds of fear.

It started with the Roman soldiers who saw the angel roll the stone away from the entrance to the tomb. They "were so afraid of him that they shook and became like dead men" (Mt 28:4). Shortly thereafter the women came to the tomb and saw two angels, who told them that Jesus had risen from the dead. "Trembling and bewildered, the women went out and fled from the tomb. They said nothing to anyone, because they were afraid" (Mk 16:8). And even though reports kept coming in throughout the day that Jesus had been seen alive, that evening "the disciples were together with the doors locked for fear of the Jews" (Jn 20:19).

That background gathered from each of the other Gospels helps to prepare us for Luke's account. The distinctive aspect of our text is Luke's emphasis on the profound fear in the hearts and minds of the disciples. The vague fog of fear which had permeated the day was suddenly and utterly intensified when Jesus stood among them.

That is why they thought they were seeing a ghost. Here and in verse 39 we have the only two instances in the New Testament of the Greek word πνεῦμα being used to mean "ghost." The more likely choice would have been φάντασμα (as in Matthew 14:26 and Mark

6:49), but the context makes the meaning clear enough. There are two witnesses that read φάντασμα for πνεῦμα, but as Arndt explains, "Evidently some copyist and perhaps even Marcion himself attempted to introduce a clarification."

As for the notion that Scripture here certifies the existence of ghosts, Lenski's comment bears repeating: "No one had ever seen one, nor had they. . . . Terror arouses all the superstition that is latent in men's minds. . . . When fear set in in a company like the present one, its contagion was hard to resist."

vv. 38,39 — *He said to them, "Why are you troubled, and why do doubts rise in your minds? Look at my hands and my feet. It is I myself! Touch me and see; a ghost does not have flesh and bones, as you see I have."*

As Jesus continued speaking, the familiar inflections of his voice began to calm the fears of the disciples, but his tone was not entirely comforting. Saint Mark says, "He rebuked them for their lack of faith and their stubborn refusal to believe those who had seen him after he had risen" (Mk 16:14). It seems unlikely that Jesus thundered at them in anger; perhaps the rebuke was delivered in soft, calm cadences, scarcely louder than a whisper. It was not so much wrath as disappointment that marked the Master's words.

The terror which had filled their hearts when he first appeared now melted into the fear which so often accompanies a guilty conscience. Jesus was right, of course; they had let him down. They ought to have been expecting his resurrection, but instead they had been depressed by his demise and apprehensive of their own.

However, Jesus' purpose was not merely to make them feel worse. It was truly meet, right and salutary that his rebuke should make them feel guilty and contrite, but Jesus was not going to leave them to wallow in their emotions. Therefore he encouraged and even commanded them not only to listen, but also to look and to touch. Whereas they had been reluctant to believe the reports of other eyewitnesses, they had now become eyewitnesses themselves. Jesus stood before them as incontestable proof that those reports had been true. This was no hallucination. They were not somehow imagining what they had been hoping would happen. On the contrary, they were taken totally by surprise. And the overwhelming evidence convinced them that the Lord is risen indeed.

Some commentators point out that Saint Luke never says in so many words that the disciples did actually touch and handle Jesus. But Lenski responds, "Let no one say that awe restrained the disciples from touching the glorified body. Do you suppose that Jesus would take the risk that the old doubts should again appear afterward? He was here to convince every one of these men of the reality of his human body, 'flesh and bones,' and he convinced them by their actually handling him." And furthermore, we have Saint John's testimony, "That which was from the beginning, which we have heard, which we have seen with our eyes, which we have looked at and our hands have touched — this we proclaim concerning the Word of life" (1 Jn 1:1).

A part of Jesus' purpose was also to enable his disciples to relate to him as a "flesh and bones" human being. The phrase is an echo of Genesis 2:23. Just as Adam recognized Eve as "bone of my bones and flesh of my flesh," so Jesus wanted the disciples to regard him as fully human and therefore closely related to each of them. Although his resurrection body is transformed and glorified, three of them had already glimpsed something similar on the Mount of Transfiguration. And Jesus wanted all of them (and through them, all of us) to realize that his glorified body is still the same physical, material, flesh-and-blood-and-bones human body that died on the cross.

v. 40 — *When he had said this, he showed them his hands and feet.*

The UBS Greek text includes this verse, but gives it only a "D" rating, which is intended to mean "there is a very high degree of doubt concerning the reading." That is because Westcott and Hort have classified this verse as a "Western non-interpolation" which they believe was not originally included in Luke's Gospel. (The same is true of verses 3,6,12,36,51 and 52 in this chapter.) Their conviction is that some copyist who was familiar with John 20:20 tried to amplify Luke's account by inserting John's words here.

But there has been substanial and widespread dissent to this view among text critics, especially in recent years. According to Bruce Metzger, "Scholars have been critical of the apparently arbitrary way in which Westcott and Hort isolated nine passages for special treatment . . . whereas they did not give similar treatment to other readings which also are absent from Western witnesses."

Leon Morris ably summarizes what needs to be said here: "Verse 40 is yet another passage omitted by RSV (and many others) on the grounds that it is missing from the Western text. Unless we are prepared to give that text a veto, the words should be read. They cannot have been derived from John, for his account speaks of Jesus' hands *and side* (Jh 20:20). They indicate that Jesus did what his words implied and showed the disciples the places where the nail-prints were."

vv. 41-43 — *And while they still did not believe it because of joy and amazement, he asked them, "Do you have anything here to eat?" They gave him a piece of broiled fish, and he took it and ate it in their presence.*

In the introductory remarks we noted the contrast between our text and John 20:19-23 in that John seems to emphasize the overwhelming joy the disciples felt while Luke focuses on their fear. Verse 41 indicates that that contrast does not constitute a contradiction. The NIV says they felt both "joy and amazement."

The Greek word rendered "amazement" is θαυμαζόντων. Commenting on the New Testament usage of this word, Kittle says, "Most of the passages occur in the Synoptists, and especially Luke. . . . The same term occurs at Luke 24:41 in immediate proximity to ἀπιστεῖν. . . . Doubt and fear are combined in this θαυμάζειν, as in the well-known conclusion of the story of the empty tomb in Mark 16:8: ἐφοβοῦντο γάρ."

Bengel dismisses the word ἀπιστούντων with the comment, "They doubtless believed, otherwise they would not have rejoiced: but a full exercise of their faith was impeded by their joy." That is too charitable, however, because it ignores the basic meaning of the word and its complete agreement with the context.

We might be inclined to describe the disciples as thinking, "This is just too good to be true," or "I can't believe my eyes." And no doubt that is what Luke means when he says "they still did not believe it because of joy. . . . " But their fear was also an important factor. Where Bengel says, "their faith was impeded by their *joy*," we would do well to add, "their faith was impeded by their *fear*." It is nearly impossible to trust a person who terrifies you.

They were all "doubting Thomases" to begin with, and unbelief dies hard. Although it is understandable that it took some time for the truth to sink in, we dare not excuse the disciples' unbelief on that account. We can sympathize with them because the same problem afflicts us, but the fact that "we all make mistakes" does not diminish either our guilt or our holy God's righteous wrath at our sin. Mark labels the disciples' lack of faith as σκληροκαρδίαν, "hardness of heart" (Mk 16:14). And Matthew tells us that this doubt still plagued some of them 40 days later as they met on the mountain in Galilee just before Jesus' ascension (Mt 28:17).

This suggests another pertinent application. If the apostles had to struggle to overcome their unbelief even with their risen Lord standing before them in the flesh, who are we to suppose that our fight against fear and doubt will be easily or quickly won? Let us pray together with the demoniac's father, "I do believe; help me overcome my unbelief!" (Mk 9:24).

For the sake of his disciples, Jesus requested, received and consumed a piece of broiled fish. Lenski sees this act directed toward the future as much as the present: "After Jesus would be gone, and sober thought would once more come back, the old doubts and new ones might return [sic!]. So Jesus does this physical eating . . . and furnishes another decisive proof for all sober minds."

It was not unprecedented for the Son of God to eat with mortals. In Genesis chapter 18 the LORD and two of the heavenly host accepted Abraham's invitation to table fellowship. Likewise here the Lord's glorified body was not subject to hunger, but he did desire to break bread with his friends — especially since they were in the middle of their meal when he appeared (Mk 16:14). Ylvisaker says, "The parched earth absorbs the water in a manner different from the glowing sunbeam."

Another textual question arises in verse 42. Did Jesus eat only fish, or also "some honeycomb"? According to a footnote in Arndt's commentary, "Hauck says Palestinian custom would favor the eating of honey after eating fish, but holds the reading may have been introduced on account of a symbolism connected with divine worship, honey according to Psalm 119:103 being a picture of the word of God and of Paradise."

We simply don't know whether in our glorified bodies we shall eat in heaven. We do know that we won't hunger (Rev 7:16). And yet we also read that the Tree of Life will be there bearing a bountiful crop (Rev 22:2) and that we are invited to partake of "the wedding supper of the Lamb" (Rev 19:9; see also Mt 8:11).

## Homiletical Suggestions

To bring out some of the distinctive features of Saint Luke's account, the preacher might use the theme:

## Looking At Easter Through Luke's Eyes

1. We see the frightened disciples (vv. 37,38,41)
2. We see the risen Lord (vv. 35,39,40,42,43)

The introduction could trace some of the background in each of the four Gospels and then point out how Luke's Gospel is both complementary to the other three and distinct from them.

The first part of the sermon would then highlight the various reasons why the disciples were so frightened: a) they feared for their own physical safety (Jn 20:19); b) their eternal salvation was in doubt since the man they had believed to be the Messiah was now dead; c) they were shocked and surprised when Jesus suddenly appeared (vv. 37,38,41 of the text).

The second part would shift attention from the frightened disciples to the glorified Jesus and concentrate on the physical proof he presented that his resurrection body was a fully human "flesh and bones" body. Combined with the promise in Philippians 3:21, that has a powerful and personal application to every one of us.

A variation on the same theme might utilize this outline:

**Behind Locked Doors**

1. They couldn't lock fear out (vv. 37,38,41)
2. They couldn't lock Jesus out (vv. 36,39,40,42,43)

The introduction might discuss the proliferation of locks and deadbolts and burglar alarms in our society as an indication that we live with certain fears every day. Something similar prevailed in Jerusalem on that first Easter evening.

The two parts would then follow much the same train of thought as outlined above.

# FOURTH SUNDAY OF EASTER

## The Scriptures

Lesson — *Acts 4:23-33*
Epistle — *1 John 3:1,2*
Gospel — *Luke 10:11-18*

## The Text — Luke 10:11-18

Jesus spoke the words of this text about six months before his suffering and death. In John 7:10 we were told that Jesus decided to go up to Jerusalem for the Feast of Tabernacles. This was observed in the month of October. It would appear that in John 7:10 through John 10:21 we have a record of Christ's activity at that feast. Since John 10:22 tells us that the Feast of Dedication came after this "Good Shepherd Sermon" of Jesus, and since that festival occurred in the month of December, we are safe in placing this word-picture of Jesus sometime in the late fall of his last year of public ministry, the so-called "Year of Opposition."

v. 11 — *"I am the good shepherd. The good shepherd lays down his life for the sheep."*

By means of masterful sentence crafting, Jesus opens this important section in such a way that all eyes will be upon him. The personal pronoun "I" (ἐγώ) stands in emphatic position at the beginning of the sentence. From the outset, we are invited to look at Jesus, only Jesus, and away from ourselves, our limitations, our worries, our problems.

Once Jesus has our attention, he makes us see him for what he really is. He is, literally, "the shepherd, the good one." Jesus is in a class all by himself. There is no other shepherd who even comes close. And this shepherd, Jesus, is καλός. Our translation of "good" is a bit bland. Jesus is not "good" in the sense that a piece of cake tastes "good," or that a student who receives a 92% on a test is doing "good" work. Jesus is, instead, "excellent," "the very best," with respect to both his personal character and the work that he does. Jesus is, after all, the only one "good" enough to merit this high mark of praise from the Father, who demands perfection: "This is my Son, whom I love; with him I am well pleased" (Mt 17:5).

Part of what makes Jesus the good shepherd is his selfless, sacrificing love for the sheep, the believers. Here again, Jesus relies on a simple picture to bring across his point so vividly. The people to whom he spoke were familiar with the work of a shepherd and with the importance of that ancient profession. Sheep have the reputation of being docile, harmless, and rather stupid animals. In storms they have been known to pile up in the corner of their pasture, actually smothering one another to death. If a sheep stumbles and falls into a ravine and rolls over on its back, the poor animal is helpless to right itself and to stand up again. And of course, a sheep does not have fangs or claws or the ferocity to defend itself from a hungry predator. In short, sheep are helpless without a shepherd.

That's where a dedicated, loving shepherd comes in. Such a shepherd will care for his sheep, provide them with pasture and water (Ps 23), go after a lamb that gets lost (Lk 15:4), and even stand between the flock and danger (1 Sm 17:34-36). A good shepherd might even make the supreme sacrifice for the sheep — that of laying down (τίθημι: a word which carried with it the idea of "risking," "hazarding") his life.

vv. 12,13 — *"The hired hand is not the shepherd who owns the sheep. So when he sees the wolf coming, he abandons the sheep and runs away. Then the wolf attacks the flock and scatters it. The man runs away because he is a hired hand and cares nothing for the sheep."*

Jesus proceeds to contrast the good shepherd with the hired hand. The word "hired hand" (μισθωτός) shows us that this individual is watching over the sheep only because of the pay. He doesn't have any investment in them. Nor does he invest any love or affection in them. He just doesn't care (μέλει is an impersonal construction with the dative αὐτῷ). We can almost hear this fellow complaining about "the lousy hours, poor pay, and smelly working conditions." It is understandable that with this kind of attitude this hired hand will turn tail and run at the first sign of danger.

This picture describes precisely the indifferent selfishness of the Pharisees of Jesus' day. They showed little concern for the welfare of others, being consumed instead by their greed (Mt 23:14). This picture also stands as a condemnation of religious leaders of our day, pastors and teachers, who have no love for souls but labor only for the paycheck (1 Tm 3:2,3).

What happens to the sheep if no one cares for them? Obviously they will be "attacked" (ἁρπάζω). We can almost see the blood dripping from the wolf's fangs as he snatches a defenseless lamb. And what about the rest of the flock? They will scatter, but without a shepherd they, too, may die.

Rather than speculate about the "wolf," who he is or what he is, we are better off staying with the simple picture. The wolf represents danger, life-threatening danger. Behind all such attacks on God's sheep, the believers, we need to recognize the devil, the "roaring lion" (1 Pe 5:8).

vv. 14,15 — *"I am the good shepherd; I know my sheep and my sheep know me — just as the Father knows me and I know the Father — and I lay down my life for the sheep."*

The opening words of verse eleven are repeated here verbatim. Notice the dramatic contrast that Jesus has set up. We have seen the tragic results of having a "hired hand" watch over the sheep. Now Jesus proceeds to bring all attention back to himself.

In the previous section, Jesus showed that he was "good" because he was so willing to sacrifice for the sheep. However, that in itself, though noble, would not be enough. What good would it do for an earthly shepherd to fight with a wolf and lose? If the shepherd is dead, if the fight is lost, then the sheep are, pardon the expression, "sitting ducks." The wolf will polish them off after all.

Jesus shows us in this section, however, that he not only loves the sheep above all else, but he has the power to do something for them. That power is evidenced, first of all, in Jesus' knowledge of his flock. Earlier in this same chapter (vv. 3-5) Jesus has described the close relationship that develops between a faithful shepherd and his flock. They learn to know their master by his voice, and because of the way he always cares for them, they trust him. They follow him wherever he leads. The shepherd, on the other hand, also gets to know his flock. He keeps track of which ones are feeble and unable to travel as quickly, which ones are sick or about to give birth, and so forth. Shepherd and sheep come to know each other so well because they have been together so long, have been through so much.

Remembering this, drink in the deep comfort of hearing Jesus say, "I know my sheep." Jesus is speaking about his followers, those who know him by faith. The word "know" that he uses to describe the close relationship between him and his church is γινώσκω. This word means "to know by experience." Jesus knows his believers, he knows us through and through. He knows us by name. He knows our needs, our wants, our desires, our pain (2 Tm 2:19). He knows us so perfectly that he keeps every hair on our heads numbered (Mt 10:30). We, in turn, can "know" and trust this Good Shepherd. As we look back in our lives, we can see how Jesus has always been beside us. His love stands firm, his protection secure. He is the Shepherd we can depend on (Ps 23; Is 40:11; Zec 9:16).

Jesus compares this relationship with believers to the unique relationship that he enjoys with the Father. There is no profit in engaging in idle speculation about the inner workings of the Trinity at this point. Stay with the simple emphasis. Jesus wants us to know how close he is to us, how completely he as our Shepherd and our Savior takes care of us.

The last phrase in verse 15 differs from verse 11 only in this: Jesus changes the sentence structure from the third person to the first person. Our Lord makes it plain as day that throughout this section, he is talking about himself as the Good Shepherd. He lays down his life "in place of" (ὑπέρ) the sheep. Here we see the substitutionary nature of Christ's work. Christ dies so the sheep can live. the Good Shepherd becomes the Lamb who takes away the sin of the world (Jn 1:29; Isa 53:5; Lev 16:8ff), the Servant who pays the debt we owed by humbling himself even to the death on the cross (Php 2:8; 2 Co 5:21; Ga 3:13; 1 Pe 3:18).

v. 16 — *"I have other sheep that are not of this sheep pen. I must bring them also. They too will listen to my voice, and there shall be one flock and one shepherd."*

To dismiss any wrong ideas the crowd before him might have about who belongs to God's flock, Jesus makes it clear that his flock will be an international one. He will gather in believers from every corner of the globe, as was promised so often in Old Testament times (Ge 12:3; Isa 60:3; Mic 4:1,2). Gentiles would also listen to Christ's voice as it went out and continues to go out through faithful messengers carrying and sharing the good news. This verse reminds us that there is only one true Christian church, the invisible church, which consists of all who are "the sons of God through faith in Christ Jesus" (Ga 3:26).

vv. 17,18 — *"The reason my Father loves me is that I lay down my life — only to take it up again. No one takes it from me, but I lay it down of my own accord. I have authority to lay it down and authority to take it up again. This command I received from my Father."*

We have already noted, in connection with verse 11, that Jesus is loved by the Father because he is a perfectly obedient Son (active obedience). Here Jesus indicates that the Father also loves him "because" (διὰ τοῦτό) Jesus willingly gives up everything, even his life, for the sheep (passive obedience). This section summarizes God's entire plan of salvation. Jesus went into death voluntarily. No one took his life from him. And although Jesus laid down his life as the sacrificial lamb, there is one important difference. Jesus had the "authority" (ἐξουσία) to lay down his life, but he also had the authority to take that life up again (Mt 28:18). According to plan, Christ would go through death, suffering even the agonies of hell on the cross, in order to make a full payment for the sins of the world. Also, according to God's plan, Jesus would rise again from the dead, having conquered the power of sin, death and hell for us (Isa 63:1; Ro 8:37; 1 Co 15:57; Rev 17:14).

At the end of this section, the word "command" (ἐντολή) may be misunderstood. We wouldn't want to leave the impression that Christ didn't want to carry out God's plan to save sinners. Therefore the translation "commission" might better reflect what transpired between Father and Son. Both were in perfect harmony in will and in purpose. Jesus did not need to be pushed off his glorious throne and dragged down to this lowly, wicked earth. He came to us willingly because he is our Good Shepherd.

## Homiletical Suggestions

This striking picture of our Savior has inspired and comforted generations of his flock. Many of us will have in our homes, our studies, our churches, artistic variations on this "Good Shepherd" theme. It seems wise to mention such pictures in a sermon on this text. They may bring to life the picture in this text, helping the listeners to "see" what Jesus paints for them.

This moving text can have a wide variety of applications and uses for God's flock. Keeping in mind that these verses are suggested for use in the Easter season, we may want to incorporate the triumphant flavor of the resurrection message into our handling of this section. One approach might be:

## Our Good Shepherd Lives On

1. Love compelled him to ultimate sacrifice (vv. 11-13)
2. Power compelled him to total victory (vv. 14-18)

In the introduction of such a sermon the preacher could remind his listeners that Jesus spoke these confident, triumphant words some six months before he suffered, died and rose again. The outcome of his battle was never in doubt. His love and purpose never wavered.

Another approach that would build much more upon the word-picture of the text, as well as upon the many pictures we might have in our homes, could be:

## We Are Safe In The Arms Of Jesus

1. Because he is the Good Shepherd (vv. 11-14a,17,18)
2. Because we are the sheep of his flock (vv. 14b-16)

In such a treatment, each listener is asked to envision himself/herself as that lamb in the Savior's arms. This is a most comforting picture.

It would be a great mistake to limit usage of this text to one particular season or Sunday of the year. Why not consider using these words for a pastors' conference? The approach could be that of a pastor's prayer:

**Lord, Make Me A Good Shepherd**

1. Give me a Christ-like love for your sheep (vv. 11-13)
2. Help me to know your sheep better (vv. 14,15)
3. Let me share Christ's voice in all I do (v. 16)
4. Encourage me with Christ's power (vv. 17,18)

It would also seem appropriate to use this text at a funeral, perhaps for a child called home to heaven suddenly and unexpectedly. What comfort could be gained from hearing:

**The Good Shepherd Has Called His Lamb Home**

1. The Good Shepherd who died, yet lives (vv. 11-13,17,18)
2. The Good Shepherd who knew this lamb and all its needs (vv. 14,15)
3. The Good Shepherd who now watches over this lamb in the fold above (v. 16)

Finally, a single verse of this text could be isolated and used with profit for a very positive mission message. On a mission festival, how encouraging it would be to hear our Good Shepherd declare:

**"I Have Other Sheep"**

1. "I must bring them also" (v. 16a)
2. "They too will listen" (v. 16b)

# FIFTH SUNDAY OF EASTER

## The Scriptures

Lesson — *Acts 8:26-40*
Epistle — *1 John 3:18-24*
Gospel — *John 15:1-8*

## The Text — John 15:1-8

Through the Apostle John God has given us a great deal of information about Maundy Thursday evening that we don't know from the other evangelists. Jesus' discourse on the vine and the branches is an example. While some speak of this as taking place in the upper room, the last words of chapter 14 imply that Jesus and the disciples were leaving the room and heading for the Garden of Gethsemane.

While the text does not exactly fit the traditional idea of Cantate, it certainly is apt for the Easter season with its stress on remaining closely connected with the living, life-giving Christ. He alone is the source of strength for his believing branches.

Maundy Thursday was the last opportunity Jesus had to teach his disciples before his death. His evening was filled with vivid examples and varied pronouncements. What he had to say about the vine and the branches is perhaps one of the best known sections.

Jeus sets up both the picture and the reality in the first verse:

v. 1 — *"I am the true vine, and my Father is the gardener."*

The vine (ἄμπελος) is often used symbolically in Holy Scripture. In the Old Testament the vine was used as a picture of fruitfulness (Ps 128:3; Zec 8:12), and even as a picture of God's people (Isa 5:1-7). Here Jesus portrays himself as the vine, in fact the "true" (ἀληθινή) vine. That adjective conveys the idea that Jesus not only has the name and appearance, but also the real nature of a vine in regard to his people. His Father is the "gardener" (γεωργός, actually the one who tills the soil). He protects and preserves what is in his vineyard.

His work is described as follows:

v. 2 — *"He cuts off every branch in me that bears no fruit, while every branch that does bear fruit he prunes so that it will be even more fruitful."*

The Father is very much a results-oriented gardener. He is looking for a response of faith and gratitude for the blessed connection to Jesus, the vine, that believers enjoy. Good works, the fruit he looks for, include everything the believer does out of faith and love for God.

The unproductive branches are cut off from the vine, while the fruitful branches are pruned to make them still more fruitful. The divine gardener trims off all the suckers and pinches off all buds that might sap the branch's strength and hinder production. This ongoing pruning is accomplished through the continuing work of the Holy Spirit. The nature of that fruit is especially well described in Galatians 5:22,23.

This work had already begun in the disciples:

v. 3 — *"You are already clean because of the word I have spoken to you."*

This was the second time Jesus said "You are clean" that night (cf. Jn 13:10). The first time was in connection with his washing of the disciples' feet. Jesus' point was that the disciples had already experienced a cleansing. It occurred when they were declared righteous by faith in Christ (Ro 5:1). It was accomplished through Jesus' "word" teaching (λόγος), the whole gospel message he proclaimed, of which he was the embodiment.

Jesus had a command for his fruitful branches that pointed them to success:

v. 4 — *"Remain in me, and I will remain in you. No branch can bear fruit by itself; it must remain in the vine. Neither can you bear fruit unless you remain in me."*

Jesus' encouragement is that the disciples "remain" (μείνατε) in him so that they might continue as fruitful branches. The command carries some implications: that the disciples were already in Jesus, but that the close connection could be broken. Since the command is in the aorist tense, it expresses the idea of "Remain always."

Jesus didn't want any misunderstanding, so he placed the picture and reality side by side. And what a comfort the reality is! Jesus would always remain in those who remain in him. That staying power is not something that the branches of the true vine can muster of their own strength. It is the power of the Holy Spirit that alone can accomplish this, but with that power in action we, the branches, remain intimately connected to Christ, the vine, so that we might produce much fruit.

In many ways verse 5 is the summary of this whole section:

v. 5 — *"I am the vine; you are the branches. If a man remains in me and I in him, he will bear much fruit; apart from me you can do nothing."*

Here Jesus' basic proposition is emphasized again. Like the vine which conveys the vital sap to its branches so they may remain productive, so Christ funtions as the source of life for his people. As long as the connection remains, there will be spiritual fruit as a result. One of the men who heard this truth expounded from our Savior's lips did not put it into practice that night. Peter thought he was a strong enough branch on his own. Relying on himself, he put himself into danger, and denied the Lord. The application to us is obvious. Once we set out on our own, there will be no spiritual fruit, and we will become dead and fruitless.

Jesus then points out what the gardener will do with all dead branches:

v. 6 — *"If anyone does not remain in me, he is like a branch that is thrown away and withers; such branches are picked up, thrown into the fire and burned."*

Fruitlessness is not a condition that is excused or ignored by the gardener. He wants to get rid of what does not produce fruit. Such branches are cut off and thrown away to wither. Such withering happens very quickly in nature, as we see in our own gardening efforts. What is cut off or uprooted quickly begins to dry up. Such dead branches are fit for nothing but burning. That fire is the well-known, oft-repeated and very real picture of hell (Mt 3:12; 18:8; 25:41; Mk 9:43ff; Rev 20:14). This judgment on the unfruitful is made by the divine gardener who has the right and ability to "destroy both soul and body in hell" (Mt 10:28). Such a warning must not be taken lightly.

Once again the illustration swings back to the positive:

v. 7 — *"If you remain in me and my words remain in you, ask whatever you wish, and it will be given you."*

When the believer remains in the vine, Jesus' message remains in him with its cleansing and freedom-giving power (Jn 15:3; 8:31,32). This is a powerful reminder to those who would claim allegiance to Jesus but then demand the right to pick and choose which truths of Jesus' message they want to believe. Jesus' branches remain in him, and his message remains in them to believe and follow.

And to the faithful Jesus gives the privilege of prayer. Now Jesus is not giving us permission to unbridle our greed, but when we ask of him as fruitful branches, he will give us what we ask. He repeated the promise later (Jn 16:23,24). In Gethsemane Jesus gave us the example of how we are to ask, praying, "Yet not my will, but yours be done" (Lk 22:42). What a comfort to know that what we ask will be answered only according to our heavenly Father's will and wisdom! This is ours as a benefit of our close relationship to Christ.

To the world a fruitful vine is a positive reflection on a green-thumbed gardener. In the same way a fruitful Christian is an honor to the divine gardener:

v. 8 — *"This is to my Father's glory, that you bear much fruit, showing yourselves to be my disciples."*

What the Christian produces — and there is "much" (πολύν) potential — is to the glory of our heavenly Father. It is proof of what he can do with sinful, scraggly branches like us. In this way the Christian shows that he is indeed one of Jesus' "learners" (μαθηταί).

(There is a slight variant in this last verse. The Nestle text prefers γενήσεσθε, a future indicative. The UBS text uses γένησθε, an aorist subjunctive, but gives that choice only a "D" rating in the apparatus. The difference doesn't really change the meaning.)

Some like to stress the idea here that the eleven to whom Jesus was speaking were already his disciples, and did not need to become such. Others remind us that believers are in a constant struggle of becoming the disciples they ought to be. As Jesus' learners and followers, we are in a state of being what we are and yet also growing in what we are.

## Homiletical Suggestions

The word "remain" (μείνω) occurs eight times in the eight verses of this text. This, then, becomes an obvious point of emphasis. The disciples would experience a separation from Jesus by death. Christ's ascension would separate them physically. Therefore the message of this text is very appropriate for the Easter season. Jesus assures his followers that he will remain with them and he calls upon them to remain in him.

A message of appropriation from this text is Jesus' role for us as the true vine, our source for all strength and blessing. He is that for us because he both lived and died for us. As believers, we are branches in Christ, and we are to produce fruit accordingly. This text encourages the Christian, "Be what you are. Remain in Christ and be productive in that blessed relationship."

This text also has excellent potential as a confirmation text. It can never be emphasized too much that confirmation is not an end, but a time when we declare that, by the grace of God, we intend to remain in Christ for life.

While Jesus, the vine, remains central, the work of the Father and of the Holy Spirit in making and keeping us as fruitful branches will be brought out in a sermon with the theme:

**Remain In Christ**

1. Planted (vv. 1,4)
2. Pruned (vv. 2,3)
3. Productive (vv. 5-8)

The same ideas could also be incorporated in a two-part sermon with the theme:

**Remain In Me**

1. That you may receive strength (vv. 1-4)
2. That you may produce results (vv. 5-8)

Another approach to this text would be to stress the contrast between the fruitful and the dead branches, something like the contrast found in Psalm 1. The division of the text would have to be synthetic, showing the difference in nature (fruitful vs. unfruitful), treatment (pruning vs. cutting off) and end (remaining vs. eternal separation):

**What Sort Of Branch Are You?**

1. There are two types of branches
2. There are two methods of treatment

Finally, for those who like contemporary themes, here is one that would supply ready introductory material, pointing out that other "grapevines" aren't reliable, but what Jesus has to say is:

**I Heard It Through The Grapevine**

1. How I have been cleansed
2. How I may produce results

# SIXTH SUNDAY OF EASTER

**The Scriptures**

Lesson — *Acts 11:19-30*
Epistle — *1 John 4:1-11*
Gospel — *John 15:9-17*

**The Text — John 15:9-17**

Jesus spoke the words of our text to his apostles on Maundy Thursday evening in the upper room. They are part of his farewell discourse (Jn 13-16) and precede his high priestly prayer (Jn 17) and his arrest in the Garden of Gethsemane (Jn 18:1-11). As Jesus addressed his apostles for the last time before his death, he gave them a source for the assurance and comfort they would need when they would witness his arrest, conviction and execution and later when they would carry out his great commission.

Jesus' allegory of the vine and the branches (Jn 15:1-8) immediately precedes our text. He reminded his apostles that just as a branch needs to be connected to its vine and to remain in it to be productive, so they needed to be connected to him and to remain in him to be productive followers. The ideas of productiveness and remaining in Jesus are also contained in the words of our text.

As our text begins, Jesus reminds his apostles of his love for them:

v. 9 — *"As my Father has loved me, so have I loved you. Now remain in my love."*

Jesus loved his apostles in the same way (καθώς) as his Father loved him, that is, with a perfect love. The Greek verb Jesus used for love is ἀγαπάω, to show ἀγάπη. Ἀγάπη in contrast to φιλία, the love of friendship, and to ἔρος, sensual love, denotes the highest type of love, a love which is sure, steadfast, heartfelt, warm. Jesus wanted his apostles to continue to enjoy his love.

What a blessing it is to enjoy the love of the Son of God. No matter what the believer experiences as he travels through life on his way to heaven, he has the assurance that his Savior is dealing with him in love.

Jesus next tells his apostles how to remain in his love. They remain in his love by obeying his commands.

v. 10 — *"If you obey my commands, you will remain in my love, just as I have obeyed my Father's commands and remain in his love."*

Obedience to Jesus' commands is the product of faith. Therefore, as the apostles had productive faith in their Savior, they would remain in his love. Jesus used his perfect obedience and his relationship with his heavenly Father as an encouraging example for his apostles. Jesus continues to be an encouraging example for his believers today.

Jesus goes on to tell his apostles for what purpose (ἵνα) he wants them to obey his commands and remain in his love. He wants them to have the same kind of joy he has:

v. 11 — *"I have told you this so that my joy may be in you and that your joy may be complete."*

Contrary to what the unbelieving world thinks, true and lasting joy comes from knowing and serving a loving Savior. While the unbeliever seeks joy in the pursuit of sinful pleasures, the believer is reminded that real, complete joy is found in the Savior. The focus of this verse on joy makes this text a fitting choice for the joyful Easter season.

Earlier (v. 10) Jesus had told his apostles to obey his commands. He now summarizes those commands for them in one word, love.

v. 12 — *"My command is this: Love each other as I have loved you."*

St. Paul expressed a similar thought in Romans 13. He listed the Fifth through Tenth Commandments and then continued, "and whatever other commandment there may be, are summed up in this one rule: 'Love your neighbor as yourself.' Love does no harm to its neighbor. Therefore love is the fulfillment of the law" (Ro 13:9,10).

Jesus told his apostles to love one another as he loved them. In the following verse Jesus explains that this means with a selfless and self-sacrificing love:

v. 13 — *"Greater love has no one than this, that he lay down his life for his friends."*

Jesus is stating a general truth. The supreme sacrifice that a person can make for his friends is to lay down his life for them. Jesus made that supreme sacrifice when he laid down his life on the cross on Good Friday. However, Jesus not only laid down his physical life, he also suffered the torments of hell, separation from his heavenly Father (Mt 27:46), to pay for the sins of the world.

Jesus now describes his friends:

v. 14 — *"You are my friends if you do what I command."*

Jesus' friends are those who believe that he laid down his life to pay for their sins. They show their faith by obeying his commands.

Only the believer, the one who in faith accepts Jesus' love, can do what Jesus commands, namely, to love others. John explains it like this: "We love because he first loved us" (1 Jn 4:19).

Jesus further describes his friends by pointing out the privilege they enjoy:

v. 15 — *"I no longer call you servants, because a servant does not know his master's business. Instead, I have called you friends, for everything that I learned from my Father I have made known to you."*

Jesus again was stating a general truth. Servants are simply doers. They do not know what their masters are trying to accomplish. Friends, on the other hand, are "in the know."

Jesus' apostles were not servants. They were friends. They were friends because Jesus had revealed to them the words of his heavenly Father, the gospel message of salvation, and they in faith had accepted them.

All people need and want friends. What a blessing it is for those who through faith have Jesus as their friend! He is the one friend who is always there when they need him. He is the one friend who completely knows and understands them. He is the one friend who never fails to give the right advice through his word. He is the one friend who will receive them into his heavenly home.

Friendships usually develop mutually. Friends choose one another. Jesus points out that this is not the case when it comes to him and his friends:

v. 16 — *"You did not choose me, but I chose you and appointed you to go and bear fruit — fruit that will last. Then the Father will give you whatever you ask in my name."*

In grace Jesus chose the apostles to be his friends. He chose them for a definite purpose (ἵνα), to go out and be fruitful ambassadors for him.

So it is with all believers. By nature they were spiritually dead, blind and enemies of God. They had neither the desire nor the ability to come to faith in Jesus and become his friend. But Jesus in grace chose them and brought them to faith through his word. Like the apostles, all believers are chosen for a definite purpose. Jesus chooses his believers to live fruitful Christian lives for him. What meaning and what challenge that purpose puts into their lives!

The last ἵνα clause of verse 16 is best taken as a result clause. One of the results of the apostles' being chosen by Jesus as his friends was that they could pray to their heavenly Father in his name. This was an important and valuable blessing as they carried out their Savior's purpose in choosing them.

Prayer is one of every believer's great blessings. In time of need or difficulty the believer can turn to his heavenly Father. Since the believer prays in Jesus' name, that is, trusting in Jesus as his Savior and desiring that his heavenly Father's will be done, he always receives an answer to his prayers.

The text concludes with a reptition of the thought of verse 12:

v. 17 — *"This is my command: Love each other."*

## Homiletical Suggestions

Since the Easter season is a season of joy in the victorious, risen Savior, the text can be focused around verse 11: "I have told you this so that my joy may be in you and that your joy may be complete." That joy is based on the Savior's love for sinners which moved him to lay down his life for them. Sinners receive that love through faith and reflect that love to others in obedience to Jesus' commands. Contrary to what the unbelieving world thinks, it is a joy to know and serve a loving Savior.

Adding to the Christian's joy is the fact that he is a friend of the risen Savior. The Savior has chosen him as a friend purely out of grace. He has revealed to him the words of his heavenly Father. He has given him a real purpose in life. He has given him the assurance that his heavenly Father will hear and answer his prayers.

In a world that is vainly looking for joy and happiness, our God has graciously given us:

## Two Keys To A Joy-Filled Life

1. Remaining in Jesus' love (vv. 9-13,17)
2. Experiencing Jesus' friendship (vv. 14-16)

This text also lends itself to use as a homily, beginning with Jesus' exhortation to "remain in his love" as a theme, and following his thoughts as he himself expands on this theme as follows:

## Remain In Jesus' Love (v.9)

1. Obediently (v. 10)
2. Joyfully (v. 11)
3. Sacrifically (vv. 12,13)
4. Knowingly (vv. 14,15)
5. Fruitfully (v. 16)
6. Demonstrably (v. 17)

210

With this kind of treament it is important to relate each part to the theme, also remembering throughout that Jesus bases this exhortation upon his picture of a Christian's relationship to himself as a branch to a vine (ch. 15:1-8). Apart from him we can do nothing (v. 5).

# ASCENSION OF OUR LORD

**The Scriptures**

> Lesson — *Acts 1:1-11*
> Epistle — *Ephesians 1:16-23*
> Gospel — *Luke 24:44-53*

## The Text — Luke 24:44-53

Our text takes us back forty days, to the first Easter evening. The disciples were gathered behind locked doors (Jn 20:19). They had heard the reports of the women who had gone to the tomb (vv. 9-11). Peter and John had checked it out but had only found the grave empty (Jn 20:3-9). Mary Madgalene had reported her visit with the risen Lord (Jn 20:18). The two Emmaus disciples had returned with the startling news of their walk and talk with the Lord (vv. 33-35).

Despite all these reports the disciples were still confused and uncertain. Was it really true? Was their dear Lord really alive? "While they were still talking about this, Jesus himself stood among them and said to them, 'Peace be with you' " (v. 36). To silence their persistent doubts Jesus invited his disciples to touch him, and he ate some fish in their presence. Then:

vv. 44,45 — *He said to them, "This is what I told you while I was still with you: Everything must be fulfilled that is written about me in the law of Moses, the Prophets and the Psalms." Then he opened their minds so they could understand the Scriptures.*

After the time when the disciples had confessed Jesus as "the Christ, the Son of the living God" (Mt 16:16), the Lord had provided information concerning the events of Holy Week (Mt 16:21; Mk 8:31,32). He repeated this information as they were making that fateful trip to Jerusalem (Mt 20:17-19). Gathered with his disciples in the upper room, Jesus added still more details (Judas as the betrayer, Peter's triple denial). Note well that with each announcement of his death Jesus added, *"On the third day he will be raised to life!"* (Mt 20:19).

Note that well, because the disciples seem to have forgotten that "little" detail. What unnecessary grief, worry and pain that caused! This world and this life bring us enough troubles and tribulations, enough pains and problems. Why needlessly make matters worse by forgetting the many gracious promises of our risen, our *ascended* Lord?

"Everything must be fulfilled" (v. 44). *Everything.* God does not keep his promises "more or less." He fulfills his word down to the last detail. Think of the details of the many Old Testament prophecies about our Lord: the birth in Bethlehem, the flight into Egypt, the thirty pieces of silver, the pierced side. He said that is the way it would be, and that is the way it was!

What a powerful statement on the inspiration and inerrancy of the Word our text is. "Everything must be fulfilled." "The Scripture cannot be broken" (Jn 10:35). (Jesus refers here to the Old Testament Scriptures in their tripartite divison.) Our ascended Lord has left us with many precious promises. "Surely I am with you always" (Mt 28:20). "We know that in all things God works for the good of those who love him" (Ro 8:28). Recall Jesus' promises in the book of Revelation of the crown of life (2:10), the new Jerusalem (21:1-5), the tree of life (22:14). Recall his promise to return and take us home to heaven (Jn 14:1-3; Ac 1:11; Rev 22:7,12,20). Certainly there is much food for our faith in this verse. Be careful not to neglect the rest of the text!

As we study the Word we must not forget that Jesus "opened their minds so they could understand the Scriptures" (v. 45). We need divine assistance to understand the divine Word. Review Paul's words on this truth in 1 Corinthians 2. Recall Luther's explanation of The Third Article in our catechism. Then rejoice in our Lord's ascension promise to send his Holy Spirit as our Counselor to guide us into all truth (Jn 16:13).

vv. 46,47 — *He told them, "This is what is written: The Christ will suffer and rise from the dead on the third day, and repentance and forgiveness of sins will be preached in his name to all nations, beginning at Jerusalem."*

Jesus of Nazareth, Mary's Son, is the Christ, the Messiah, the Anointed One. As such he was sent by God, anointed and empowered with the Holy Spirit (Ac 10:38) to be our Prophet, Priest and King. (Cf. Christ's office under The Third Article in our catechism.) As our Christ, the Anointed One, Jesus had to suffer, die and rise again. Thus the good news of God's love and forgiveness for us sinners — proclaimed by Jesus our Prophet — was established. Thus as our Priest, Jesus presented himself as the atoning, all-sufficient sacrifice for the sins of the world (Jn 1:29; He 7:27; 9:28; 1 Jn 2:2). Thus — by suffering, dying and rising again — has Jesus our King delivered us from our sins, destroyed death's power and rescued us from Satan's slavery. Since this is an Ascension Day text it would be well to emphasize Jesus as our Christ in his exaltation. As our Prophet he sends us out to preach the gospel (v. 48; Mk 16:15) and provides his church with pastors, etc. (Eph 4:11). As our Priest he lives to intercede for us (Ro 8:34). As our King he rules this world for the good of his church (today's Epistle reading).

Verse 47 confronts us with a variant reading. The Greek text offered by the United Bible Societies (1975), weakly (a "D" rating), prefers the reading μετάνοιαν εἰς ἄφεσιν ἁμαρτιῶν (repentance *for* the forgiveness of sins). The AAT and the NASB follow this reading. The NIV, KJV, TEV and Luther adopt the second reading of μετάνοιαν καὶ ἄφεσιν ἁμαρτιῶν (repentance *and* forgiveness of sins). The manuscript evidence seems to prefer this reading.

The difference reflects the use of repentance (μετάνοια) in its broad (AAT, NASB) and narrow (NIV, KJV) meanings. In the *broad* sense repentance includes not only recognition and confession of sin, but also faith in Christ as the Savior from sin. (Cf. Lk 13:3,5 for a similar usage of the word.) The *narrow* definition limits repentance to recognition and confession of sin. Of course such repentance does not lead to life and salvation (cf. Judas). Nor is this the chief proclamation of the church. To such repentance there must be added (καί) the announcement of God's gracious forgiveness for Jesus' sake.

While preaching on this verse, keep in mind the picture behind the Greek word for repentance. Repentance is a "change of mind." We see sin for what it really is. Sin does not bring pleasure and satisfaction (except to the Old Adam, and then only temporarily). Sin is deadly, destructive, damnable. It is defying the holy, righteous God. With that realization, and the confession that *I* am a sinner, the message of God's full and free forgiveness in the Lord is indeed good news. Jesus' perfect life is God's answer to our unholy lives. His innocent death paid for our sins. His Easter victory is our victory. His ascension assures us that his work as our suffering Savior is complete.

This message of repentance and forgiveness is to be "preached in his name to all nations" (v. 47). Forgiveness is only in connection with Jesus' name (all that we know about him from the Word). His forgiveness is for all nations. Our faith-wrought conviction of God's forgiveness is built on the universal, objective facts of justification. Jesus is the Savior of the world (Jn 1:29; Ro 3:23,24; 2 Co 5:14-19). All need to hear this good news.

With Christ's work completed, ours begins:

vv. 48,49 — *"You are witnesses of these things. I am going to send you what my Father has promised; but stay in the city until you have been clothed with power from on high."*

Witness — that is our work and calling as Christians. A witness speaks what he has seen and knows. That's it! That is our gospel

214

ministry. We share what we know about Jesus from his Word. "Always be prepared to give an answer to everyone who asks you to give the reason for the hope that you have," Peter tells us in his first letter (3:15). "But do this with gentleness and respect."

A clear understanding of this point can help alleviate the potential fear of sharing the Savior. Witnessing need not involve delivering a detailed theological treatise. Witnessing is not necessarily a regurgitation of Christian dogmatics. It is stating the simple (albeit profound) facts of law and gospel, our sins and God's grace in Christ. It is explaining what Christ means *to me*, stating the hope *I* have because Jesus is the Savior. The rest is up to the Holy Spirit. We are witnesses. Conversion is his work.

Jesus reminds us of the promise of the Spirit and Pentecost. The Father had already given this promise through Joel (2:28,29; Ac 2:16-21). Jesus spoke at length about the Spirit and his work on Maundy Thursday evening (Jn 14-16). Since Pentecost is only ten days away, Ascension Day is not the time to elaborate on this point. Concentrate on the promise but not the fulfillment.

The remaining verses take us from these words of Easter evening to Ascension Day.

vv. 50,51 — *When he had led them out to the vicinity of Bethany, he lifted up his hands and blessed them. While he was blessing them, he left them and was taken up into heaven.*

Acts 1 identifies the site of the ascension as the Mount of Olives, a Sabbath day's walk (about three-quarters of a mile) from Jerusalem (v. 12). Nearby the Lord had prayed in the Garden of Gethsemane and was betrayed. Within sight of the city that scorned him, within sight of that place called Golgotha and the empty tomb, the rejected, the *risen* Jesus ascended in triumph. He who was mocked as the King of the Jews (Jn 19:3; Lk 23:37; Mk 15:31,32) is the King of kings and Lord of lords (Rev 19:16).

While expounding on the ascension of Christ, care must be taken to avoid giving any false impressions. Our Lord, the God-man, is not confined to a limited space in heaven. While we cannot see him with our eyes, cannot walk and talk and eat with him as the disciples did, we know that he is ever with us. He is everywhere (cf. today's Epistle reading). We cannot explain this mystery, but what comfort it offers us!

Jesus left with a blessing. There was no mere handshake of goodbye. He blessed them, his hands lifted high. These are the hands of forgiving grace, still bearing the marks of the nails (Jn 20:27). These hands reach out to gather us safely to our Savior's side (Mt 23:37). These are the protecting hands of our Good Shepherd (Jn 10:28). These hands are firmly in control of our life and our world (Mt 28:18). His hands are still lifted high to bless us.

"Parting is such sweet sorrow," it has been said. Our lives can testify to that. Yet we read about the disciples:

vv. 52,53 — *Then they worshiped him and returned to Jerusalem with great joy. And they stayed continually at the temple, praising God.*

The doubts of Easter evening had vanished. Joy — *great joy* — filled the disciples' hearts and lives. They had not been left orphans (Jn 14:18). Their Savior was still with them. His peace filled their hearts (Jn 14:27). They had his promise of the Spirit. Their lives had meaning and purpose. Ascension bids us worship our God, obey him (they stayed at the temple), praise him.

### Homiletical Suggestions

Prayerful meditation on this text will dispel any Ascension Day "blahs" (low attendance, etc.). This day is just as exciting, as important, as festive as Christmas, Easter or any other church holiday.

Care must be taken not to get bogged down in the exposition of the text. There is much meat here, enough for several sermons. For example, verse 44 reminds us that the *whole* Old Testament (Law, Prophets, Psalms) speaks of Christ (Jn 5:39), not just the direct Messianic prophecies. The sermon cannot include "everything" written in the Old Testament about Christ. Instead, carefully chosen references should be made.

These verses do not tell us what our Lord is doing now as he "sits at the right hand of God the Father Almighty." However, the session at the right hand is closely connected to the ascension. It, too, is a truth of great importance and comfort. Christ is not idly sitting by waiting for judgment day to come. He is actively involved in this world and in our daily lives. Make that point clear. Ending our ascension celebration with Jesus "taking off" will leave our hearers hanging in the air. Reference to today's Epistle reading can supply the needed facts.

The ascension is part of Jesus' exaltation. The sermon should reflect this. So we can encourage God's saints to:

**"Crown Him With Many Crowns"** (TLH 341)

1. Crown him the Lord of the Word (vv. 44,45)
2. Crown him the Lord of the church (vv. 46-49)
   a. The church he purchased
   b. The church he commissions
   c. The church he empowers
   d. The church that obeys (stay/stayed)
3. Crown him the Lord of the world (vv. 50-53)
   a. The session at the right hand (Epistle reading)
   b. He daily and richly blesses us
   c. This is cause for great joy

With the ascension our Lord withdrew his visible presence from this earth. This may prompt us to ask:

**Where Is Jesus?**

1. Look for him in his Word (vv. 44,45)
2. Hear him speaking through his witnesses (vv. 46-49)
3. See him blessing us in this world (vv. 50-53)

A variation on these thoughts can be stated as:

**Our Ascension Prayer: Lord, Open Our Minds** (v. 45)

1. To see you in your Word (vv. 44,45)
2. To hear you through your witnesses (vv. 46-49)
3. To receive your blessings with joy (vv. 50-53)

A final suggestion focuses on the Lord blessing his disciples (vv. 50,51):

**Our Ascended Lord Blesses Us**

1. With the truths of his Word (vv. 44-47)
2. With the Spirit's power to witness (vv. 47-49)
3. With joy in his ascension (vv. 50-53)

# SEVENTH SUNDAY OF EASTER

**The Scriptures**

> Lesson — *Acts 1:15-26*
> Epistle — *1 John 4:13-21*
> Gospel — *John 17:11b-19*

**The Text — John 17:11b-19**

John 17:11b-19 forms the second portion of Jesus' High Priestly Prayer, the prayer our Lord spoke on the night he was betrayed. In the first portion of the prayer Jesus prays for himself (17:1-5). In the second portion he prays for his disciples as he prepares to leave them. The third portion of the prayer (17:20-26) is a prayer for those who would believe in him "through their message." Concerning the entire prayer Luther remarks: "It is truly a fervent and sincere prayer, in which he opens and pours out his soul to us and to his heavenly Father. But I fear that we cannot properly estimate and describe the power, the characteristic quality and virtue of this prayer; for however simple and unadorned, it is nevertheless impossible to fathom its profound significance, its wealth and its compass."

v. 11b — *"Holy Father, protect them by the power of your name — the name you gave me — so that they may be one as we are one."*

Twice before in the prayer Jesus has said "Father." However, here he addresses his Father as "Holy Father." God's holiness stands in stark contrast to the world. Jesus is leaving this world to return to the Father. But his disciples will remain in the world though they are not "of the world" (v. 14). As Jesus prays for them, he addresses the one whose holiness overcomes any power the world brings against his children.

This power to protect is vested in "the power of your name (ὄνομά σου) — the name you gave me," the revelation of the word, particularly as the disciples have been privileged to hear it from the Word made flesh. Jesus notes earlier in the prayer (vv. 6-8) that the disciples have received this revelation; just as they have been protected by this name while Jesus was with them (v. 12), the Savior prays that this name will continue to protect them after he leaves.

The power of the word has always been the Christian's protection. Paul's description of the word as the offensive and defensive weapon Christians possess comes quickly to mind (Eph 6:17). Similarly, Luther frequently stated that the word is the Christian's strength and protection: "Yes, indeed, it is the power of God which causes the devil the deepest anguish but strengthens, comforts and helps us beyond measure."

The Savior states that the purpose behind his prayer for protection is that his disciples "may be one as we are one." While these words are often mustered in support of a false ecumenism, Jesus' meaning is clear. He is not praying that they may "become one," but that their unity already established (cf. vv. 7,8) may continue in the face of the world's opposition (the Greek ὦσιν is a present subjunctive with durative force).

v. 12 — *"While I was with them, I protected them and kept them safe by that name you gave me. None has been lost except the one doomed to destruction so that Scripture would be fulfilled."*

Jesus has consistently shown himself to be the true Shepherd of his sheep. His ministry has succeeded: not one of those "you gave me" was lost by him. Jesus kept them constantly in his protection (note the imperfect, ἐτήρουν) so that all are safe *now* (aorist, ἐφύλαξα).

But what about Judas? Is he the exception? Did the Lord's protection succeed in every case except his? Jesus notes that the one lost was ὁ υἱὸς τῆς ἀπωλείας, the "son of destruction," a Hebraism (compare Mt 23:15) that denotes his character as being the "product of eternal damnation" (Lenksi). Judas' destruction was the result of what he already was (Ac 1:25). While this happened "that the Scripture would be fulfilled," it would be unscriptural to infer that Judas' destruction was somehow "fated." His sin and his damnation remain his own fault; Jesus' observation serves rather to remind us that God's word is absolutely true in all that it foretold about the Messiah.

v. 13 — *"I am coming to you now, but I say these things while I am still in the world, so that they may have the full measure of my joy within them."*

Jesus is speaking his prayer in the hearing of his disciples. As they listen to him in intimate discourse with the Father, as they are (and have been!) forewarned of Jesus' imminent departure, they are to have joy, not sorrow. Jesus speaks his words in his prayer in combination with all that they have heard him say earlier in the evening, in order that the disciples may see all that is unfolding before them is entirely in keeping with the Father's will. In this regard, the gospel holds no surprises. Jesus' course was sure and certain: the Scriptures, the name that had protected them to this point, were being fulfilled for their benefit! The words of Jesus should always be our source of joy because they are true and certain as they promise every grace and mercy.

This joy, however, would be theirs in the midst of a world that would hate them. Thus Jesus continues:

v. 14 — *"I have given them your word and the world has hated them, for they are not of the world any more than I am of the world."*

"The world is bound to crucify whatever is of God," states Luther in words that echo these words of Jesus. The Savior has given the disciples his precious Word, a gift of purest grace, for their protection and as their message to proclaim. But the gift freely given nonetheless will exact a cost from those who hold it: the hatred of the world. Why? Because through it "they are not of the world any more than I am of the world." The Greek aorist ἐμίσησεν is ingressive: as soon as the disciples were transformed spiritually, "the world *began* to hate them," the inevitable reaction of unbelief to faith.

This reaction is founded upon the fact that Christians, like their Lord, are different from "the world" (ἐκ τοῦ κόσμου). Lenski points out that ἐκ denotes an "ethical force" "of the same nature, kind and quality." But Christians are not ἐκ τοῦ κόσμου. Sometimes one sees bumper stickers that imply that the only difference between believers and unbelievers rests in the forgiveness of sins. Jesus says that there is a greater difference; believers have a new nature created within by grace, and this is something the world also perceives and despises.

So Jesus prays for the holy Father's protection of his disciples because they will remain in the world to do the work he has commissioned them to do:

vv. 15,16 — *"My prayer is not that you take them out of the world but that you protect them from the evil one. They are not of the world, even as I am not of it."*

One might expect in view of the hatred of the world that Jesus would ask the Father to spare the disciples by taking them from the world. But "I have sent them into the world" (v. 18) to be messengers, ambassadors of the kingdom. The disciples have a "great commission" to fulfill, a race to run before they will be called home. Protection, not removal is called for.

The NIV translates τοῦ πονηροῦ as "evil one," opting for the masculine as it did in the Lord's Prayer. This is preferable to viewing it as a neuter, which would yield the more general translation "protect them from evil." Paul reminded the Ephesians that the Christian's struggle in the world is against Satan and his forces (Eph 6:12). However, in the final anaylsis either translation amounts to much the same thing since Satan's hand is so inextricably found in the evil that surrounds us.

Jesus repeats the thought of verse 14, "they are not of the world . . . ," as the basis for his prayer for protection.

v. 17 — *"Sanctify them by the truth; your word is truth."*

Jesus began this section of his prayer with the address, Πάτερ ἅγιε *"holy* Father." His prayer is that the Πάτερ ἅγιος now *sanctify* (ἁγία-σον) the disciples. *Sanctify* means to "set apart," specifically for God, the one who is *sanctus*. The disciples will remain in the world, but they are no longer part of it. In the previous verses the Lord had requested protection from the evil one, the "negative" part of his prayer for the disciples. Here the matter is stated positively: set them apart, conse-crate them, keep them separate as they do the work given them.

As Jesus has said earlier, this is all to be accomplished through the blessed operation of the word of truth. "If you hold to my teaching, you are really my disciples. Then you will know the truth, and the truth will set you free" (Jn 8:31,32). Truth declares in the word the liberating message of the gospel; by the truth of the word the disci-ples have been given grace upon grace. Paul could say of the truth he had been given in the word: "It is the power of God for the salvation of everyone who believes" (Ro 1:16). It was truth given by the wisdom of God that had operated on the disciples' hearts to create saving faith; the same truth would preserve them in their sanctifying faith.

"Your word is truth" is more than just saying "it is true." The Word equals truth. The Bible is more than a true book; it is truth, the ultimate standard of teaching and life. "How precious is the Book Divine, By inspiration giv'n! Bright as a lamp its doctrines shine To guide our souls to heav'n" (TLH 285:1).

v. 18 — *"As you sent me into the world, I have sent them into the world."*

Jesus is the one sent who now sends. He had received a "great commission" from his Father which was near completion; he will soon give a "great commission" to the small group of men with him to proclaim the message of truth. Both Jesus and the disciples were sent "into the world" (εἰς τὸν κόσμον). The story of amazing grace from the Father's heart was to continue: Christ came to save a world in rebellion against God; the disciples were to proclaim reconcilia-tion to a world that would hate them for it. Yet God's grace in Christ would be proclaimed "to save the world through him" (Jn 3:17).

v. 19 — *"For them I sanctify myself, that they too may be truly sanctified."*

Jesus closes this portion of his prayer with the reminder that it is truly the prayer of a priest: Christ "sets himself apart"(ἁγιάζω ἐμαυτόν), consecrates himself, for the sake of (ὑπὲρ) the disciples, so that they, in turn, may produce an act of consecration. Jesus refers plainly to what is about to take place. His redemptive work on the cross would complete and complement the redemptive work of his active obedience to gain full and sure salvation to all who would believe in him, in particular at this juncture, the disciples.

Jesus states that his consecration as the high priest would accomplish a consecration in his disciples for their work that would not be a mere outward consecration. They would be consecrated ἐν ἀληθείᾳ, "in truth." In view of Jesus' prior use of this word in connection with the Scriptures, to translate "truly" would appear weak. The disciples were to be continually protected, strengthened and motivated — in a word, *consecrated* — in connection with "the truth." One would expect the actual adverbial form, ἀληθῶς, if Jesus' only point were that the disciples' consecration would be genuine.

## Homiletical Suggestions

This reading fits well the emphases usually attached to this Sunday of the church year. We have just celebrated the Ascension of the Lord; this portion of the High Priestly Prayer is reminiscent of Jesus' promise at the ascension to continue to guard and keep his disciples. It also looks forward to the celebration of Pentecost as Jesus emphasizes the power of the word.

It is this latter thought that appears to be most important in the text. As Jesus prays for his disciples, he constantly appeals to his heavenly Father to grant protection to them, to sanctify them by the word, "that name you gave me." We could synthesize the thrust of the text as: Jesus, the great High Priest, prays for the power of the word for the protection and consecration of his disciples.

Under such a synthesis the importance of the word for the disciples is elevated as the main thought. Jesus, the great High Priest, prays for his disciples' protection from evil and consecration in their work — all to be accomplished in connection with the word. The Lord's disciples today need the same word for their protection and consecration. The same High Priest continues to supply their need.

Sermons emphasizing the need for the word are (and should be) a staple item for Christian congregations. This particular text reinforces the fact that the Lord himself sees this need as a top priority for his people. Gathering these thoughts together leads to an outline along these lines:

**The Word Is For His Workers**

1. By it they are protected from evil (vv. 11b-16)
2. By it they are consecrated in service (vv. 17,18)

If we wish to emphasize Jesus' role in praying for these blessings of the word, the following outline along the same lines might be used:

**Your Priest Prays For You**

1. That his word will protect you (vv. 11b-16)
2. That his word will lead you in service (vv. 17,18)

Shifting the emphasis slightly to reflect Jesus' observation that the word separates his disciples from the world yields a different treatment. Keying off Jesus' words, "Your word is truth," is this outline:

**The Truth Brings Consequences**

1. It separates us from the world (vv. 11b-16)
2. It sends us to the world (vv. 17,18)

# PENTECOST

## The Scriptures

Old Testament — *Ezekiel 37:1-14*
Epistle — *Acts 2:22-36*
Gospel — *John 7:37-39a*

## The Text — John 7:37-39a

John chapter seven gives the time setting and theological setting for these words of Jesus chosen as a Pentecost text. The time setting is not Pentecost but the Jewish Feast of Tabernacles (Jn 7:2). The theological setting is that there is great confusion about Jesus (Jn 7:3-52). Even Jesus' brothers do not understand his kingdom; in fact, although Jesus' brothers know he is someone great, John states that at this point they do not believe in him (Jn 7:5). There is theological confusion about Jesus also among the people in Jerusalem celebrating the Feast of Tabernacles. The views about Jesus' character range from "He is a good man" to "No, he deceives the people" (Jn 7:12). The views about Jesus' ranged from "He is the Christ" to "He is the Prophet" to "He is an imposter who should be removed from influencing the people" (cf. Jn 7:40-44). In this setting Jesus preaches.

v. 37 — *On the last and greatest day of the Feast, Jesus stood and said in a loud voice, "If anyone is thirsty, let him come to me and drink."*

The Feast of Tabernacles was celebrated from the fifteenth to the twenty-first day of the Jewish month Tisri, which generally corresponds to our month of October. The Feast of Tabernacles was a thankgiving festival for the harvest of corn and wine (Dt 16:13) and a festival of remembrance for the Lord's abiding presence when the Israelites wandered in the wilderness and lived in booths (Lv 23:39-43). The Jews reenacted for one week the living in booths by constructing thousands of booths and tents outside the walls of Jerusalem.

John says that Jesus made his loud invitation for the thirsty to drink from him "on the last and greatest day of the Feast." Most commentators think this "greatest day" refers to the "closing assembly" held on the eighth day (Lv 23:36).

When we know the customs followed at the Feast of Tabernacles, we can appreciate the aptness of Jesus' use of word-pictures involving thirst and drinking. As Jesus fittingly used the illustration of "living water" when he spoke to the Samaritan woman at the well (Jn 4) and the illustration of "bread of life" when he spoke to the five thousand whom he had miraculously fed with five loaves and two fish (Jn 6), so here Jesus' use of water fits the custom followed at the Feast of Tabernacles. In his work *The Gospels*, Ylvisaker writes about a custom observed at the Feast of Tabernacles:

> On each of the seven festal days, the officiating priest took a golden vessel at the morning service, and filled it with water from the fountain of Siloam in the Kidron valley, mixed the water with the wine of the drink offering, and poured it into two perforated silver bowls on the west of the altar for the burnt offering, while the trumpets were sounded and praise was sung. The people chanted Isa. 12:3: "Therefore with joy shall ye draw water out of the wells of salvation."

As the one of whom Moses and the prophets wrote, Jesus, who is the world's salvation described by Isaiah, stood and proclaimed in a loud voice: "If anyone is thirsty, let him come to me and drink."

The importance of the message as well as the confusion of the populace called for Jesus to stand and shout. This was not the type of controlled setting he had when he sat down and preached in Nazareth's synagogue (Lk 4) or when his disciples came to him on the mount and he sat and taught (Mt 5:1). Certain times call for a standing and "shouting" preacher.

Such was the case at the first Pentecost Festival after Jesus had ascended into heaven. In fulfillment of Jesus' promise that the apostles would receive power when the Holy Spirit came on them (Ac 1:8), when the day of Pentecost came there was a sound like the blowing of a violent wind, and then what seemed to be tongues of fire came to rest on the disciples. The sound of the wind caused a crowd to gather in bewilderment. Some were amazed and perplexed and some mocked. At such a time of confusion Peter stood up and raised his voice and addressed the crowd (Ac 2:14).

The message of Peter at the Feast of Pentecost was the same as the message of Jesus at the Feast of Tabernacles, and it is our message today: salvation!

In our text Jesus proclaimed: "If anyone is thirsty, let him come to me and drink." Are men by nature thirsty? Yes, but for what? We agree with Job's friend Eliphaz that man is by nature vile and corrupt and "drinks up evil like water." Man is thirsty — for evil. By nature dead in transgressions and sins (Eph 2:1), every man enters life like the dead and dry bones that Ezekiel saw in our Old Testament lesson. "If a man is thirsty," shouted Jesus. Jesus knew how to make a man thirsty; he could unmask man's sin like no other. In fact, before he went up to the Feast of Tabernacles, he had told his brothers, "The world cannot hate you, but it hates me because I testify that what it does is evil" (Jn 7:7). To those who despaired of their own righteousness through contrition for sin Jesus said: "Come to me and drink." He invited all such thirsty ones to come to him for forgiveness of sins, life and salvation.

And so Peter preached at Pentecost. The Pentecost people were not thirsting for Jesus Christ, religious though they were. But Peter stood up and made many thirsty: " 'Therefore let all Israel be assured of this: God has made this Jesus, whom you crucified, both Lord and Christ.' When the people heard this, they were cut to the heart and said to Peter and the other apostles, 'Brothers, what shall we do?' " (Ac 2:36,37).

Like Jesus, Peter cut through the outward religious piety of the Pentecost crowd and by setting their evil works before them revealed to them their parched, bone-dry, dead condition before God. And Peter directed thirsty ones to God's salvation in Jesus in the means of grace: "Repent and be baptized, every one of you, in the name of Jesus Christ for the forgiveness of your sins. And you will receive the gift of the Holy Spirit" (Ac 2:38). And about three thousand drank from the well of salvation.

And so in our twentieth century when man is religious but not repentant, preachers must cut through the smugness and pride of man to expose his sin-parched condition, that people might become contrite and thirsty. And to the thirsty penitent we will proclaim the Water of Life, the well of salvation: Jesus Christ, "the atoning sacrifice . . . for the sins of the whole world" (1 Jn 2:2).

vv. 38,39a — *"Whoever believes in me, as the Scripture has said, streams of living water will flow from within him." By this he meant the Spirit, whom those who believed in him were later to receive.*

As already pointed out in this study, the Apostle John in chapter 7 shows that the festival crowd held a variety of opinions about Jesus: good man, deceiver of people, the Prophet, the Christ. The last, of course, is the correct view; Jesus is the promised Christ. (It seems in John 7 that those who said "the Prophet" did not equate this with "the Christ." We know that when Moses mentions "the Prophet" in Deuteronomy 18 he is referring to Jesus, the Christ.)

But we also know that even the apostles, who in their self-appointed spokesman Peter confessed Jesus as "the Christ, the Son of the

living God" (Mt 16:16), did not fully understand how the kingdom of
the Christ would come. Peter did not understand the need for the
cross, as Matthew 16:21-23 indicates. And even after the resurrection
and before the ascension the apostles did not fully understand the
kingdom of Christ. Before Jesus ascended the apostles had asked
him, "Lord, are you at this time going to restore the kingdom to
Israel?" (Ac 1:6). Why had not Jesus set them straight at that point?
Well, they would not fully understand his kingdom until the outpouring of the Holy Spirit. He had said to them in the upper room, "I have
much more to say to you, more than you can now bear. But when he,
the Spirit of truth, comes, he will guide you into all truth" (Jn
16:12,13).

And in our sermon text: " 'Whoever believes in me, as the Scripture
has said, streams of living water will flow from within him.' By this
he meant the Spirit, whom those who believed in him were later to
receive."

After the outpouring of the Holy Spirit at Pentecost the apostles
had no more questions about "restoring the kingdom to Israel." In
his Pentecost sermon Peter preached that Jesus by his resurrection
from the dead was placed on David's throne and now was exalted to
the right hand of the Father (Ac 2:29-33).

And believing in Jesus and having a Holy Spirit-given understanding of the kingdom caused "streams of living water" to flow
from the apostles and the other Jerusalem Christians. Scattered
throughout Judea and Samaria by the persecution of Saul, the Jerusalem Christians "preached the word wherever they went" (Ac 8:4).
Philip preached in Samaria, followed by Peter and John (Ac 8). Peter
preached to a gathering of Gentiles at Cornelius' house. And after
the persecutor Saul was baptized and filled with the Holy Spirit, the
streams of living water flowed throughout the Roman world. The
promise of Jesus at the Feast of Tabernacles was fulfilled in a special
way at the Feast of Pentecost. And to this day the Holy Spirit poured
out at Pentecost works in Christians the attitude expressed by Peter
and John: "We cannot help speaking about what we have seen and
heard" (Ac 4:20).

## Homiletical Suggestions

The preacher will want to bring out the festival note common to
the text from the Feast of Tabernacles, and to the Pentecost Festival
after Jesus' ascension, when the great outpouring of the Holy Spirit
took place. Both Tabernacles and Pentecost were harvest festivals
and were celebrated at the time when crops were gathered in. John

the Baptist and Jesus himself used harvest illustrations for the calling and gathering of God's elect. Pentecost began the great ingathering into the holy Christian church, the communion of saints.

But how can spiritually dead men respond to the harvest call? Luther expressed best the Christian's acknowledgment to the Holy Spirit, the Lord and Giver of life, for the gift of faith: "The Holy Ghost has called me by the gospel."

This text teaches us that the Holy Spirit uses us Christians to reach others to show them their spiritually parched condition and to point the thirsty to Jesus Christ.

So each Christian is to be like the child who is the first to find the park's drinking fountain on a hot summer's day. The child drinks and drinks, quenching his thirst. And then he calls out to his playmates scattered throughout the park searching for the fountain, "Here it is; come and drink; it's good!"

Our suggested outlines:

## Join The Pentecost Celebration

1. Let Jesus quench your spiritual thirst (v. 37)
2. Let the Holy Spirit use you to invite others to drink of salvation (vv. 38,39a)

## Pentecost Still Refreshes

1. Come to Jesus if you are thirsty for forgiveness (v. 37)
2. Point the spiritually dry to Jesus (vv. 38,39a)

# HOLY TRINITY —
# FIRST SUNDAY AFTER PENTECOST

## The Scriptures

> Old Testament — *Deuteronomy 6:4-9*
> Epistle — *Romans 8:14-17*
> Gospel — *John 3:1-17*

## The Text — John 3:1-17

The words of our text are the second of three testimonies concerning Jesus. In chapter two John relates how Jesus cleansed the temple. This incident meant something more than purifying the temple area. It was also a sign that Jesus was the Messiah, for the Old Testament Scripture had promised that the Messiah would suddenly come to his temple (Mal 3:1) and in place of the sanctuary would raise up his own glorious temple (Zec 6:12,13). Following out text is John the Baptist's testimony about Jesus. Jesus is the bridegroom, while John as the best man prepares the way and gives way to his Lord.

The testimony in our text is a conversation between Jesus and Nicodemus, a man who represented the best in Jewish religion and learning. Jesus' testimony to Nicodemus begins with a preachment of repentance. Then follows an explanation of Jesus' mission. God became a man to win salvation for all, and the only way to that salvation is faith in his work. This conversation is a grand summary of the gospel.

v. 1 — *Now there was a man of the Pharisees named Nicodemus, a member of the Jewish ruling council.*

As a Pharisee Nicodemus was accustomed to practicing religious puritanism, separating himself from the Gentiles, and following the law of Moses fanatically. He was a member of the Sanhedrin (7:50), and he was a scribe, a rabbi learned in the Old Testament Scriptures. Jesus calls Nicodemus "Israel's teacher" (v. 10).

v. 2 — *He came to Jesus at night and said, "Rabbi, we know you are a teacher who has come from God. For no one could perform the miraculous signs you are doing if God were not with him."*

Nicodemus may have visited Jesus at night simply because that was the normal time for quiet discussion of deep subjects, or his visit may have been conditioned by fear. Other teachers of the law had denounced Jesus as one who was "possessed by Beelzebub" (Mark 3:22). They obviously did not share Nicodemus' opinion of Jesus.

What effect Jesus' words had on Nicodemus we are not told. John is not so concerned about providing all the historical details as he is about offering testimonies concerning Jesus.

Nicodemus addressed Jesus as "Rabbi," the usual title of respect given to Jewish teachers. The word comes from the Hebrew רַב which means "great or mighty" and was made a title of honor meaning "master" or "teacher."

When Nicodemus says οἴδαμεν, "we know," he means not the other members of the Sanhedrin, but rather the "many people" referred to in 2:23.

A Jewish maxim stated that no sinner, i.e. a breaker of the law, could perform a miracle. Many believed God was with Jesus when they saw the miraculous signs which he did, but Jesus wanted Nicodemus to understand that believing is more than being impressed by signs or having a sincere interest in him as a teacher.

The Greek phrase μετ αὐτοῦ means that God was with Jesus in the sense of association; the preposition σύν would mean God was with Jesus to help him.

The warning is in place that people not look to Jesus as only a teacher of God's law or a great leader of men. They need to know him as the Savior from sin.

v. 3 — *In reply Jesus declared, "I tell you the truth, no one can see the kingdom of God unless he is born again."*

The two Greek verbs ἀπεκρίθη and εἶπεν reveal that what Jesus is about to say to Nicodemus is very important. Jesus knows Nicodemus' innermost thoughts (2:25) and understands exactly what he needs to hear. With the words ᾽Αμὴν ἀμὴν λέγω σοι Jesus assures Nicodemus that his words are absolutely true, for he speaks with authority.

Jesus disregards Nicodemus' compliment about being a teacher from God. He will talk about his person later. His first words to Nicodemus are a preachment of repentance. A person needs to be born again. A spiritual birth is required. Jesus shatters all ideas of work-righteousness. Being a Jew, being a Pharisee, being a member of the Sanhedrin, being famous as a scribe have not gotten Nicodemus into the kingdom.

Entrance into the kingdom of God is of vital importance. This kingdom is unlike the kingdoms of the world. It is a kingdom established by Jesus and existing only where he rules with his power and grace. It is the holy Christian church, which consists of all believers in Jesus throughout the ages. Unless Nicodemus is born again he will not see (ἰδεῖν) the kingdom, i.e., have an experience of it.

Before Jesus proclaimed the sweet message of the gospel he impressed upon Nicodemus the need for repentance. Those who feel they are in the kindom of God because of who they are or what they have done need the stern preachment of repentance today too.

v. 4 — *"How can a man be born when he is old?" Nicodemus asked. "Surely he cannot enter a second time into his mother's womb to be born!"*

Nicodemus realizes that Jesus is not speaking about physical birth. The Greek interrogative beginning with μὴ reveals that Nicodemus understands the answer to his question to be "no." He understands that Jesus has some other kind of birth in mind. Nicodemus is actually asking how such a birth can take place. He is looking for an explanation of what Jesus has just said.

v. 5 — *Jesus answered, "I tell you the truth, no one can enter the kingdom of God unless he is born of water and the Spirit."*

A person can contribute no more to his spiritual birth than he did to his physical birth. The Holy Spirit must give a person the new birth. The Spirit does this in baptism. It is important to note that Jesus does not separate the Spirit from the water of baptism, as if baptism were just a sign of repentance and that the Spirit came later. The Greek preposition ἐξ (denoting source) has as its object the words ὕδατος καὶ πνεύματος ("water and Spirit"). Jesus says God's Spirit works in the water of baptism to accomplish the new birth.

Nicodemus knew only the baptism of John the Baptist, but this sacrament admitted people to the kingdom as surely as did the baptism which Jesus instituted later.

Baptism is not optional in the church. Anyone who despises and refuses baptism, Jesus says, cannot enter his kingdom, for such willful disobedience to Jesus' clear command and invitation is an expression of damning unbelief. Those inclinded to think lightly of their own baptism or the baptism of those over whom God has given them charge need to take note.

v. 6 — *"Flesh gives birth to flesh, but the Spirit gives birth to spirit."*

Flesh, mind, human will or imagination cannot bring about the new birth. Flesh can only give birth to what it is, namely flesh. A stream never rises higher than its source. The contrast between the Greek words σάρξ (flesh) and πνεῦμα (spirit) underscores that the former does not merely refer to the human body but to flesh in opposition to spirit. Σάρξ thus includes the soul, the seat of sin. If it is to be regenerated, flesh must be acted on by the Holy Spirit, and this, Jesus has just said, the Spirit does in baptism.

These words of Jesus teach the biblical doctrine of original sin. Though it isn't pleasant to hear, we need to be reminded that we were sinful from conception, for we inherit the guilt and depravity of our parents.

vv. 7,8 — *"You should not be surprised at my saying, 'You must be born again.' The wind blows wherever it pleases. You hear its sound, but you cannot tell where it comes from or where it is going. So it is with everyone born of the Spirit."*

Nicodemus marveled that Jesus insisted on this new birth. He had spent his whole life thinking that works were the way to God and heaven. Jesus tells him not to marvel only, because that might lead to a denial of the possibility of being born again.

Jesus says an analogy for the mystery of the Holy Spirit's working can be found in the wind, whose sound we hear and whose reality we feel, but whose coming and going we cannot explain. The Greek word πνεῦμα may mean either "wind" or "spirit," as may the Aramaic רוּחַ, the word Jesus no doubt actually used. Jesus makes the point that the believer knows the Holy Spirit has been at work in him by the very fact that he believes. This is the point of comparison. We ought not conclude from Jesus' words that the Spirit works arbitrarily or without means.

vv. 9-11 — *"How can this be?" Nicodemus asked. "You are Israel's teacher," said Jesus, "and do you not understand these things? I tell you the truth, we speak of what we know, and we testify to what we have seen, but still you people do not accept our testimony."*

Jesus had pointed Nicodemus away from the *manner* of the Spirit's working to the essential *fact* that the Spirit works, but Nicodemus insists on asking *how* the Spirit works.

As a teacher of the Old Testament, Nicodemus should have understood the things about which Jesus spoke. The word γινώσκεις means not only intellectual comprehension but a knowing which involves the heart. Nicodemus knew quite a lot but still did not understand in his heart because he stressed the how instead of the fact.

There are still those, like Nicodemus, who insist on explanations about the mysteries of the Spirit rather than taking them on faith and finding in them their great comfort and joy.

By use of the word "we" Jesus as *the* Prophet associates himself with the prophets, including most recently John the Baptist, who have provided valid witness of heavenly things. Jesus and the prophets had not only spoken what they knew but had testified to what they had seen. One naturally tells what he knows, but to testify one must have seen.

Jesus does not directly accuse Nicodemus of being an unbeliever, but by the words he uses Jesus gives room for Nicodemus to include himself among those who do not believe if he is still determined to do so. Jesus speaks about the reason for unbelief in verse 19: "Light has come into the world, but men loved darkness instead of light because their deeds were evil."

v. 12 — *"I have spoken to you of earthly things and you do not believe; how then will you believe if I speak of heavenly things?"*

Jesus now refers to himself alone, not because John the Baptist and the prophets had no knowledge of heavenly things, but because he could testify as one who has seen them directly. The earthly things about which Jesus had spoken included faith, repentance, baptism, regeneration, etc. If Nicodemus did not believe upon hearing of these earthly things, Jesus expects that he would not believe either if he spoke to him about heavenly things, such as God's love which moved him to send his Son for our salvation.

v. 13 — *"No one has ever gone into heaven except the one who came from heaven — the Son of Man."*

If an ordinary man were to become a witness of heavenly things, he would first have to ascend into heaven, but no one has ever done this. Jesus, however, was in heaven to begin with, and all he needed to do was to come down from heaven. Man could not rise to God, so God descended to man by means of the incarnation. Jesus identifies himself as the "Son of Man" to underscore that he, the Son of God, assumed human flesh and became a man for the salvation of all mankind. "Son of Man" is Jesus' favorite name for himself and is used over fifty-five times in the four Gospels.

The NIV does not translate the last words of this verse: ὁ ὤν ἐν τῷ οὐρανῷ, "who is in heaven." There is a strong textual evidence for including these words. Jesus did not merely change his place of residence. Though he came down from heaven and now speaks to Nicodemus, he is still in heaven forever united in essence with the Father and the Holy Spirit.

vv. 14,15 — *"Just as Moses lifted up the snake in the desert, so the Son of Man must be lifted up, that everyone who believes in him may have eternal life."*

Jesus has testified to Nicodemus about the way into the kingdom of God. But Jesus is more than a witness; he is the very Savior himself. To describe the salvation he is about to accomplish, Jesus refers to the Old Testament type of the brazen serpent and holds the great antitype of his own crucifixion next to it.

Like the Pharisees of Jesus' day the Children of Israel in the wilderness had rebelled against God. To chastise those who murmured against him God sent fiery serpents, whose bite caused many to die. When the people repented, God directed Moses to make a brazen serpent and to place it on a pole. He promised that all who looked upon it when bitten would be cured (Nu 21:4-9).

God sometimes works through visible signs, so that people may see the invisible by faith. The brazen serpent in the wilderness, like many other signs in the Old Testament, found its full meaning in the person and work of the Son of God, who became a man. When Jesus was lifted up on the cross, he provided salvation for all. In John 12:32 Jesus says, "But I, when I am lifted up from the earth, will draw all men to myself." John adds in verse 33, "He said this to show the kind of death he was going to die."

It is doubtful that all of this was clear to Nicodemus at this time. It was not clear to Jesus' disciples either. They did not understand until after Jesus died and rose again.

"Everyone who believes" (πᾶς ὁ πιστεύων) is like a blank check signed by God himself. Jesus invites Nicodemus to write in his own name. He extends the same invitation to every other sinner in this world. Note the singular. Salvation is always an individual matter.

"Life" (ζωή) is a word that means the life principle. Here it refers to that which makes us alive spiritually. Whoever looks to Jesus in faith is made alive in and through him, and this life goes on forever. Death is only a transition from life in this world to life in the next.

v. 16 — *"For God so loved the world that he gave his one and only Son, that whoever believes in him shall not perish but have eternal life."*

The Greek particle γάρ, used here and again in verse 17, reveals that these verses are also Jesus' words and not John's reflections on what Jesus has said. Consequently it seems inappropriate to begin a new paragraph at verse 16, as the NIV does.

In this verse Jesus sums up the entire gospel message. It has rightly been called "the gospel in a nutshell." If a person knows and believes only these truths, he is saved; he has eternal life. This is God's plan of salvation; he who came down from heaven confirms it!

The Greek word οὕτως indicates the manner and degree to which God loved the world. The verb ἠγάπησεν is placed ahead of the subject to emphasize it: God *loved* the world. This verb refers to the love of

God which understands how wicked and helpless mankind is but still is determined to rescue mankind. The aorist reveals that it is a love which extends back into eternity and culminates in Jesus' coming into the world.

The universality of this salvation has been revealed in the name "Son of Man" in verse 13 and the words "everyone who believes" in verse 15. It is underscored by the object of God's love, namely, "the world." God's love extends to all people of the world without exception.

The verb ἔδωκεν ("he gave"), which is aorist indicative, says that the gift planned from all eternity was actually made. The Savior is there before Nicodemus. The gift includes all that God has done for our salvation: the incarnation, the crucifixion, etc.

The word μονογενῆ (translated here as "one and only") is used by John to express the eternal relation of the Son to the Father. The AV translation "only begotten" expresses better, perhaps, the unique relationship of Jesus to the Father.

The verb ἀπόληται never means to suffer annihilation, but denotes instead total and eternal rejection by God. It is defined further as the opposite of being saved (verse 17), as being condemned (verse 18), and as having one's deeds exposed (verse 20).

v. 17 — *"For God did not send his Son into the world to condemn the world, but to save the world through him."*

The gift referred to in verse 16 is the mission of God's Son in the world. The giving of the Son, instead of being an act of justice or judgment, was entirely an act of love. If God's purpose had been to judge the world, it would not have been necessary to send his Son into the world. He could have sent a flood or a fire or some other destructive force.

The verb σωθῇ is passive, with God as the agent. He will use a Mediator, namely his Son, "so that the world might be saved through him."

**Homiletical Suggestions**

Nicodemus represents those in any age who express curiosity about Jesus and the message of God's Word. He was curious about Jesus' person, he questioned how a person could be born again, and he wondered about the work of the Spirit. Jesus, in every case, directed Nicodemus to the essential matters of salvation.

People today may ask questions about the church building and the advantages of membership in the church. They may be attracted by the music, the forms of worship, or the pastor's personality and speaking ability. They may look only at outward things and like Nicodemus have difficulty dealing with the really important matters of repentance, regeneration and salvation. Long-standing members of congregations may sometimes suffer the same malady. This text stresses the importance of looking beneath the outer shell and seeing God's way of salvation.

## Behold The Gospel In A Nutshell

1. Consider the outer shell (vv. 1-9)
2. Enjoy the meat (vv. 10-17)

The curiosity of Nicodemus could serve as the focus of the sermon. The questions of Nicodemus reveal that curiosity can be good if it is inspired by an honest searching for the truth, but curiosity is dangerous when it questions God's way or demands answers that God has not seen fit to provide for us.

## Exercise Your Curiosity Aright

1. The curiosity of unbelief questions God's ways (vv. 1-9)
2. The curiosity of faith accepts God's answers (vv. 10-17)

The First Sunday after Pentecost, coinciding as it does with the historic observance of Trinity Sunday, also affords the opportunity to preach about the Trinity. This text suits that purpose beautifully. The work of each person of the Trinity is clearly defined by Jesus in his conversation with Nicodemus. A synthetic outline of the text is necessary to treat the work of the three persons in the order in which we usually speak of them.

## The Triune God Has Provided Your Salvation

1. The Father gave his Son for you (vv. 16-17)
2. The Son died on the cross for you (vv. 10-15)
3. The Spirit gives you life (vv. 1-9)

# SECOND SUNDAY AFTER PENTECOST

**The Scriptures**

> Old Testament — *Deuteronomy 5:12-15*
> Epistle — *2 Corinthians 4:5-12*
> Gospel — *Mark 2:23-28*

**The Text — Mark 2:23-28**

The Pharisees were often looking for ways to trap Jesus. They were jealous of him because the common people were paying more attention to him than to them. They had spent long years of study in the rabbinical schools, while Jesus had not. They were the experts in the law, and yet the common people listened more eagerly to Jesus. The people were giving him the honor and respect the Pharisees thought they deserved. And they didn't like it.

But there was more behind these hostile confrontations than mere jealousy. The Pharisees trusted in a way of salvation that was contrary to God's plan. They perverted God's plan. They viewed the Old Testament as a book of rules and regulations to be kept in order to earn salvation. They did not recognize that the law with all its rules and regulations dramatically demonstrated that they could not save themselves because they were sinful human beings. For God demanded perfect obedience in the Old Testament as well as in the New. He declared, "Be holy because I, the LORD your God, am holy" (Lev 19:2). Nothing less than perfect obedience was acceptable.

Nor did they grasp the significance of the Old Testament sacrifices or understand the many promises and prophecies concerning the Savior. God had promised to send a Savior who would render the perfect obedience he demanded and who would suffer the punishment which sin deserved. But the Pharisees wanted to earn their own salvation. They wanted to be honored by God and man for their piety. Jesus pointed out their hypocrisy and demonstrated that it is impossible for a human being to save himself. Jesus came to save sinners. The Pharisees didn't realize they needed a Savior from sin. Their opposition to Jesus was a result of this lack of understanding.

That lack of understanding and their legalistic approach are very evident in the text we are considering. Our Savior addressed those problems because he had an important truth for them to learn.

vv. 23,24 — *One Sabbath Jesus was going through the grainfields, and as his disciples walked along, they began to pick some heads of grain. The Pharisees said to him, "Look, why are they doing what is unlawful on the Sabbath?"*

Jesus and his disciples were walking along a path that led through a grainfield. Since they were hungry, the disciples began to pluck some of the ripe heads of grain and eat them. The Sinaitic law code permitted this (Dt 23:25).

But the Pharisees objected to what the disciples were doing, because it was the Sabbath. God had commanded that on the Sabbath no work was to be done (Ex 20:8-10; Dt 5:12-15). Over the years the Jewish legal experts had gone to great lengths to define exactly which activities were permissible on the Sabbath and which were to be forbidden. The law did not permit harvesting of grain. According to their way of thinking, the disciples, by picking the heads of grain, were harvesting. So they were doing work forbidden by the tradition of the elders.

The Pharisees called Jesus' attention to this apparent violation of Sabbath law. But their remarks were really aimed at Jesus. In effect they were saying to him, "What's wrong with you? You're supposed to be a great religious teacher, and you're allowing your disciples to do something contrary to the law."

Jesus' disciples were not guilty of any wrongdoing. The Pharisees were in the wrong. They had added their own rules to God's law; and some of their rules were not only additions to God's laws, they directly contradicted God's Word. As Jesus told them on another occasion, "Isaiah was right when he prophesied about you hypocrites; as it is written: 'These people honor me with their lips, but their hearts are far from me. They worship me in vain; their teachings are but rules taught by men.' You have let go of the commands of God and are holding on to the traditions of men" (Mk 7:6-8).

Not only had the Pharisees gone beyond what God's law required, they had misunderstood the purpose of the law altogether. They claimed to be experts in the Old Testament, but were ignorant of what the Scriptures really taught. Jesus pointed out their error by reminding them of a well-known incident from the life of King David:

vv. 25,26 — *He answered, "Have you never read what David did when he and his companions were hungry and in need? In the days of Abiathar the high priest, he entered the house of God and ate the consecrated bread, which is lawful only for priests to eat. And he also gave some to his companions."*

When David was fleeing for his life from Saul, he and his companions were hungry and had nothing to eat (cf. 1 Sa 21:1-6). When they arrived at the tabernacle, they were given the bread of presentation even though only the priests were supposed to eat this bread (cf. Lev 24:5-9). And yet no one, not even the Pharisees, would have accused David and his men of sin. For "in the case of necessity, above all, love is the fulfillment of the Law, and no one ever thought of censuring David for his action" (Kretzmann). Jesus' point was clear — if David wasn't guilty of sin when he ate the bread of presentation when he was hungry, Jesus' disciples weren't guilty either for picking heads of grain on the Sabbath when they were hungry.

There is, however, an apparent problem in our text that needs to be addressed briefly. Jesus speaks of Abiathar as the high priest, while the account in 1 Samuel says that Ahimelech was high priest at that time. Unbelieving scholars try to use this as proof that either Jesus was mistaken or that the Bible is fallible.

But there are possible solutions of this so-called "problem." Ahimelech was the father of Abiathar. It is quite possible that they each had the same name — Ahimelech/Abiathar. This was not uncommon in ancient times. If this was the case, then Jesus was merely calling Ahimelech by his other name. But another and perhaps better solution also presents itself. We know that Abiathar became high priest after his father's death. Abiathar undoubtedly served with his father. Jesus mentions him as the better known of the two. Even though he was not yet high priest, Jesus refers to him as high priest because that is what he later became. It is much the same as if we said that King David killed Goliath even though we know that David was not yet king when that event took place.

v. 27 — *Then he said to them, "The Sabbath was made for man, not man for the Sabbath."*

Jesus states an important principle: "The Sabbath was made for man, not man for the Sabbath." God created man first. Then he established the Sabbath for the benefit of man. The Sabbath was meant to serve man, not to enslave him. God had man's best interests in mind. There is, of course, value in taking a day off from work for the sake of one's physical and emotional well-being. But our Lord also had a more important purpose in mind. He intended the Sabbath observance to benefit his people spiritually — not by slavish observance of the letter of the law, but by offering the believer a special opportunity to worship, to study God's Word and meditate on his plan of salvation. God intended the Sabbath to be a regular opportunity for man to learn God's way of salvation as well as God's will for his earthly life. He did not intend it as a legalistic requirement that man would have to meet in order to save himself.

As part of the ceremonial law the Sabbath also served as a type of the far greater rest God was providing his people ("sabbath" means "rest"). As a type its function would cease when its antitype appeared. When Jesus' redemptive work on this earth was done, the Old Testament ceremonial law was abrogated. As Paul wrote to the Colossians, "Therefore do not let anyone judge you by what you eat or drink, or with regard to a religious festival, a New Moon celebration or a Sabbath day. These are a shadow of the things that were to come; the reality, however, is found in Christ" (Col 2:16,17).

The writer to the Hebrews tells us, "There remains, then, a Sabbath-rest for the people of God" (Heb 4:9). The Old Testament Sabbath pointed ahead to the rest that our Savior would bring — the rest that we have in the forgivness of sins and the ultimate rest we will enjoy fully in heaven. Jesus invites us to partake of that rest when he says, "Come to me, all you who are weary and burdened, and I will give you rest. Take my yoke upon you and learn from me, for I am gentle and humble in heart, and you will find rest for your souls" (Mt 11:28,29).

But the Pharisees did not understand any of this. They had no grasp of God's plan or purpose. Neither did they understand who Jesus really was. And so Jesus continues:

v. 28 — *"So the Son of Man is Lord even of the Sabbath."*

Jesus referred to himself as the "Son of Man" — the Messianic title he preferred because of all the false political hopes attached to the title "Christ." He told them, "So the Son of Man is Lord even of the Sabbath." As true God from all eternity he had instituted the Sabbath and as the long promised Messiah he was the fulfillment of the Sabbath. If only the Pharisees had known who he was, they never would have accused him of letting his disciples violate the Sabbath. If only the Pharisees had recognized him as their Savior, they would have been willing to sit at his feet and listen to his teaching. But they did not want the kind of Savior Jesus came to be, and so their opposition to him intensified.

## Homiletical Suggestions

This text deals with the problem of legalism. By nature all of us are legalists. We're born that way. Our sinful nature wants us to think that we can earn our own salvation. It wants us to think that the purpose of God's law is to show us how we are to save ourselves. Like the Pharisees, we also have the tendency to want to add human rules and regulations to the holy will of God. This text serves as a warning to watch out for that tendency. We want to avoid legalism in everything we do and say.

Sunday is not a New Testament Sabbath. Nor is there any ceremonial law for people living in the New Testament era. So we do not want to turn Sunday into a New Testament Sabbath by making all kinds of rules and regulations for Sunday observance. In Christian freedom Sunday was chosen by the early Christians as their regular day for worship, but not as the only permissible day. In the Old Testament God commanded, "Worship on the Sabbath!" To us in the New Testament he merely says, "Worship!" We want to be careful about making statements like, "All God requires of us is one hour a week" — as if our Sunday worship were some sort of legal requirement that we are to meet in order to gain God's favor. God wants our whole life to be a life of worship. Faithful Christians will therefore want to study God's Word and sing his praise every day of their lives.

We might want to deal with the subject of legalism on the basis of this text in this way:

**Beware Of Legalism**

1. Understand the meaning of God's law (vv. 23-26)
2. Recognize its purpose (vv. 27,28)

We might also want to explain the meaning and purpose of the Sabbath and how it applies to us today by pointing to the one who both established it and fulfilled it. Using the last verse of the text as our theme we can treat the text in this way:

**Jesus Is The Lord Of The Sabbath**

1. He established it (vv. 23-27)
2. He fulfilled it (v. 27)

The Sabbath was meant not to enslave God's people, but to benefit them. That is especially true for us who live in the New Testament era. We know the blessed rest we have in the forgiveness and salvation our Savior won for us on the cross. Therefore, we want to be careful not to slip into dead formalism in worship or legalistic observance of religious holidays or outward forms. Rather we want to express our appreciation for all the blessings God has given us by glorifying God in everything we do and by daily meditating on the blessing of forgiveness. We can express those thoughts by using this outline:

**Enjoy Your Sabbath Rest**

1. In true worship, not dead formalism (vv. 23-27)
2. In deliverance from sin, not legalistic observance (vv. 23, 24,27,28)

One final suggestion:

## Look To The Lord Of The Sabbath Day

1. For its correct interpretation
2. For its perfect fulfillment

242

# THIRD SUNDAY AFTER PENTECOST

**The Scriptures**

Old Testament — *Genesis 3:9-15*
Epistle — *2 Corinthians 4:13-18*
Gospel — *Mark 3:20-35*

**The Text — Mark 3:20-35**

According to the parallel account in Matthew 12:22-37, the visit by Jesus' family and scribes from Jerusalem came after Jesus made it possible for a blind and mute demon-possessed man to see and talk.

This miracle occurred after Jesus had returned to Capernaum from the borders of Galilee on his second tour of Galilee. By this time many were asking, "Could this be the Son of David?" (Matthew 12:23).

Jesus' visitors, however, came to different conclusions. Jesus' family decided he must be out of his mind. The scribes from Jerusalem accused him of being in league with Satan.

v. 20 — *Then Jesus entered a house, and again a crowd gathered, so that he and his disciples were not even able to eat. When his family heard about this, they went to take charge of him, for they said, "He is out of his mind."*

Jesus was beginning to attract attention from many people. Among them were sincere inquirers, bitter opponents and curiosity seekers.

Jesus' family became concerned about the attention Jesus was getting. Jesus' brothers (half brothers or cousins) didn't believe in him at first (Jn 7:5). Later some did (Ac 1:14). They heard about his miracles, about the people's desire to make Jesus king, and about the hostility of the religious leaders of Israel toward Jesus. The family thought Jesus was "out of it" (ἐξέστη). They decided to take him home for his own protection. They resolved to do this by force, if necessary.

People also accused Paul of being insane (Ac 26:24; 2 Cor 5:13). Committed Christians today are sometimes called deluded.

v. 22 — *And the teachers of the law who came down from Jerusalem said, "He is possessed by Bellzebub! By the prince of demons he is driving out demons."*

The Greek has *Beelzeboul*. Beelzebub was the Ekron god, the "Lord of the Flies." The Jews mocked the false god and his worshipers by changing one consonant. Beelzeboul means "Lord of Dung." Beelzeboul became a nickname for Satan.

The scribes from Jerusalem were "heavy hitters" who'd come down to assist the local religious leaders as they challenged Jesus. They accused Jesus of using the power of Satan to cast out demons.

They couldn't deny Jesus' powerful miracle, so they questioned the source of his power. They concluded that his power was evil.

vv. 23-26 — *So Jesus called them and spoke to them in parables: "How can Satan drive out Satan? If a kingdom is divided against itself, that kingdom cannot stand. If a house is divided against itself, that house cannot stand. And if Satan opposes himself and is divided, he cannot stand; his end has come."*

Jesus loved his enemies and graciously tried to win them. Yet he did so with a parable or comparison. Those who were seeking the truth would find it, but those looking to trap him would be confused and dumbfounded.

The charge was ridiculous. Civil wars don't make a country strong. Patricides, matricides and fratricides don't benefit royal families or common ones.

It is preposterous to suggest Satan advances his kingdom by plundering his allies, the demons. When a ruler attacks his own army, his days as ruler are surely numbered. Satan would be cutting his own throat if he helped Jesus or anyone else cast out demons.

Evil is what some modern men call the God who punishes every sin with hell and forgives every sin only through the death of his Son on the cross. Do you ever call God evil for the good he does in your life through troubles?

v. 27 — *"In fact, no one can enter a strong man's house and carry off his possessions unless he first ties up the strong man. Then he can rob his house."*

Would anyone let a robber take his goods if he could overpower the robber? Robbers, using surprise or a deadly weapon, first try to kill, knock unconscious or tie up the person they intend to rob. Then they can proceed unhindered.

If Jesus can cast out demons, it must be because he has defeated Satan and rendered him powerless to resist. This Jesus was already doing by his preaching and his miracles. But the final battles were still in the future: to endure Calvary's cross and to loosen the cold grip of death. These battles, too, would be won. Satan would be powerless to stop Jesus from plundering his kingdom. Mankind would be freed from the devil's hold through sin.

The gates of hell won't prevail against the church! All demons are subject to Christ (cf. Eph 1:21-22). "The one who is in you is greater than the one who is in the world" (1 Jn 4:4).

vv. 28-30 — *"I tell you the truth, all the sins and blasphemies of men will be forgiven them. But whoever blasphemes against the Holy Spirit will never be forgiven; he is guilty of an eternal sin." He said this because they were saying, "He has an evil spirit."*

Jesus' family came to wrong conclusions; Jesus' enemies attacked deliberately and maliciously. The Spirit had testified the truth about Jesus to them. They knew it, but still spoke evil of Jesus. So Jesus warned them about the terrible sin they were flirting with.

Blaspheming the Holy Spirit is unforgivable because it is a stubborn resisting of the activity of the Holy Spirit, who seeks to work regeneration. It is a persistent sin against better knowledge. The Holy Spirit's testimony has been heard and understood, perhaps even believed. Blaspheming the Holy Spirit is not only *thinking* evil of God, but continuing to *speak* evil of him until death. It will end a person's time of grace before the end of his earthly life and will guarantee his eternal damnation. Obviously, then, no one who worries whether he may have committed this sin has actually committed it.

Take note of the wonderful gospel in the middle of this frank warning: "I tell you the truth, *all* the sins and blasphemies of men will be forgiven them."

vv. 31-35 — *Then Jesus' mother and brothers arrived. Standing outside, they sent someone in to call him. A crowd was sitting around him, and they told him, "Your mother and brothers are outside looking for you." "Who are my mother and my brothers?" he asked. Then he looked at those seated in a circle around him and said, "Here are my mother and my brothers! Whoever does God's will is my brother and sister and mother."*

Remember *why* the members of Jesus' family were coming. They intended to stop his work, by force if necessary. Jesus wasn't disparaging the blessing of a family. He submitted to his parents' authority (Lk 2:51,52). He later provided for Mary from the cross (Jn 19:27). But no one, not his enemies, not Peter (Mt 16:22), not his own relatives or mother would be allowed to interfere with his mission to save us.

Jesus' *real* family are all people who do God's will. "You are all sons of God through faith in Christ Jesus" (Ga 3:26). Those "seated in a circle around him" were those disciples who came to hear him, learn from him, believe him and follow him. They were his *real* family.

Those who *do God's will* are Christians. "I am the vine; you are the branches. If a man remains in me and I in him, he will bear much fruit; apart from me you can do nothing" (Jn 15:5). Baptism is God's way of adopting individuals into his family. God's children, who believe in him, will do his will as a natural result of their faith.

## Homiletical Suggestions

One approach is to focus on the word "family." Usually, we are close to our birth-families. But sometimes we meet others and become even closer to them than we are to our blood relatives. Jesus was closer to believers not of his birth-family than to unbelievers from his natural family.

Jesus' *natural family* misunderstood his mission (vv. 20,21). They tried to stop Jesus from preaching. He had to resist them because he was determined to do the will of his heavenly Father.

The world calls salvation by grace unreasonable, illogical. It may even accuse those who faithfully follow Jesus of being out of their minds.

Jesus' enemies accused him of belonging to *Satan's family* (vv. 22-30). They did this against their better knowledge. But still Jesus dealt patiently with them and tried to warn them. Certainly, Jesus also warns us not to sin against our conscience or speak against what we know God's Word says.

Finally, Jesus shows that *Christians are his real family* (vv. 31-35). Certainly the preacher will call to mind what blessings are ours now because Jesus is our brother and what eternal blessings will be ours. He will also stress that God adopted us by his grace. We didn't earn our way into his family or deserve a place because of blood, or church membership or past performance.

An outline reflecting these thoughts might be:

## Who Is Jesus' Real Family?

1. His birth family? (vv. 20,21,31-33)
2. Satan's family? (vv. 22-30)
3. His adopted family! (vv. 34,35)

Or one could downplay the idea of family and focus on three questions the text might suggest:

## Questions Addressed To Jesus

1. Are you out of your mind? (vv. 20,21)
2. Whose side are you on? (vv. 22-30)
3. Is that any way to treat your family? (vv. 31-35)

The answers are: "No, I'm going to save you. I'm on *your* side against the devil. You're my real family, if you listen to me, believe in me, and thereby do my will."

A final approach focuses on the great humiliation our Savior endured for us. Part one treats the slander of his enemies, how he graciously answered them and warned them. Part two covers the misconceptions of his well-meaning family. He had to continue his work and carefully explained who his real family is. Both parts would allow an application about how to react to evil remarks made about us. An outline would be:

**Behold, Our Slandered Savior**

1. His enemies said, "He is in league with the Devil" (vv. 22-30)
2. His family said, "He's insane" (vv. 20,21,31-35)

One last comment. Let the listener **not** be a spectator in the sermon thinking "Stupid family!" or "Wicked enemies!" Help the listener to see himself as one who consistently fails to understand Christ, who makes impossible demands on him, and who accuses him of evil even though he does all things well. And, of course, let the listener bask in the sure promises of forgiveness shown by Jesus' refusal to back off of his mission; by his power and victory over Satan; by his oath (v. 28) about the forgiveness of all sins and by his declaration that believers are his real family.

# FOURTH SUNDAY AFTER PENTECOST

**The Scriptures**

Old Testament — *Ezekiel 17:22-24*
Epistle — *2 Corinthians 5:1-10*
Gospel — *Mark 4:26-34*

**The Text — Mark 4:26-34**

Jesus is teaching the crowds by the lake (Mk 4:1) and uses the occasion to instruct them on the nature of God's kingdom. Many of the Jews, even Jesus' disciples to a degree, thought that the kingdom of God was a visible entity. They believed that the Messiah would come and restore Israel to a place of prominence among the nations of the world, establishing a replica of the glorious kingdom of David and Solomon. He had to remind them again and again that God's kingdom is not an earthly kingdom. It is a spiritual kingdom. "The kingdom of God does not come with your careful observation, nor will people say, 'Here it is,' or 'There it is,' because the kingdom of God is within you" (Lk 17:20,21). God's kingdom is his rule of grace in the hearts of people. He establishes that rule through the powerful working of his word.

Jesus instructs us concerning the kingdom of God through a wide range of parables. Each parable teaches us about a particular aspect of God's kingdom. The parable of the sower (Mt 13:1-9) shows us how God's word is received. The parable of the weeds (Mt 13:24-30) teaches us that the kingdom is not identical to the visible church, lest we be unduly upset by the hypocrites we might encounter there. The parables of the hidden treasure and the priceless pearl (Mt 13:44-46) teach us to value the kingdom of God as our most valuable possession. The parable of the net (Mt 13:47-50) teaches us to cast out the net of the gospel and leave the judging of results to God on the last day. This is just a sampling of the parables Jesus used to teach the concept of the kingdom of God.

Looking at the parables in this text, we have to ask ourselves, "What particular aspect of the kingdom is Jesus teaching here?" The parable of the mustard seed can be found in Matthew 13:31,32 and Luke 13:18. In these instances, it is paired with the parable of the yeast. The parable of the mustard seed shows how God's kingdom had small beginnings but grew to great proportions. The parable of the yeast applies the same principle to the heart of the individual believer. It starts small but eventually takes over the whole heart. The emphasis in both instances is the remarkable growth of the kingdom.

Only Mark records the parable of the growing seed. By placing it alongside the parable of the mustard seed, he also emphasizes the growth of the kingdom. But there is a subtle difference which gives this text its particular preaching value. The emphasis is on the power of God's word to achieve that growth — both in the heart of the individual and in the world.

vv. 26-29 — *He also said, "This is what the kingdom of God is like. A man scatters seed on the ground. Night and day, whether he sleeps or gets up, the seed sprouts and grows, though he does not know how. All by itself the soil produces grain — first the stalk, then the head, then the full kernel in the head. As soon as the grain is ripe, he puts the sickle to it, because the harvest has come."*

The seed is the word of God. The point of comparison in the parable is this: Just as the seed has some mysterious and wonderful power to grow and produce a harvest, so God's word has a mysterious and wonderful power to grow in the hearts of people and produce a harvest for the Lord. The man who sows the seed has nothing to do with the power which gives growth. So also, anyone who plants the seed of God's word can only stand by and let the word work by itself. We can hinder its growth by planting it carelessly, but we cannot cause it to grow. That is why we pray, "Thy kingdom come." Only God can create faith in the heart of man. As Paul said, "So neither he who plants nor he who waters is anything, but only God, who makes things grow" (1 Co 3:7). (For further support see He 4:12; 1 Pe 1:23; 1 Co 2:4,5.)

Some argue at great length that the one who sows the seed must be, or must not be, Jesus himself. Those who argue it must be Jesus point out that the sower is also pictured as the one who does the harvesting, which is the Lord's work. Those who argue to the contrary say that Jesus could not be pictured as one who is powerless to cause the seed to grow. You will always have such difficulties when you try to press interpretations from the details of a parable instead of sticking to the point of comparison.

The same is true of the Greek word αὐτομάτη ("all by itself"). The adjective modifies "the earth," but is used more in the adverbial sense. Interpreting the earth as the heart of man, which must in some way be responsible for the growth of the seed, would give this parable the exact opposite of its intended meaning. Neither the one who sows the seed nor the one in whom the seed has been planted is responsible for its growth. Instead, the power is in the seed itself, the word of God.

In verses 28 and 29 we see a progression — the stalk, the head, the full kernel in the head, then the harvest. Again, we have a problem if we press the details of the parable into the interpretation. We do see a progression in a Christian's life from the beginning of faith to Christian maturity. "The path of the righteous is like the first gleam of dawn, shining ever brighter till the full light of day" (Pr 4:18). The problem lies in the timing of the harvest. God doesn't always wait for us to reach Christian maturity before he takes us to heaven. The seed which has just sprouted and the seed which has reached maturity have an equal place in God's kingdom. There is no problem, however, if you use the details to embellish the main point rather than creating a separate point for each detail. The point is not when God does the harvesting, but how he prepares the harvest — through the power of his word. When we witness the growing and maturing process in our fellow Christian's life, and in our own lives, we can stand in awe of the power of God's word.

There are two ways we can apply the truth of this parable. For the church as a whole and for everyone who is busy planting the seeds of God's word (be it a pastor, evangelist, teacher, parent, or friend), the message is clear. Our job is planting. God, in his own way and at his own time, will provide the growth.

There is also rich comfort given to the individual Christian in his life of sanctification. We don't always see the progress in our Christian life we would like to see. We can see such progress in others more easily than we can see it in ourselves. But if we apply ourselves to the word of God, the growth will come. We have God's promise (Isa 55:10,11).

vv. 30-32 — *Again he said, "What shall we say the kingdom of God is like, or what parable shall we use to describe it? It is like a mustard seed, which is the smallest seed you plant in the ground. Yet when planted, it grows and becomes the largest of all garden plants, with such big branches that the birds of the air can perch in its shade."*

The mustard plant in Israel grows to ten or fifteen feet, dwarfing its neighbors in the garden and giving the birds a chance to "tent" in its branches. All this from the tiniest seed!

There is no need to argue whether the mustard seed refers to God's word or to Christ. To preach God's word is to preach Christ. Note the similarity with the Old Testament lesson from Ezekiel. "All the trees of the field will know that I the LORD bring down the tall tree and make the low tree grow tall" (Eze 17:24). A different picture with the same message is found in the vision of Nebuchadnezzar, where a stone the Lord cut out destroyed the statue (symoblic of earthly kingdoms) and "became a huge mountain and filled the whole earth" (Da 2:35).

Remember, a parable reveals to us a spiritual truth that would otherwise be hidden from our sight. Who would have believed that the child born in Bethlehem's stable would someday rule such a vast kingdom? Or who could have guessed that a handful of disciples preaching a simple message of salvation through Christ would spread a religion to followers on every continent and in every century? And who knows what God will accomplish through the seeds we plant today?

vv. 33,34 — *With many similar parables Jesus spoke the word to them, as much as they could understand. He did not say anything to them without using a parable. But when he was alone with his own disciples, he explained everything.*

Jesus used parables in his teaching for two reasons. First, the parable was designed to make spiritual truths easier to understand and easier to retain. Likewise today, people may forget much of the sermon we preach to them. But they will remember the timely illustrations we use and the spiritual truths they illustrate. Secondly, Jesus' parables served as a judgment against those who stubbornly remained in the darkness of unbelief (Mk 4:10-12).

These last two verses do not add any thoughts which are central to the text, but they do serve to bring the point of the parables into sharp focus. Jesus' ministry is characterized by his teaching and preaching the word. God's kingdom grows through the power of the word. At times, we foolishly wish that there were more we could do to make God's kingdom grow, as if using the word alone were a limitation. It is not a limitation. It is the means which God ordained and which Jesus used and still uses to establish his kingdom. These parables serve to open our eyes to the unlimited potential of using God's word.

## Homiletical Suggestions

One of the suggestions of this text is to preach a sermon which is personal and practical, not just theoretical. Our specific failure or malady (law) is doubting the power of God's word. So we catch ourselves saying things like, "If my parents had given me a better example when I was young, being a Christian wouldn't be so hard for me." Or, "If my spouse were more cooperative, it would be easier for me to grow in my faith." But God's gospel message can work and does work in spite of the circumstances.

The same kinds of doubts can easily hinder kingdom work. "If only our congregation were larger and had better facilities, maybe more people would visit us." Or "If only I could speak more fluently, maybe I could persuade my neighbor to come to church." But Jesus didn't have a church building to preach in and Moses wasn't fluent. The power to save is in the word. This truth gives us an encouragement to plant the seeds of the gospel, without being discouraged by its apparent lack of success. It does not, however, give us an excuse to present the word carelessly, or to settle for an unwholesome atmosphere in which it is preached.

In preaching on this text, it is important to keep in mind that God's kingdom is invisible. God's church of all believers can never be identified with one visible organization, nor can it ever be measured with statistics. It is a matter of faith. That is why we confess, "I believe in . . . the holy Christian church."

In the following outline, part one would stress our personal use of the word while part three would deal with our using the word to reach out to others.

## God's Word Is Powerful

1. Powerful enough to change a human heart (vv. 26-29)
2. Powerful enough to create a vast kingdom (vv. 30-32)
3. Powerful in the hands of those who use it (vv. 33,34)

The following outlines stress the invisible nature of God's kingdom and how the kingdom grows. In the first outline, Jesus' use of parables together with examples from his ministry could serve as examples of how kingdom work is done in faith.

## Kingdom Work Is A Matter Of Faith

1. Faith that God's word is working (vv. 26-29,33,34)
2. Faith that God's church is growing (vv. 30-32,33,34)

## Look At The Kingdom Through God's Eyes

1. We see the planting; he sees the harvest (vv. 26-29)
2. We see the small seed; he sees the mature plant (vv. 30-32)

## Kingdom Work Takes Patience

1. Patience to let God work (vv. 26-29)
2. Patience to see the end result (vv. 30-32)

# FIFTH SUNDAY AFTER PENTECOST

The Scriptures

Old Testament — *Job 38:1-11*
Epistle — *2 Corinthians 5:14-21*
Gospel — *Mark 4:35-41*

The Text — Mark 4:35-41

The miraculous stilling of the storm is recorded in all three synoptic Gospels (Mt 8:23-27; Lk 8:22-25; and here in Mark ). It probably occurred several months after Jesus began his Galilean ministry. By this time the disciples should have come to know Jesus as the Son of God. They fully deserved it when Jesus rebuked them for their lack of faith.

Mark alone tells us that this incident happened on "that day" that he taught the previously described parables. Other similar "unnecessary" details give the impression of an eyewitness account and support the theory that the source of Mark's Gospel is Peter.

vv. 35,36 — *That day when evening came, he said to his disciples, "Let us go over to the other side." Leaving the crowd behind, they took him along, just as he was, in the boat. There were also other boats with him.*

Large crowds were following Jesus, and he was apparently preaching to them from the boat as he had on other occasions. Small bays with rising hillsides form several natural amphitheatres on the east shore of the Sea of Galilee.

He was in the boat (ὡς ἦν ἐν τῷ πλοίῳ) when he decided to go over to the other side. The sea offered the only relief from the large crowds. But even that route was crowded as indicated by the other boats which were around him (ἄλλα πλοῖα ἦν μετ᾽ αὐτοῦ).

v. 37 — *A furious squall came up, and the waves broke over the boat, so that it was nearly swamped.*

The Sea of Galilee is notorious for its sudden storms, but this one was special. It may have been raised by Jesus to allow an escape from boats that were following. It was certainly raised by him for the purpose of teaching his disciples another lesson.

v. 38 — *Jesus was in the stern, sleeping on a cushion. The disciples woke him and said to him, "Teacher, don't you care if we drown?"*

"In the stern" (ἐν τῇ πρύμνῃ) and "on a cushion" (ἐπὶ τὸ προσκεφάλαιον) are two more details which suggest the vivid reminiscence of an eyewitness. Commentaries offer other translations besides "cushion" for προσκεφάλαιον.

Jesus' peaceful "sleeping" stands in sharp contrast to the disciples' worry and fear. This is the only place where sleep is attributed to Jesus. It lends strong support to his nature as true man.

The rudeness in the disciples' question, "Don't you care" (οὐ μέλει σοι), is an eloquent pointer to their lack of understanding regarding Christ's person. The Son of God is subjected to the rudeness of men.

The storm must have been of unusual force to frighten such veteran fishermen, but that they are "drowning" (ἀπολλύμεθα) is their opinion, not factual assessment of the situation.

v. 39 — *He got up, rebuked the wind and said to the waves, "Quiet! Be still!" Then wind died down and it was completely calm.*

The Greek present imperative "Quiet!" (Σιώπα) is addressed to the wind, and the perfect passive imperative "Be still!" (πεφίμωσο) is spoken to the waves. The cosmic overtones in Mark's Gospel account are evident here by his careful choice of the same terminology which describes Jesus' encounters with demons (1:25; 3:12; 9:25). Compare also the role of the word of God in the creation accounts of Genesis 1 and John 1, as well as in the exodus and the crossing of the Red Sea.

Jesus' commands are followed by a great calm. The man in the boat speaks to the inanimate forces and elements of nature, and they obey him! Others have commanded nature and failed. The Persian King Xerxes had the sea whipped and cursed to no avail. His fleets were destroyed by storms and Greece was saved. There can be only one explanation for this calm. The man in the boat is the LORD of Israel, the God of history and the King of the universe.

vv. 40,41 — *He said to his disciples, "Why are you so afraid? Do you still have no faith?" They were terrified and asked each other, "Who is this? Even the wind and the waves obey him!"*

Two grammatical points are worth noting in verse 40. The present tense "are" (ἐστε) in Jesus' first question and the adverb "still" (οὔπω) in his second question narrow the focus of both questions. He is not rebuking the disciples for the unbelief just displayed by their terror in the boat and the rudeness of their question, which implied that he didn't care about them. Rather, he is inquiring about the fear and unbelief which he reads in their hearts after the storm is over. "Why **are** you so afraid? Do you **still** have no faith?"

Mark's comments in verse 41 confirm this understanding. He notes that the disciples are still terrified and are asking themselves who this is that even the wind and the waves obey him.

Jesus' two questions are not so much an angry rebuke as they are a loving call to repentance, similar to the hurt look which he gave to Peter after the denial, or the repeated question, "Do you love me?" The "faith" (πίστις) which Jesus is looking for is not an intellectual acknowledgment of his divine person and power. Rather it is "faith" in God's helping power present and active in Jesus. When Jesus asks, "Do you still have no faith?" he means specifically faith in God's saving power as this is present and released through him. He is looking for faith in the Old Testament Messiah, the Savior God of Israel and the world.

The disciples still fail to grasp the true nature of Jesus' identity and mission. The revelation of God's love in nature does not change men's hearts and create saving faith. As Luther often points out, natural knowledge of God is law knowledge which inspires fear. The disciples' terror and question confirm what Jesus reads in their hearts.

## Homiletical Suggestions

The stilling of the storm is not merely a demonstration of power. It is a manifestation through which Jesus begins to unveil himself as mankind's Savior from all troubles. It is a Pentecost text through which the Holy Spirit calls people to faith in Jesus. The last sentence of the text is a rhetorical question which invites the response of faith:

### Jesus Is Our Savior God

1. He stills storms in our lives (vv. 35-39)
2. He stills storms in our faith (vv. 40,41)

Law applications in the first part would be drawn from verse 38 and the disciples' accusation that Jesus does not care about them. The storms which God brings into our lives often give us the impression that he is sleeping and doesn't care about us.

The gospel applications are in the fact that even as God "sleeps," he is in control and governing events for our benefit. Just as he lets the storms come into our lives, so he stills them when they have served his purpose.

Law applications in the second part would be drawn from verse 41 and the disciples' continued fear and lack of faith. In spite of all the storm-stilling that God does for us, we continue to doubt him and question him.

The gospel applications are in Jesus' power to read their hearts and his loving questions. He never rebukes them for their rude question in verse 38. With his power and with his questions he continues to display his love for them. The most revealing display, the one which will put his power, his identity, his mission and his love beyond question, will be the display on the cross. His atoning work on the cross will still the storms in the disciples' faith and change their hearts forever.

For those who might like a more catchy theme, the same two parts can be treated under the title:

## Jesus Is Our Storm-Stiller

Other thoughts to flesh out the above skeleton outline would center around faith and doubt. For example, it could be pointed out that faith is little when the object of faith grows little. The disciples' faith was "small" because they let the stormy sea become greater than Jesus sleeping in the bottom of the boat.

Additional material is offered by the use of this miracle in the early Christian church. Art of this period often depicts the church as a boat driven upon a perilous sea. Jesus as the pilot or at the tiller shows that there is nothing to fear. The early Christians took great comfort in this incident as the assurance of Jesus' saving presence during the persecution which threatened to overwhelm them.

Other outlines with which some preachers might be more comfortable include the following:

## Who Is This Whom Even The Winds And Sea Obey?

1. He is the Son of God
2. He is the Christ

The first part would emphasize Jesus' divinity and power; the second, the use of that power as our Savior.

A simple law-gospel outline might be:

## Jesus Is The Storm-Savior

1. He raises storms to expose our doubts
2. He stills storms to remove them

Both the introduction and the sermon itself could be woven around the ancient world's common belief in a storm-god. He was often the chief deity in ancient pantheons. Baal, for example, was the Canaanite and Phoenician storm-god. All the thoughts in the first outline can easily be arranged under this theme, showing the difference between pagan storm-god and Christian Storm-Savior.

All the outlines present the main point of the text, namely, that Jesus is looking for saving faith in him, the Savior God.

# SIXTH SUNDAY AFTER PENTECOST

**The Scriptures**

> Old Testament — *Lamentations 3:22-33*
> Epistle — *2 Corinthians 8:1-9,13,14,21-24a*
> Gospel — *Mark 5:21-24a,35-43*

**The Text — Mark 5:21-24a,35-43**

The events of our text follow those of last Sunday's text by only a few — but most eventful — days. On the east side of the sea of Galilee Jesus had driven the demons out of a man into a herd of pigs. As a consequence, he was asked to leave and went back to Capernaum. From the book of Matthew we learn that on his return he healed a paralytic, then called Matthew and accepted Matthew's invitation to a feast with "sinners." During the discussions which followed Jesus' acceptance of this invitation, Jairus came to Jesus with a special request, and our text begins:

> vv. 21,22a — *When Jesus had again crossed over by boat to the other side of the lake, a large crowd gathered around him while he was by the lake. Then one of the synagogue rulers, named Jairus, came there.*

Mark makes this account extremely vivid by using present tense verbs throughout. Jairus (his name means "Jehovah enlightens") had the important and honored position of synagogue ruler. Such rulers were members of a board which managed the services and other affairs of the synagogue. Jesus had healed the centurion's servant and the nobleman's son in this vicinity. He had also taught in the synagogue. So Jairus had good reason to hope Jesus would help.

> vv. 22b-23 — *Seeing Jesus, he fell at his feet and pleaded earnestly with him, "My little daughter is dying. Please come and put your hands on her so that she will be healed and live."*

"Little daughter" is a term of endearment. Luke tells us that she was an only child. Later in our text we are told she was twelve years old, the age when Jewish girls reached the age of majority. But she is still her father's little girl. This dear child is ἐσχάτως, "at the last," at the point of death. We might ask, "Why did Jairus wait so long?" We are not told. His coming to Jesus might have been a last resort and might explain why the Ruler of all things allowed death and a delay to become a part of the picture, so that Jairus' faith might be tested and thereby strengthened.

His request begins with a Greek ἵνα clause. This ἵνα gives the sense of a courteous imperative to what follows. Although Jesus had healed sick persons from a distance in Capernaum, he had also put his hands on others when he healed them. Jairus asks for the laying on of hands "in order that she may be saved" (ἵνα σωθῇ). In her present state "to be saved" would be the equivalent of being healed, and so the NIV translates.

v. 24a — *So Jesus went with him.*

Here is a man with a serious need. Jesus recognizes the need and immediately goes along with him.

Now comes an interlude in the story (vv. 24b-34). We are told that a large crowd pressed around him. The crowd was curious, but was also inconsiderate, since the press must certainly have delayed Jesus' progress.

But there is yet more delay. A woman subject to bleeding touches him and is healed. Jesus stops to take care of this need. This delay probably is not more than five or ten minutes, but a minute can seem like an eternity in an emergency. But this delay is not accidental. Jesus is putting the faith of Jairus to a wholesome test. The more helpless we are the more distinctly we see that our help comes from the Lord.

v. 35 — *While Jesus was still speaking, some men came from the house of Jairus, the synagogue ruler. "Your daughter is dead," they said. "Why bother the teacher any more?"*

The worst has happened. Some men, either relatives or friends, come to say that the girl is dead. While there is life, there is hope, but now, "No life — so no hope." As far as they are concerned, to take more of Jesus' time would be to bother him (σκύλλεις) unnecessarily. Since the child is dead, Jesus can no longer do what they had hoped for. We note that they give Jesus the title "teacher."

v. 36 — *Ignoring what they said, Jesus told the synagogue ruler, "Don't be afraid; just believe."*

The Greek παρακούω means "hear aside, be unwilling to hear, pay no regard to." Before Jairus is able to say a word, Jesus takes command of the situation. He knows what is going on in the heart of Jairus. He does not want Jairus to give up under the blow of the message. The durative imperatives encourage Jairus, "Do not give way to fear; keep on believing."

v. 37 — *He did not let anyone follow him except Peter, James and John the brother of James.*

For the very personal events that are to follow, it is inappropriate that there be a huge crowd milling around. The crowd is curious, but such is the force of Jesus' personality that he is able to disperse them forthwith. The only ones who are to witness the coming miracle are the inner circle of his disciples, the three who later witnessed his great exaltation on the mount of transfiguration and his most abject humiliation in Gethsemane. Jewish law required two or three witnesses to establish a fact, and these three disciples were those witnesses.

vv. 38-40a — *When they came to the home of the synagogue ruler, Jesus saw a commotion, with people crying and wailing loudly. He went in and said to them, "Why all this commotion and wailing? The child is not dead but asleep." But they laughed at him.*

The Greek θόρυβον means "a noise or uproar." What a scene! Every people has its funeral customs, some very fitting, but also some whose purpose is to mask the reality of death. At that time even the poorest man felt obligated to have a minimum of two flute players and one mourner at the death of his wife. Jairus was a prominent man, and so there would be many more professional mourners there. Matthew mentions the flute players. Luke speaks of those wailing and beating their breasts. It was the custom to have paid professionals, and we may be sure they staged their best performance for this prominent family. The Greek term ἀλαλάζοντας, an onomatopoeic term, is used for wailing.

Jesus tells them their demonstration is out of place, for the child is not dead but asleep. Modern critics seize on the word "asleep" and say that the girl was in a coma. But Jesus also said of Lazarus, "He has fallen asleep." There is no doubt that the girl really was dead. The mourners were so sure of it that they laughed at Jesus (κατεγέλων means "laugh against, deride").

To us the word "asleep" presents a wonderful promise, not only for the family of Jairus, but to every believer. Jesus keeps everything in perspective for us.

vv. 40b-42 — *After he put them all out, he took the child's father and mother and the disciples who were with him, and went in where the child was. He took her by the hand and said to her "Talitha koum!" (which means, "Little girl, I say to you, get up!"). Immediately the girl stood up and walked around (she was twelve years old).*

The dignity of the moment demands proper silence, so the mourners are put out.

Jesus used his hands freely in touching those he healed, but not always. Jairus had asked Jesus to lay hands on his daughter. This

Jesus did not do, but he used the very appropriate gesture of taking her hand to assist her in getting up.

"*Talitha koum*" — words of the mother tongue are most fitting in this solemn moment. Mark wants us also to hear the very Aramaic words Jesus used. Must we not say that the words have also remained imbedded in our memory?

The results are immediate. Death has been conquered. So has the illness. She is alive and healthy once more. What a miracle! See the reaction of the parents. They are "ecstatic with great ecstasy" (ἐξέστησαν ἐκστάσει μεγάλῃ).

v. 43 — *He gave strict order not to let anyone know about this, and told them to give her something to eat.*

In their ecstasy the parents might have forgotten that the girl would be hungry after her illness. What tender thoughtfulness on the part of Jesus to remind them of her physical need.

There could be no possibility of covering up the fact that the dead girl was brought to life. But Jesus did not want the details of how it was done to be spread abroad to people who did not yet understand his Messianic mission.

## Homiletical Suggestions

Jesus' miracles of raising persons from the dead justly are considered his greatest and most convincing of miracles. This account is the only one in this series of texts that recounts one of these miracles. This is the first such miracle that Jesus performed: raising a child dead for a very short time. Later followed the raising of the youth of Nain, dead probably about a day. Then comes the raising of Lazarus, dead four days and beginning to decompose. We dare not forget the greatest of all miracles, Jesus raising himself from the dead.

Jesus' power over death must be in the forefront in our treatment of this text. Since death also comes into our lives, this text affords us the opportunity to help our members cope with death when it takes their loved ones and also when it comes to them personally.

Our text has three striking statements, each of which can serve as a theme for us.

## Don't Be Afraid; Just Believe

1. Come to Jesus in fearful times (vv. 21-24)
2. Don't become discouraged (vv. 35-40a)
3. Your faith will not be put to shame (vv. 40b-43)

## The Child Is Not Dead, But Sleeps

1. Without Jesus, only mourning (vv. 35,37,38,40a)
2. With Jesus, there is hope (vv. 21-24,36)
3. That hope is not in vain (vv. 36,39,40b-43)

## "Talitha Koum"

1. Death strikes again (vv. 21-24,35,36)
2. Mourning cannot allay the tragedy (vv. 37,38,40a)
3. But "Talitha koum" (vv. 39,40b-43)

# SEVENTH SUNDAY AFTER PENTECOST

## The Scriptures

Old Testament — *Ezekiel 2:1-5*
Epistle — *2 Corinthians 12:7-10*
Gospel — *Mark 6:1-6*

## The Text — Mark 6:1-6

The rejection of Jesus by his home town of Nazareth may have happened twice. Edersheim (*The Life and Times of Jesus the Messiah*) feels that Matthew 4:12,13 and Luke 4:14-30 describe the first event in Nazareth and that Matthew 13:53-58 and Mark 6:1-6 describe a second event occurring about eight months later. Lenski believes the passages describe only one rejection in Nazareth. Whichever the case, this dramatic return home illustrates our Lord's grace in ministering to those who he knew would reject him. The attitude of the Nazarenes teaches us about our own human nature, warning us not to let familiarity breed contempt when it comes to our knowledge of God.

v. 1 — *Jesus left there and went to his hometown, accompanied by his disciples.*

Picture the small hometown, "the tenacious narrowness and the prejudices so characteristic of such a town, with its cliques and petty family pride" (Edersheim). The mention that his disciples accompanied him on this trip to Nazareth is one reason some commentators distinguish this visit from that described in Luke 4:14-30.

v. 2 — *When the Sabbath came, he began to teach in the synagogue, and many who heard him were amazed. "Where did this man get these things?" they asked. "What's this wisdom that has been given him, that he even does miracles!"*

The people of Nazareth readily acknowledged that Jesus spoke "wisdom" and that he did "miracles." The indication that something is amiss is their question, "*Where* did this man get these things?" It is as though they had never heard of a prophet who was given words by God. They should have been looking for such a prophet on the basis of Moses' prediction in Deuteronomy 18:18,19: "The Lord said . . . 'I will raise up for them a prophet like you from among their brothers; I will put *my words in his mouth*, and he will tell them everything I command him. If anyone does not listen to my words that the prophet speaks in my name, I myself will call him to account.' " Jesus' words and deeds pointed to the obvious answer to the question, "Where?"

Yet the people of Nazareth, impressed (ἐξεπλήσσοντο) though they were, refused to reach the logical conclusion. Far from suspecting that "this man" (expressed with contempt in the Greek) might be the Messiah, they even refused to consider that he might be an inspired prophet. The obvious conclusion would be the one reached by Nicodemus, who reasoned: "Rabbi, we know that you are a teacher who has come from God. For no one could perform the miraculous signs you are doing if God were not with him" (Jn 3:2).

The Nazarenes' excuse for dismissing this man in spite of his wisdom and power is given in the following verse:

v. 3 — *"Isn't this the carpenter? Isn't this Mary's son and the brother of James, Joseph, Judas and Simon? Aren't his sisters here with us?" And they took offense at him.*

Remember the family history: Joseph and Mary had grown up in this town, after marrying had left to register in Bethlehem, had sojourned in Egypt, and then had returned to Nazareth with the little boy, Jesus. The child's miraculous conception was not commonly known (Lk 3:23). He apparently drew no particular attention to himself while growing up as the God-man, but quite normally "grew in wisdom and stature, and in favor with God and men" (Lk 2:52).

Jesus no doubt worked as a carpenter in Nazareth until he was about thirty years old — the minimum age for becoming a rabbi. The most natural understanding of the people's remarks about his family is that Joseph and Mary had children after Jesus was born. The "sisters here with us" had no doubt married local men and settled in Nazareth. The omission of Joseph's name probably indicates he had died some time ago. We might well imagine that many in Nazareth had furniture made by "this man." It would be amazing to have this familiar neighbor return home teaching brilliantly and performing miracles. But the Nazarenes quite unreasonably pointed to their familiarity with Jesus as an excuse to reject his message (see also Jn 6:41,42).

"And they took offense at him." The Greek verb is ἐσκανδαλίζοντο, from the noun σκάνδαλον, which means "a trap." The passive verb form is used here figuratively, referring to the fact that people were "tripped up" by their familiarity with Jesus and so failed to reach the logical conclusion about him.

v. 4 — *Jesus said to them, "Only in his hometown, among his relatives and in his own house is a prophet without honor."*

Jesus found their response to be so typical of people as to be proverbial. The irony of being rejected by his own is expressed poignantly in John 1:10,11. His rejection by all men in general and by his chosen people in particular had long been predicted (Isa 53:1-3). Even his own family disbelieved and considered him "out of his mind" for a while (Mk 3:21; Jn 7:3-6), although later some of them — notably James — became prominent disciples (1 Co 9:5; Ga 1:19; 2:9; Ac 15:13).

This familiar prophet was "without honor" (ἄτιμος). They attached no value to him. To honor him would have been to esteem him a prophet, to pay attention to his words, believe them, and act upon them.

v. 5 — *He could not do any miracles there, except lay his hands on a few sick people and heal them.*

The unbelief of the people in Nazareth prevented them from accepting the miraculous blessings Jesus had brought to so many other towns. He could work only a few miracles because only a few people came to him for help. (May we not, through weakness of faith, prevent Jesus from bringing to our lives the blessings he wants to bring!)

v. 6 — *And he was amazed at their lack of faith.*

Even Jesus with his understanding of human nature marveled at their unbelief. "In view of their own reasoning it was most unreasonable" (Edersheim). In a similar way, the man born blind was amazed at the unbelief of the Pharisees in the face of his healing: "Now that is remarkable! You don't know where he comes from, yet he opened my eyes.... If this man were not from God, he could do nothing" (Jn 9:30,33).

### Homiletical Suggestions

This text along with the attendant Epistle and Old Testament readings has to do with people's attitude toward God's word spoken by men. The human prophet's weakness (Paul, Ezekiel) or familiarity (Jesus) do not change the character of the message. However, for those who choose not to believe, externals are made to provide an excuse for dismissing the message. Pointing to Jesus' family was the only escape for these people of Nazareth who had been backed into a corner by God's truth, the only alternative to repenting and believing.

A sermon might warn the listener of this sinful tendency so that he will not allow "familiarity to breed contempt" in the matter of his religion. Young people might be warned against the tendency to rebel against their inherited faith simply because it was the one they were born into, the one their parents hold. We all must beware of the appeal of the exotic, the foreign, the mysterious. It would be astoundingly unreasonable to dismiss our church and our holy book, the Bible, on the excuse of their familiarity.

The event in Nazareth illustrates the unreasonable nature of unbelief. Modern unbelief, ushered in during the "Age of Reason," is no more reasonable than ancient unbelief. "The more strongly negative criticism asserts its position as to the person of Jesus, the more unaccountable are his teaching and the results of his work" (Edersheim).

A sermon might explain that unbelief is not a reasonable conclusion based upon intelligent observation of the facts. Rather, unbelief is the choice of our sinful human will, which persists blindly in spite of the facts — as in Nazareth. Since the fall into sin our wills are bound in unbelief until the Holy Ghost miraculously calls us to faith through the gospel (Mt 23:37; 1 Co 12:3; 2 Cor 4:3-6; Ro 1:16; 10:17; and especially relevant to this text, Jn 6:41-45).

The rejection of Jesus in Nazareth provides the preacher with an opportunity to illustrate the amazing grace of our Lord, who knew he would be dishonored but came anyway — came to earth, came to Israel, came to Nazareth (Ro 5:6-10). This offers firm assurance that he wants to come also to us with forgiveness, life and salvation.

An outline for this text could be:

**Honor the Carpenter-Prophet**

1. Note Nazareth's excuse for unbelief
2. Beware of following their example

This is a simple approach in which part one is exposition and part two is application. The listener will enjoy thinking his way into the viewpoint of Jesus' neighbors; then the road is paved for drawing the point home to modern Christians.

Another possibility:

**Amazing Unbelief**

1. Amazingly unreasonable (vv. 1-4)
2. Amazingly harmful (v. 5)
3. Amazingly disappointing to our Savior (v. 6)

# EIGHTH SUNDAY AFTER PENTECOST

## The Scriptures

Old Testament — *Amos 7:10-15*
Epistle — *Ephesians 1:3-14*
Gospel — *Mark 6:7-13*

## The Text — Mark 6:7-13

On his third tour of Galilee, Jesus brought his good news to the smaller towns and villages. He had compassion on the people (Mt 9:36) and took action to cover "all the towns and villages" of Galilee (Mt 9:35).

In keeping with this plan, he called (προσκαλεῖται) his twelve disciples to himself.

v. 7 — *Calling the Twelve to him, he sent them out two by two and gave them authority over evil spirits.*

The word προσκαλεῖται may be used either for the call to faith in Christ (Ac 2:39) or the call to service in his name (Ac 13:2). Here the Lord is calling to faith in himself. After this calling to himself, he sends them out. In the same way today the Lord invites his disciples to all that he is and offers before he sends them out to do his bidding.

Of special importance is that the doer of all these actions is Christ. It was Christ's choice when, after he called his disciples to himself, he sent them out. It was not a matter of their decision to go but of Christ's decision to send. The voice of our Lord not only invites in grace, but in grace impels, so we appreciate the good works in which he moves us to walk.

The fact that Jesus does the sending drives the sinful flesh to service, eases the mind of the person who questions the situation in which the Lord has placed him, and encourages him to go forward. The one sent does not need to be paralyzed by laziness or worldly concerns, to be driven to sorrow by sin and doubt, or to be blinded by fear.

But it is the hearers of those sent who primarily benefit from Jesus' act of sending. They hear God's message and receive the assurance of salvation and the courage to live godly lives. They receive comfort and hope, while having their stubborn selves overcome.

In addition to calling his disciples to himself and sending them out, Jesus gave them power over evil or unclean spirits and authority to heal diseases (Lk 9:1). These were exceptional or miraculous abilities. God gave them this authority, not at the apostles' request, but because he saw fit. St. Paul tells us the reason God gave him his authority (ἐξουσίαν) was to "build up" (2 Co 13:10) the church, not tear it down. That was Christ's objective here. Since the Christ was to come with all manner of signs and wonders, it should not surprise us that he gave his apostles this power.

Neither should it surprise us that, since the Christ has come and has established the authority of his word in this world, his gospel is still a powerful message, God's power (δύναμις) for our salvation (Ro 1:16).

In applying these words to ourselves, it is very appropriate that we thank God for having given such miraculous gifts to the church and that we exercise our authority in the word to "demolish arguments and every pretension that sets itself up against the knowledge of God, and . . . take captive every thought to make it obedient to Christ" (2 Cor 10:5). In this way our Lord builds his church.

Yet Jesus not only gave his apostles authority, he also gave them instructions:

vv. 8,9 — *These were his instructions: "Take nothing for the journey except a staff — no bread, no bag, no money in your belts. Wear sandals, but not an extra tunic."*

These instructions sound strange to the 20th-century ear. But consider that the staff was a practical tool, not only for the old and infirm, but also for the traveler in Galilee. Low-lying brush was the habitat for snakes and rodents. The staff afforded ready protection.

On the other hand, a money belt or bag might give the impression that the disciples were out for financial gain. They were, instead, to display the trust that the Lord would provide their bread, for "the Lord has commanded that those who preach the gospel should receive their living from the gospel" (1 Cor 9:14). Sandals were to be worn, but the apostles were not to carry extra ones along. They would deserve to have their needs supplied as they carried out their mission (cf. Mt 10:10), and the Lord would see to it that they would lack no necessity. While travelers generally wore two tunics — the one a lighter shirt, the other a longer overcoat — the apostles were to trust that the Lord would provide added warmth as necessary.

Jesus was essentially saying that the apostles were to travel wisely, using the goods at their command (i.e., sandals and staff), but were not to be burdened by anything that might impede their journey or mission (i.e., extra sandals and money belt).

Ministers are to use practical, common sense measures to avoid injury, at the same time avoiding whatever might stop them from preaching the gospel or whatever might give the wrong impression about their intention of saving souls. They are to display trust in the Lord's providence.

That providence generally was to come through those to whom the gospel was preached.

vv. 10,11 — *"Whenever you enter a house, stay there until you leave that town. And if any place will not welcome you or listen to you, shake the dust off your feet when you leave, as a testimony against them."*

Jesus did not want his apostles to move around within a city in a search for special accomodations. A look at St. Matthew's Gospel gives the added thought that the person with whom they stayed was to be "worthy" (Mt 10:11). Such worthiness would basically mean a willingness to listen to their message. Their primary message, of course, was the saving gospel.

But the law needed to be preached as well. Shaking the dust from their feet was a preachment of the law. Jews would shake the dust from their feet when leaving Gentile cities. The implication here is that those who refused to hear the gospel were no better off than Gentiles without the revealed Word. This action had the added benefit of keeping the apostles aware of the seriousness of their task.

Today's task is no less serious. The pastor of a congregation should not have to be greatly concerned for his material needs. Those who hear the gospel are to provide for their pastor's bodily needs. Paul states the same principle when he declares that "those who preach the gospel should receive their living from the gospel" (1 Co 9:14).

Those on the other hand who openly despise and reject the gospel should have the word taken from them. This is a "testimony against them," a stern preachment of the law.

This text concludes with a simple summary statement: the apostles went and did as Jesus instructed them to do.

vv. 12,13 — *They went out and preached that people should repent. They drove out many demons and anointed many sick people with oil and healed them.*

We are not told how many they converted or how they felt about their task. St. Mark simply tells us that the apostles faithfully carried out the ministry to which Jesus called them. That is all that Jesus asks of any of his called servants.

### Homiletical Suggestions

This text applies both to ministry in general and the minister specifically. The day's Epistle fits in well with the general theme.

The Old Testament lesson speaks more of the specific call to the ministry. The preacher will need to exercise care to deal with the principles the text is based on and yet not lose the flavor of the text.

The more general theme will deal with the ministry of all Christians, stressing the importance of Christ's calling, keeping goals and priorities clear, and measuring success on the basis of faithfulness.

The more specific theme of the called public servant may reiterate the same thoughts, but show how his ministry is related to theirs and encourage a spirit of dedication and humility as each Christian serves his Lord and his fellow believers with the talents God provides.

These themes reflect the fact that God establishes the ministry, not we. Understanding this, we preach that

## Jesus Reaches Sinners Through His Messengers

1. He sends his messengers (v. 7)
2. He instructs them (vv. 8-11)
3. He blesses them (vv. 12,13)

One may focus on the public ministry in this way:

## God Gives His Church Ministers

1. Whom he has sent
2. Whom he has instructed
3. Whom he will bless

Here is a synthetic approach, which emphasizes the apostles' response:

## Jesus Wants The Gospel Preached

1. Without hindrance (vv. 8-11)
2. With authority (vv. 7,12,13)

# NINTH SUNDAY AFTER PENTECOST

**The Scriptures**

Old Testament — *Jeremiah 23:1-6*
Epistle — *Ephesians 2:13-22*
Gospel — *Mark 6:30-34*

**The Text — Mark 6:30-34**

The region of Galilee was being swept by news that thrilled and shocked and stirred the people. Jesus, the prophet of Galilee, had seemingly stepped up his activity: not only was he himself teaching and traveling vigorously, he had also commissioned the Twelve to go out two by two. Their call to repentance was backed up by the same power their Lord displayed, for they too drove out demons and healed the sick.

But at the same time grievous news came from Herod's palace. The proud and boastful king had yielded to Herodias' hatred and had ordered the execution of John the Baptist.

Into the maelstrom of joy and grief comes this calm and comforting work of the Savior, which culminated in feeding the 5,000 with only five loaves of bread and two fish. All four evangelists report that mighty miracle (the only event reported in all four Gospels in the time between Jesus' baptism and Palm Sunday). Matthew, Luke and John mention this part of the sequence only in passing, or not at all; but Mark offers this insight into how Jesus helped his followers to cope.

v. 30 — *The apostles gathered around Jesus and reported to him all they had done and taught.*

This is the only time St. Mark refers to the Twelve as "apostles." It is an appropriate term to describe men who had been "sent out two by two" (verse 7 of this chapter). Perhaps the term is familiar enough; or perhaps its use here will provide opportunity to review its specific meaning. If the preacher wishes to do that, he might consider whether the similarity to an "epistle" should also be noted, along with our role as "living letters."

The report of the apostles concerned the mission committed to them in verses 7-11 of this chapter. Mark describes the events in verses 12 and 13. The disciples preached repentance, as their Lord did. God gave his stamp of approval on their words by miraculous signs and wonders, the same signs that marked Jesus' ministry. Clearly these men were his men; their message was his message.

Just as clearly we see that those who go in his name are accountable for what they say and do. The disciples returned and gave reports — a solemn thought, worth pondering by the preacher whether or not he dwells on it in his sermon to others.

Why did the disciples return at this particular time? Was it the day appointed in advance as the end of their first preaching tour? Or was it the dreadful news about John's death that sent them scurrying back to their Lord? There is no word in the record to specify. We are left to realize that both factors were probably in the picture. Christ is dealing with excited men who have made their first evangelism visits and preached their first sermons; and he is dealing with friends of John the Baptist who are grieving at the loss of their former teacher. How many of them are also saying: "That's what happened to a preacher of repentance; do I still want to go out in public as a preacher of repentance in Jesus' name?" Christ will have to deal with both the experiences of their travels and the fears that threaten their souls.

v. 31 — *Then, because so many people were coming and going that they did not even have a chance to eat, he said to them, "Come with me by yourselves to a quiet place and get some rest."*

Counseling was simply impossible. Jesus' headquarters-home in Capernaum was filled with so many people coming and going that there wasn't even a chance to hold a dinner meeting. From that circus atmosphere he invited his apostles to a more secluded place for some rest.

"Rest" is a word that echoes in our hearts. We teach the Third Commandment and expound the joy of God's true rest in the Savior. We memorize Jesus' invitation in Matthew 11:28. But it is wise to be a bit restrained about introducing those references too soon.

The rest Jesus offered the disciples certainly means first of all the kind of rest that weary bodies and minds need after the physical and mental exertion of traveling and teaching. There are valuable lessons for us when we note that this rest followed their hard work. As the harvest follows the planting, so on earth God's plan summons us to arduous labor before the good times follow. After work has wearied us, then comes the time for rest and ease.

We also should recognize that rest is not now a permanent state. The period of rest precedes and prepares for more work. The next order of business for the Twelve is going to be pondering the needs of 5,000 supperless hearers. This perplexing mental activity is followed by carrying to them the bread and fish the Lord Jesus provided so miraculously. No, earth is not a place for extended idleness; earthly rest restores the energy we expended in labor and reinvigorates us for continued labor.

On that foundation we may properly point out that the "rest that remains" (Hebrews 4) remains our hope and God's heavenly gift. And till we enter that perfect rest the peace of forgiveness in Christ brings rest and comfort during our weary days on sin-stained earth.

v. 32 — *So they went away by themselves in a boat to a solitary place.*

St. Luke mentions a place near Bethsaida as the destination. That is Bethsaida Julia, north and east of the point where the Jordan enters the Sea of Galilee. It wasn't even the humble village that was the goal, nor was it a country club resort. He who, unlike the foxes, had no place to lay his head, who had no preaching place but a boat, also had nothing but an unpopulated wilderness for his resort motel.

v. 33 — *But many who saw them leaving recognized them and ran on foot from all the towns and got there ahead of them.*

The throng from Capernaum followed. In all the cities along the way they added to their numbers. It didn't require superior agility to keep up with the boat. After all, following the shoreline was the natural course for the boat. And the passengers in that boat were not striving for any speed record; they were seeking rest and private conversation with the Lord. Possibly most of their rest came on the cruise rather than at the destination. (John 6:3-5 does indicate that there was at least some time alone for Jesus and his disciples on the hillside. That raises the question whether "ahead of them" is really the best translation from the original; it might be overstating the verb a bit.)

Those who followed along the shore were indicating a strong enthusiasm for Jesus. They desired more from him, more teaching, more miracles. Yet we fear that their joy in him may have been only an "ecstasy without root" (Ylvisaker). After they were miraculously fed it was their plan to take him by force to make him an earthly king. That's the direction their enthusiasm was taking; they should have listened more closely.

v. 34 — *When Jesus landed and saw a large crowd, he had compassion on them, because they were like sheep without a shepherd. So he began teaching them many things.*

It was rude of the crowd to impose on Jesus in Capernaum; it was rude of them to follow where others had been invited. Yet it was not rude treatment that their victim returned to them. Jesus had compassion on them. "Undeserved love" is the basis for the Savior's dealings with sinners, all sinners. Compassion and grace and a shepherd's care are the gifts, the good news, that Jesus brings.

The other evangelists note that Jesus' compassion on the crowd included miracles of healing. Mark's report does not exclude that. The faithful Shepherd's care provided whatever was needed.

## Homiletical Suggestions

Can a simple paragraph about harried people taking a boat ride serve as material for a sermon? Only if the preacher faithfully concentrates on the central figure and not on the setting. Our focus is on Christ, the Shepherd, the Compassionate, the Rest-giver.

Certainly the setting is one that attracts attention. Even if we ignore the miracle that this introduces, to hear an invitation to travel to a place of rest is an attention-getter. This text is assigned for use on a Sunday that will fall at the height of the vacation season north of the equator. Summer Sundays are a great time to think of all the ways we have for getting rest and recreation. Let us use that well-understood idea of rest properly; let us be sure our enthusiasm is directed to the Lord's gifts, not just to our own ease.

Indeed Jesus offered physical rest to his tired disciples. As they were tired from their journeys, spent from their preaching, and drained by the sad news about John, he offered them the rest and recuperation they needed.

Applying this to ourselves, we realize with joy that life is not all work. A day of rest was the Creator's example and gift. Though sin has spoiled much, it has not repealed that truth.

At the same time we need to counter the thinking of the old Adam; life now is not meant to be all rest either! The Savior's will had sent the apostles out to tire themselves. His teaching while they rested had prepared them to go forth again, to become tired again and again as they would go to all nations. Indeed, that very day ended with them hard at work carrying baskets of food to the hungry.

This truth that earthly rest is not yet perfect serves as a transition to those other thoughts about rest, the perfect rest still to come.

The Twelve needed to hear of a better rest. Their earthly rest was fragile and vulnerable. Sheer numbers had foiled rest in Capernaum. How much uneasiness filled their work reports as they told Jesus not only of welcomes for their words but also of rejection? After all, Jesus had prepared them (v. 11) for people who would refuse to listen. All their life there would come days when messages would come about the death of friends. All their life they would be dealing with demanding, discourteous actions by some of earth's citizens.

The crowd that followed was also in need of rest that went beyond the usual food and shelter. Did they really understand why Jesus was important to them? If they were thinking of making him king so they could straighten out affairs in Jerusalem, what other incorrect ideas were they holding?

To the needy Jesus gave rest far beyond physical rest. He had compassion. The simple answer of God to human weakness and inadequacy is his love. He will be our helper.

Let earthly vacations then fall short of perfection. It doesn't really matter if the mosquitoes are too plentiful and the fish too scarce. Such rest can only last till the next work schedule begins. As Christians we can rejoice in Jesus' gift of perfect rest! Viewing the wonders of God's creation shows us the splendor and power he has available to show his love for us. Enjoying the technology of our day bids us to humble ourselves as we receive benefits we cannot understand, much less deserve. We find our rest in God's compassion, in the assurance of the forgiveness of our sins and the sure hope of everlasting life.

To present these thoughts in outline form we might use wordings like these:

**Accept Jesus' Offer Of Rest**

1. He recognizes the need for physical rest (vv. 30-32)
2. He brings rest for troubled souls (vv. 33,34)

Or:

**"Come With Me ... And Get Some Rest"**

1. Jesus offered physical rest for his tired disciples (vv. 30-32)
2. Jesus brought rest to troubled souls (vv. 33,34)

274

# TENTH SUNDAY AFTER PENTECOST

**The Scriptures**

Old Testament — *Exodus 24:3-11*
Epistle — *Ephesians 4:1-7,11-16*
Gospel — *John 6:1-15*

**The Text — John 6:1-15**

vv. 1-4 — *Some time after this, Jesus crossed to the far shore of the Sea of Galilee (that is, the Sea of Tiberias), and a great crowd of people followed him because they saw the miraculous signs he had performed on the sick. Then Jesus went up on a mountainside and sat down with his disciples. The Jewish Passover Feast was near.*

John presents important background material leading up to the miracle that Jesus is about to perform. Additional background material is supplied by the synoptic Gospels, all of which include this miracle (Mt 14:13-21; Mk 6:30-44; Lk 9:10-17).

In the previous chapter John tells us that Jesus was at Jerusalem "for a feast of the Jews" (5:1). Now in chapter 6 we hear of Jesus up in Galilee. Evidently there is a gap of six months to a year during which Jesus finished his Judean ministry, as reported by the synoptic writers, and now he goes north for his Galilean ministry.

Luke notes that Jesus and his disciples were now at the city of Bethsaida along the northeastern coast of the Sea of Galilee. What John reports in our text took place prior to this, when "Jesus crossed to the far shore of the Sea of Galilee." Jesus and his disciples left the crowds at Tiberias, along the western coast of the Sea of Galilee, and traveled by boat to the northeastern coast of the lake. However, many of the people followed him on foot, and some even arrived at Bethsaida before Jesus and the disciples. The people had been attracted to Jesus because of the miraculous signs that he had performed on the sick. Desiring to spend some time alone with his disciples, Jesus took them to a desolate area outside of Bethsaida, on a mountainside. Jesus felt it important to get away with his disciples for some rest (Mk 6:30-34).

We might add a few side notes. John is the only evangelist to refer to the Sea of Galilee as "the Sea of Tiberias." At this time the reigning emperor of Rome was Tiberias Caesar (A.D. 14-37). The city of Tiberias had been built in his honor, and the sea along which it was located also came to be known by his name. John mentions it again in 21:1.

As far as the time period is concerned, John mentions that "the Jewish Passover Feast was near." This would then be the spring of A.D. 29, approximately a year before Jesus' passion at Jerusalem.

vv. 5,6 — *When Jesus looked up and saw a great crowd coming toward him, he said to Philip, "Where shall we buy bread for these people to eat?" He asked this only to test him, for he already had in mind what he was going to do.*

As soon as Jesus sat down with his disciples, he looked up and saw a great crowd approaching. John is the only evangelist who notes what Jesus said before the entire crowd arrived. Jesus addressed a question to Philip: "Where shall we buy bread for these people to eat?" The purpose in asking this question was to "test" (πειράςων) Philip, and with Philip all the disciples. Jesus was "trying out" his disciples to see what kind of response they might give.

It was a way of teaching them a very important lesson. Would they be able to distinguish between the inability of human provision and the almighty power of their Lord to provide for the physical needs of that great crowd of people? Would they think beyond the question of Jesus concerning the "buying" of bread to the possiblity that he had another solution in mind? Hours later they would discover that Jesus "already had in mind what he was going to do." In the meantime they would have plenty of opportunity to consider all the alternatives to "buying bread."

vv. 7-9 — *Philip answered him, "Eight months' wages would buy enough bread for each one to have a bite!" Another of his disciples, Andrew, Simon Peter's brother, spoke up, "Here is a boy with five small barley loaves and two small fish, but how far will they go among so many?"*

It would appear that these responses of Philip and Andrew to the "test question" of Jesus were given much later in the day after they had had time to consider it. It is obvious that they thought Jesus was very serious about having to buy enough bread or food to feed that great crowd of people.

During the interval the synoptists reveal what occupied the time and attention of Jesus. His heart went out to the people "because they were like sheep without a shepherd" (Mk 6:34). Thus he cared for their spiritual needs by teaching them about the kingdom of God and revealing his divine power and authority by healing those who were sick.

It was now late in the day with evening approaching. The people had been there much of the day, and the disciples suggested that Jesus send the crowds away so that they might buy food for themselves (Mt 14:15). This was their first "solution" to the problem Jesus had posed to Philip. But Jesus replied, "They do not need to go away. You give them something to eat" (Mt 14:16). Again Jesus was "testing" his disciples to see their reaction.

This was no doubt the time when Philip came up with his response. The "eight months' wages" of the NIV translation is the equivalent of the literal "two hundred denarii" (Διακοσίων δηναρίων). One denarius was the usual wage for a day's work. The amount that a man could earn in two hundred work days could not begin to provide the amount of food that five thousand men (plus thousands of women and children) would need for a single meal.

Andrew had another suggestion. He had noticed a boy in the crowd who had five small loaves of barley bread and a couple of small fish. But even he could see the hopelessness of this suggestion: "How far will they go among so many?"

Both Philip and Andrew had failed their "tests" miserably, but Jesus had accomplished a part of his purpose in testing them. He wanted them to realize the hopelessness of the situation. There was not enough money to buy the food necessary to feed such a crowd. There was not enough food available to feed such a crowd.

Their realization of the hopelessness of the situation, however, did not lead them to the solution that Jesus wanted them to reach. He wanted them to look to him as their "bread of life." But their faith and trust in him had not yet advanced to the point where they would immediately think of him as "the perfect solution" to the problem at hand.

vv. 10,11 — *Jesus said, "Have the people sit down." There was plenty of grass in that place, and the men sat down, about five thousand of them. Jesus then took the loaves, gave thanks, and distributed to those who were seated as much as they wanted. He did the same with the fish.*

Jesus then revealed what he had in mind all along. He told his disciples to have the people sit down on the ground. Since it was early spring, there was plenty of grass for the people to sit on. John mentions that the crowd numbered "about five thousand." This number was only "the men" and did not include the women and children who were also present (Mt 14:21). Mark notes that the people sat down in groups of hundreds and fifties.

Jesus then had the five loaves of bread and two small fish brought to him. Giving thanks for them, he had the disciples distribute the food to the people so that they could have as much as they wanted. What is not said, but is certainly implied here in John's account, is that the food kept on multiplying as it was being distributed. "Jesus gave and gave and gave,and as he gave, there was always more to give" (Lenksi). It was a miracle, pure and simple!

vv. 12,13 — *When they had all had enough to eat, he said to his disciples, "Gather the pieces that are left over. Let nothing be wasted." So they gathered them and filled twelve baskets with the pieces of the five barley loaves left over by those who had eaten.*

The miracle was not finished. All the people had eaten and were filled — and there was food left over! The leftovers were not to be wasted. So Jesus directed his disciples to gather them up. When they did this, it was discovered that there were twelve full baskets of food, more than there was to begin with.

The purpose Jesus had in gathering the fragments that remained was not only to teach a lesson in conservation and good stewardship, but above all to impress upon the disciples the magnitude of the miracle they had just witnessed. Now they could not miss the point. He is able to give in unlimited measure what is needed for this life. But even though his ability to provide is limitless, he promises to provide only what we really need.

vv. 14,15 — *After the people saw the miraculous sign that Jesus did, they began to say, "Surely this is the Prophet who is to come into the world." Jesus, knowing that they intended to come and make him king by force, withdrew again to a mountain by himself.*

The result of this "miraculous sign" was predictable. The people drew the wrong conclusion from this miracle. They recalled the prophetic words of Moses in Deuteronomy 18:15 about "the prophet who is to come into the world." While many regarded this prophet to be the promised Messiah, their Messianic hopes were more worldly than spiritual. They were looking for a king who would deliver them, not from sin, but from the tryranny of Rome. It was thus the intent of the people to reestablish the throne of David in all its former glory. As they were about to go up to Jerusalem for the feast of the Passover, this seemed to be the ideal time to do this. If Jesus proved unwilling, they would try to take him by force.

The synoptists report that Jesus now has his disciples sail back to Bethsaida. Jesus remains to dismiss the crowd, and then he departs alone to a mountainside where he can spend much needed time with his Father in prayer. Opposition to Jesus grows in Galilee, as Jesus makes it increasingly clear that he will not be the kind of king that the people want.

## Homiletical Suggestions

This text provides an excellent opportunity to focus the attention of the people on the grace and goodness of God as revealed in the person and work of his Son, Jesus Christ. Jesus is that living bread from heaven who has come to give life to all mankind.

There are three important points that are brought out in the text: the need of the people, the predicament of the disciples, and the miraculous solution which Jesus provides out of the abundance of his grace. Theme and parts for the sermon may advance along these lines:

### Leave It To Jesus

1. To recognize the need (vv. 1-9)
2. To provide the solution (vv. 10-15)

Or:

### Jesus Has The Answer

1. In addressing the needs of the people
2. In spite of the weaknesses of his followers
3. In keeping with the abundance of his grace

Some other suggestions:

### The Lord Never Stops Giving

1. He gives to supply our earthly needs
2. He gives to strengthen our faith in him.

One idea that would be in keeping with the thoughts of the other lessons for the day:

### Find True Fellowship With Jesus

1. He freely gives of himself to us
2. We receive of him to give to others

# ELEVENTH SUNDAY AFTER PENTECOST

## The Scriptures

Old Testament — *Exodus 16:2-15*
Epistle — *Ephesians 4:17-24*
Gospel — *John 6:24-35*

## The Text — John 6:24-35

The sixth chapter of John records the events and teachings connected with Jesus' miraculous feeding of the 5,000. Attracted by his miracles, a large crowd of people had followed him when he set sail to the eastern shore of the Sea of Galilee. Jesus taught them on the barren shoreline throughout the day. Toward evening he fed them with five loaves of bread and two small fish. Immediately after the miracle Jesus sent his disciples sailing back to Capernaum. He rejoined them later that night by walking upon the water.

v. 24 — *Once the crowd realized that neither Jesus nor his disciples were there, they got into the boats and went to Capernaum in search of Jesus.*

These people had been fed by the miracle Jesus worked the day before. During the night, however, Jesus and his disciples had left because of the crowd's desire to proclaim Jesus their Messiah, an earthly deliverer from Roman rule. At least a portion of the crowd still hotly pursued Jesus. They hired boats and returned to Capernaum. Perhaps these boats were blown over from Capernaum by the storm the night before. Or, what is more likely, numerous fishermen had sailed across the sea to earn quick cash by ferrying the crowd back. Whatever the case may have been, the crowd arrived in Capernaum on the day after Jesus had fed them.

They press on with their search for Jesus.

v. 25 — *When they found him on the other side of the lake, they asked him, "Rabbi, when did you get here?"*

The crowd politely gives Jesus the traditional greeting of "Rabbi" (Teacher). The subsequent dialog, however, shows that they are unwilling to let Christ be their teacher. They are the masters, the ones who will judge Jesus' credentials and dictate what miracles he is to perform.

Already this attitude of unbelief shows through when they ask Jesus, "When did you get here?" They are really asking Jesus how he got to Capernaum. In such a short time Jesus could hardly have walked around the northern shore of the Sea of Galilee. They themselves had seen the disciples leave without Jesus, and there had been no other boats on the scene until morning. Judging from the prominence they give to the miraculous in their following words, they are asking Jesus to fill them in on the latest miracle he performed to reach Capernaum. They search not for knowledge, but for an unending stream of titillating miracles by which Jesus can entertain and sustain them.

v. 26 — *Jesus answered, "I tell you the truth, you are looking for me, not because you saw miraculous signs but because you ate the loaves and had your fill."*

Jesus directs his reply not to their question, but to the motive for the question. In a solemn declaration he exposes the true condition of their hearts. They did not come back to Capernaum to find the Savior Jesus claimed to be. They had come looking for the Savior they wanted Jesus to be. They had not really "seen" (εἴδετε) the miracle that had taken place on the other side of the Sea of Galilee. Although they saw it with their outward eyes, even felt and tasted the miracle's results, they did not grasp its significance with the eyes of faith. Their belief in an earthly Messiah had blinded them to the true significance of the miracle.

The miracles he had performed in their presence — the healing of the sick (Jn 6:2) and the multiplication of the bread and fish — Jesus calls "signs" (σημεῖα). These were signals that Jesus, the one who performed these miracles, was the Son of God. Faith in Christ would see these miracles as Jesus' credentials, the proof that he was who he claimed to be, the Savior of the world. Faith would not focus on the miracles, but rather on the performer of those miracles and his teachings. But the crowd lacked faith. Instead of being drawn closer to Jesus and his teachings, they were simply enthralled by the miracles. They had plenty to eat the day before, and now they wanted more. They forgot the giver and marveled at the gifts.

Having exposed them for what they really are, Jesus now directs their attention to the real miracle, the Son of God in their midst:

v. 27 — *"Do not work for food that spoils, but for food that endures to eternal life, which the Son of Man will give you. On him God the Father has placed his seal of approval."*

The crowd had exerted itself to obtain bread that wasn't worth the effort. Yesterday's bread was gone. It had given no lasting benefits. They were hungry again.

Recalling the miracle of the preceding day, Jesus calls every human effort to support oneself "food." All human endeavors carried out apart from God's saving purpose produce fruits that spoil. "What good is it for a man to gain the whole world, yet forfeit his soul?" (Mk 8:36). Every earthly goal and ambition the sinful mind sets up in place of God is bread that spoils. It all comes to nothing and can only leave the soul that pursued it tormented in hell.

But there is a food that does not spoil, which has eternal benefits. This bread exists for the purpose of (εἰς) bestowing eternal life on its eater.

Ζωή is life in the highest sense. God alone gives it and God alone sustains it through faith in Christ. It is the exact opposite of death, separation from God's blessings. It is an existence untouched by sin and unaffected by the consequences of sin. Holiness, innocence, purity of heart and hand lie in that word "life." Once a person has that life, he is content. He is at rest with God because of trust in the loving Savior. All our efforts to justify and preserve ourselves grind to a halt once that life from God is ours.

The Son of Man gives this life. The crowds wanted to see Jesus as a Messiah, who would be an earthly deliverer. They were willing to call him the Son of God, cloaked with a heavenly glory which could translate itself into earthly glory both for himself and his loyal band of partisans. But the title "Son of Man" carried no such thoughts of earthly glory. It was a term of humility which downplayed all that was miraculous and glorious about Jesus. It stressed his serving and suffering nature.

By saying the Son of Man will give this life, Jesus rules out all thoughts of work-righteousness. The gift of eternal life cannot be earned by sinners. It can be received only through faith in the merits of the sinless Savior.

Jesus knew his words would not sit well with the crowd. They were eager to work and sacrifice to attain earthly glory. He told them the glory they sought was vanity. Their enthusiasm was misplaced. Because of the sudden change of attitude Jesus' words demanded, he sets forth the authority by which he makes these demands. The crowd ought to listen to the Son of Man because God has set his "seal of approval" upon Jesus.

Interestingly enough, this also is hinted at by the "signs" which Jesus had earlier mentioned. The bearer of a letter would be given a distinguishing mark (σημεῖον) by which the recipient of the letter could be assured of the bearer's commission. The angels, in instructing the sheperds to seek the baby Jesus in a manger, gave a sign by which the shepherds would know that they were true messengers from God (Lk 2:12). Jesus also has credentials which should have won him a hearing even from this crowd. At his baptism God the Father placed his seal of approval upon Jesus. "You are my son, whom I love; with you I am well pleased" (Lk 3:22). With each miracle God placed Jesus' credentials before the world for all to see. "The miracles I do in my Father's name speak for me" (Jn 10:25).

Jesus at least accomplished this much: he succeeded in turning the minds of the crowd temporarily away from the miraculous and toward God's will for them.

v. 28 — *Then they asked him, "What must we do to do the works God requires?"*

Once again their sinful nature entraps them. First of all, they imagine that there actually exists a class of works, human actions, which by their very nature are so praiseworthy that they can earn eternal life. Their second mistake is thinking they can perform those works. Jesus has been speaking words of spirit and life to them. Being earthly and enslaved by sin, they fail to grasp his words.

v. 29 — *Jesus answered, "The work of God is this: to believe in the one he has sent."*

Since they are determined to talk about work, Jesus tells them about the one work which will truly gain eternal life. Since they want to talk about something that God requires, Jesus will tell them what truly pleases God — faith.

One work does exist which bestows eternal life. But that work is not something a human being can accomplish. It is the "work of God." The subjective gentive denotes the agent. God does the work. God creates faith. Because it is a working of God, it pleases him.

Saving faith makes the blessings of Christ's suffering and death ours. Through faith in his atoning death on the cross we receive the forgivenness of sins he earned for all people. "Where there is forgiveness of sins, there is life and salvation," as Luther put it. Stop looking for the easy answers. Don't imagine that you can bribe God to gain his favor. Stop working. Start believing. With these words Jesus not only offers salvation through faith, but provides the means by which that faith comes about, the living and powerful gospel.

v. 30 — *So they asked him, "What miraculous sign then will you give that we may see it and believe you? What will you do?"*

The crowd fails to take Jesus at his words. He has set before them a work which strikes them as absurdly simple. Faith is too little for God to ask of them. It does not flatter their "eager beaver" sinful human nature. Because Jesus' demand for faith, a faith which God himself provides, is so extraordinary, they ask to see Jesus' credentials once more. They are back where they started. Their old, unhealthy craving for the miraculous once again occupies their thinking. With pointed emphasis, they lay the blame for their unbelief on Jesus. They haven't taken him at his words because he hasn't done enough. If only he will perform another miracle that they can feast their eyes on, they will believe, they promise. So great is the "cheek" of these people that they even suggest the miracle which Jesus should perform:

v. 31 — *"Our forefathers ate the manna in the desert; as it is written: 'He gave them bread from heaven to eat.' "*

The crowd rejects the miraculous feeding of yesterday as an inferior miracle. Jesus had simply taken bread which already existed and had multiplied it for them. If he could keep on providing food from nothing, like the manna the Israelites ate in the desert, that would certainly convince them. They would recognize him as one greater than Moses.

vv. 32,33 — *Jesus said to them, "I tell you the truth, it is not Moses who has given you the bread from heaven, but it is my Father who gives you the true bread from heaven. For the bread of God is he who comes down from heaven and gives life to the world."*

Once more Jesus corrects their misconceptions. Moses did not miraculously feed the Israelites for forty years in the wilderness —God the Father did. Moses could take no credit for it. The unspoken implication is that Jesus is greater than Moses, for he had through the power of his own person miraculously fed them on the other side of the Sea of Galilee. Manna could not impart heavenly life. It only sustained earthly life. Those who ate of that manna eventually died — the desert was littered with their bodies for forty years.

At this point Jesus tantalizes the crowd with his words. He does not yet choose to reveal himself as the true bread of God. Rather, his words emphasize the glorious blessings this bread gives. Manna came from the cloud, but this bread comes from heaven itself. Manna did not give spiritual life, but this bread gives real life, spiritual life with all the blessings of God. Manna fed the Israelites. This bread feeds the entire world. No matter how much the crowd marvels at the manna, something far greater than manna is available to them.

v. 34 — *"Sir," they said, "from now on give us this bread."*

The word of God is powerful. At least some in the crowd are moved by the majesty of this bread from heaven and desire it. To be sure, their understanding is weak, as weak as that of the Samaritan woman at Jacob's well who asked Jesus for the water of life so she would not have to draw water anymore. Yet a willingness now exists to hear more about this bread. They want this bread in their lives. They recognize that Jesus can give this bread. Such a remarkable change has been worked in them not because of the sternness of the law, but by the winsome words of the gospel Jesus has just uttered.

Now Jesus feels they are ready for the full truth about the bread from heaven.

v. 35 — *Then Jesus declared, "I am the bread of life. He who comes to me will never go hungry, and he who believes in me will never be thirsty."*

Jesus is this bread. It is not a thing, it is a person, the Son of God himself. Eating this bread, drinking this water of life, is believing in Jesus as the Savior. Strange that those who mistakenly see later in this chapter a reference to the eating which goes on in the Lord's Supper fail to notice Jesus isn't talking about eating at all here. He is talking about faith, the only thing that saves.

When by the working of the Holy Ghost through the word a person believes, he is satisfied. Eternal life is his. There is no more working for it, no more longing for it. Why thirst for something we already have? The words and works of Christ last for all eternity. Never again need we suffer from the thirst and hunger of not knowing that our sins are forgiven by the gracious will of God through the work of Christ.

## Homiletical Suggestions

This text's rapid conversational give-and-take focuses on one element: the necessity of faith in Jesus Christ. Yet that is the overriding feature of the entire bread of life discourse. Close attention to the specific content of the text will prevent needless repetition over the series and will bring out the unique feature of each pericope.

One approach might be:

### The Lasting Work Of God

1. The fuss over miracles fades (25-27,30-33)
2. Faith in the Messiah endures (28,29,34,35)

Part one would stress how sinful human nature, caught up in the miraculous and the external, wastes even the miraculous gifts God bestows on mankind. The miracle of life itself is taken for granted, not to mention how God sustains that life. Part two would stress that God-given faith does endure the trials and unexpected turns of events in this life. Faith counts. Everything else that passes for "religion" doesn't.

A slightly different way to look at the conflict the between the people's view of the Messiah and who he really is might be:

## Believe In The True Messiah

1. More than daily bread (25-27,30-33)
2. He gives life eternal (28,29,34,35)

The heart of the crowd's problem was an insistence that humans could earn their way to heaven. A sermon attacking the work-righteous attitude in every sinful human being would also hit the nail on the head. The preacher's line of thought would be:

## Enduring Food Is Ours

1. Human efforts fail to gain it (25,26a)
2. Superhuman efforts fail to give it (30,31)
3. Jesus' efforts alone can provide it (26b-29,32-35)

Part one views the futility of natural man trying to earn his way to heaven. Part two stresses that even Christians with their best efforts will never attain eternal life. Part three stresses the gospel message of forgiveness offered freely through the death of Jesus Christ.

# TWELFTH SUNDAY AFTER PENTECOST

## The Scriptures

Old Testament — *1 Kings 19:4-8*
Epistle — *Ephesians 4:30-5:2*
Gospel — *John 6:41-51*

## The Text — John 6:41-51

This is the third of five consecutive Gospel readings from John 6. While crafting a series of sermons on these readings, the preacher will want to identify the special emphasis of each. The analysis below may prove to be helpful:

Jn 6:1-15 — the marvel of a miraculous meal
Jn 6:24-35 — the bread that gives life — the search for it and the source of it
Jn 6:41-51 — the bread that gives life — heavenly ingredients and eternal benefits
Jn 6:51-58 — the bread that gives life — eating it (believing)
Jn 6:60-69 — the bread that gives life — an offense to some, an assurance to others

John 6:1-3 indicates that the events surrounding Jesus' bread of life sermon took place at the time of Passover. Jesus had one year left in his public ministry before he would sacrifice himself as our Passover Lamb. The bread of life sermon proved to be a turning point in his ministry. It marked the end of Jesus' popularity among the majority of his countrymen. No longer did large crowds of curiosity-seekers follow him. Only the faithful few remained. As intense opposition set in, Jesus began more intensive training of the disciples. He made more specific predictions of his suffering and death, and he occupied himself with more outreach to non-Jews.

v. 41 — *At this the Jews began to grumble about him because he said, "I am the bread that came down from heaven."*

Jesus had led the Jews who were listening to his bread of life sermon along a logical path of reasoning: food for the soul is more important than food for the body (27); food for the soul comes from God in heaven (32); this bread of God is a *person* who comes from heaven and gives life to the world (33); and then the clincher, "I am the bread of life" (35) . . . "I have come down from heaven" (38).

The Jews arrived at the correct conclusion: Jesus was claiming that he had come from heaven. This fact they refused to accept.

Instead of pursuing the point to uncover the truth about his heavenly origins and miraculous birth, instead of seeking a fuller explanation from Jesus, they began to grumble about him (ἐγόγγυζον) under their breath. Their grumbling was not just a little inquisitive whispering but a caustic, cold-hearted mumbling aimed at Jesus. Their reaction to the words and works of the Son of God reminds us of the actions of their forefathers in the wilderness (Ex 15:24; 16:2; 17:3; Nu 11:1; 11:4; 14:2; 17:5; 21:5).

v. 42 — *They said, "Is this not Jesus, the son of Joseph, whose father and mother we know? How can he now say, 'I came down from heaven'?"*

The Jews refused to be certain of what they did not see: "How can this Jesus say, 'I came down from heaven?' We know that he came from Nazareth. We know his parents!"

But ever searching to reclaim straying sheep, the Savior attempted to head off their rancorous mumbling. He continued to build his case in support of the claim that he had come from heaven.

vv. 43,44 — *"Stop grumbling among yourselves," Jesus answered. "No one can come to me unless the Father who sent me draws him, and I will raise him up at the last day."*

It is impossible for a sinful human being without divine intervention to pull himself into a right relationship with God. Only God by a miracle of his grace can "draw" (ἐλκύσῃ) people close to himself. However, it is possible for a human being to push himself away from God. That's what Jesus observed as he stood in front of these mumbling, grumbling Jews. He was looking at people who considered themselves to be spiritually well-fed. But they had been eating spiritual junk food. They had sated themselves on the notion that they had the inborn ability to get close to God. Remember, they had asked, "What must we do to do the works God requires?" (28).

With a precise and emphatic statement Jesus negated their notions and pinpointed God's plan for bringing people close to himself: "No one can come to me unless the Father who sent me draws him." "Stand before God empty of your own good; let God fill you up with his love and forgiveness" (cf. Mt 5:6; Lk 1:53).

This passage punches a hole in "decision theology." It parallels other pronouncements from our Lord such as, "You did not choose me, but I chose you" (Jn 15:16). When it comes to the doctrine of conversion, God is the one doing all the work. As Luther wrote, "I believe that I cannot by my own thinking or choosing believe in Jesus Christ my Lord or come to him, but the Holy Spirit has called me by the gospel."

The last phrase of verse 44 ("I will raise him up on the last day") gives us a glimpse ahead at the topic Jesus will emphasize in verses 47-51. Once the Father has drawn a sinner to Jesus, that sinner is given eternal life. Instead of being condemned to eternal doom on the last day, a believer can claim this promise from the Savior: "I will raise him up at the last day." Many grammarians assume that the use of the Greek personal pronoun ἐγώ automatically adds special emphasis to the pronominal subject ("I *myself* will raise him up"), but other grammarians contend that the use of the personal pronoun actually throws added weight toward the action of the verb. For instance, in this passage Jesus is speaking emphatically, "I *really* will *raise* him up." The latter grammatical explanation fits well into the context of the Savior's bread of life sermon.

v. 45 — *"It is written in the Prophets: 'They will all be taught by God.' Everyone who listens to the Father and learns from him comes to me."*

As verse 44b looked ahead to the main point of verses 47-51 (namely, that the benefit that is offered by the bread of life is eternal life), so verse 45 looks ahead to the main point of verses 66-69 (namely, the words of God are the means by which this eternal life is channeled into our hearts). Here our Lord musters scriptural support, "It is written in the Prophets," for his claim that conversion takes place only when God performs a miracle of grace on the heart of a sinner. No doubt the ears of many people perked up when Jesus asserted, "It is written in the Prophets." Their religious leaders were accustomed to saying, "It is written in our laws," "This is what our forefathers said," "This is what we, the teachers, say." The Lord Jesus, on the other hand, knew God's words, used God's words, and applied God's words, and he did so with authority.

"It is written, 'They will all be taught by God.' " The context of this quotation from Isaiah indicates that the prophet was speaking about believers. All believers become believers and remain believers because the powerful words of God's forgiveness have turned their hearts of stone into hearts of flesh. The words of God are the living, active tools by which God creates faith and strengthens faith. The apostle Paul echoed this truth in his letter to the Romans: "Faith comes from hearing the message, and the message is heard through the word of Christ" (10:17).

But in any discussion about faith we recognize that the most important aspect of the discussion is the *object* of faith. We don't believe in our believing. We believe in the Lord Jesus, our only helper and hope, our only rescuer and redeemer. In this bread of life sermon Jesus focused attention on the proper object of faith when he stated that everyone who actually listens (aorist participle) to the Father's words and actually learns (aorist participle) comes to Jesus. This statement no doubt startled the Jews who had gathered around Jesus on this occasion. Most of them had incorrectly assumed that listening to God's words and learning from him would lead them only to laws and more laws. Others in their midst misread God's words and didn't learn from him at all; instead they leaned on their own works as the object of their faith. But there is only one proper object of faith — the Lord Jesus Christ.

v. 46 — *"No one has seen the Father except the one who is from God; only he has seen the Father.*

To understand why Jesus added this comment we will want to picture how his hearers would react to the words he had just spoken. He had claimed to be the only proper object of faith. The Jews reasoned, "Why should we put our trust in this teacher from Galilee in order to get close to God? Certainly we enjoyed the free food he provided yesterday. We wouldn't mind it if he continued to duplicate the feat and made our life a little easier. But what right does he have to say that we need him to get close to God? Who does he think he is?"

Jesus makes it very clear who he is. He is the one sent from God, the only one who has seen the Father, the only one who has an eternal, intimate unity with the Father. The words of verse 46 clinch the argument which Jesus stated in verse 41. If anyone is looking for bread that gives life, look to Jesus. He is the heavenly ingredient of that bread; he is the bread of life.

vv. 47,48 — *"I tell you the truth, he who believes has everlasting life. I am the bread of life."*

With a double ἀμὴν (occurring 25 times in John's Gospel) Jesus introduces a weighty and momentous statement. In the preceding verses he emphasized the truth that he is the heavenly ingredient of the bread of life (he is the bread of life). Now he emphasizes the eternal benefits of eating that bread. The one who believes in Jesus has and enjoys eternal life. Note that eternal life is not some distant, far-away benefit but a present reality (ἔχει) for a believer. Whether young or old, in good health or ill, whether rich or poor, a believer in Jesus enjoys God's forgiveness and mercy. And one day he will enjoy God's love in perfection.

vv. 49,50 — *"Your forefathers ate the manna in the desert, yet they died. But here is the bread that comes down from heaven, which a man may eat and not die.'*

The Jews were searching for some sort of magically produced earthly bread that would improve the quality of their physical life, or at least make it less of a burden and bore to put bread on their tables. "Our forefathers picked up free food for forty years during their wilderness wandering. They didn't have to labor and sweat for it. Wouldn't it be a luxury to have someone put us on easy street by providing a steady supply of free food?" But Jesus was offering himself as spiritual bread that would benefit their souls spiritually and eternally. Eat of this bread and you won't die. For "God has given us eternal life, and this life is in his Son. He who has the Son has life" (1 Jn 5:11,12). As Jesus told Martha, "I am the resurrection and the life. He who believes in me will live, even though he dies; and whoever lives and believes in me will never die" (Jn 11:25,26).

v. 51 — *"I am the living bread that came down from heaven. If a man eats of this bread, he will live forever. This bread is my flesh, which I will give for the life of the world."*

Verse 51 offers a magnificent, sweeping summary of this portion of Jesus' bread of life sermon. He reinforces and restates the truth of his heavenly origins. He is the one and only heavenly ingredient of the bread of life (he is the bread of life); and he reinforces and restates the wonderful benefit of eating this bread (believing in Jesus gives eternal life).

This portion of the Savior's bread of life sermon closes with a statement that startled his hearers and touched off their spiritually infantile question about cannibalism. Had the Jews been looking at him and listening to him with the eyes and ears of faith, they would have shouted to the heavens for joy at this pronouncement of good news, "This bread is my flesh, which I give for the life of the world." The Jews simply could not and would not understand that his death was for their eternal good. They present to us a foretaste of the spiteful rejection Jesus suffered at his trial. At that time their chief spokesman, Caiaphas, announced his conviction that Jesus ought to die. But couched in Caiaphas' decree was an unwitting parallel with the words of Jesus. Caiaphas declared, "It is better for you that one man die for the people than that the whole nation perish" (Jn 11:50).

What eternal benefits we enjoy because of Jesus! He gave his flesh, his life as a payment for all the sin of all people of all time. "In him we have redemption through his blood, the forgiveness of sins" (Eph 1:7). Oh, praise the bread of life, our Savior Jesus Christ!

## Homiletical Suggestions

As mentioned earlier, the preacher will want to note the special emphasis of each portion of Jesus' bread of life sermon when preaching on this series of texts from John 6. John 6:41-51 seems to divide itself nicely into two major thoughts. The first section (6:41-46) emphasizes the fact that Jesus can be called the true bread of life because he is from heaven. By way of application the preacher will want to remind his hearers that it is important for them to nourish their souls with spiritual food consisting of the proper ingredients. Many of them are concerned enough about bodily nutrition that they carefully read the labels of grocery items in order to detect artificial ingredients and to avoid ingredients that clog the arteries and add unnecessary calories. Won't they also want to check the ingredients of the spiritual food that goes into the soul? "Make sure you eat only the bread of life!" Jesus is the only proper soul-food.

The second section (6:47-51) emphasizes the benefit of eating the bread of life. There is plenty of artificial, non-nourishing spiritual food offered in the spiritual marketplace of the world's religions. But nothing can satisfy the soul with the comfort and confidence of eternal life like the true bread of life.

With those major points in mind we offer this outline:

## Jesus Is The Bread That Gives Life

1. Note the heavenly ingredients (vv. 41-46)
2. Enjoy the eternal benefits (vv. 47-51)

Along the same lines, another wording:

## Heavenly Bread Is Yours

1. Bread that came from heaven (vv. 41-46)
2. Bread that leads to heaven (vv. 47-51)

# THIRTEENTH SUNDAY AFTER PENTECOST

The Scriptures

> Old Testament — *Proverbs 9:1-6*
> Epistle — *Ephesians 5:15-20*
> Gospel — *John 6:51-58*

**The Text — John 6:51-58**

"This is a hard teaching. Who can accept it?" (Jn 6:60). Such was the response of many disciples to Jesus' lesson on the bread of life. No doubt many other listeners in the Capernaum synagogue that day felt the same way.

Their attitude toward Jesus of Nazareth had undergone a dramatic change since only the previous evening. Just a few miles away and only a few hours before, Christ had fed five thousand men with five small barley loaves and two small fish (Jn 6:1-15). At that time he filled the role of Messiah much to the liking of the Jews. They wanted an earthly king. They wanted a leader who would feed them by miraculous means every day. So when Jesus withdrew from the crowds and returned to Capernaum, many followed him.

Those who sought earthly bread from an earthly king were very disappointed once they caught up with Jesus back in Capernaum, however. He gave them no new miracles. He produced not a single new loaf of miracle-bread. Instead he used their curiosity to go into a discourse on much more important matters. "I am the bread of life," he announced. This was a "hard teaching" for many; it still is. Yet it is a gospel gem for those who hunger for eternal life.

Jesus' lesson on the bread of life reaches its climax in the following verses:

> v. 51 — *"I am the living bread that came down from heaven. If anyone eats of this bread, he will live forever. This bread is my flesh, which I will give for the life of the world."*

The Jews had been trying to get another miracle out of Jesus. They had been talking about how the Lord had once fed their forefathers with manna. Still impressed by that event in the desert many centuries earlier, they challenged Jesus, "Can you top this?" So Jesus reminded them of something they were overlooking: Their forefathers had died. Even with a steady diet of manna from heaven, an entire generation of their ancestors had died!

How much better if a man has "the living bread" — ὁ ἄρτος ὁ ζῶν). Once again Jesus directs his listeners away from earthly food whose nutrients are temporary. The heavenly bread with eternal food value is so much more precious! Jesus Christ is the food that people need! Christ had said this very thing many times before (Jn 3:16-18; 5:24-26; repeatedly in 6:25-50). Here he says it again with expressions that are only partly figurative. The following parallel might be an appropriate summary of this passage: As a starving man may eat bread and live for a few days longer, so may the dying sinner believe in Christ's sacrifice for all sinners and live forever.

The flesh (ἡ σάρξ) of Christ is essential to this statement. After "the Word became flesh and made his dwelling among us" (Jn 1:14), he gave his flesh as the sin-atoning sacrifice on the cross. A man will eat that flesh as his only bread of life; he will believe it.

v. 52 — *Then the Jews began to argue sharply among themselves, "How can this man give us his flesh to eat?"*

Did the Jews actually think that the great miracle-worker from Nazareth was urging cannibalism? A handful of them may have been turned off by such an implication. Yet undoubtedly there were others there who used that tack simply because they found the concept of Christ as their bread of life much too hard to swallow. They preferred the bread of their own righteousness to the righteousness of Jesus Christ. Their question earlier had been, "What must we do to do the works God requires?" (Jn 6:28). It did not appeal to their tastes merely to receive a bread which was already done. Besides, Jesus of Nazareth was too much a local boy for some of them (Jn 6:42). Then, too, he was too much a flesh-and-blood person like themselves to be their bread of life.

For several reasons "Christ crucified" was "a stumbling block to Jews" (1 Cor 1:23) already at this stage in his public ministry.

vv. 53,54 — *Jesus said to them, "I tell you the truth, unless you eat the flesh of the Son of Man and drink his blood, you have no life in you. Whoever eats my flesh and drinks my blood has eternal life, and I will raise him up at the last day."*

The arguments among his listeners did not prompt the Savior to back off. He continued to confront them with the truth about himself, making these two verses the core of this text.

To begin, Christ takes his promise of eternal life out of the future tense. He says, "Whoever eats my flesh and drinks my blood *has* eternal life" (ἔχει ζωὴν αἰώνιον). The gift of life without end is the believer's possession already in this life. Although he eagerly looks forward to the time when Christ "will raise him up at the last day," he need not wait till some future date to be certain of it.

As a matter of fact, sinners who do not "eat and drink" the crucified Son of God can be equally certain of their status. Christ speaks to them directly: "You have no life in you." He voices a similar warning in John 8:24: "I told you that you would die in your sins; if you do not believe that I am the one I claim to be, you will indeed die in your sins."

To make sure that there is no misunderstanding, the Savior mentions the other component part of the bread of life: his blood. The two references he makes to drinking his blood do not add any new ideas to his message, but they certainly intensify it. Of course, for many of Christ's Jewish listeners these references to blood only increased the crisis, and a number of them further hardened themselves against their Savior.

In verse 54 there is a change in wording which the reader of most English translations will not catch. Earlier Jesus was commanding hungry sinners to "eat" his flesh, using the aorist of the more common Greek verb ἐσθίω; here he speaks of eating with the present participle of τρώγω, which means "to gnaw" or "crunch" and is often used of animals feeding. Animals eat audibly, enthusiastically, intent on their food. Could it be that Christ wants sinners to take him in with the same intensity?

These verses have a parallel in verse 40 of this same chapter. They convey a similar idea, but the graphic words of these verses make the necessity of faith much more striking.

v. 55 — *"For my flesh is real food and my blood is real drink."*

The bread which nourishes and supports the repentant sinner's soul unto life eternal is real flesh and blood. Saving faith, then, is not merely a matter of believing in Jesus Christ as our highest moral example. Nor can saving faith be equated with taking hold of his ethics for oneself or trusting him as our leader. No, one will know and believe in the incarnate Son of God. More than that, one will look in faith to the cross, where the flesh-and-blood offering was once made for the world's sins. Jesus Christ crucified, really God yet really man, remains the object of saving faith. Nothing is more real than that!

St. John also writes about the sacrificed Christ in Revelation. There he points out that "the Lamb who was slain" is the object of praise and honor even among the angels (Rev 5:2). After all, with his blood Christ "purchased men for God from every tribe and language and people and nation" (Rev 5:9).

vv. 56,57 — *"Whoever eats my flesh and drinks my blood remains in me, and I in him. Just as the living Father sent me and I live because of the Father, so the one who feeds on me will live because of me."*

Some have taken this and previous verses as references to the Lord's Supper. All of the evidence, however, is to the contrary.

First, neither Christ nor his Scripture writers employ the terms "flesh and blood" (ἡ σάρξ, τὸ αἷμα) for the Lord's Supper. It is always "body and blood" (τὸ σῶμα, τὸ αἷμα).

Secondly, it is very unlikely that the Savior would command the sacramental eating of his body and blood before he had instituted his Holy Supper. Here we would have to ask Luther's question: "Why should Christ here have in mind that Sacrament when it was not yet instituted?" (St. Louis XI: 1143).

Thirdly, nowhere does Scripture "enjoin the sacramental eating and drinking of Jesus' body and blood as an absolute requirement to gain the life" (Ylvisaker, The Gospels, p. 342). Yet in several verses here it is required that we eat and drink his flesh and blood. Again, this flesh and blood cannot be the Lord's Supper.

Finally, Christ here guarantees that "whoever eats my flesh and drinks my blood has eternal life." It is the same guarantee that he makes in such well-known passages as Mark 16:16, John 3:16 and John 11:25,26. Yet Scripture does not issue such a guarantee to everyone who partakes of his body and blood in the Lord's Supper. A person may eat and drink the sacrament unworthily and thus drink judgment on himself (1 Co 11:29).

All who insist that these are comments on the Lord's Supper are missing the point. It is a spiritual eating and drinking to which Christ here is inviting us; he is encouraging a very intimate union between the sinner and the Savior, established through the Holy Spirit's gift of faith. To "eat and drink" his "flesh and blood" is to believe in the crucified Christ with all of one's being. It is a union of the most intimate kind.

This discourse on saving faith, of course, does not make Holy Communion unnecessary. On the contrary, the oral eating and drinking of Christ's body and blood in the bread and wine of the sacrament all the more awakens and stimulates the spiritual eating and drinking. Partaking of the Lord's Supper strengthens the union already established by faith.

v. 58 — *"This is the bread that came down from heaven. Your forefathers ate manna and died, but he who feeds on this bread will live forever."*

The masterful Teacher from Nazareth circles back to the Jews' challenge of verses 30 and 31 as he concludes his explanation of the bread of life.

The Israelite forefathers had received manna from heaven to sustain them during their wilderness wanderings. Christ had duplicated that feat the evening before on the other side of the lake, but could he surpass it? One more time he refers to himself as "the bread that came down from heaven." Like the manna, Christ came from the Father and gave glory to him. Unlike those manna-eaters, though, those who take in Christ by faith have life *eternal*. They experience the greatest miracle of them all through the bread of life!

The later manuscripts include τὸ μάννα in this verse. The NIV translators have also named "manna" as the food of the Jewish fathers, although they have placed the word in brackets. It is not necessary that τὸ μάννα be considered part of the inspired text, but the comparison which Christ makes between himself and manna is vital to his message. The preacher will be sure to mention this comparison.

## Homiletical Suggestions

This text is an outstanding attention-getter! Those who hear a meaningful reading of it will be eager for a more complete understanding. Jesus makes some very thought-provoking statements about eating his flesh and drinking his blood. The preacher does well if he can knock out the misconceptions that may arise without eliminating the shocking impact Christ intended.

While his listener is still asking himself, "Did I hear that right?" the preacher may begin his address by repeating some of Christ's more startling remarks (vv. 51,53,55). Humanly speaking, a difficulty with these statements is quite understandable. Only when we go to the foot of the cross and once again view the Savior's flesh-and-blood sacrifice does the Holy Spirit bring these words into focus. They still shock us. May they never stop stirring up our stomachs. Nevertheless, at Calvary we can clearly see what the Savior expects: Eat and drink my flesh and blood. Take it into your inmost being. Sinner, believe that this sacrifice is for you.

This discourse on the bread of life affords one of the Savior's many powerful assurances of eternal life for sinful mankind. It makes the believer's "living forever" as real and certain as Christ's death. In an age when nothing seems certain and nothing seems to last, the Lord's direct promise that the gift of life eternal is ours to consume by faith is most comforting.

Above all, this text defeats the notion that a good "head knowledge" of the teachings of Scripture is the highest level of Christian faith. "Head knowledge" is too distant from the Savior. He requires something much more "up close and personal" than that. Could we call it "stomach faith" in the flesh-and-blood Christ? Why not? As they "learn and inwardly digest" the words of Christ, the preacher will urge his hearers to "inwardly digest" the Lord Jesus with their "stomach faith" and include him in their daily diet plan. The following outline may give the preacher this opportunity:

## Today We Eat And Drink At The Table Of Our Savior

1. Where the conversation is stimulating (vv. 51-55)
2. Where the food is exactly what we need (vv. 51,54,56-58)

In using this approach the preacher will, of course, make sure that the people are fully aware that he is speaking about *spiritual* eating and drinking by faith, as has been pointed out in our exposition.

Another way is to emphasize the great blessings which only Christ can offer:

## Only Jesus Offers Living Bread

1. The only life which really counts (v. 53)
2. The only life which offers fellowship with God (vv. 56,57)
3. The only life which lasts forever (vv. 51,54,58)

Emphasizing the importance of faith in this section of John 6, as Jesus does, suggests the following treatment:

## Believe In The True Bread Of Life

1. For true life to begin (v. 53)
2. For true life to remain (vv. 56,57)
3. For true life to endure (vv. 58,59)

# FOURTEENTH SUNDAY AFTER PENTECOST

**The Scriptures**

Old Testament — *Joshua 24:1,2a,14-18*
Epistle — *Ephesians 5:21-31*
Gospel — *John 6:60-69*

**The Text — John 6:60-69**

This is the fifth successive selection based on John chapter six. From Pentecost 10 to Pentecost 13 the Gospel readings have presented the feeding of the 5,000 (1-15), the discussion of the miracle (24-35), Jesus' bread of life statements (41-51), and Jesus' encouragement to eat and drink of him (51-58). The verses which form the Gospel selection for Pentecost 14 are the conclusion of the entire incident and chapter (60-69).

If this is the fifth sermon in five weeks based on John 6, an attempt should be made to build on the earlier four, especially by referring to the verses of the chapter which have so recently been expounded.

If this is the fifth sermon in five weeks based on John 6, there is the very real danger that the preacher has reached ahead and used thoughts which should have been reserved for this text. Previewing what is coming is always important.

v. 60 — *On hearing it, many of his disciples said, "This is a hard teaching. Who can accept it?"*

By this time in his ministry Jesus had attracted three sets of people who followed him around. One group (Jews — vv. 41 and 52) reacted argumentatively to his discussion of the bread of life. We are dealing with the reactions of parts of the other two groups in these verses.

Verse 60 presents the reaction of some of the disciples. Jesus' miracles and preaching had attracted many people to assume the status of learners from this rabbi (25). In order to do that, these individuals had to become part of the group which regularly followed Jesus, observed him and listened to him. This required commitment on the part of the learners. The learners also had certain expectations of the commitment they had made.

Many of the disciples with this kind of commitment and expectation heard Jesus' discussion about the bread of life, and their intellect rebelled. What Jesus had said was not hard to understand. It was plain, but it was hard for them to accept. They had attained the understanding that Jesus of Nazareth was a special rabbi, sent from

God, who could do godly actions and thus could have been a candidate for Messiah. But they objected when Jesus called himself the bread of life come down from heaven, whose flesh they must eat and whose blood they must drink for eternal life.

"Who can accept it/him" (αὐτοῦ); both are possible. If they didn't accept Jesus' teaching, they were at the same time not accepting him. Therefore, don't make an issue of changing the NIV translation from "it" to "him."

v. 61 — *Aware that his disciples were grumbling about this, Jesus said to them, "Does this offend you?"*

"Aware" might not adequately reflect εἰδὼς ἐν ἑαυτῷ. Although grumbling usually has outward telltale signs, Jesus didn't need those indicators to know the inner workings of the minds of these disciples. He "knew all things in himself," including the grumbling of these people.

"Does my discussion ensnare you, scandalize you, cause you to fall into a spiritual death trap (σκανδαλίζει)? Do you object to my references to myself as the true bread from heaven? Does my encouragement that you eat and drink of me so greatly scandalize you that it is leading you to abandon me in unbelief? Are you so ensnared by my words that you can't catch on to the meaning from the intertwined references about believing in me (vv. 29,35,36,40,47)?"

v. 62 — *"What if you see the Son of Man ascend to where he was before!"*

We continue to paraphrase Jesus' argumentation: "Does my discussion drive you to unbelief? It should, if I were only a man. It should, if I weren't the bread of life from heaven. It should, if I couldn't give you eternal life. But my discussion shouldn't scandalize you if I am the Messiah, Son of God, true God myself. What will you do if you see me, the Son of Man, ascend to where I was before? That will be further proof that I am God. Won't that prove that I came down from heaven as the true bread of life? Will you still be scandalized then? Or, will you be convinced?"

v. 63 — *"The Spirit gives life; the flesh counts for nothing. The words I have spoken to you are spirit and they are life."*

The NIV translation capitalizes the first use of Spirit, but not the second. Our continuation of Jesus' argument can go in two directions, depending on whether you opt for "Spirit" or "spirit." With "spirit": "Don't you realize I wasn't asking you to literally eat my physical body? The flesh counts for nothing. Without the spirit in a person, human flesh is just meat. Spirit is always what gives life, what animates the person, what gives meaning to existence. I was referring to myself when I used the terms "body" and "blood." My flesh itself also counts for nothing. But when it's coupled with my spirit, when it's coupled with my willingness to carry out the Father's orders, then my body and blood, my entire being as the Messiah, can give the spiritual life, the eternal life promised by the Father. The words I spoke to you were about having life (53) and remaining in me and I in you (56). They were spiritual words. They were not talking about physical things. They were words full of spiritual meaning, able to offer to people the eternal life which the Father wants them to have. In my words I offer myself to you so you might have life (17:3)."

With "Spirit": "Don't you realize I wasn't asking you to literally eat my physical body? The fleshly, physical side of life counts for nothing. It isn't even real life. Only the Holy Spirit gives real life, spiritual life. Eating my physical flesh won't give you spiritual life. Only the Holy Ghost can do that by bringing you to faith in the Messiah. He does that through the words which I spoke. In fact, because he works through my words, I can say that those words themselves are spirit. They have the Spirit working in them. They are also life. They grant to people the new life, the eternal life, which God wants them to have."

It is interesting to do a comparison of translations here. Most interesting is the fact that some translations use both "Spirit" and "spirit." In order not to confuse the listeners, perhaps the preacher should stay with whatever interpretation is obvious from the capitalization in the translation he is using in the worship setting.

v. 64 — *"Yet there are some of you who do not believe." For Jesus had known from the beginning which of them did not believe and who would betray him.*

"Yet" seems to say, "Although my words are filled with spiritual meaning and are the channel of God's gift of eternal life, some of you who have been following me do not believe." Again it is obvious that God's message, even when it is spoken by Jesus, is able to be rejected.

An editorial comment by John follows. Jesus' knowledge of what was going on in the spiritual lives of people is not a new phenomenon. He had known who Nathaniel was before they had ever met (1:47,48). He had not entrusted himself to the crowds at Jerusalem (2:24,25).

Here a brief explanation of the difference between divine approval and divine foreknowledge would be in order. Jesus knew that Judas would be the betrayer, but Jesus did not approve of Judas' treachery, nor was Jesus in any way responsible for it.

v. 65 — *He went on to say, "This is why I told you that no one can come to me unless the Father has enabled him."*

To those who were still listening Jesus explained what was happening in the lives of those who did not believe. He had pointed out this same truth previously in this discussion (v. 44). Nobody on his own comes to Jesus to believe in him as the Messiah. By nature people just don't want to be his followers. They would much rather be on their own, do their own thinking and living. The desire to come to Jesus is worked in a person only by the Lord himself. The many pictures we use fit nicely. A spiritually blind person can't see where he is supposed to go. A spiritually dead person can't go anywhere. A spiritual enemy doesn't want to go following Jesus. Only when the Lord turns on the light, makes a person alive and reverses the hostility, will a person come to Jesus and desire to follow him.

v. 66 — *From this time many of his disciples turned back and no longer followed him.*

"From this time" might rather be rendered "From this" (ἐκ τούτου) meaning "because of this incident or discussion." "Many" of course doesn't mean all. There were some learners outside of the small group of the Twelve who continued to follow Jesus. But some turned back and did not follow Jesus anymore. "Turned back" might be strengthened a little into "returned to the things behind or past" (τά ὀπίσω). Some who had given up their past lifestyle and had committed themselves to following Jesus now returned to what they had been before.

v. 67 — *"You do not want to leave too, do you?" Jesus asked the Twelve.*

This question is directed to the third group — not to the Jews, not to the disciples, but to the Twelve, the inner circle of specially called followers. The question is based on the immediately preceding circumstance, the abandonment of Jesus by some of his former followers.

The Greek question particle (μή) expects a negative answer to the question. But the question really is: "Do you still want to be followers? Even after my comments on the bread of life? Even after many have left? Will you go along with the crowd?" With this question Jesus was pushing them to evaluate their reasons for following him. He was giving them a chance to assess their relationship with him and the basis for it. He was calling on them to verbalize what they believed. That would help them remain strong in the midst of all this defection.

v. 68 — *Simon Peter answered him, "Lord, to whom shall we go? You have the words of eternal life."*

Peter's answer acknowledges man's need to go somewhere for spiritual answers to life's spiritual needs. He admits man can't stand spiritually by himself or on his own. But he sees nobody besides Jesus who can satisfy man's spiritual needs. No one had been able to provide what Jesus had been supplying for them as they had followed him. From Jesus' words to them they had experienced new life with the Lord, the eternal life for which God had originally created man, interaction with the Lord, and enjoyment of his unending blessings. How could they abandon this source of life to which Jesus had referred (v. 63)?

v. 69 — *"We believe and know that you are the Holy One of God."*

Peter's statement that Jesus was the one to follow was based on something else. He and the other disciples had been led to believe and learned to know from their own experience with Jesus that he was the Holy One of God. "We" is emphasized in contrast to the conclusion which many had reached about Jesus. Peter is saying he and the rest of the Twelve had concluded that Jesus was correct in his claims about himself. He was specially set apart by God as Messiah. He had come into our sinful world to do what was necessary to accomplish salvation for mankind while at the same time remaining separate from the sinfulness of the world in which he spent his 33 years.

## Homiletical Suggestions

As previously mentioned, our text concludes a series of selections from John chapter six. It brings the aftermath of Jesus' testimony concerning himself as the bread of life. In the final analysis the result of this testimony was twofold. Some because of their own unbelief found Christ unacceptable and ceased to follow him. Others, moved by a Spirit-filled faith, found in Christ all that he offered.

It is interesting to note again that both reactions came not from the hostile Jews referred to earlier on in the chapter (v. 41 an v. 52), but from those who wished to be considered as "disciples" (v. 60). A total acceptance of Jesus as the only way to eternal life was the issue.

Reactions to Christ's testimony are the same today. Many of those who want to follow him as "great teacher" are offended by the claims which Christ clearly makes concerning himself in his word. Others find in these claims the only real assurance of eternal life.

Which brings us to our theme:

**Christ's All-Decisive Testimony Concerning Himself**

1. A hard and offensive word to some (vv. 60-66)
2. A word of assurance and eternal life to others (vv. 67-69)

A similar treatment of this text can be carried out on the basis of questions with which the Lord himself confronts his presumed followers:

**Two All-Decisive Questions Asked By Jesus**

1. "Does my teaching offend you?" (v. 61)
2. "You do not want to leave too, do you?" (v. 67)

In carrying out the thoughts indicated above the preacher will carefully point out that the "decision" for or against Christ lies exactly where the text itself places it. It is man's own stubborn unbelief which rejects the word of Christ (v. 64). It is the Holy Spirit, enabled by the Father, who moves the sinner to accept him as Savior (v. 63 and v. 65).

Although this still confronts us with the "why some and not others" mystery, we as Lutheran Christians will want to rest our assurance upon the *sola gratia* of Scripture rather than upon the shaky foundation of a sin-blinded reason.

# FIFTEENTH SUNDAY AFTER PENTECOST

**The Scriptures**

Old Testament — *Deuteronomy 4:1,2,6-8*
Epistle — *Ephesians 6:10-20*
Gospel — *Mark 7:1-8,14,15,21-23*

**The Text — Mark 7:1-8,14,15,21-23**

The text records another confrontation between Jesus and the Jewish leaders. At least five such confrontations had occurred earlier. The Jewish leaders had questioned him about his ability to forgive sins (Mk 2:7), about his association with tax collectors and sinners (Mk 2:16), about fasting (Mk 2:18), about work on the Sabbath (Mk 2:24) and about the casting out of demons (Mk 3:22). Here the issue is hand-washing and the traditions of the elders.

Presumably, this event took place near Capernaum. It fits into the period of "withdrawals" in Jesus' ministry, shortly after the great Galilean ministry.

Our text begins with a question from the Pharisees:

vv. 1-5 — *The Pharisees and some of the teachers of the law who had come from Jerusalem gathered around Jesus and saw some of his disciples eating food with hands that were "unclean," that is, unwashed. (The Pharisees and all the Jews do not eat unless they give their hands a ceremonial washing, holding to the tradition of the elders. When they come from the marketplace they do not eat unless they wash. And they observe many other traditions, such as the washing of cups, pitchers and kettles.) So the Pharisees and teachers of the law asked Jesus, "Why don't your disciples live according to the tradition of the elders instead of eating their food with 'unclean' hands?"*

"Uncleanness" (κοινός/κοινόω) is the unifying motif in this lesson. According to the Old Testament ceremonial law certain foods and animals were inherently unclean. People, objects and places could acquire uncleanness through contact with anything unclean. Uncleanness brought guilt, sin and a loss of holiness. It often required a sin offering for atonement (Lev 5:2-6). The Old Testament said nothing, however, about a person becoming unclean by eating with unwashed hands. It gave hand-washing regulations only to the priests in their ministry at the Tabernacle (Ex 30:19,21) and to a man with a discharge (Lev 15:11).

A rule against eating with unwashed hands developed in the Jewish oral tradition. Many such extra laws accumulated in the centuries prior to the time of Jesus, designed to "build a hedge around the written Torah and guard against any possible infringement of the Torah by ignorance or accident." Insight into these traditions of the elders can be gleaned from reading the *Mishnah*, a written compilation of Jewish traditional law compiled around A.D. 200. One tractate of the *Mishnah* is entitled "Yadaim" ("hands"). Here the hair-splitting casuistry of the rabbis is evident as they stipulate how much water needs to be used, how the water is to be applied, what makes a person's hands unclean, and so on (cf. Danby, pp. 778ff). Perhaps a solution to the Greek word πυγμῇ (literally: "fists; handfull") of verse 3 is found in the *Mishnah*, however, when it talks about pouring water "up to the wrist" (Yadaim 2:3). In verse 3 Beck translates: "without washing their hands up to the wrist."

The Pharisees at the time of Jesus considered this oral law to be as inspired and authoritative as the written law. They therefore fasted frequently (Mt 9:14), tithed their herbs (Mt 23:23), wore conspicuous phylacteries (Mt 23:5) and made distinctions about oaths (Mt 23:16-22). It was natural for them to ask, "Why don't your disciples live according to the traditions of the elders instead of eating their food with 'unclean' hands?"

Incidentally, it can be noted that the Greek word βαπτίζω in this lesson very definitely does not mean "immerse." Since the Jews certainly did not immerse themselves after returning from the market, the word βαπτίζω here simply means to "wash." Though this point will probably not come up in a sermon on this text, it is an important point in teaching the doctrine of baptism.

We hear Jesus' response to the Pharisees:

vv. 6-8 — He replied, "Isaiah was right when he prophesied about you hypocrites; as it is written: 'These people honor me with their lips, but their hearts are far from me. They worship me in vain; their teachings are but rules taught by men.' You have let go of the commands of God and are holding on to the traditions of men."

What Isaiah said as a prophet of God about the Jews of his generation applied also to the Pharisees of Jesus' day, according to Jesus. The Pharisees had two failings. First of all, they honored God with their lips, while their hearts were far from him. Secondly, they followed teachings taught by men.

The latter of these two charges was very evident. The Pharisees openly taught and practiced the traditions of the elders. What was most tragic was the fact that these man-made rules often were allowed to supercede the written law of God. For example, the Fourth Commandment was sidestepped in order to make a "Corban" (vv. 9-13). In giving a tenth of their garden herbs, justice and the love of God were neglected (Lk 11:42). Quite brazenly, the *Mishnah* asserted, "Greater stringency applies to [the observance of] the words of the Scribes than to [the observance of] the words of the [written] Law" (Sanhedrin 11:3). Jesus could say, "You have let go of the commands of God." "They worship me in vain."

The Pharisees were also guilty of offering outward lip service to God, without a pure heart. They were very much concerned with outward appearance. They made a show of their giving, praying and fasting (Mt 6) and were respected by others as outstanding examples of piety. They looked irreproachable in their actions. Yet, Jesus could see that their hearts were rotten. Inwardly they loved money (Lk 16:14), they were proud (Lk 18:11), they were plagued by selfish ambition (Lk 11:43), and they practiced self-indulgence (Mt 23:25). Most importantly, they refused to be baptized by John (Lk 7:30) and rejected Jesus as their Savior from sin (Jn 7:48). They were like whitewashed tombs (Mt 23:27) and like cups clean on the outside while dirty on the inside (Mt 23:25). In an astonishing display of their character, they refused to enter the palace of Pilate on Good Friday morning lest they become unclean, while at the same time they were fostering hatred toward the Son of God in their hearts (Jn 18:28).

Jesus properly gives them the label "hypocrites." The word "hypocrite" is an interesting one. In Attic Greek it was the word for an actor, "one playing a part on the stage." It came to refer to any person who pretended to be something he wasn't. This is how we use the term today. We define "hypocrite" as "one who pretends to be a believer but really isn't." This title fits the Pharisees. The yeast of the Pharisees was hypocrisy (Lk 12:1). Though they may not have consciously been "playing a part," yet, in reality, they were tremendous actors. They acted as God's favored followers, while they, in reality, were on the way to hell (Mt 23:15).

Our text now brings us the verses which give Jesus' elaboration:

vv. 14,15,21-23 — *Again Jesus called the crowd to him and said, "Listen to me, everyone, and understand this. Nothing outside a man can make him 'unclean' by going into him. Rather, it is what comes out of a man that makes him 'unclean'... For from within, out of men's hearts, come evil thoughts, sexual immorality, theft, murder, adultery, greed, malice, deceit, lewdness,*

*envy, slander, arrogance and folly. All these evils come from
inside and make a man 'unclean.' "*
Jesus had criticized the Pharisees for following man-made rules
about uncleanness. Here he goes a step further by saying, "Nothing
outside a man can make him 'unclean' by going into him." With
these words Jesus is abolishing the distinction between clean and
unclean foods as it was given by God in the ceremonial law of Moses.
Mark, in his significant editorial comment, says, "In saying this,
Jesus declared all foods 'clean' " (v. 19b). Jesus is saying the same
thing as Acts 10:13-15; Romans 14:14-20; Colossians 2:13-17; 1 Timo-
thy 4:3-5; and Hebrews 9:10. The Old Testament dietary laws (Lev 11;
Nu 19; Dt 14) are transcended now that the Savior has come. Certain
foods no longer make a person unclean. The implications of this
assertion most definitely were not understood by the disciples until
much later. Otherwise there would not have been such hesitation
and uncertainty in the primitive church about unclean foods (Ac
10:14; 11:2,3).

But even more importantly, Jesus with these words — in this
setting as he is dealing with the hypocritical Pharisees — is making
the point that the inner attitude is all important in God-pleasing
living. Uncleanness is not just a matter of externals. It is not a
matter of hand washings and food. It is a matter of the heart.
William Barclay offers this pertinent comment: "There is no greater
religious peril than the peril of identifying religion with outward
observance. . . . Church-going, Bible-reading, careful financial giving, even time-tabled prayer do not make a man a good man. The
fundamental question is, how is a man's heart towards God and
towards his fellow-men? And if in his heart there are enmity, bitterness, grudges, and pride, not all the outward religious observances
in the world will make him anything other than a hypocrite."

Worthy of note in regard to these verses is an observation made by
Hugo Odeberg in his book *Pharisaism and Christianity*. He suggests
that the fundamental difference between Pharisaism and Christianity lies in their teachings about the natural condition of man's heart.
The Pharisees taught that man has a "good disposition" by nature
and a free will to choose what is good. For Jesus the starting point is
just the opposite. According to Jesus, man's heart is by nature evil.
"From within, out of men's hearts, come evil thoughts, sexual immorality, theft. . . . " The *Mishnah* said that there must be a "Father
of Defilement" on the outside if a person is to become unclean.
According to Jesus, there is no need for an outside source of contam-
ination. Man's heart is corrupted by original sin.

## Homiletical Suggestions

With this text an interesting and edifying sermon could be preached about the errors of the Pharisees. It is in this text that Jesus exposes the two failings of the Pharisees — their allegiance to man-made rules and their hypocrisy.

In such a sermon the preacher would encourage his hearers to avoid making the same errors, inasmuch as Pharisaism is still a very real tempation. There are other religious groups which set forth man-made rules. There is a temptation within our own congregations to elevate human traditions to a level of authority. We need to cling solely to the commands of God in the Bible and avoid man-made rules. Also there is a temptation for all of us to externalize our religion and become hypocrites. We are tempted just to "go through the motions" in our worship and Christian living, while our hearts are far from the Lord. We need to be reminded that the inner attitude is all-important.

In talking about the heart, the preacher would want to stress what it is which makes a person's heart "near to God." It is Jesus. The Pharisees rejected their "only Mediator and Redeemer, Jesus Christ," so whatever they did, they were still far away from God (Heb 11:6). We need to confess our own unworthiness and look to Jesus as our Savior. Through him we are reconciled and "brought near" to God (Eph 2:13).

### Don't Be A Pharisee

1. They followed rules taught by men
2. They honored God with their lips, but their hearts were far from him

These same thoughts could be developed in a sermon with a more positive approach, focusing on what is necessary for a God-pleasing life. The Pharisees were intensely interested in leading a God-pleasing life, but they were misguided. Through the admonition of Jesus we can learn what is really necessary.

### Live A God-pleasing Life

1. Follow God's word, not human traditions
2. Have a pure heart, not just outward actions

Another suggestion would be to center on the concept of cleanness and uncleanness. This motif pervades the lesson and is a common theme in the entire Bible (just check a concordance on "clean" and "unclean").

A complete presentation of the concept as it appears in the lesson would have three parts. Jesus indicates that human tradition doesn't make a person unclean. Jesus indicates that the ceremonial law of Moses no longer makes a person unclean. Rather, it is the evil which comes from within which makes a person unclean.

Many passages from other parts of the Bible could be employed to develop the fourth point — that Jesus alone makes us "clean" in the eyes of God. (Cf. Eph 5:26; Heb 9:14; 10:22; 1 Jn 1:7,9; Rev 7:14.)

## Spiritual Cleanness And Uncleanness

1. Uncleanness does not come from unwashed hands or certain foods
2. Uncleanness comes from evil thoughts and actions
3. Cleanness comes alone from Jesus

A final suggestion would be to focus on the biblical doctrine of original sin. In the 1970 survey of 5,000 American Lutherans published in *A Study of Generations*, 50% of the respondents answered "yes" to the statement: "A person at birth is neither good nor bad." Perhaps a greater emphasis in Lutheran preaching needs to be placed on our inherent sinfulness.

The Pharisees felt that man is able to do good in and of himself. They felt that a person becomes evil only after being corrupted by forces from the outside. This is the belief of many today. It can be countered by Jesus' words, "All these evils come from inside and make a man unclean."

Such a sermon, of course, would need a third part, presenting the glorious truth of the gospel. God has redeemed us from our natural sinfulness through the atoning work of Jesus.

## The Natural Condition Of The Human Heart

1. Was thought to be good by the Pharisees
2. Was exposed as evil by Jesus
3. Has been redeemed by Jesus

# SIXTEENTH SUNDAY AFTER PENTECOST

## The Scriptures

Old Testament — *Isaiah 35:4-7a*
Epistle — *James 1:17-22,26,27*
Gospel — *Mark 7:31-37*

## The Text — Mark 7:31-37

Our text is included in a series of miracle accounts leading up to Peter's confession of Jesus as the Christ in Mark 8:29. After observing the miracle reported in this text, people were moved to confess with amazement, "He has done everything well" (v. 37). The narrative is unique to Mark. Jesus' journeys brought him from the northern region of the Holy Land to the area of the Decapolis in present-day Jordan, west of the Jordan River. It was here that our Lord met people seeking his help on behalf of a deaf man with an impediment in his speech.

v. 31 — *Then Jesus left the vicinity of Tyre and went through Sidon, down to the Sea of Galilee and into the region of the Decapolis.*

The Decapolis (Δεκαπόλεως) was a league of 10 cities established by the followers of Alexander the Great (as one might surmise from the Greek name, "ten cities") and rebuilt by the later Roman governors. The region had its own coinage and army. Like the previous pericope on the Syrophoenician woman, this text demonstrates our Lord's interest in people beyond Palestine proper. Since Mark was written for Gentile readers, Mark has an evangelistic concern in including this fact.

v. 32 — *There some people brought to him a man who was deaf and could hardly talk, and they begged him to place his hand on the man.*

The Savior's reputation had gone before him, even to this remote place (see Mark 5:20 and context for another miracle in the same location). Thus a group brought to Jesus a man who was deaf (κωφόν) and unable to speak clearly (μογιλάλον).

The text, of course, deals with the physically deaf, but it may be applied to the spiritually deaf (1 Co 2:14,12:3) without violence to its original intention. In Mark 8:18 Jesus asks, "Do you have eyes but fail to see, and ears but fail to hear?" Jesus made spiritual applications of physical miracles in places such as John 9, especially verse

39. Spiritual deafness is much more serious than physical hearing impairment, for its result is eternal death. So Jesus calls to us also, "If anyone has ears to hear, let him hear" (Mk 4:9,23).

v. 33 — *After he took him aside, away from the crowd, Jesus put his fingers into the man's ears. Then he spit and touched the man's tongue.*

Jesus took the man "aside" before healing him. Ever considerate of the feelings of others, he did not want to embarrass him in front of others. Deaf people are often embarrassed by the frustration of having others talk to them without being able either to understand or to reply. Blindness is usually quite evident, and so are most other physical handicaps, but we often are not aware of a person's deafness until we attempt to speak with the person.

Our Lord's use of miracles contrasts starkly with the techniques of some of today's "miracle workers." Instead of quietly taking a sick or disabled person aside, they prefer to perform before TV cameras. Instead of using their "gifts of healing" for the benefit of chronically or terminally ill who are confined to hospitals or nursing homes, they often use advance teams to interview patients before "healing" them on TV. They want to find those who will most likely respond positively to the healer's ministrations.

In contrast, Jesus did not publicize his signs and wonders, although he often (especially in John's Gospel) pointed to them as a basis for faith. Some of those writing about our Lord's "Messianic Secret" do so for reasons of unbelief (so Wrede), but it is clear that Mark's Gospel especially stresses his reluctance to be known as a miracle-working Messiah. This text is no exception (cf. 7:36). Neither demons (Mk 1:34; 3:12) nor his disciples (Mk 8:30; 9:9,10) nor those healed (Mk 1:43,44; 5:43) are permitted to speak of his miracles. He must go the way of the cross (Mk 8:31-34), not the way of glory, attracting enthusiastic crowds. Luther's "theology of the cross" in contrast to the "theology of glory" is manifested here.

Jesus worked miracles of healing as marks of his Messianic office and out of compassion for the victims of various maladies, but never for sheer sensationalism.

v. 34 — *He looked up to heaven and with a deep sigh said to him, "Ephphatha!" (which means, "Be opened!").*

One is struck by the very specific and detailed description of the actions and emotions of the Savior in the healing miracle recorded here. Since ancient tradition has it that Mark might really be called "the Gospel of Peter as told to Mark," it is likely that we see the marks of an eyewitness description here. Although at times Jesus healed instantaneously even at a distance with only a word (cf. Mk 7:24-30; Mt 8:5-13; Jn 4:46-54), at other times he healed very deliberately and with meaningful gestures, as in this case.

Each action was an invitation to faith, dealing gently and lovingly with the deaf man. Those who brought the man to Jesus begged him to place his hand on him. Our Lord goes beyond this, involving the very organs affected by the man's malady: his ears and his tongue.

Mark also gives us a deep insight into the emotions of the Savior, a glimpse indeed into the very heart of God. Jesus looks up into heaven and utters a deep sigh. We are reminded by the mood, if not the exact words, of the scene in John 11 where Jesus is at the tomb of his beloved friend Lazarus. Here we witness the profound sympathy of the God-man over our earthly troubles. The preacher would do well to note the theological parallels in Hebrews 2:14-18 and 4:14-16. He indeed is the "man of sorrows, and familiar with suffering" (Isa 53:3). Jesus agonizes over the results of the fall in the physical suffering of mankind, profoundly moved by what is rather than what might have been.

Scripture sees all illness and death as evidence of our fallen state and of Satan's power in the world. In his sigh (ἐστέναξεν) Jesus echoes the sigh of creation, of all Christians, and of the Holy Spirit (Ro 8:22-27). How different our state is from what Eden was and what heaven will be!

Then Jesus healed this man's deafness with a single Aramaic word, "Ephphatha! Be opened!" The same divine power which brought the universe into existence when God spoke brought healing to this man!

v. 35 — At this, the man's ears were opened, his tongue was loosened and he began to speak plainly.

This miracle heralds the Messianic age, prophesied in Isaiah 35:5,6, appropriately selected as the Old Testament reading for this Sunday. Miracles are the signs, "the calling cards of the Messiah," indicating who Jesus was (cf. Acts 2:22). Each miracle constitutes a miniature restoration of Paradise and a reversal of the effects of the fall. God did indeed visit his people.

The words of Christ "opened" (διανοίχθητι) his ears completely and literally "loosed the band of his tongue" (ἐλύθη ὁ δεσμὸς τῆς γλώσσης αὐτοῦ). The fetters of Satan were cast off of the poor man. Perhaps for the first time he could hear sounds, words, music! How much this must have felt like being released from a prison, a prison of silence. Now also he could speak "plainly", or rather "correctly, straightly" (ὀρθῶς).

v. 36 — *Jesus commanded them not to tell anyone. But the more he did so, the more they kept talking about it.*

As noted above, our Lord is not interested in being a heroic "man on horseback," ushering in a millennium, manifesting his glory before the crowds. Yet, the tongues of the people had also been loosened, and they "could not help speaking about what" they had "seen and heard" (cp. Ac 4:20). True faith shows itself in witness (1 Pe 2:9) and worship, praising God for what he has done.

v. 37 — *People were overwhelmed with amazement. "He has done everything well," they said. "He even makes the deaf hear and the dumb speak."*

This last verse of our text is its climax. Everything has been leading up to this marvelous confession of faith: "He has done everything well." Note the emphasis given by the Greek word order: καλῶς πάντα πεποίηκεν. There can be no doubt that this verse is a conscious reflection of the verdict of Genesis 1:31, "God saw all that he had made, and it was very good." God had made all good in the first place; only man's sin and its consequences have made it otherwise (Ro 8:18-23). Now, in Christ, God was putting into effect "Plan B": the reconciliation and restoration of God's original good in the work of Christ. It had all been καλῶς before, it would be καλῶς again!

Now the promise of Isaiah 35 had been fulfilled before their eyes. As Jesus deliberately said, the prophecies of Isaiah 61:1-6 had come to pass: the Messianic age was among them, for the Messiah had given evidence of the power and authority of his kingdom in the midst of a world ruled by Satan.

But the best is yet to come. There will again be a time when all weeping, all ailments, all death will be banished forever, and there will be no more need for sighing. This is in heaven, as Revelation 7:11-17 and 21:1-7 joyfully declare.

Thank God that Jesus still utters his "Ephphatha" for us also, opening the eyes and ears closed by unbelief and the mouths silenced by sin, in captivity to the power of Satan. He still does it through word and sacrament as here and throughout the world he releases prisoners from their captivity, opens the eyes of the blind and the ears of the spiritually deaf so that they might hear the gospel, turn and be forgiven (Mk 4:12). As a new creation (2 Co 5:17), we praise him now and forever.

## Homiletical Suggestions

Our text is full of preachable clues for both law and gospel, especially as it is applied to mankind's spiritual blindness. Here is one suggestion:

### Jesus Still Says "Ephphatha: Be Opened!"

1. Our spiritual deafness — stubbornly refusing to hear
2. The Savior opens our ears through the gospel
3. Opened mouths praise him now and forever

A theme taken from the text suggests:

### "He Does All Things Well"

1. At creation, God says, "Very good"
2. The fall corrupts God's good creation
3. The Messiah restores in his miracles
4. The Savior restores in the gospel
5. The final restoration of heaven

A simpler way, perhaps, of presenting these truths would be:

### Jesus, The Divine Healer, Takes Us Aside

1. Individually
2. Compassionately
3. Powerfully

# SEVENTEENTH SUNDAY AFTER PENTECOST

**The Scriptures**

Old Testament — *Isaiah 50:4-10*
Epistle — *James 2:1-5,8-10,14-18*
Gospel — *Mark 8:27-35*

**The Text — Mark 8:27-35**

Do we see our Savior clearly? The reading before us directs disciples of Jesus to a careful examination of the person and work of Christ. Have we made a positive identification concerning Jesus of Nazareth? Have we recognized his mission? There is still some confusion among the twelve disciples in our text — and among countless people today. Yet our salvation depends on a solid identification of the Savior and his work. There must be no confusion concerning his identity!

In connection with this text it is especially helpful to consider the context. Despite the miraculous provision of food at the beginning of the chapter, the disciples were still sidetracked in their understanding of Christ and his real task (cf. Mk 8:14-21). Following still another miracle, this time a healing miracle, Jesus asked what people were saying about him. Peter answered with a clear confession about his person but revealed a warped understanding of his work (cf. Mk 8:32). He still had much to learn.

About one week later the transfiguration took place (cf. Mk 9:2). Jesus vividly revealed his glory, discussed his upcoming death (Lk 9:31) and predicted his resurrection (Mk 9:9,10). As his public ministry drew to a close, Jesus patiently instructed his followers on some basic questions: Who was he? What did he come to do? Our Scripture provides the answers to those questions, answers which are the very core of the gospel.

v. 27 — *Jesus and his disciples went on to the villages around Caesarea Philippi. On the way he asked them, "Who do people say I am?"*

Jesus and the Twelve were up north, away from Judea and Galilee. Toward the close of his ministry Christ withdrew from the open unbelievers and concentrated on privately instructing the chosen ones. The unbelief of the majority was clearly hardening. The Pharisees even had the gall to ask Jesus for a miracle to substantiate his claims. Hadn't Christ just fed the thousands? No sign would reward their unbelief (Mk 8:11-13). Even the populace viewed Jesus as a "meat and potatoes" Messiah and tried to make him a king (Jn 6:14,15). No doubt his fame was widespread, but the people were still in darkness. By asking the disciples this identity question, he gave them the chance to air the popular opinions and to consider for themselves the current explanations. But Christ did not want them swayed by a public opinion poll mentality.

v. 28 — *They replied, "Some say John the Baptist; others say Elijah; and still others, one of the prophets."*

The common notion was that Jesus of Nazareth was indeed someone special. In keeping with prevalent Jewish apocalyptic expectations, some identified Jesus as the reincarnation of John the Baptist or Jeremiah. They looked for a reincarnation of the prophet right before the physical return of the Messiah. Others thought of Jesus as another great prophet carrying on the same work as the Old Testament prophets. Do opinions today have such variety? Of course they do. Consider how Jesus' message is distorted in favor of the latest trend in religious opinion or the newest theory for social reform.

v. 29 — *"But what about you?" he asked. "Who do you say I am?" Peter answered, "You are the Christ."*

Jesus wants them and us to search our own hearts. The question he asks is of eternal importance. The Greek has "you" (ὑμεῖς) in emphatic position. No longer talk about others' ideas. Jesus asks each of us, "But you, who do you say I am?" It is a key question for each individual. Who is the Jesus? A disciple needs a clear answer. The answer will determine the commitment.

Peter provides a bold confession for the group. There is no dissension among them, no disagreement. Jesus is the Christ. The other synoptic writers provide a fuller reply, but there is certainly no contradiction with Mark's abbreviated account. The title, Christ, means "the anointed one," "the anointed of God." The prophets of old had clearly foretold this Messiah. By using the title Christ (the Greek name, Christ, is identical to the Hebrew name, Messiah), Peter confesses that the disciples have made a positive identification. Jesus is the one promised, true God and true man.

v. 30 — *Jesus warned them not to tell anyone about him.*

In the light of the centuries that had passed while the people waited for the Christ, this request comes as quite a surprise. If the disciples have made the positive identification, why conceal it? Yet Christ's words are forceful. The Greek ἐπιτιμάω ("warned") implies a censure or rebuke. At times the rebuke is a sign of disapproval, as in verses 32 and 33. Peter disapproves of the idea that Jesus should suffer harm. Jesus then rebukes Peter and sternly disapproves of any attempt to dissuade him from his mission. However, in verse 30 ἐπιτιμάω seems to have a different focus. Jesus rebukes the disciples in order to forbid what might happen if they should tell others. Jesus does not disapprove of Peter's clear confession, but the time is not ripe for the Redeemer to be revealed. Neither the disciples nor the people can fully perceive what the Christ has come to do. Only after the cross and tomb will they be brought to an understanding of these matters.

v. 31 — *He then began to teach them that the Son of Man must suffer many things and be rejected by the elders, chief priests and teachers of the law, and that he must be killed and after three days rise again.*

Jesus now plainly speaks to his followers about the real purpose of his ministry. He has come to die for all, and to rise for all. God had foreordained this rescue mission and had promised it immediately after man's rebellion (Ge 3:15). God then sent prophet after prophet to enlighten the people about the champion to come, the one anointed to save. He would be a prophet (Dt 18:15-18), and a king (2 Sa 7:11-16; Zec 9:9,10), yet one rejected by men (Isa 53:2,3). He would be true God and true man, come to serve not subjugate (Eze 34:23,24). He would be perfect and sinless, yet suffer for the crimes of others — our crimes (Isa 53:6-12)! He would come to die, but through that death he would destroy death forever (Isa 25:7-9). Jesus knew it had to be thus. God's law is not mocked. It must be obeyed and sin must be punished. Only then is God's holiness vindicated. So Jesus came to fulfill the law and suffer the penalty for our transgressions of God's law. Jesus came to do what no mere human could do, to rescue us from ruin. He had to do this for us. The key word in this verse is δεῖ ("it is necessary"). It was absolutely necessary that God's plan would be carried out for our salvation. To change his plan or to fail to carry it through would mean the damnation of every man, woman, and child. To keep Christ from the cross would achieve Satan's ultimate victory.

vv. 32,33 — *He spoke plainly about this, and Peter took him aside and began to rebuke him. But when Jesus turned and looked at his disciples, he rebuked Peter. "Get behind me, Satan!" he said. "You do not have in mind the things of God, but the things of men."*

Is it any wonder that Jesus so sternly admonished Peter? How shocked the disciple must have been! After all, Peter had spoken out of concern. He wanted nothing evil to happen to his teacher. It hurt Peter to hear Jesus talk about rejection, suffering, death. Yet if Peter's misguided admonition were followed, salvation for the world would be thwarted! It was necessary for Jesus to rebuke Peter in no uncertain terms.

The reaction of Peter confronted Jesus with a real temptation. Such concern for his physical well-being was a temptation for Jesus. Must the cup be drunk so fully? Could he not just keep teaching and preaching? Such thoughts were Satan's attacks in an effort to abort Jesus' mission. Jesus, the perfect Son of God, knew the source of the temptation and also knew how to deal with it and overcome it. "Get behind me, Satan!" he said to Peter. Peter did not yet understand God's plan, for his sinful flesh still blinded his understanding. It was only later, after the outpouring of the Spirit, that the pieces of God's plan fit into place for Peter. Consider his beautiful Pentecost sermon (Ac 2). Through the Spirit's work Peter was led to see the things of God. He was able to clearly identify the person and purpose of the Christ.

## Homiletical Suggestions

This text provides a powerful opportunity to concentrate on the Bible's basics. No listener should leave without knowing who Jesus really is and what he really came to do. For Christians of every spiritual maturity level, these basic truths need to be applied. Don't we sometimes try to redefine Jesus according to our preconceived notions? Do we ever try to redirect his mission more to our liking? Do we try to shape the Savior to our patterns? Any such attempts are from Satan. Our reading helps us remember God's plan and how Christ must fulfill every part of his calling. The first two outlines concentrate on this proper identification and have an identical verse breakdown.

### Who Is This Jesus?

1. Identify the person (vv. 27-30)
2. Identify his purpose (vv. 31-33)

### Issues And Answers

1. About the most important person (vv. 27-30)
2. About the most important work (vv. 31-33)

Another direction one can easily pursue is taken from verse 31. The preacher could tie in the promises and fulfillments of Scripture as being all part of God's great plan to save. Here the emphasis would be on the Christ as the central theme of both testaments. "These are written that you may believe that Jesus is the Christ, the Son of God, and that by believing you may have life in his name" (Jn 20:31). The plan to save mankind centers on Christ, and it cannot be changed.

**God's Got A Plan** (v. 31)

1. The plan cannot be changed (vv. 32-33)
2. Only Jesus can fulfill it (vv. 27-30)

Some of the pericope listings add verses 34 and 35 to this Sunday's text. Jesus goes on in those verses to show us the character of a disciple. Our life, too, has a purpose and mission that centers on the cross. The two outlines below are given with that addition.

**Dare To Be Disciples Of Jesus!**

1. Bold to confess him (vv. 27-29)
2. Bold to believe his mission (vv. 30-33)
3. Bold to follow his cross (vv. 34,35)

**Do We Have The Scriptures Straight?**

1. The facts about our Lord? (vv. 27-29)
2. The facts about his life? (vv. 30-33)
3. The facts about our life? (vv. 34,35)

# EIGHTEENTH SUNDAY AFTER PENTECOST

**The Scriptures**

> Old Testament — *Jeremiah 11:18-20*
> Epistle — *James 3:16-4:6*
> Gospel — *Mark 9:30-37*

**The Text — Mark 9:30-37**

The opening words of our text indicate the situation and set the scene:

vv. 30-31a — *They left that place and passed through Galilee. Jesus did not want anyone to know where they were, because he was teaching his disciples.*

Jesus and the Twelve were returning from a visit to the villages around Caesarea Philippi (Mk 8:27-38) and from the Mount of Transfiguration (Mk 9:2-13), where Jesus had revealed himself to Peter, James and John in glory. At both places the Lord had talked to the disciples about the events soon to take place in Jerusalem involving his suffering, death and resurrection.

After Jesus healed a boy with an evil spirit (Mk 9:14-29), they "passed through Galilee." It was the Lord's last visit to this area before his death, a private visit away from the crowds which had surrounded him on many previous trips through this area. Jesus "was not wanting" (ἤθελεν — imperfect tense) anyone to know where they were.

The reason for this somewhat protracted period of privacy is told us in the words of our text which follow:

v. 31b — *He said to them, "The Son of Man is going to be betrayed into the hands of men. They will kill him, and after three days he will rise."*

Public preaching was now to be relegated to the background. The private instruction of the disciples was the priority item on Jesus' agenda. R. C. Lenski summarizes the situation well: "In these out-of-the-way places Jesus was devoting himself to the last, intensive training of the Twelve, especially also preparing them for the end" (*The Interpretation of Mark's Gospel*, p. 387).

Although the Lord had on other occasions directed his conversation toward the climactic events about to take place in Jerusalem, this was a more intensive effort on his part to concentrate on this matter. "He was teaching his disciples," our text says. The use of the

Greek imperfect tense of the verb (ἐδίδασκεν) indicates an ongoing process of instruction. This related to what would happen to "the Son of Man," the Redeemer, in his divine-human natures. He who by his many miracles had demonstrated his power over all things was going to "be betrayed into the hands of men." Did Judas catch the implied warning?

Jesus would be "killed" and would "rise again." That which had been prophesied concerning him from the beginning was about to be fulfilled. This was no oblique reference to the series of events which would earn salvation for all mankind. Jesus spoke directly about the events that would soon come to pass. This was a matter of intensive private instruction.

How disappointing, therefore, the words of our text which follow:

v. 32 — *But they did not understand what he meant and were afraid to ask him about it.*

Again Mark uses the imperfect tense of the Greek verbs for "did not understand" and "were afraid," describing a continuing state of ignorance and fear on the part of the Twelve. They simply did not grasp what seemed incredibly horrible to them. Unfortunately, their thoughts seemed to stop with the words "be killed." This did not fit into their ideas of how Jesus would establish his Messianic rule. That is also why they even feared to ask about it. Don't we do the same when we hesitate even to discuss matters that worry us or frighten us?

One might look upon this reluctance to accent the necessity of the cross in God's plan of salvation as a matter of stubborn obtuseness. But should it surprise us? The preaching of the cross, as Paul reminds us, is a "stumbling block to Jews and a foolishness to Gentiles" (1 Co 1:23). Many who wish to be classified as Christians today imagine that the chief purpose of the Christian church is to be found in activities which relegate into the background the message of a Savior crucified for sin. They suppose that the chief purpose of Christianity lies in spectacular demonstrations for social and political reform, or in making this a "better world" in which to live, or in engaging in activist programs which show that the church is a real "force for good" in this world. The central message of the Bible is clear, but "blood religion" does not appeal to the people of this world. They don't want to hear repeated references to the ugliness of personal sin and the divine necessity of a sacrificial cross to atone for that sin.

Yet, as Jesus reminded the Twelve repeatedly, these were inescapable requirements of his mission. As Paul adds, "The foolishness of

God is wiser than man's wisdom, and the weakness of God is stronger than man's strength" (1 Co 1:25). Christ's sacrificial death and glorious resurrection are mankind's only way of justification before a holy and righteous God.

The incidents which are reported in the next portions of our text show the kind of response Christ wants to find in those who accept his way of the cross:

> vv. 33,34 — *They came to Capernaum. When he was in the house, he asked them, "What were you arguing about on the road?" But they kept quiet because on the way they had argued about who was the greatest.*

That the disciples were still filled with false hopes concerning the Messianic kingdom became even more apparent in their discussions on the way to Capernaum. As Jesus entered this Galilean city for the last time on his way to Jerusalem, he felt it necessary to speak privately to the Twelve about these discussions of "who was the greatest." Perhaps their argument had arisen because Jesus had granted only Peter, James and John the privilege of seeing him in his glorious transfiguration. In any case, the disciples did not want to say what they had been arguing about. "They kept quiet." They must have sensed that their ideas of greatness did not agree with what Jesus had been talking about when he spoke of the necessity of his death.

And how right they were! Knowing all about their discussions pertaining to worldly recognition and grandeur, Jesus decided it was high time to take them aside and tell them what true greatness was all about in God's kingdom:

> v. 35 — *Sitting down, Jesus called the Twelve and said, "If anyone wants to be first, he must be the very last, and the servant of all."*

What a paradox — to be first one must be last! True greatness is determined, not by deeds which receive the greatest outward attention, but by humble service which is often scarcely recognized. The word "servant" (διάκονος) generally implies some type of servile waiting upon others, doing this service in simplicity of heart and without thought of earthly return. In later church terminology a "deacon" or "deaconess" was a person placed rather low on the register of church officialdom, rendering some type of practical service as a helper or agent in behalf of others. The essence of true spiritual greatness in Christ's kingdom is determined by the amount of humble, selfless service which a person contributes in behalf of others, not for any kind of personal gain, but simply out of thankfulness for grace already received. How different from the standards which the unbelieving world uses in determining greatness!

In order to illustrate this principle of greatness among Christian disciples, the Lord gives a striking object lesson:

vv. 36,37 — *He took a little child and had him stand among them. Taking him in his arms, he said to them, "Whoever welcomes one of these little children in my name welcomes me; and whoever welcomes me does not welcome me but the one who sent me."*

This "little child" (παιδίον) was young enough for Jesus to take in his arms. What an object lesson for the Twelve!

Whoever receives one of these little children "in my name" —literally "upon" (ἐπί) my name, "on the basis of" my name — welcomes Jesus himself. The name of Jesus includes the entire revelation of Scripture pertaining to his person. To receive a child in the name of Jesus means more than giving it a lot of physical tender-loving care. It involves spiritual care as well, being concerned about the child's eternal welfare. Jesus says that the business of taking care of this need is the highest kind of ministry in his kingdom. What Jesus calls greatness in his kingdom is also greatness in the eyes of the Father who sent him. What an encouragement for Christian parents and for those involved in the work of Christian education!

## Homiletical Suggestions

This text divides itself neatly into two chief parts.

In the opening verses Jesus impresses upon his disciples the way he must walk in order to carry out his mission, a way which leads to a cross and a crown (vv. 30-32).

In the succeeding section Jesus relates this way to that of his disciples, who were arguing about "who was the greatest." Through words and an impressive object lesson he shows that the way to true greatness in his kingdom lies in humble service (vv 33-37).

Theme and parts based on this division might be expressed as follows:

### The Way Of True Discipleship

1. By faith centered in the cross and the crown (vv. 30-32)
2. By a life which responds in humble service (vv. 33-37)

### True Greatness In The Kingdom Of God

1. What this meant for Christ (vv. 30-32)
2. What this means for his followers (vv. 33-37)

# NINETEENTH SUNDAY AFTER PENTECOST

**The Scriptures**

> Old Testament — *Numbers 11:4-6,10-16,24-29*
> Epistle — *James 4:7-12*
> Gospel — *Mark 9:38-50*

**The Text — Mark 9:38-50**

The preceeding portion of chapter 9 provides us with a picture of the majesty and power of our Lord Jesus. On the Mount of Transfiguration the three disciples shielded their eyes from the divine brilliance of the Savior. Upon leaving the mount, they witnessed a healing miracle as Jesus drove an evil spirit from a young boy's body.

With such a powerful and caring master the disciples began to feel the temptation to pride and jealousy. While traveling down the road, they argued with one another about who was the greatest disciple among them. As we saw in last Sunday's text, Jesus took them aside and set them straight on that idea. In this text John provides an opening for another lesson from Jesus:

> v. 38 — *"Teacher," said John, "we saw a man driving out demons in your name and we told him to stop, because he was not one of us."*

The way in which John addresses Jesus gives us insight into the disciples' relationship with him. He was first and foremost their teacher. John's question is the question of a student and follower who is looking for information and approval.

The disciples had seen a man who knew of Jesus and the power connected with Jesus' name. Whether the man knew Jesus as his Savior through faith, we are not told. Yet the man was using the name of Jesus as his source of authority and power over evil spirits. His intentions were honorable, and his goal appears to have been a proper honoring of Jesus' name.

When they saw him, the disciples took issue with the man. They criticized his use of Jesus' name, because he was not one of the Twelve. John was upset because the man was not acting "officially" as a representative of Jesus. The conative imperfect of the Greek κωλύω shows that they were attempting to stop or hinder the man from continuing to use the name of Jesus.

> v. 39 — *"Do not stop him," Jesus said. "No one who does a miracle in my name can in the next moment say anything bad about me,"*

If John was looking for "a pat on the back," he was not going to get it from Jesus. The present prohibition (μὴ κωλύετε) implies that the disciples were to discontinue their negative behavior toward this man. Jesus points out the facts of the situation to them. The man's use of Jesus' name would bring honor to Jesus. The use of Jesus' name reveals something about the man's heart. He also loved the name of Jesus. Even though his knowledge may have been limited, he was still on the "right side of the fence."

v. 40 — *"for whoever is not against us is for us."*

In his relationship to Christ a person is either with him or against him. There is no middle ground. Even though this man did not have the same associations or credentials as the disciples, he was not an enemy of Jesus. He should not be treated like an enemy. The disciples should rather rejoice in his success and not hinder his activities.

v. 41 — *"I tell you the truth, anyone who gives you a cup of water in my name because you belong to Christ will certainly not lose his reward."*

Faith in the heart is evident through the actions that it produces. Even a cup of water given to someone because that person is a disciple of Jesus is a display of faith and love. The kindness done for a disciple is really done for his master too. Jesus gives the solemn promise that love for Christ in the heart and demonstrated by actions of the hands will not go unrewarded.

v. 42 — *"And if anyone causes one of these little ones who believe in me to sin, it would be better for him to be thrown into the sea with a large millstone tied around his neck."*

The general nature of this conditional statement should cause every Christian to take notice. The phrase "little ones" includes not just small children, but all who are infants in faith, regardless of their physical age. The Greek word σκανδαλίζω refers to the trigger stick attached to the bait in a deadfall trap. When the bait is moved the stick is dislodged and the heavy weight comes crashing down.

The picture here refers to someone causing another person to stumble and fall away from faith in Jesus. The Lord will hold that person accountable who injures another person's faith. For that reason, it would be better for the offending person to be removed from the scene before the offense occurs. The μύλος ὀνικὸς was the upper millstone. It was a large stone turned by a donkey. Such a stone hung around a person's neck and dragging him to the bottom of the sea would remove any possibility of harming someone else in faith.

vv. 43-48 — *"If your hand causes you to sin, cut it off. It is better for you to enter life maimed than with two hands to go into hell, where the fire never goes out. And if your foot causes you to sin, cut it off. It is better for you to enter life crippled than to have two feet and be thrown into hell. And if your eye causes you to sin, pluck it out. It is better for you to enter the kingdom of God with one eye than to have two eyes and be thrown into hell, where their worm does not die, and the fire is not quenched."*

Falling away from faith has deadly consequences. It must be avoided at all costs. The verses picture what a surgeon might do to save a person's life. If a hand or foot or eye is badly infected and presents a life-threatening danger to the whole body, the surgeon will remove the infected member to save the person's life.

Jesus means exactly what he says here. If any member of your body causes you to sin and endangers your salvation, get rid of the offending member! A closer self-examination, however, will show that the source of the problem is in the heart, not in the hand or foot or eye. Anything that leads us away from God needs to be dealt with. Often the only solution is a radical removal. It may be necessary to turn off the television, throw away the magazine or book, break a friendship or association or even change jobs. It may require changing a personal habit that is leading one away from faith in Jesus Christ.

If cutting off, tearing out and throwing away sounds too terrible, just consider the alternative, the result of falling away from faith —an eternity in hell. Consider the description of hell. The Greek word σβέννυμι means to "extinguish." The fire of hell cannot be extinguished. It is eternal. It burns without consuming. Endless torment is also pictured by the worms or maggots that do not die. They feast on rotting flesh, also without consuming the body and putting it out of its misery. This picture of hell is taken from Isaiah 66:24.

When the eternal consequences are considered, the goal of maintaining one's own faith and encouraging the faith of others is greater than any other goal in life.

vv. 49,50 — *"Everyone will be salted with fire. Salt is good, but if it loses its saltiness, how can you make it salty again? Have salt in yourselves, and be at peace with each other."*

The picture of salt used as a preservative is found several times in the Scriptures. In Matthew 5:13 Jesus calls his disciples the salt of the earth. Here the salt is something in the disciples. The powerful word of God in their hearts and minds is the salt that will preserve them in faith. While they have the salt now, they must be aware of the possibility of losing it. In the physical world salt might lose its saltiness through a chemical reaction. Believers can lose their spiritual "saltiness" if they stop using God's word to preserve them in faith and guide them in Christian living.

If the disciples were going to be ambassadors of the gospel, they would need to be full of salt. When their hearts were filled with the "salt" of the gospel, they could lay aside questions of who was greatest among them. When their actions were controlled by the same "salt," they would live at peace with one another and with others who spoke the name of Jesus. Filled with the salt of God's word, they would enjoy the peace of God together and spread God's good news to the world.

## Homiletical Suggestions

The sermon might develop the idea of "salt" in the Christian's life. Only the word of God can lead to a well-balanced, positive, productive life. Only through this "salt" can we follow Jesus. When the gospel is on our lips and in our hearts, the negative defensiveness falls away. We look for and give thanks for all words and actions that bring honor to Christ. Likewise, the growing disciple deals gently and humbly with others, so that their faith is not disturbed or damaged. Through the "salt" we gain wisdom for life.

### The Well-Seasoned Disciple

1. Encourages the weak (vv. 38-41)
2. Causes no one to stumble (vv. 42-48)
3. Is filled with the word (vv. 49,50)

Another outline might develop the idea of disciples being at peace with each other. All disciples of Jesus share a precious truth and gift. Jealousy and infighting should be unheard of. The only way it can be overcome is through growth in the word. This "salt" will preserve the individual and the whole body of believers.

### Live At Peace With All Others

1. Putting aside all jealousy and pride (vv. 38-41)
2. Being filled with the word of God (vv. 42-50)

# TWENTIETH SUNDAY AFTER PENTECOST

**The Scriptures**

> Old Testament — *Genesis 2:18-24*
> Epistle — *Hebrews 2:9-11*
> Gospel — *Mark 10:2-16*

**The Text — Mark 10:2-16**

The events recorded in Mark 10 took place some time after Jesus had left Capernaum (Mark 9). He was gradually making his way to Jerusalem for the last time. His route was indirect as he traveled from Galilee through the eastern portion of Judea and into the region beyond the Jordan River.

At this point in his ministry Jesus' reputation was well established. Even in this remote area people flocked to him. The terrible events awaiting him in Jerusalem must have occupied his thoughts, but this did not prevent him from taking the time to instruct those who came to him.

Jesus' popularity had increased among the people, but so had the hatred and opposition of the Pharisees. His enemies followed him with zeal — not to hear and learn, but to challenge and undermine his work.

The Gospel reading includes accounts of two separate incidents. First (vv. 2-12) we hear the Pharisees' question about divorce and Jesus' response. Then (vv. 13-16) follows the familiar story of Jesus blessing the children. Since these two incidents are not inherently related, and since each contains a wealth of homiletical material, it may be wise to treat them in two different sermons. However, if you choose to combine them, several outlines incorporating the entire reading are offered at the end of this study.

v. 2 — *Some Pharisees came and tested him by asking, "Is it lawful for a man to divorce his wife?"*

The enemies of Jesus approached him as he taught, and directed a question to him. On the surface it seemed like a legitimate question, but the inspired writer of the Gospel comments that their purpose was to "test" (πειράζω) him. Their purpose was not to learn but to catch Jesus in an inconsistency or falsehood. They wanted to know whether it was lawful or right (ἔξεστι) for a man to divorce his wife. If Jesus would answer that divorce was permitted, they would be able to accuse him of being "soft" on divorce. If Jesus would answer that divorce was wrong, they would be able to accuse Jesus of contradicting Moses. So Jesus, aware of their game, answered their question with one of his own:

v. 3,4 — *"What did Moses command you?" he replied. They said. "Moses permitted a man to write a certificate of divorce and send her away."*

Jesus was not trying to evade their question. Rather, he wanted to lead the discussion beyond the question of divorce to the underlying principles of marriage itself. In their answer to him, the Pharisees quoted Deuteronomy 24:1, but they interpreted Moses' words in a typically legalistic and self-serving way. The complete context of that passage in no way gives God's approval for divorce. Through this law God was rather working to regulate and limit the harm that would inevitably be caused when people ignored God's will for marriage.

Jesus points out their faulty interpretation when he continues:

v. 5 — *"It was because your hearts were hard that Moses wrote you this law," Jesus replied.*

The law written by Moses was not a statement of permission for divorce. Rather, God recognized that even among his chosen people there would be those who would harden their hearts to God's will for marriage. God did not speak out of both sides of his mouth concerning marriage. The problem was that some of his people simply refused to listen. This command in the law of Moses was never intended to encourage or permit divorce; it was intended to protect those who in civil life would be harmed by the failure of spouses to recognize the sanctity and permanence of marriage. Ancient Israel, we remember, was under a theocratic system of government.

Jesus then directed their attention to the underlying principles of marriage itself:

vv. 6-9 — *"But at the beginning of creation, God 'made them male and female.' 'For this reason a man will leave his father and mother and be united to his wife, and the two will become one flesh.' So they are no longer two, but one. Therefore what God has joined together, let man not separate."*

Jesus answered the question by referring to God's word. He pointed to God's original plan and purpose for marrige by quoting from Genesis, and he added his own commentary about the implication of those words. Jesus made the following points:

1) Marriage was established by God when he created Eve for Adam and brought them together as husband and wife.

2) The first marriage and every subsequent marriage involved the intimate union of one man and one woman. The two individuals in marriage are joined by God in a union of love, trust and faithfulness.

3) This union is intended by God to be a *lifelong* union, with God alone having the right to end a marriage.

4) While man has the terrible power to dissolve a union which God has made, man is not to exercise that power, since this is contrary to God's will.

We see the contrast in the ways that Jesus and his enemies used Scripture. The Pharisees used God's Word as it suited them. They appealed to it only when it served their purposes. They approached it with the rigid legalism for which they are known. On the other hand, Jesus focused on the essence of God's plan and purpose for marriage. He let God's Word speak for itself. He courageously proclaimed God's will for marriage and joyfully outlined God's promises connected with it.

vv. 10-12 — *When they were in the house again, the disciples asked Jesus about this. He answered, "Anyone who divorces his wife and marries another woman commits adultery against her. And if she divorces her husband and marries another man, she commits adultery."*

The discussion with the Pharisees had raised some further questions in the minds of the disciples. We aren't told whether they had some doubts about what Jesus had said or whether they simply wanted him to expand on it. Jesus again emphasized that the breaking of the marriage bond would be a sin against the Sixth Commandment. He added that subsequent remarriage would also be a violation of God's design for marriage. Mark does not report that Jesus mentioned here the exceptions mentioned elsewhere in Scriptures (see Mt 5:32 and 1 Co 7:15), but this silence does not mean that he did not discuss it with his disciples. Nor does Mark report that Jesus brought up the matter of remarriage in the case of repentant and forgiven sinners.

v. 13 — *People were bringing little children to Jesus to have him touch them, but the disciples rebuked them.*

Some time later (we don't know exactly when or where) parents began to bring their young children (παιδία) to Jesus. They came not out of superstition, thinking that a touch by Jesus would bring magical benefits. They simply brought their children with the hope that Jesus would place his hands on them and bless them. While our attention is correctly fixed on Jesus' love for the children and on the insensitivity of the disciples, we do not want to overlook the admirable efforts of the parents. They recognized that the Savior was not only for them, but that he had also come for their children. They went to great lengths to give their children what they needed most — the blessing and love of the Savior.

We aren't told exactly why the disciples objected to the parents' efforts. Perhaps they felt that the Savior was too busy with other matters. Perhaps they felt that the Master could not take the time for something that appeared to them so trivial. But Jesus showed them how wrong they were:

vv. 14-16 — *When Jesus saw this, he was indignant. He said to them, "Let the little children come to me, and do not hinder them, for the kingdom of God belongs to such as these. I tell you the truth, anyone who will not receive the kingdom of God like a little child will never enter it." And he took the children in his arms, put his hands on them and blessed them.*

The Scriptures make it abundantly clear that the blessings of Christianity are *inclusive* rather than *exclusive*. God so loved *the world* that he gave his one and only Son. The Son of God came to seek and to save sinners who were lost. The Son showed his all-inclusive love by instructing prostitutes and sinners, calling them to repentance, and assuring them of God's forgiveness. He crossed into the borders of Samaria to bring foreigners into God's kingdom. He rejoiced when a Roman centurion confessed his faith. And here Jesus showed that little children are also the objects of his searching grace. It was his love for the souls of these children that moved him to scold his disciples. Once again they had failed to understand why Jesus had come and what his kingdom really was.

Here Jesus saw a double opportunity. He was able to bless the children who had been brought to him. And he was able to teach his disciples two important lessons: First, he demonstrated for them that God's kingdom (God's gracious rule in the hearts and minds of believers) was meant also for children. Faith is not primarily a matter of the intellect or the will, but a matter of trust in Jesus and in the promises of a gracious God.

To underscore this first point, Jesus made a second. Not only were these children a part of God's kingdom through faith in him, but it is precisely that kind of faith which God looks for in all of his believers — the simple, humble, trusting faith that looks only to him.

What a reminder of Jesus' selfless love! Just over the horizon loomed the dark shadow of the cross. Jesus' mind must have been filled with the thoughts of what his last visit to Jerusalem would mean. Yet, with the smile of love on his face, Jesus took the little children in his arms, one by one and blessed them.

## Homiletical Suggestions

Thirty years ago divorce was relatively rare. It was the exception to the rule. Today, however, our society has come to view marriage as little more than a temporary agreement by two people to remain together "as long as we both shall love."

We are painfully aware that this same attitude has begun to infiltrate and influence the members of God's church. But changes in society and changes in the attitudes of Christians do not change the will of the one who instituted marriage. This text provides the preacher with a beautiful opportunity to proclaim and teach what God has said about marriage and divorce. It is, admittedly, a difficult subject, but it is one that God's people need to hear about repeatedly.

The sermon will seek to combat the attitude of the Pharisees which sometimes surfaces among God's people today. The Pharisees had missed the point of God's plan for marriage — or ignored it. They had obscured the blessings and sanctity of marriage in their attempts to justify the dissolution of marriage. These attitudes were a result of their hardness of heart, their unwillingness to let God's word speak to them and move them.

The same hardness of heart is evident today when a person refuses to recognize that marriage has been instituted by God; that every marriage is a union which God himself establishes; and that only God has the right to end a marriage. This hardness of heart shows itself even among Christians when they refuse to change their attitudes and actions which have been harmful to their marriages, and when they fail to show the kind of selfless love that God wants them to show for their spouses. This hardness of heart shows itself when people view their marriage problems as hopeless, convincing themselves that they cannot change and that God cannot make their weak marriage into a strong one.

A sermon based on this text will confront these underlying sinful attitudes which lead toward problems in marriage and which lead to an "easy" conscience toward divorce. But the sermon will also center on the positive. It should remind God's people of his wonderful plan and design for marriage. It should hold out to them the unchanging and unbreakable promises that God gives to those who follow his will in their married lives. It should assure them of God's constant help, protection and strength in good days and in bad.

The second half of the text provides other opportunities. Christian education — actively leading children to know and believe in Jesus as their Savior — can be encouraged and stressed. The important role of parents in Christian education should be stressed. The obstacles for carrying out this work (lack of money, lack of commitment, lack of knowledge) should be identified.

Above all, this portion of the text centers on Christ's love for us *and for our children.* His is a love which is ours — and theirs — through a simple, humble, trusting faith in his promises.

As mentioned earlier, the two parts of the text may be treated individually. Suggestions for vv. 2-12:

## Marriages Are Made In Heaven

1. God brings couples together (v. 6)
2. God guides couples together (v. 7)
3. God keeps couples together (vv 2-5,8-12)

## God's Guide For A Happy Marriage

1. Recognize who joined you (vv. 2-6)
2. Rejoice as God blesses you (vv. 7,8)
3. Live as God guides you (vv. 9-12)

## Problems In Your Marriage?

1. Understand the cause (vv. 2-5,10-12)
2. Know the solution (vv. 6-9)

## Divorce Is Not The Answer

1. Because it denies God's plan for marriage (vv. 2-5,10-12)
2. Because it ignores God's promises for marriage (vv. 6-9)

Suggestions for vv. 13-16:

## Let The Children Come

1. Jesus came to save them (vv. 13,14)
2. Children can and do believe in him (vv. 15-16)

## Christian Education: Are You Helping Or Hindering?

1. Watch out for the obstacles (v. 13)
2. Look for the blessings (vv. 14-16)

## Jesus Touches Children With His Blessings

1. Through faithful parents (vv. 13,14)
2. Through his word (vv. 15,16)

Using the entire Gospel reading, two possible themes would be:

**Parents: Love Your Children**

1. By cultivating a strong marriage (vv. 2-12)
2. By bringing your children to Jesus (vv. 13-16)

**God Wants Parents Who Love**

1. Each other (vv. 2-12)
2. Their children (vv. 13-16)

# TWENTY-FIRST SUNDAY AFTER PENTECOST

**The Scriptures**

Old Testament — *Amos 5:6,7,10-15*
Epistle — *Hebrews 3:1-6*
Gospel — *Mark 10:17-27*

**The Text — Mark 10:17-27**

Three Gospel accounts record the visit from the rich young ruler, occurring immediately after Jesus blesses the little children. The love we see in the Savior who takes the little ones in his arms and blesses them is amplified even more as he reaches out in patience and understanding to a misguided young man. "Jesus looked at him and loved him."

v. 17 — *As Jesus started on his way, a man ran up to him and fell on his knees before him. "Good teacher," he asked, "what must I do to inherit eternal life?"*

To walk with Jesus on the dusty paths of Palestine must have been exciting. What miracle would come next? Who would be the next visitor? What memorable words would come from the Savior's lips?

As Jesus is walking (ἐκπορευομένου), a man runs up (προσδραμών) to him and falls on his knees before him. Matthew says that he was young (19:22), and Luke tells us that he was "a man of great wealth" (18:23). Enthusiastic, energetic, polite and deeply religious are words we can use as we draw from our text a profile of the young man who came to Jesus. He was loved by people, and he thought he was loved by God for the sterling life he had endeavored to live. He had a zeal for God, but as Paul says, it was "not based on knowledge" (Ro 10:2). He considered himself an heir by works and did not know about being an heir by promise (Ga 3:29). He thought he had found the way, but the way he had chosen would end in eternal death (Pr 14:12). He loved Jesus as a good teacher to help him on that way (Jn 3:2), but did not know Jesus was the way.

v. 18 — *"Why do you call me good?" Jesus answered. "No one is good — except God alone."*

Matthew includes Jesus' question, "Why do you ask me about what is good?" (19:17). It appears that there was a longer conversation on why the young man called Jesus "good." Jesus did not want his admiration but rather adoration. He did not want to hear the words "good teacher," but rather he wanted to hear him say, "My

Lord and my God." The enslaving chains of trust in self will be broken if the transition can be made from believing that Jesus is a great teacher to believing that he is God. Note how Paul was changed by the Lord God identifying himself with the words, "I am Jesus" (Ac 9:5). Seeds of truth about the Messiah are planted which can later offer hope to a sad young man.

v. 19 — *"You know the commandments: 'Do not murder, do not commit adultery, do not steal, do not give false testimony, do not defraud, honor your father and mother.'"*

The first table of the law is not mentioned. The approach of Jesus is slightly different from his approach with the lawyer in Luke 10:26. The lawyer felt the sting of God's law from the second table with the parable of the Good Samaritan. This man would be broken down by seeing how miserably he had failed to keep the first commandment.

v. 20 — *"Teacher," he declared, "all these I have kept since I was a boy."*

There is no idle boasting and bragging here, not even a hint of doubt about his keeping of the law as in Luke 10:29. He is sure of himself. From his youth he has "kept" (ἐφυλαξάμην) these laws of God. He has been complimented for his kindness, his obedience to parents, his clean living. He is the young man every Jewish mother would love to have as a son-in-law. Here was a "Hebrew of the Hebrews," someone deeply religious and faultless in the eyes of others (Php 3:5,6). His limited understanding of sin allowed him to see himself as righteous before God (Ro 7:7).

Illustration: A family was traveling from the Midwest to the coast of California. A hundred miles away from home the three-year-old asked, "Daddy, are we there yet?" So it was with the rich young ruler who thought "he was there" because of the "good life" he lived.

v. 21 — *Jesus looked at him and loved him. "One thing you lack," he said. "Go, sell everything you have and give to poor, and you will have treasure in heaven. Then come follow me."*

Jesus "looked" at him (ἐμβλέψας) and "loved" (ἠγάπησεν) him. We think of Jesus looking at Peter, turning to the dying thief, and gazing on the little children he took in his arms to bless. To gaze in the eyes of God's Son and see his love for you was a sight never to be forgotten.

The words seemed to be so demanding. Deeply ingrown self-trust is in need of radical surgery. His money could be used for heavenly treasures (Mt 6:19,20). His life would be so much richer leaving all behind to follow Christ. The demands are not excessive; they are exciting. Opportunity knocks, not oppression. The demands are intended to unveil ugly greed and selfishness, destroying the man's illusions of grandeur with God. As Luther said, before God can make us glad he must make us sad. This is the "strange work" of the Holy Spirit (cf. Formula of Concord, Thorough Declaration, V, 11). How hard it is to bring the thunderings of God's law to those who are kind, loving and caring!

v. 22 — *At this the man's face fell. He went away sad, because he had great wealth.*

The original Greek says that "he became appalled (στυγνάσας) in this thing." The happy, radiant face of a nice young man is suddenly turned sad. He went away (ἀπῆλθεν). Did he simply walk a short distance away, or did he remain to hear more? We do not know. We do know the Savior's words about himself as "the one who is good" combined with the loving gaze would be the seed to work saving faith. The door of mercy is always open (Mt 11:28; Lk 15).

v. 23 — *Jesus looked around and said to his disciples, "How hard it is for the rich to enter the kingdom of God!"*

The eyes of the Savior had looked into the faces of little children and looked at the young man. They now "look around" (περιβλεψά-μενος) for disciples to instruct. Here is another opportunity to teach a lesson about money. Riches have caused Christians to lose their place in the kingdom of God. The warnings abound (Ps 62:10; 1 Ti 6:6-10).

v. 24 — *The disciples were amazed at his words. But Jesus said again, "Children, how hard it is to enter the kingdom of God!"*

The disciples "were amazed" (ἐθαμβοῦντο). They had heard Jesus talk about this before. His words to this nice young man were so devastating, so crushing. The reaction was similar after the Sermon on the Mount (Mt 7:28,29).

It is hard to enter the kingdom of God. All self-righteousness and sin must be left behind to enter through the narrow door (Lk 13:24; Mt 7:13,14). Old things must pass away before all things can become new (2 Co 5:17).

v. 25 — *"It is easier for a camel to go through the eye of needle than for a rich man to enter the kingdom of God."*

There is no need to think the "eye of the needle" was some low door in the wall of Jerusalem which required the camel to have its baggage removed. This is a proverbial expression for something impossible. We would say, "You cannot put a square peg in a round hole."

It is humanly impossible for a rich man to enter heaven, because no matter how good he may be, he will always have moments when he thinks more of his riches than of God. To gain heaven by our works we must walk the tightrope of God's law without ever moving slightly to the right or left. The heavy load of riches can easily cause a person to lose his balance, waiver and disqualify himself for God's kingdom. Thus the declaration in Romans 3:11,12.

v. 26 — *The disciples were even more amazed, and said to each other, "Who then can be saved?"*

The disciples are amazed, literally "totally knocked off their feet" (περισσῶς ἐξεπλήσσοντο). Such a feeling comes over us when we discover we must be perfect for a perfect and holy God (Mt 5:48). The self-righteous person who comes to a knowledge of what God expects for eternal life will also be knocked off his feet and led to ask, "Who then can be saved?"

v. 27 — *Jesus looked at them and said, "With man this is impossible, but not with God; all things are possible with God."*

There is hope for mankind. God is able to do the impossible. As the angel told Mary, "Nothing is impossible with God" (Lk 1:37). A virgin was able to bear a son; five thousand people were fed with five barley loaves and two small fish; the world came into existence by God's word; and God came to this earth as a man with human flesh. The Christian faith is built on miracles, or mysteries (1 Co 4:1). All sin is cleansed by the blood of Christ. Faith can be created where a heart is dead in trespasses and sins. Faith takes hold of a God who is able to do the impossible. Even a rich man trusting in his good works can be brought to repentance. Then he is forgiven by Christ and he acquires treasures which last forever.

## Homiletical Suggestions

These verses give us an outstanding example of preaching law and gospel. Jesus proclaims the law fearlessly, leaving his disciples stunned. He proclaims the gospel briefly, but with ringing comfort and clarity, as he says, "All things are possible with God." The preacher must constantly strive to preach the law, not about the law, and preach the gospel, not about the gospel. A poor theme and parts would be "How Jesus Preached the Law and Gospel" 1. He preached the law to break a man down. 2. He preached the gospel to lift him up. This kind of sermon would easily drift towards preaching **about** the law and the gospel, instead preaching law and gospel.

Since pride and riches are an ever present threat to Christian faith, warnings can be drawn from the life of this young man. The pride and riches which kept him from the kingdom of God could pull us away from the kingdom of God.

The following outlines are suggested:

## Two Dangerous Extremes

1. Overestimating ourselves (vv. 17-22)
   a. The pride of the rich man
   b. The love of Jesus
   c. The result of Jesus' words
   d. Challenges which reveal our sinful nature

2. Underestimating God (vv. 23-27)
   a. The disciples were stunned
   b. The impossible becomes possible
   c. God has done the impossible in your life. Faith is based on what is not seen, the miraculous

## Jesus' Love For A Rich Man

1. He loved him enough to tell him the truth
2. He loved him enough to make the impossible possible

## When You Feel Proud

1. Remember the rich young ruler
2. React like the disciples

# TWENTY-SECOND SUNDAY
# AFTER PENTECOST

## The Scriptures

Old Testament — *Isaiah 53:10-12*
Epistle — *Hebrews 4:9-16*
Gospel — *Mark 10:35-45*

## The Text — Mark 10:35-45

This text is found in the Eisenach pericope for Quinquagesima Sunday (the Sunday before Ash Wednesday). It fits well there as a text which speaks of our Savior's suffering. In the ILCW Series B it works well for the twenty-second Sunday after Pentecost as a text which points to the Christian's discipleship. The lesson is meant for every Christian. If he wishes to be a disciple of Christ, then he must learn that a disciple of Christ is a servant.

vv. 35-37 — *Then James and John, the sons of Zebedee, came to him. "Teacher," they said, "we want you to do for us whatever we ask." "What do you want me to do for you?" he asked. They replied, "Let one of us sit at your right and the other at your left in your glory."*

James and John were good men who had served their father Zebedee until the time Jesus called them to follow him. These two brothers were privileged, together with Peter, to be with Jesus at special times during his life on earth, such as the Lord's transfiguration.

Yet these sons of Zebedee made an error in their request to Jesus. They asked him to do whatever they would ask. They were hoping to be first and second in importance and honor right after Jesus. It is noteworthy that Jesus did not condemn these two disciples for their ambition, but he did correct them where they were at fault and sought to purify their motives.

vv. 38-40 — *"You don't know what you are asking," Jesus said. "Can you drink the cup I drink or be baptized with the baptism I am baptized with?" "We can," they answered. Jesus said to them, "You will drink the cup I drink and be baptized with the baptism I am baptized with, but to sit at my right or left is not for me to grant. These places belong to those for whom they have been prepared."*

When Jesus talk about the "cup" (τὸ ποτήριον) he is referring to suffering, and the word "baptism" (τὸ βάπτισμα) here means death. Could James and John go through suffering and death as Jesus would? They boldly replied, "We can."

Whether the brothers John and James understood Jesus or not, they would indeed undergo suffering and death for their Lord's sake. James was put to death with the sword by wicked King Herod (Ac 12:1,2), and John was imprisoned on the island of Patmos "because of the word of God and the testimony of Jesus" (Rev 1:9). John drank the cup of suffering and James went through the baptism of death.

The way of discipleship is one of suffering and, for some, of martyrdom. When we follow Christ we must deny ourselves, take up our crosses and wholeheartedly follow him. A disciple of Christ is a suffering servant.

But he is also a servant who is rewarded by his Lord. There are rewards here on earth. We have peace and comfort because we know that our sins are forgiven and that we are children of God through faith in Christ Jesus. There will be rewards in heaven. We will sit with our Lord Jesus eating and drinking at his table. We will be in God's home singing the praises of the Almighty and enjoying his protection day and night. These rewards we will have because Christ Jesus suffered and died for us.

When the other ten disciples heard what the two sons of Zebedee had asked and how Jesus had responded to them, they were upset with James and John.

vv. 41-44 — *When the ten heard about this, they became indignant with James and John. Jesus called them together and said, "You know that those who are regarded as rulers of the Gentiles lord it over them, and their high officials exercise authority over them. Not so with you. Instead, whoever wants to become great among you must be your servant, and whoever wants to be first must be slave of all."*

The Lord Jesus still had some things to teach the Twelve! He told them that their attitude should not be like that of the Gentile rulers or their high officials, but rather that they should desire to be servants and slaves among their brothers and sisters in Christ. Concerning the phrase "Not so with you," R. C. H. Lenski says, "Jesus states this as a fact, which is even stronger than making it a demand." The positions of "servant" (διάκονος) and "slave" (δοῦλος) are not very enviable, and yet that is what Christ wants his disciples to be.

Here is another application. A disciple of Christ is a humble servant. To be a servant for others is not easy, but those who humble themselves and serve others receive special honor from the Lord. We recall that at another time, when the disciples were arguing over who would be the greatest, Jesus took a little child and said to them, "Whoever welcomes this little child in my name welcomes me; and whoever welcomes me welcomes the one who sent me. For he who is least among you all — he is the greatest" (Lk 9:48). Humble service can be as simple as welcoming a little child in Jesus' name. We can humbly serve our fellow believers, and everyone, when we speak not of ourselves, but of our Savior, Jesus Christ.

We can learn to humble ourselves by following Christ's example.

v. 45 — *"For even the Son of Man did not come to be served, but to serve, and to give his life as a ransom for many."*

Christ Jesus is the very Son of God, and yet he became a man to be our Savior. Jesus humbled himself to serve us and others. He was conceived by the Holy Ghost and born of the virgin Mary in order that he could place himself under God's law. He humbled himself, even getting down on his knees to wash the feet of his disciples. He suffered the agony of hell as he hung from the cross with our sins laid upon him. He gave his life as a ransom for all, that all might be saved. Out of thanks for what Christ has done for us, let us *serve* our brothers and sisters in Christ.

## Homiletical Suggestions

Although this text refers to Christ's suffering and death, its chief emphasis lies in the area of Christian discipleship. A Christian will want to serve others out of love for Christ. That is the aim we want to proclaim to our listeners. Of course, in order to serve others a Christian looks to his Lord for the perfect example and for the proper motivation.

The following outline is suggested:

## A Disciple Of Christ Is A Servant

1. He is a humble servant (vv. 41-44)
2. He is a suffering servant (vv. 38,39,45)
3. He is a servant rewarded (vv. 35-37,40)

Another outline concentrates on Jesus' example:

## Following Jesus' Example On How To Serve

1. Be humble (vv. 43,44)
2. Be ready to suffer (vv. 38,39)
3. Be ready to die (v. 45)

The following outline is by the Rev. J. Sheatsley from his book, *Sermons on the Eisenach Gospels* (Lutheran Book Concern, 1915):

**The Way To True Greatness**

1. The way of suffering
2. The way of service

While this text deals with many of the same thoughts as the one of the Eighteenth Sunday after Pentecost, the fact that a situation like this arose among the Twelve so soon after the previous one shows how important *repeated* encouragements toward humble service among Christians are. The preacher will take care, of course, that his illustrations and applications are not simply a repetition of those presented four weeks ago.

# TWENTY-THIRD SUNDAY AFTER PENTECOST

## The Scriptures

Old Testament — *Jeremiah 31:7-9*
Epistle — *Hebrews 5:1-10*
Gospel — *Mark 10:46-52*

## The Text — Mark 10:46-52

On his way to Jerusalem for the last time, Jesus traveled through Jericho, having crossed the Jordan River from Perea. The parallel accounts of this healing of a blind man (Mt 20:29-34; Lk 18:35-43) have raised critical questions in the minds of many commentators. Did it happen as they left the city (Matthew and Mark) or as they entered (Luke)? Were there two blind men (Matthew), or was there just one (Mark and Luke)? Any good commentary will have no difficulty in dealing with these supposed discrepancies. The two cities of Jericho (Old Testament and New Testament) may help explain whether they were coming or going. The topical arrangement of Luke, who positions the story of Zacchaeus (not told by Matthew or Mark) after the healing of the blind man, may also resolve the issue. And the word he uses for approaching the city may simply mean that Jesus was in the vicinity of Jericho. The fact that two evangelists mention but one blind beggar does not exclude the possibility that there were two. Thus the differences in the three accounts are not really problems for us, for they simply demonstrate that the gospel-writers wrote independently of each other about the same historical incidents.

v. 46 — *Then they came to Jericho. As Jesus and his disciples, together with a large crowd, were leaving the city, a blind man, Bartimaeus (that is, the Son of Timaeus), was sitting by the roadside begging.*

The Jericho of the Old Testament was destroyed by Joshua. Despite attempts to rebuild it, no doubt it remained mostly in ruins at the time of Christ. But a new city called Jericho had been erected nearby, one of the winter residences of King Herod. In this tropical paradise the tax-collector Zacchaeus lived. Jesus and his disciples spent some time at his house. Then a large crowd was attracted to the popular and controversial Jesus, and they accompanied him as he made his way out of the city. Sitting by the road was a blind man, whose name Mark alone tells us was Bartimaeus, which meant "Son of Timaeus" in the native tongue. The tragic condition of blindness in that society almost invariably left one a beggar.

v. 47 — *When he heard that it was Jesus of Nazareth, he began to shout, "Jesus, Son of David, have mercy on me!"*

The commotion caused by the parade of people accompanying Jesus did not go unnoticed by blind Bartimaeus. When he learned that Jesus of Nazareth was passing by, he began to cry out: "Jesus, Son of David, have mercy on me!" The reports of his miraculous signs and wise teaching had enabled even the blind to recognize Jesus as the promised Messiah, as the title, "Son of David," denoted. This title Jesus accepted as the climax of his Messianic work drew so near. "Have mercy" recalls the origin of our liturgical chant known as the *Kyrie.* It is a plea for help from the Lord.

v. 48 — *Many rebuked him and told him to be quiet, but he shouted all the more, "Son of David, have mercy on me!"*

Why the surrounding spectators tried to stifle his shouts is speculative. Were they annoyed by the disturbance? Did they regard this beggar as unworthy of the great prophet? Whatever the case, the son of Timaeus would not be silenced. He raised his voice even louder to get the attention of the Son of David. And he succeeded.

v. 49 — *Jesus stopped and said, "Call him." So they called to the blind man, "Cheer up! On your feet! He's calling you."*

His persistent prayer paid off. Jesus halted the procession and beckoned the supplicant. Adding details the others omit, Mark inserts the bystanders' sudden words of encouragement in vivid tones: "Cheer up! On your feet!" (literally, "Get up!"). How quickly a comment by Jesus could change the mood of the multitude! Obviously, no one was too insignificant for him.

v. 50 — *Throwing his cloak aside, he jumped to his feet and came to Jesus.*

The excitement is depicted as if related by an eye-witness. (Remember, Mark wrote for Peter, according to reliable tradition.) His "cloak" may have been the sole possession of this beggar, a ragged robe which served as the roof over his head and the bed for his body on many a cold night. Leaping from the ground, he rushed over to Jesus as fast as the parting throng and directing hands allowed. This was the moment he had been waiting for.

v. 51 — *"What do you want me to do for you?" Jesus asked him. The blind man said, "Rabbi, I want to see."*

Jesus' question was asked as much for the benefit of the onlookers who may not have known the man was blind as it was for Bartimaeus. The gracious invitation is an open-ended opportunity to beg for blessing. "Rabbi" (ῥαββουνεί) is a Hebrew/Aramaic term of respect for a teacher, equivalent to "Master." (Matthew and Luke have "Lord.") His request for sight is couched in the humble language of faith.

v. 52 — *"Go," said Jesus, "your faith has healed you." Immediately he received his sight and followed Jesus along the road.*

Mark abbreviates the Lord's response, omitting the action of touching his eyes (Matthew) and the order, "Receive your sight" (Luke), and settling for the single imperative, "Go!" Now Bartimaeus could see where he was going. This was the result of his faith. The object of his faith, which plainly was the Jesus the Messiah, was reponsible for the healing. His personal trust was merely the means of receiving that blessing. The grace of God, not the degree of man's conviction, is the operative cause of all miracles.

His sight was restored at once, negating any suspicion of coincidental gradual remission. "Healed" is the implied meaning of the Greek (σέσωκεν, literally, "has saved"). Surely, his sight was rescued.

Consequently, the now-sighted recipient of mercy joyfully and thankfully followed Jesus down the road which led to Jerusalem and the dramatic events of the final week of Jesus' earthly ministry.

## Homiletical Suggestions

In a sermon the pastor need not devote much time to solving the apparent discrepancies in the three accounts of this story. (Bible Class would be a better setting.) Only in filling out Mark's rendition of the incident might reference to Matthew and Luke be constructive. The main lesson of the miraculous healing of blind Bartimaeus should stay in focus: Jesus reveals His divine identity to support his claims to be the God-sent Savior of mankind. This is the underlying purpose of all his miracles.

However, the unique features of this episode dare not be overlooked. Bartimaeus seems to be singled out because he acknowledged Jesus as the Son of David (even before the miracle) while others rejected his credentials. This was prior to Palm Sunday, when many people parroted the refrain, "Hosanna to the Son of David." Two blind men were healed; only the son of Timaeus was named. Also the energy with which he pleaded for the Lord's mercy, not taking "hush" for an answer, appears to be commended to us. We ought to be as persistent and as bold in prayer as he was.

The interesting sidelight of his throwing aside his cloak suggests some applications for today. How many "cloaks" hinder us from running to Jesus for help? The cover-ups of pet sins, the burdens of material acquisition, the smokescreen of self-righteous pride — these and more may prevent us from "jumping" at the chance to receive blessings from the Lord! A sense of urgency to go to Christ while he is nearby pervades this scene. That moment was Bartimaeus' day of salvation.

Preaching on this text, one will naturally mention the miracle of our enlightenment by the Holy Spirit. By his illumination we have also seen Jesus as the Son of David and our Savior.

The personal side of Bartimaeus' predicament may also be brought out. Individuals in the congregational audience may have felt so destitute and depressed at times — as if they were living in the dark. There is hope, too, for them in Christ. It may be appropriate to draw the parallel between the misery of illness and the despair of poverty some experience in our time and the hardship blind beggars suffered in A.D. 30. Christians do not want to discourage the "huddled masses" from seeking the Lord's comfort and aid as the citizens on that street near Jericho did initially. Rather, we want to assist the poor and needy in coming to Christ for physical and spiritual sustenance.

This must be the lasting memory of the sermon: Jesus has power to heal and to save (σέσωκεν). Not many blind people will receive sight, perhaps, but every blind soul can receive light. The good news of Jesus extends it, and the faith it produces embraces it. In that way our faith has healed us also.

As a result, the listener will be moved to join Bartimaeus in following Jesus along the road. He is the way. The journey will take one to the cursed cross, but it also leads to the triumphant tomb. We can trust him to guide us safely home where we shall see him face to face.

The colorful description of Mark's Gospel offers a variety of lively sermon outlines. One in keeping with the action of the account:

### A Blind Man's Leap Of Faith

1. A hop for help (vv. 46-48)
2. A jump for joy (vv. 49-52)

Identifying with Bartimaeus:

### When You Hear Of Jesus

1. Cry out for his help (vv. 46-48)
2. Believe in his blessing (vv. 49-52a)
3. Follow in his footsteps (v. 52b)

A synthetic treatment of verse 50:

## Throw Aside Your Cloak!

1. The cloak of despair (vv. 46,47)
2. The cloak of doubt (vv. 48,49)
3. The cloak of denial (vv. 50-52)

349

# TWENTY-FOURTH SUNDAY AFTER PENTECOST

**The Scriptures**

Old Testament — *Deuteronomy 6:1-9*
Epistle — *Hebrews 7:23-28*
Gospel — *Mark 12:28-34*

**The Text — Mark 12:28-34**

We are approaching the end of another church year. Another year of grace is drawing to a close. Another year of opportunities to see ourselves as sinners and Jesus as our Savior is coming to an end. With out text we return to the Tuesday of Holy Week, a day on which the renowned rabbi Jesus is grilled with question after question. Most are "trick questions" used in an effort to trap the Christ and trip him up (Mk 12:15). Those who ask the questions see themselves as godly, while they view Jesus as a godless enemy.

One questioner is in for a surprise. A teacher of the law comes to test Jesus, as we learn in Matthew's Gospel (22:34-40), but he leaves with the Savior's words ringing in his ears: "You are not far from the kingdom of God" (Mk 12:34). What happened? This man had raised a valid question, a most important question. This question and God's answer in the Word is fundamental in teaching us and our people the doctrines of sin and grace.

What is that question?

v. 28 — *One of the teachers of the law came and heard them debating. Noticing that Jesus had given them a good answer, he asked him, "Of all the commandments, which is the most important?"*

Jesus had just silenced the Sadducees, telling them they were in error since they did not know "the Scriptures or the power of God" (Mk 12:24). They had asked a question about a woman who had been married to seven husbands during her lifetime. Each husband had died, and then the woman also passed away. This was their question: "At the resurrection whose wife will she be, since the seven were married to her?" (Mk 12:23). Their question did not come from a sincere, answer-seeking heart. They used their query to cast doubt and ridicule on the biblical teaching of the resurrection. The Sadducees were hoping to score a point in favor of their contention that there is no resurrection. They failed. Jesus scored a smashing victory, using the word of God to defeat them in debate.

Jesus answered well, and the teacher of the law recognized the value of Jesus' answer. He stepped forward to test the Teacher further. But his question was different. As a teacher of the law, he appeared sincerely interested in finding out where Jesus stood on the importance of the commandments. His question, if paraphrased and personalized, would sound like this: "What especially does God expect of me?" or "What most of all does my Maker require of me?" It's a good question, a very important question, one that every human being needs to ask!

To this crucial question Jesus has the perfect answer. He has God's own answer in the Word.

vv. 29,30 — *"The most important one," answered Jesus, "is this: 'Hear, O Israel, the Lord our God, the Lord is one. Love the Lord your God with all your heart and with all your soul and with all your mind and with all your strength.' "*

Jesus is quoting from Moses' sermon to the people of Israel as recorded in Deuteronomy 6:4,5, part of our Old Testament lesson for this day. Maybe we think our Lord quoted too much. Verse 4 in Deuteronomy isn't a commandment, after all. It's a statement of fact. But it is such a vital fact that the Teacher makes a point of stressing it: "The Lord is one." The Lord is the God revealed in Holy Scripture. He is the God of the promise, the God of grace and faithfulness. He is the only God that exists!

As the Lord, the only Lord, he is worthy of his creatures' total love and devotion. "Love the Lord!" is the foremost commandment and is a fitting caption over Commandments 1-3, the so-called first table of the law. The *alls* stand out in Jesus' answer. They are significant. They leave no room for a half-hearted effort at loving God. And the whole being is involved — heart, soul, mind and strength. Can anyone truthfully say, "I have always loved the Lord God with my whole being!"? No, "*all* have sinned and fall short of the glory of God" (Ro 3:23).

All but one, that is! The rabbi who cited this foremost commandment also kept it perfectly. Twice the heavenly Father commended his Son saying, "With him I am well pleased" (Mt 3:17; 17:5). Jesus loved his Father with a perfect love and obedience. The temptation in the desert is evidence, and even more convincing proof can be found in the Garden of Gethsemane and on Calvary. Thus Jesus was the only fulfiller of this chief command. All this he did for us as our substitute under the law. "Christ is the end of the law so that there may be righteousness for everyone who believes" (Ro 10:4).

In further response to the scribe's question, our substitute goes on to give the second key commandment from God:

*v. 31 — "The second is this: 'Love your neighbor as yourself.' There is no commandment greater than these."*

What Jesus states now is commonly referred to as the second table of the law and covers commandments 4-10. In summary of those seven commands which deal with human relationships Jesus quotes Leviticus 19:18, "Love your neighbor as yourself." The Apostle Paul offers a worthwhile commentary on this passage when he writes under inspiration: "Let no debt remain outstanding, except the continuing debt to love one another, for he who loves his fellowman has fulfilled the law. The commandments, 'Do not commit adultery,' 'Do not murder,' 'Do not steal,' 'Do not covet,' and whatever other commandment there may be, are summed up in this one rule: 'Love your neighbor as yourself.' Love does no harm to its neighbor. Therefore love is the fulfillment of the law" (Ro 13:8-10).

But again, who of us can truthfully say, "I have never harmed my neighbor!"? Recall that our neighbor is the person we are "next to" in life. The Greek word is πλησίος. So "neighbor" includes our marriage partners, children, and parents, those people we are closest to in life. It also includes people we don't even know and yet come in contact with — the woman ahead of us in line at the check-out counter of a grocery store, the owner of a parked car which we notice has its headlights left on, the children we meet when we go to the pool or skating rink, for just a few examples. Thus the term "neighbor" encompasses every single person with whom we come in contact, whether that contact lasts only a few minutes or many years.

Now, this command to show love to the people I meet in life makes me ask myself some questions. Have I ever spoken words that tore like a knife into the heart of a family member or friend? Have I never gone by thoughtlessly when I saw that a neighbor was in need of my help? Have I ever pushed and shoved to get my way and thereby inflicted pain on someone else? Have I always put all my neighbors' needs and concerns on the same level as my needs and concerns? And the greatest need everyone has is the need for a Savior and the forgiveness of sins. I know that Savior. I have him as mine. Do my neighbors know this? If not, do I love them enough to share Jesus with them? I am a sinner! We all are! We haven't loved anyone as ourselves.

The mirror of the law shows us what we look like to God. The wise Teacher has added this second key commandment to the first to make the picture even clearer to us all. Maybe we think we are doing a pretty good job of loving the invisible God, but our Lord would ask, "How are you doing in this responsibility of loving the people in your life? And if you don't show them love, how can you say that you love God?" The Apostle John uses this same logic: "If anyone says, 'I love God,' yet hates his brother, he is a liar. For anyone who does not love his brother, whom he has seen, cannot love God, whom he has not seen" (1 Jn 4:20). Thus Jesus speaks of these two commandments as one, for they interlock and together condemn us as sinners.

Jesus is sinless though. He also kept this second command to love. His very presence on earth as a human being is proof of his great and perfect love. In love this heaven-dweller became a "neighbor" to the world of sinners. He put all of our needs first, loving us to the point of taking all our loveless thoughts, words and actions to the cross and suffering the punishment for them as if he had lived a loveless life. That is love, perfect love, and by that love we and all mankind have been saved.

Our loving Savior has given his answer. Now it is his questioner's turn to respond and react to what he has heard. He does so with commendation.

vv. 32,33 — *"Well said, teacher," the man replied. "You are right in saying that God is one and there is no other but him. To love him with all your heart, with all your understanding and with all your strength, and to love your neighbor as yourself is more important than all burnt offerings and sacrifices."*

The teacher of the law agreed with Christ. He knew there were many laws found in the Scriptures and in the rabbinical writings. Yet he also realized and believed that all of God's laws could be summed up in just one word, "love."

Such an idea has never been popular. The Pharisees led many of their fellow Israelites to put a strong emphasis on the letter of the law and mere outward obedience to it. Today many people feel they are doing God a big favor by sacrificing a part of their time and money to him. But really love him? They know no reason to; they are only doing what they think they have to in order to stay on God's good side.

But it doesn't work that way, and this man recognized that fact. God is not interested in our mere outward obedience, our sacrifices. Perhaps this man, who knew his Bible well, was thinking of what Samuel said to Saul: "Does the Lord delight in burnt offerings and sacrifices as much as in obeying the voice of the LORD? To obey is better than sacrifice, and to heed is better than the fat of rams" (1 Sm 15:22). Perhaps, too, he was mindful of God's lament spoken through the prophet Hosea: "I desire mercy, not sacrifice, and acknowledgment of God rather than burnt offerings" (Hos 6:6). Our Creator wants our hearts, not just our hands and heads. He wants to see our hearts alive with faith and aglow with his love. That much wisdom the Holy Spirit had given this man through his study of the law. For this reason Jesus had a favorable comment to make to him.

v. 34 — *When Jesus saw that he had answered wisely, he said to him, "You are not far from the kingdom of God."*

What does our Savior mean? Jesus can see that the law of God has done its job. The man knows what God expects of him — a love he cannot render. He realizes that his Creator isn't interested in seeing a "good show" on his part. Therefore the law has brought this scribe's heart to sense a deep need for a Savior. And of course, Jesus, who stands before him, is that Savior. Jesus is, in effect, saying, "You know the law, and I, who am so close to you, am the gospel."

The theological discussion ends at this point, and the Bible account closes this way:

v. 34b — *And from then on no one dared ask him any more questions.*

Christ Jesus is Wisdom personified. No one could stymie or stump him. No one could trip him up or trap him in his words, for he took his stand on the Word of God. That Word is a rock, a solid foundation, and anyone who takes his stand on what God says will not stumble. He will not be put to shame! Christ's opponents, however, were making fools of themselves. They were stumped and stymied. They were tripped up and must have felt trapped in the foolishness of their unbelief. Ask this rabbi any more questions? They didn't dare! That much they were smart enough to recognize!

### Homiletical Suggestions

We pastors might be surprised to have this sermon text come up in the waning phase of the church year. The last days, death, judgment day, heaven and hell are usual focal point at such a time. Our text, as well as its accompanying readings, has no such emphasis. That's not bad. The concerned pastor of souls can use this account with its basic law-gospel message to his own and his people's great advantage. Here is an opportunity to say again what you have said countless times before, but to say it in a way that may sound different to your members. Quietly lay out the law before your listeners and let that law penetrate their hearts. Your law-message will sound something like this: "God wants us to love him and everyone else perfectly. Do you? Do I? For us to render perfect love is as impossible as for us to walk on water. We need someone who can do the impossible. We desperately need a Savior."

Where is that Savior? He is standing right in the forefront of this word of our God. He is standing there in divine wisdom, perfectly answering this question and each question before it from the Scriptures. He is standing there in divine love, patiently putting up with all these questions and patiently pointing out the truth even to his bitter enemies. The Savior is standing there on the brink of hell's fierce torments. It's Tuesday of Holy Week. We know what Friday brings. He, too, knows what is coming. His was and is a perfect love for us and our neighbors, sinners all.

Perfect love — keying off that idea, let us announce to our people:

**Perfect Love Is The Perfect Answer**

1. To a most important question (v. 28)
2. To a most dreadful dilemma (vv. 29-31)
3. To a most precious opportunity (vv. 32,33)

Another approach which would be effective in driving out the work-righteous attitude in all of us is this:

**God Wants You!**

1. He gave his heart
2. To win yours

Or the homiletician may take his cue from Jesus' words to the scribe, "You are not far from the kingdom of God." Perhaps we would start by telling our people, You've heard all this before. But it's so important that I have to tell you again. Let us together ponder anew:

**The Spirit's Way Into God's Kingdom**

1. He brings us face to face with the mirror of the law
2. He then brings us face to face with the Keeper of the law

Finally, we can come up with a totally different angle on this text if we step back and consider from a distance how this tested rabbi fielded each question. He did so wisely, standing always on the Word. He did so lovingly, pointing out the truth for the salvation of souls. Like Jesus, we and our people are being questioned and tested more and more in these last days. How fitting it is to urge our members to follow Jesus' own example, encouraging them:

**Tested Christians, Take a Stand!**

1. On the wisdom of the Word
2. In the love of the Lord

# TWENTY-FIFTH SUNDAY AFTER PENTECOST

## The Scriptures

Old Testament — *1 Kings 17:8-16*
Epistle — *Hebrews 9:24-28*
Gospel — *Mark 12:41-44*

## The Text — Mark 12:41-44

It is a joy to find the new treasures of Scripture, but it is an equal joy to bring forth the old, such as this text which has become proverbial, although perhaps misnamed, as "The Widow's Mite." Familiarity will not breed contempt in this case.

The event provided Jesus with a good deal of joy. It must have "made his day." Surrounded by pride, hypocrisy, ignorance and rejection of the Scripture (cf. Mk 11 and 12:1-40), he justly had been engaged in verbal denunciation of the people, especially their hypocritical leaders. The strain must have been great. Prophets appointed to tear down as well as to build up do not have an easy time of it. But then the ray of sunshine, the oasis in the desert, appeared.

v. 41 — *Jesus sat down opposite the place where the offerings were put and watched the crowd putting their money into the temple treasury. Many rich people threw in large amounts.*

We know about this place in the temple from Scripture (Ne 10:37,38; 12:44; 13:7; Jn 8:20), from apocryphal and rabbinical writings and from such writers as Josephus and Philo. Edersheim brings much of this together in *The Temple.* He tells us that the offering chests were thirteen in number, trumpet-shaped, clearly marked according to object, nine being for the "receipt of what was legally due by worshipers, four for strictly voluntary gifts" and placed around the Women's Court, which "covered a space upwards of 200 feet square."

While the focus of our New Testament worship is the perfect sacrifice already made, the focus of Old Testament worship was the sacrifice yet to be made. Offerings were therefore of great importance to the Lord and his people, offerings of money primarily as substitutes for symbolic animal offerings. A review of the principles and specifics of Old Testament law would open many doors for the proclamation of law and gospel. It would lead naturally to a discussion of the widow's motives for bringing her sacrificial offering. The Old Testament law had done its job effectively in her heart. And so had the Old Testament gospel.

First mentioned in our text, however, are the crowd and the many rich people who threw in large amounts. Because of the last verse of the text, we may immediately categorize it as one in which familiar rich/poor contrasts are drawn. The letter of the Old Testament law was evidently engrained in the hearts of many, but the spirit was often sadly lacking. Warnings of how riches deceive, how the love of riches is a root of all kinds of evil and how difficult it is for a rich man to enter the kingdom of God — such warnings are always in place. In Jesus' teaching a rich man seldom appears who is not living proof of these dangers of wealth. His "woe" of Luke 6:24 sounds frighteningly general in nature.

In our churches we may have few who fit Jesus' description of a rich man and his offerings in Matthew 6:2. Yet the poor *and* the rich we have always with us. And with what relish do we not *receive* the larger amounts in contrast to the small amounts! With whom in our text, then, do we find ourselves in sharp contrast?

Mark presents this contrast here also, but it is mainly the principle of proportional giving that is supported by the text. The rich are not criticized for giving much. That is expected of them. The Lord receives their offerings gladly if given cheerfully out of a pure heart. Was not the substance of Mary Magdalene very useful to his work, and was it not a rich man from Arimathea who provided necessary ministrations later on? The Lord's comments in our text are related to the staggering proportion of the widow's offering and the contrasting typical and insignificant proportion of the offerings of the rich.

The Lord definitely has concern for the offerings of his people. "Careful observation by an interested observer" is how one lexicon defines the Greek verb θεωρέω. And judging from its literal use in a passage like Matthew 27:55 and its figurative use in John 6:40 and elsewhere, that definition seems correct. Jesus observed the offerings. He commented critically upon them. He saw them as fruits of faith. Like words or children's songs or expensive ointment they were external evidence of what was within. Externals did not impress. His was a righteous judgment of the people. And he knew a thing or two about sacrifice.

v. 42 — *But a poor widow came and put in two very small copper coins, worth only a fraction of a penny.*

The widow's "mite" is a misnomer. There were two coins. She could have given only one and still have given a greater percentage of her wealth than the rest of the crowd. She would have had a little left for herself, which would have been by far the more "sensible" approach. But no, she put in both her coins, both λέπτα.

These were not valuable coins. As the original Greek text tells us, it took two of these Jewish-minted λέπτα to equal one *quadrans*, the smallest Roman copper coin. There were four *quadrans* in an *as*, sixteen *as* in a *denarius* and a *denarius* was a day's wage for an ordinary working man. (The preacher could give his hearers some background on the coins in circulation, Greek, Roman and Jewish, and recall how Jesus had recently driven the money changers out of the temple.) No, these were not gold pieces or even silver dollars, but neither were they worth only "a fraction of a penny," as the NIV states. An average working man today, at least in the United States, makes far more than 128 pennies a day. In buying power they equaled about a half dollar. This makes the widow's offering even more of a sacrifice. She may not come out quite as poor if we figure the worth of her coins in this way, but her offering comes out as even more remarkable. She was not throwing in some coins with which you could not even buy bubble gum; she was offering egg or bread or milk money, as did the widow of Zarephath, her last meal's worth.

vv. 43,44 — *Calling his disciples to him, Jesus said, "I tell you the truth, this poor widow has put more into the treasury than all the others. They all gave out of their wealth; but she, out of her poverty, put in everything — all she had to live on."*

Out of the abundance of his heart Jesus' mouth spoke. He taught his disciples and he teaches us. The disciples might have been engaged in private meditation upon Jesus' denunciation of the teachers of the law. They might have been looking around them and thinking the thoughts one of them would soon put into words about the impressiveness of the temple. Jesus calls them together, however, for another lesson, a lesson not unlike those he was accustomed to give, a lesson from something lowly, like the birds or a shepherd or a little child or a mustard seed. Jesus could get excited, exuberant about the meanest things. They seemed to hold the greatest lessons.

Jesus used the word "Amen," not as we do, at the end of a statement, but at the beginning, and most likely said it like more of a forethought than an afterthought too. As long as the word is so commonly used in prayers and hymns among us, why don't we use it at other times? It hits a lot harder than translations like "truly," "verily," etc.

What Jesus had to tell them was so opposed to human reasoning that it had to be introduced emphatically. And while Christians today accept it mentally as a "given" because they know this Bible lesson, and while we pay it lip service by singing such verses as, "Take my life and let it be. . . . Take my silver and my gold, not a mite would I withhold," how far from practicing what we preach are we not most of the time! If widows' mites were all that common in the church, Jesus would not have said what he said.

That such givers are indeed "rare birds" was underscored by Dr. Neelak Tjernagel in an article in the *Lutheran Sentinel* (Nov. 1982) entitled "Give and It Shall Be Given Unto You." Citing *Profiles of Lutherans*, which revealed that Lutherans generally give 2.6 percent of their income for purposes related to missions and the maintenance of the church, he then contrasted that with the fifteen percent we give to waitresses and the up to twenty percent we have paid in interest in recent times. While the author suggested practical steps pastors and churches can take to help Christians improve, the most important step mentioned was what God has done for us. If the poor widow was so inspired and filled with gratitude because she had the picture and symbolic promise of the animal sacrifices before her eyes, how much more inspired should we not be who have Jesus Christ, God's only-begotten Son, and his sacrifice before us!

Believers do not need commendation. They do not expect it. They do not believe they are deserving of it. It will surprise them on judgment day. It is unlikely that Jesus conveyed his praise personally to the widow. It stands nonetheless in Scripture, for this widow, for the widow of Zarephath, for Abel, for Mary at Bethany. By faith they offered better sacrifices. By faith they were commended as righteous. And by faith they still speak. They speak important testimony. Their money talks louder than words. Are we listening to what they say — about faith and putting our faith into action?

## Homiletical Suggestions

One is torn, laboriously yet determinedly sweating over bills, traipsing covetously yet curiously through malls, loathing yet living the "Yuppies' " credos, and then along comes this story of the widow's mites. What a breath of fresh air! It blows the smog away, uplifting and inspiring. It spurs us on to love and good works, dispelling our diffidence. It crucifies the flesh and nourishes the fruits of the Spirit. It makes a bigger impact on our minds and hearts than the glitzy soaps and the "lifestyles of the rich and famous." It makes us want to sing hymn 400 as if we really mean it.

The power of this poor widow's example is not that of a saccharine, merely human-interest saga of sacrifice. This story breathes the spirit of David and his Psalm 51 about sacrifice, and the spirit of Paul in 2 Corinthians 8:9. It's about a nearly perfect sacrifice, but it's more about the Perfect Sacrifice. It tells of a widow poor materially, but even more about being poor in spirit. For we know the grace of our Lord Jesus Christ.

Our outlines will reflect this:

## A Sacrifice Of Staggering Proportions

1. Given in anticipation of an even greater Sacrifice (vv. 41,42)
2. Commended by the Lord (vv. 43,44)

## How The Widow Brought Her Offering

1. It was of great concern to Jesus (vv. 41,42)
2. It was a study in contrasts to Jesus (vv. 43,44)

## A Penny Given Is More Than A Penny Earned

1. It tells a lot about the giver (vv. 41-44)
2. It tells even more about the cause (vv. 41-44)

## Offeringstyles Of The Poor And Lowly

1. Worthy of comparison with those of the rich (vv. 41-44)
2. Worthy of Jesus' commendation (vv. 43,44)

## Our Offerings: A Subject Not Too Touchy To Handle

1. Jesus takes a good deal of interest in it (vv. 41,42)
2. He teaches his disciples about it (vv. 43,44)

## Pennies For Heaven?

1. Ask yourself more basic questions first (vv. 41-44)
2. Then this question will answer itself (vv. 41-44)

## The Truth About Offerings

1. The truth easily obscured (vv. 41,42)
2. The truth clearly defined (vv. 43,44)

## Offerings Speak Louder Than Words

1. They tell whether we are giving out of our abundance (vv. 41-44)
2. They tell whether we are giving out of our poverty (vv. 41-44)

## The Nitty-Gritty Of Giving

1. Many give from the pocketbook (vv. 41-44)
2. A few give from the heart (vv 41-44)

360

We add a hymn which could be sung to the tune "Stuttgart":

## How The Widow Brought Her Off'ring

1. How the widow brought her off'ring
   To the temple, to the Lord!
   All she had she offered freely,
   Hands and heart in one accord.

2. Small it was by human standards —
   Pennies — nothing in our sight.
   Large it was by heav'nly measure,
   To the Savior pure delight.

3. "What to give?" we ask and wonder.
   "What to offer? What to bring?"
   "See this woman," says the Savior,
   "She brought all, brought ev'rything!"

4. Give us faith, give us your Spirit!
   Give us trust in you, our Friend!
   Give us hearts to love you, Jesus,
   Hands our all to you to lend!

5. Lending is it, for you tell us
   You will handsomely repay.
   Yes, what grace, what love, what mercy
   We can see from day to day!

# TWENTY-SIXTH SUNDAY AFTER PENTECOST

**The Scriptures**

> Old Testament — *Daniel 12:1-13*
> Epistle — *Hebrews 12:26-29*
> Gospel — *Mark 13:1-13*

**The Text — Mark 13:1-13**

When one reads through the events of Holy Week, one is impressed with all Jesus said and did in those seven days. The worshiper is well acquainted with the main events of Palm Sunday, Maundy Thursday, Good Friday and Easter Sunday. However, the worshiper may not realize what else Jesus said and did during that week. Jesus' present discourse on the end times also falls into that first Holy Week. This makes these warnings of Jesus all the more intense.

vv. 1-4 — *As he was leaving the temple, one of his disciples said to him, "Look, Teacher! What massive stones! What magnificent buildings!" "Do you see all these great buildings?" replied Jesus. "Not one stone here will be left on another; every one will be thrown down." As Jesus was sitting on the Mount of Olives opposite the temple, Peter, James, John and Andrew asked him privately, "Tell us, when will these things happen? And what will be the sign that they are all about to be fulfilled?"*

The disciples begin this episode with small talk which the Lord uses as a springboard for a very weighty discourse. The small talk is about the beauty and size of the temple complex. Even the building stones are mentioned. Some of these stones were up to forty feet long and weighed over a hundred tons. This, in part, accounts for the fact that it had already taken forty-six years to build the temple and that it still wasn't complete. But Jesus' response was even more astounding. This temple which took decades to build would be completely destroyed. Not one of these huge stones would be left upon another.

This statement would need further explanation. Somewhat later, when Jesus was with four of his disciples sitting on the Mount of Olives, in full view of that temple, Jesus was asked to explain. These four disciples were especially concerned with the time and sign of this catastrophe. Jesus' answer was given in prophecy typical of many prophecies of the Old Testament. His words would have a

362

preliminary fulfillment in the destruction of Jerusalem and a future fulfillment in the destruction of the world. (For such an Old Testament prophecy, see 2 Samuel 7:12-16.)

In Jesus' response there are two passages which begin with the Greek imperative βλέπετε, "Watch, be on your guard!" Verse 5 introduces a section which encourages Christians to be on guard for events in the secular world. Verse 9 introduces a section in which Jesus encourages Christians to watch what is happening to the church. Let's look at the first section:

vv. 5-8 — *Jesus said to them: "Watch out that no one deceives you. Many will come in my name, claiming, 'I am he,' and will deceive many. When you hear of wars and rumors of wars, do not be alarmed. Such things must happen, but the end is still to come. Nation will rise against nation, and kingdom against kingdom. There will be earthquakes in various places, and famines. These are the beginning of birth pains."*

Jesus begins with the problem of false christs. Galilee was famous as a haven for such false messiahs. Others would follow, not the least of whom would be the Antichrist, the opposition christ in the church. That "secret power of lawlessness" was already at work (2 Th 2:7). This sign holds true for the final destruction of creation also. In our own country we have such false messiahs in Charles Manson and Rev. Moon. We have also had the beginnings of cults based on false christs, cults like the Jehovah's Witnesses and Mormons. We have philosophies which are meant to replace Jesus, philosophies such as humanism and evolution. The tragedy behind these false messiahs is that so many souls are lost eternally. That's why Jesus warns us to watch out for them.

The Savior continues by mentioning "wars and rumors of wars" as well as "nation [rising] against nation, and kingdom against kingdom." The word translated "nation" is ἔθνος. There were ethnic or racial problems within the Roman Empire, as well as problems between Rome and her satellite nations. The Bible documents such ethnic tensions between the Jews and Samaritans. The events of Holy Week underscore the problems betwen Rome and Judea. Such problems have only intensified with time and the sophistication of weapons. We have already marked the twenty-fifth anniversary of the infamous Berlin wall. There are racial tensions in South Africa, bombings in Beirut, and guerrilla warfare in Nicaragua. Only a Christian can understand Jesus' words concerning these "wars and rumors of war." He says, "Do not be alarmed. . . . the end is still to come." Jesus has reserved for himself the right to decide when the final time of judgment shall come.

Now our attention is turned to the signs in creation. Jesus speaks of earthquakes in various places and famines. History documents earthquakes in Crete, in Rome, at Apamaia in Phrygia, and at Campania between the telling of this sign and the destruction of Jerusalem. Scripture speaks of the "severe famine [that] would spread over the entire Roman world" in the reign of Claudius (Ac 11:28). In recent years earthquakes have been reported in Italy, Turkey, Mexico, the United States and other countries. Our television screens are filled with pictures of hungry children in Ethiopia and the Solomon Islands. New emphasis is being placed on the hungry in our own land of plenty.

A variant reading adds "mental anguish" to this list of signs. While not necessary for a complete understanding of the text, we can see why mental anguish is a sign of the end also. Man prides himself in his great accomplishments, whether it be the construction of the temple complex in Jerusalem or placing a man on the moon. There can be nothing more perplexing to the human psyche than to see the evidence of a greater power than mankind.

Jesus also helps us put these signs into proper perspective. He says, "These are the beginning of birth pains." Birth pains imply pain and suffering, intense at times, but they also imply a new life about to begin. Jesus had already told the disciples that wars and rumors of wars did not mean that the end was at hand. Along with these other sufferings and signs, they are simply the final pains through which the church goes as it approaches the time for the new life in the new heaven and earth. No wonder Jesus says that we should not be disturbed by such signs. For the Christian, they signal not only an end, but a beginning, a beginning of a world wherein righteousness dwells.

Now follows the section in which Jesus tells his followers to watch themselves for signs concerning the end.

vv. 9-13 — *"You must be on your guard. You will be handed over to the local councils and flogged in the synagogues. On account of me you will stand before governors and kings as witnesses to them. And the gospel must first be preached to all nations. Whenever you are arrested and brought to trial, do not worry beforehand about what to say. Just say whatever is given you at the time, for it is not you speaking, but the Holy Spirit. Brother will betray brother to death, and a father his child. Children will rebel against their parents and have them put to death. All men will hate you because of me, but he who stands firm to the end will be saved."*

This section begins with the information that one of the signs of the coming destruction is that "the gospel must first be preached to all nations." There is sobering news about this otherwise happy prospect. The sobering news is that the church will meet persecution as her pastors and people go out to make disciples of all nations. They will be called before Jew and Gentile alike. Jesus mentions the Jewish councils and synagogues. The Savior had already felt the heat in his hometown synagogue at Nazareth. Within a few days, he would be standing before the highest Jewish council, the Sanhedrin. There he would be condemned to death. The Savior also mentions governors and kings. Again, Jesus would soon stand before Pilate and Herod, both in position by the good graces of Rome.

The message of the Savior to his disciples is, "If they persecuted me, they will persecute you also" (Jn 15:20). Peter and John felt this persecution in Acts 4. Christians of all ages feel on a daily basis the consequences of being believers. This is true of a Martin Luther standing before Charles V at the Diet of Worms, and it's true of the Christian harassed by a modern government. David Barrett's *Christian Encyclopedia* lists among its statistics an estimated 300,000 Christian martyrs in 1986! It is a sign of the end of the world.

But there is good news too when it comes to preaching the gospel throughout the world. Even standing before council or in synagogue, or before governor or king, the Lord's word will be proclaimed. It is a testimony to them. The Jewish Sanhedrin had to listen to the advice of Gamaliel (Ac 5:34-39). They had to admit that the teaching of the apostles might be from God. Felix was almost converted by Paul (Ac 24:25). Ungodly rulers of today cannot say that Christians have not told them that they are offending God in promoting such ideas as homosexuality, abortion and easy divorce. And to further encourage Christians, Jesus promises that his Spirit will assist God's people to testify to their Savior in these worst of circumstances. What encouragement this gives us too as we live in times which have the characteristics of the last days.

Christians will also notice traumatic decisions being made in their own families. One family member will betray other family members — even handing them over to be killed by enemies. This underscores what the prophet Micah (7:6) had written, "A man's enemies are the members of his own household."

Human nature knows no depths to which it cannot stoop. It is a disgrace to the human race that the Lord saw it necessary to include a command among the Ten Commandments to "honor your father and your mother." Such honor does not come naturally. So Christians must expect even close relatives to join the unbelieving world against them and other believers. Already Christian parents are asking how their sons and daughters could hurt them so badly. Jesus indicates the situation will get worse, not better. This suffering at the hand of immediate family members seems to be rock bottom as far as morals are concerned.

This entire text underscores the veracity of Jesus' words, "All men will hate you because of me" (Mt 10:22). The preceding verses clearly show that the enemies of the believers will be found in the church, where false christs will abound; in the state, before whose magistrates believers would be tried; and in the home, where one would least expect it. The bottom line is that nobody likes Christians. Nobody, that is, except the Lord. Listen to his promise, "But he who stands firm to the end will be saved." "Stands firm" appears in the aorist, although it is translated as a present. The aorist implies that this standing firm is an accepted fact. Without a doubt, the believer who remains faithful to the lord in all this will be saved. This is the comfort of the child of God in the face of the end of the world: "Be faithful, even to the point of death, and I will give you the crown of life" (Re 2:10). In spite of everything else, the gospel will prove victorious. Jesus' suffering, death and resurrection, only a day or two away, are all the child of God needs as he faces the end of the world.

## Homiletical Suggestions

In preparing a sermon for this Sunday based on this text there is a temptation to see the signs of the end as the focal point of the sermon. Indeed, a very interesting dissertation could be made about the signs of the end of the world. But the message for this Sunday is the gospel, just as it is for every other Sunday. Before settling on theme and parts for this text, it is better to review its gospel content.

First, the context of this reading is Holy Week. This underscores that this text can be understood only in the light of the cross. Also, there are the words "birth pains," words which suggests the new life of the believer in heaven. In addition there is the promise that the Holy Ghost will be present with the believer even in the worst of circumstances. Finally, there is the closing promise of salvation through faith by grace. Nor can we overlook that this gospel will be preached throughout the world.

One idea for a sermon picks up on the fact that the signs for the end of the world are found in the church, the state, and the home. We might outline as follows:

## The End Of The World In The Light Of The Cross

Introduction (vv. 1-4)
1. No triumph for false christs (vv. 5,6)
2. No success for ungodly nations (vv. 7-11)
3. No victory for unbelieving relatives (vv. 12,13)

Using the two sections which begin with the warning to "watch or be on your guard" as natural divisions, we might start with this outline:

## When To Get Your Hopes Up

Introduction (vv. 1-4)
1. When you see the world at its worst (vv. 5-8)
2. When you see the Christian at his best (vv. 9-13)

The intent of these parts is to show that when the world is at its worst, the gospel hope is so much more vivid to the believer. Also, the Christian is at his best when he preaches the gospel to the world, relies on the Spirit and endures unto salvation.

Another outline comes to mind which treats the text this way:

## Some Good News For Turbulent Times

Introduction (vv. 1-4)
1. There will be an end of suffering (vv. 5-8)
2. There is a promise of salvation (vv. 9-13)

# TWENTY-SEVENTH SUNDAY AFTER PENTECOST

**The Scriptures**

> Old Testament — *Daniel 7:9,10*
> Epistle — *Hebrews 12:1,2*
> Gospel — *Mark 13:24-31*

**The Text — Mark 13:24-31**

vv. 24,25 — *"But in those days, following that distress, 'the sun will be darkened, and the moon will not give its light; the stars will fall from the sky, and the heavenly bodies will be shaken.' "*

Throughout chapter 13 the reader is faced with the difficulty of distinguishing between "those days" of the destruction of Jerusalem (vv. 18,19) and "those days" which end in the world's judgment. One simply cannot neatly dissect the text into "past" and "future" fulfillment sections. The exegete must treat both in any presentation in an attempt to do justice to the Lord's prophecy.

The words, "that distress," do little to alleviate the problem. The apostles had just been told by Christ that they would be arrested and beaten for the sake of the Lord (v. 9). He told them that family members would turn against one another because of the faith (vv. 12,13). False signs, false prophets, even false christs would appear on the scene, and from the epistles we know this started already in apostolic times. But verses 26 and 27 show quite plainly that Christ's attention here turns completely to the end times.

Jesus is talking quite literally about the end of the universe as we know it. The signs of verses 24 and 25 will be the inescapable reality of judgment day itself. "The heavens will disappear with a roar" (2 Pe 3:10), "and the sky [will be] rolled up like a scroll" (Isa 34:4). As horrible as the destruction of Jerusalem sounded to the apostles, the last day would be a day of destruction beyond the imagination of man. Yes, even beyond the imagination of those who picture a world engulfed in nuclear war. They see only this world, but Christ will devastate the universe — and all because of sin.

It is under the burden of sin that all creation groans. All creation has been twisted by that fateful action in the Garden. Yet all creation was given hope when in another garden a stone was overturned to reveal a Savior vanished, a foe vanquished. That living Lord promised that those who believe in him would not perish. Everlasting life would belong to everyone who trusts in him alone. A place in heaven is reserved for his own — for us. With his love as our motivation and this hope our energy, we can face whatever "distress" may come. That too shall pass. It is but temporary. Christ will return before it is too late.

vv. 26,27 — *"At that time men will see the Son of Man coming in clouds with great power and glory. And he will send his angels and gather his elect from the four winds, from the ends of the earth to the ends of the heavens."*

While false prophets hawk their wares, like Tetzel selling indulgences in order to appease consciences, Christ will come. While man goes about his daily routine of warring with his neighbor and with his spouse, while he continues being the self-centered creature that sin made him, the Lord will come. As in the days of Noah, man may indeed forecast the rain, but not the consequences. He knows that death will come, but he refuses to prepare himself to meet his Maker on the Maker's terms. So he bedecks himself with his philosophical platitudes and his fatalistic attitude of "Eat, drink and be merry; tomorrow we die." Some hug the tattered robe of what little righteousness they feel they can claim for themselves and then tell themselves that as long as they've "done their best," they'll get what they deserve. They're right. And they'll find out its full unpleasantness when Christ comes.

The Savior will make an appearance unmatched by anything Spielberg or DeMille could ever picture. As promised by the angels, the Son of Man will come as he left: visibly appearing in the clouds. It will be a sight beheld by all, even those who pierced him (Rev 1:7).

Some who rejected him will try to tell themselves, "This man cannot be the one we rejected. We rejected a baby born in a stable, a carpenter who had delusions of grandeur, a prophet who let things get out of control and died."

Others will say, "We pictured him as a man who meant well, a great religious leader on the order of Moses or Mohammed. But this . . . ." Their words will ring hollow in their ears even as they speak, for they will know as soon as they see him that this *is* he. He had been their only hope. Some never sought him. Some refused to listen to him. Some even used his name but changed his word. But all such truly rejected him. All those he will now reject before his Father in heaven. For them, it will be too late.

But when the Christian looks up, all doubt will be removed, all hope fulfilled, every prayer answered. The Son of God, who had humbled himself for our salvation, returns in all his power and glory. The angels will sweep the Christian from his feet to meet the Lord in the air. Judgment day will not be the frightening day he had feared it might be. Rather, it will be the day which will end all the fearful times he's ever had.

Tribulation will be left behind. All the time spent worrying about what tomorrow might bring will be over. He will laugh to think he had actually wanted to cling to temporal life a bit longer, to see his children grow up or to be with his wife a moment more. For he now knows that since Christ has come, he not only has all the time in the world to get to know his children better, he has all eternity.

Every believer from every corner of the earth, indeed from every age gone by, will be gathered by those angels. The Lord of life will give new life, eternal life to all his children. They will have glorified bodies and lives of joy unlike anything they've ever experienced, because **this** time the joy will not end.

This is something worth preparing for. God has been preparing for it since before the beginning. We had better spend some time preparing for it as well.

vv. 28,29 — *"Now learn this lesson from the fig tree: As soon as its twigs get tender and its leaves come out, you know that summer is near. Even so, when you see these things happening, you know that it is near, right at the door."*

Remember the purpose of a parable (cf. Mk 4:11,12). Our physical eyes can observe the signs of spring and summer such as the fig tree would show. Jesus now uses a parable (παραβολή — NIV "lesson") to teach the importance of using the eyes of faith, that type of sight which sees the signs of the times and responds to them. Never mind that some say the Christian has his head up in the clouds. Actually, the Christian lives each day looking to the clouds, but not like the Thessalonians who spent their time staring at the sky. The angels told the disciples to stop doing that on the Mount of Olives. There is work that needs to be done, they were reminded. That work still needs to be done, urgently. The Savior is near. A world needs his word. Jesus emphasizes our responsibility to that world in verse 29 when — after telling this brief parable — he verbally points to his followers with "so also **you** . . . " (οὕτως καὶ ὑμεῖς). We haven't a moment to lose!

The reference to Christ's being "right at the door" brings to mind two pictures: one positive, the other negative. A family has been waiting eagerly for the father to return home from work. He has the kind of job in which regular hours are unheard of. Still, it's his birthday. They've planned the party for a long time. They've been waiting for a long time. The littlest one keeps asking if Daddy is really coming tonight or not. Then mother makes the announcement: "Get ready, everyone! He's right at the door!" You can almost feel the excitement, the eager anticipation of a wonderfully happy time.

But I mentioned another picture, a negative one. Again, there's a group of people in a home, only they are not supposed to be there. The teenage son is having a party while his parents are gone for the weekend. The place is a mess. The music is wild. The glasses contain more than soda pop. And almost no one notices the sound of a car door slamming in front. Almost no one. The room goes quiet when one of the girls sitting at the front window cries out, "Hey, your dad's at the door!" You can almost feel the fear, the sudden panic of knowing that it is too late to escape. Which picture will fit our lives? Will we "learn this lesson from the fig tree"?

vv. 30,31 — *"I tell you the truth, this generation will certainly not pass away until all these things have happened. Heaven and earth will pass away, but my words will never pass away."*

The problem of past and future fulfillments again arises with Christ's promise concerning "this generation" (ἡ γενεὰ αὕτη). There are those who interpret this literally, identifying "all these things" as the destruction of Jerusalem. You are then dealing with the standard 40-year generation. Others, however, look at the "all" (πάντα) in "all these things" (ταῦτα πάντα) and ask how the concept of judgment day could possibly be considered missing. In understanding "all these things" as including not only the destruction of Jerusalem but also the tribulations of Christians through the ages, the signs of the end times, and the judgment, the reference to "this generation" has to be rethought. There is precedence in Scripture to interpret "generation" as being not people of the same age group, but people of the same mind (Ps 12:7; Jr 7:29; Lk 16:8).

There will always be those who know the name of Jesus but flat out reject him as their Lord and God. This is what many of the Jews did during his ministry and that of his apostles. "This generation" could thus refer to the Jewish race, the majority of whom still recognize the reality of Jesus without accepting him as God and Savior. They and others will still be voicing their self-confident rejection of Christ when he appears, the God and Judge of all.

The disciples' minds must have been reeling from this discourse on the last days. They were told that nearly everything they had thought unchangeable would change. The change from being "fishermen" to being "fishers of men" probably seemed minor to them in comparison to the universal changes and calamities described by Christ.

We, too, have been overwrought by a world which changes too fast for most of us. People we trusted have proven to be less than trustworthy. Jobs we thought we'd have for life have disappeared as the business packed up and moved out. Morals we grew up taking for granted are forgotten and scorned. Even our church is not untouched by change: different translations are read, new liturgies are sung, "the quick and the dead" has been replaced in our children's memory work, and so on.

If we attempt to anchor our trust upon such mutable things, we will find ourselves sorely disappointed. Jesus has said that heaven and earth will "pass away" (παρελεύσονται). The Greek literally means "to pass by, to progress." We have seen that all creation has been affected by sin, now it will be changed by God. The universe as we know it will pass away, and our Lord will make for us a new heaven and a new earth. But such a change for the sure Word is unnecessary. It is complete and perfect in itself.

So Jesus would have us trust in that which does not change: his Word. Oh, the world has tried to hide it, to pervert it, to subdue and even destroy it. But it has failed. The Word still endures. The heavens themselves will go through dramatic changes, but "your Word, O LORD, is eternal; it stands firm in the heavens" (Ps 119:89). Whether one says "whosoever believeth in him" or "whoever believes in him," the Word remains the same. The promises are just as sure. Our faith rests on an unshakable foundation: the Word of our Savior and God.

When he returns, may he find us faithfully holding to that Word and sharing it as well.

## Homiletical Suggestions

Being the second last Sunday in the Church Year, anticipation needs to be heightened for the coming climax of the New Testament era: the return of Christ. The Christian watches the news, discouraged by all the bad news he hears. He needs the encouragement that comes from knowing God is still in control, that all the events on the 6:00 o'clock Eyewitness Report are in accordance with God's plan for the world. In fact, the tribulations of life should be a reminder to the Christian, first of all, of the presence of sin in the world and in us, and then of the promises of Christ concerning our salvation and his return.

The nearness of the judgment is emphasized in the text when we are told that the Lord is "right at the door."

## The End Is Right Around The Corner

1. The prophecies point to it (vv. 24-29)
2. The Savior promises it (vv. 30,31)

Millennialists do much in interpreting the signs of the times — too much. With their fundamental overemphasis on literal interpretation of apocalyptic prophecies so prevalent now on Christian radio and TV shows, perhaps we'd do well to simply stress that — not unlike a parable — every sign has but one main message: "Be ready, judgment ahead." Signs may be helpful, but it is dangerous to stare at them when you're supposed to be driving.

## Keep Your Eyes On The Road To Eternity

1. Read the signs carefully (vv. 24,25,28-30)
2. But don't lose sight of the goal (vv. 26,27,31)

Even many Christians fear the thought of a day of judgment. We need to remember that Christ is coming to judge those who have rejected him and to save those whom he has adopted by faith. God has assured us that there is no condemnation for those who believe in the payment made by Christ on Calvary's cross. The joyful anticipation of the elect can be contrasted with the fatal apathy of the world. One would do well to stress the Christian's responsibility to spread the word, so that as many as possible may look forward to the judgment day with joy. The parts of this outline could be switched around, depending upon your desire to go "law/gospel" or "gospel/law/gospel."

## The Judgment: A Day Of Sorrow, A Day Of Joy

1. Work to avoid the sorrowful tragedy of the unbeliever (vv. 24-26,28-30)
2. Give thanks to God for the joyful gift of faith (vv. 26,27,31)

The last verse of this text could easily stand alone and give more than ample material for this part of the church year.

## No, All Things Do NOT Change (v. 31)

1. The whole universe needs a change
2. But not the Word of God (and it never will)

# LAST SUNDAY AFTER PENTECOST

## The Scriptures

> Old Testament — *Isaiah 51:4-6*
> Epistle — *Revelation 1:4b-8*
> Gospel — *John 18:33-37*

## The Text — John 18:33-37

Beginning with the 15th Sunday after Pentecost, all of the texts in this Gospel series are taken from Mark. The Gospel texts for the 24th through the 27th Sundays emphasize the Christian's sanctification — love for God and neighbor (Mk 12:28-34); complete trust in God and the stewardship of his gifts (Mk 12:41-44); the need for being firm in faith, aware and ready for judgment day (Mk 13:1-13 and 13:24-31).

For this Last Sunday after Pentecost the text is from John's Gospel. The emphasis here is not on the Christian's work or readiness for the last day but on the fact that Jesus' kingdom is from above, and that those who believe in him have a place in his kingdom. Traditionally the Sunday is known as "Christ the King Sunday." Jesus establishes his kingdom of grace through his suffering, death and resurrection. It was for this that he came into the world. In this world Jesus, the judge of all, is on trial. The Jews have handed Jesus over to Pontius Pilate and have brought their charges against him.

Having heard the accusations of the Jews against Jesus and their demand for his execution, the text continues:

v. 33 — *Pilate then went back inside the palace, summoned Jesus and asked him, "Are you the king of the Jews?"*

The chief priests and leaders of the Jews have already brought their false accusations against Jesus. They have accused him of "subverting our nation" claiming "to be Christ, a king" (Lk 23:2). Is Jesus a threat to Roman power in Palestine? Hardly! Pilate soon recognizes that the charges against Jesus are the result of jealousy on the part of the Jewish leaders (Mt 27:18) and that there is "no basis for a charge against him" (Jn 18:38).

Pilate enters the Praetorium, his official residence (the NIV translates it as "palace"). He summons Jesus for questioning. The aorist of the Greek verb φωνέω ("call") has here the meaning of "summoning someone." Jesus, the King of heaven and earth, is summoned by this earthly ruler for interrogation. Pilate asks Jesus, "Are you the king of the Jews?"

v. 34 — *"Is that your own idea," Jesus asked, "or did others talk to you about me?"*

Jesus is not challenging Pilate, but he is extending an invitation to him. "Are you saying this from yourself?" (Note the emphasis on the second person:' Ἀπὸ σεαυτοῦ σὺ ... λέγεις;) We assume that Pilate was not ignorant about Jesus. We assume that Pilate knew about Jesus' reputation as healer and preacher, just as did Herod (Lk 23:8). It was Pilate's responsibility as the Roman governor to know what was going on in Palestine. Jesus' question is not a challenge but, rather, an invitation. Jesus had extended similar invitations to others, including his disciples: "Who do people say the Son of Man is? . . . . Who do you say I am?" (Mt 16:13,15); to Martha, "Do you believe" that "I am resurrection and the life?" (Jn 11:25,26). Through this question, "Are you saying this from yourself?" Jesus is giving Pilate the opportunity to confess faith in him. Pilate, however, rejects this opportunity and this invitation.

v. 35 — *"Am I a Jew?" Pilate replied. "It was your people and your chief priests who handed you over to me. What is it you have done?"*

Pilate says, "Your own nation, Jesus, your own people handed you over to me." Scoffing at this invitation and opportunity to believe in Jesus, he rejects Jesus as a "Jew" and also rejects him as his own King and Savior.

Pilate's next question indicates that perhaps Jesus has done something of which Pilate was not aware. Pilate asks Jesus about his activities. Jesus' answer reveals the true nature of his kingdom.

v. 36 — *Jesus said, "My kingdom is not of this world. If it were, my servants would fight to prevent my arrest by the Jews. But now my kingdom is from another place."*

Jesus is a King, but his kingdom is not of this world. In a worldly kingdom the servants of that kingdom fight for their king and his kingdom. Jesus' servants are not fighting for him, however. The Greek verb for "fight," ἠγωνίζοντο, an imperfect middle, is used to indicate action which would customarily be expected to happen. Note also the term used for "servants" (οἱ ὑπηρέται). It was a term used of synagogue helpers (Lk 4:20); the attendants of pagan priests; John Mark as the helper of Paul and Barnabas (Ac 13:5); believers in general (1 Co 4:1); and used here as a king's retinue. Jesus does have servants. But just as Jesus and his kingdom are not of this world, neither are his servants. Furthermore, the weapons used by Jesus as King and by his servants are different from earthly weapons. There is, in fact, only one weapon: the word of truth. This fact is brought out as Pilate continues his interrogation.

v. 37 — *"You are a king, then!" said Pilate. Jesus answered, "You are right in saying I am a king. In fact, for this reason I was born, and for this I came into the world, to testify to the truth. Everyone on the side of truth listens to me."*

The Greek particle οὐκοῦν is formally argumentative and inferential: "So then you are a king are you?" Jesus answers in the affirmative. "You are saying (it), I am a king." But just as Jesus' kingdom is not of this world, so also Jesus' function as king does not serve a worldly purpose. Jesus states that he "was born" and "has come" into the world "to testify to the truth." The truth is that mankind is doomed without him. The truth is that only through faith in him can a person become a member of his heavenly and eternal kingdom. Everyone who has that truth in his heart by the power of the Holy Spirit (1 Co 12:3) hears Jesus' word and is a member and servant in Jesus' kingdom. It is only Jesus who is "the way and the truth and the life" (Jn 14:6).

### Homiletical Suggestions

The last Sunday of Pentecost is referred to as "Christ the King Sunday." During these last days of the existence of the kingdoms of this world it is important for believers to remember that Jesus' kingdom is not of this world. Jesus' kingdom is a heavenly kingdom, established for believers, his servants, by the truth. Thus God's Word, the truth, testifies to mankind's need for a Savior and to Jesus' fulfilling that need.

Emphasizing that Jesus' kingdom is from above, we will want to view different aspects of the establishment of that kingdom. Such a treatment could be handled as follows:

### Jesus' Kingdom Is From Above

1. Established by Jesus
   v. 36 — "my kingdom is from another place"
   v. 37 — "for this reason I was born, and for this I came into the world, to testify to the truth"
2. Established through the truth
   v. 37 — "You are right in saying I am a king. . . . I came . . . to testify to the truth"
3. Established for all
   v. 35 — "your people and your chief priests . . . handed you over to me"

376

v. 34 — "Is that your own idea [that Jesus is a king] . . . or did others talk to you about me?"
v. 36 — "my servants" [Jesus has servants, disciples, believers]
v. 37 — "Everyone on the side of truth listens to me"

Since Christ the King Sunday emphasizes that we are to take advantage now of hearing his word and believing in him, this text could also be outlined as follows:

## Jesus' Heavenly Kingdom Is Proclaimed In This World

1. It is a kingdom of truth (v. 37)
2. It is a kingdom of rejected by many (v. 35)
3. It is a kingdom accepted by faith (vv. 36,37)

## Jesus' Kingdom Is Established By His Truth

1. Truth extended to all (vv. 34,35,36)
2. Truth received by believers, his servants (v. 37)
3. Truth proclaimed by believers, his servants (v. 36)

In these days of Liberation Theology, when Christian church bodies everywhere are promoting a social gospel and contributing money to "combat racism" (World Council of Churches in Africa), even encouraging revolutionary movements in order to establish in this world an "egalitarian society" (Roman Catholics in Latin America), it becomes increasingly important to reemphasize the Lutheran principle of the Two Kingdoms, and that we must clearly distinguish between the two — the kingdoms of this world and the kingdom of Christ.

This principle the King himself enunciates so clearly as he stands on trial before an earthly ruler, Pontius Pilate:

## Christ's Kingdom Is Not Of This World

1. It is of spiritual origin (vv. 33-36)
2. It uses spiritual weapons (vv. 37,38)
3. It has a spiritual purpose (vv. 37,38)

377

# REFORMATION DAY

**The Scriptures**

Old Testament — *Jeremiah 31:31-34*
Epistle — *Romans 3:19-28*
Gospel — *John 8:31-36*

**The Text — John 8:31-36**

John 8:13 begins a section of verbal warfare between Jesus and some Jews, led by the Pharisees, on the temple grounds in Jerusalem. The controversy centered on the validity of Jesus' message and who had the backing of the Father. Not everyone, however, was antagonistic toward him, for "even as he spoke, many put their faith in him" (v. 30). It was to these people, "the Jews who had believed in him" (v. 31), that Jesus addressed the words of our text. In this section Jesus strongly emphasizes that true discipleship means persevering in his Word — all of it. It is easy enough to be superficially attracted to Jesus; genuine discipleship consists of much more — and yields many more blessings.

Before proceeding with the exposition, we might just as well tackle an issue that inevitably arises in connection with this section. Is there a transition within these verses from one group to another, from believers to unbelievers? A variety of commentators believe that either in v. 31, 33 or 37 the focus of attention shifts from believing to unbelieving Jews. Some find it difficult to believe that the believers in v. 30 could change from faith to opposition (v. 33), to verbal abuse (v. 48), to attempted murder (v. 59) in such a short time.

It seems best, however, to maintain just that, for the following reasons:

1) The perfect participle πεπιστευκότας (v. 31) should be construed, according to Robertson, as a past perfect: "had believed." The people in v. 30 "had believed" in Jesus, but by the end of the chapter it is evident that they no longer do.

2) The condition Jesus uses ("if you hold ... ") is one of probability (note the subjunctive). There is the lively hope, but by no means the certainty, that the people in v. 30 would hold to Jesus' word.

3) Thayer notes that John uses πιστεύω to represent various degrees of faith, from its beginnings up to full conviction. The former seems to fit well here.

4) Nowhere is there any indication in the text that there is supposed to be a transition from one group of people to another. The same persons are referred to throughout these verses.

All this does not mean that there is no transition here. The transition is one of attitude. Once the new believers discover that the essence of faith in Jesus involves deliverance from the bondage of sin, they lose their new-found faith and begin violently to oppose him. A similar transition from faith to unbelief occurs in John 6.

vv. 31,32 — *To the Jews who had believed him, Jesus said, "If you hold to my teaching, you are really my disciples. Then you will know the truth, and the truth will set you free."*

"Holding to Jesus' teaching" (μείνητε) implies both quality and quantity. Putting your faith in man-made teachings, human reason or scientific hypotheses that deviate from Scripture does not qualify as holding to Jesus' teaching. There is the ever-present threat today, just as in Luther's day, just as in Jesus' day, to include the teachings of man along with the teachings of Jesus.

Quantity is important as well. Bible study doesn't stop at confirmation (contrary to what 90% of our congregations seem to think!). Holding to Jesus' teaching means that we will "hear, read, mark, learn and inwardly digest" the Word of God on a regular, yes, daily basis. There is the very real danger that Christians today hold more to the values of our culture as expressed through the media than to God's Word.

Jesus' teaching (λόγος) includes everything he taught. More than mere intellectual acceptance of that teaching is required. Head knowledge must translate to trust, personal application, and a response of loving obedience (cf. Mt 7:21; Lk 11:28; Jas 1:22).

Beginning believers can fall away unless they become grounded in the Word. Those of us who have watched new converts and confirmands gradually stray back to the world are painfully aware of that possibility. When a raw recruit becomes so fixed in the Word of God that it becomes a way of life for him, then he is really a disciple of Jesus. God's Word becomes the governing force of his life.

When Jesus' word is in our hearts, Jesus is in our hearts. The written word always points us to the living Word. He is in us and we are in him. That is true discipleship! (Jn 15:7; 1 Jn 2:4). Discipleship, then, is a relationship of faith with Jesus. We live each day conscious of his presence within us.

To be grounded in Jesus' teaching means that we will also "know the truth" (v. 31). This transcends a merely intellectual knowledge of the truth. True disciples will know the truth from personal experience. As they put the word into practice they will find that it is valid, effective and in accordance with reality (Jn 7:17). Moreover, believers will experience the truth that Jesus keeps his promises in our lives in a very personal way. Ultimately, to know the truth is to know Jesus, for he is the truth (Jn 14:6).

That truth "will free" us (v. 31). When the truth of Christ (and therefore Christ) dwells in us richly, we are free. Although the exact nature of this freedom is not spelled out in this verse, it is evident from the following verses that Jesus is referring to freedom from the power of sin. Sin no longer dominates us. Now we live for God.

Freedom is not being able to do what we *want* to do. That is, in fact, bondage. Real freedom means that we are now able to do what we *ought* to do and *want* to do it. We are now free to live our lives as God originally intended.

Luther certainly was a living example of these words. Once he discovered the essence of Jesus' teaching, the gospel of justification by grace through faith, he knew the truth. And the truth set him free, free from the guilt of sin that haunted him for so much of his previous life.

But it is the truth and nothing but the truth that frees us. That is why it is so important to hold to Jesus' teaching and never let go. **Sola Scriptura!**

v. 33 — *They answered him, "We are Abraham's descendants and have never been slaves of anyone. How can you say that we shall be set free?"*

The Jews object, as they are wont to do, especially in John's Gospel. Although Jesus' words initially sounded pretty good and sparked the beginnings of faith, further elaboration as to the real intent of his mission halted the progress of faith dead in its tracks. "Slaves? Us? How can you say that? We are descendants of Abraham!"

Did the Jews refer to physical or spiritual slavery in their retort to Jesus? As usual, the commentators are split in their decision. The spiritual sense appears to have more in its favor. When any appeal is made to Abraham, it is usually with a spiritual inference. Moreover, Jesus seems to understand their objections in spiritual terms (vv. 37-39).

Their argument would then be, "We are in a unique religious standing. We know the one true God. We already have the truth. We are heirs of the covenant of Abraham. Children of Abraham are not slaves, but sons of God! (Ex 19:6). The heathen are the ones in bondage. They serve idols and are ignorant of the truth. But we don't. How can you say that we need to be set free?"

It is rather ironic that some of the more enlightened among the heathen recognized something that the Jews refused to admit: everyone is enslaved. Seneca, for example, once said, "Show me anyone who is not a slave. One is a slave to lust, another to avarice, a third to abomination, all alike to fear." There are many in our own congregations who are struggling with the domineering effects of sin as well.

Jesus goes on to declare the truth of the matter:

v. 34 — *Jesus replied, "I tell you the truth, everyone who sins is a slave to sin."*

The "I tell you the truth" (ἀμήν ἀμήν) of Jesus has the force of a superlative: "Know for a fact that what I am about to tell you is part of holding to my teaching and the truth, which constitute true discipleship." Jesus is claiming divine authority with these words.

And the statement is that the one committing sin is a slave to sin. The translation of the NIV technically takes Jesus' words farther than the Greek allows. The present participle (ποιῶν) indicates a continuing state of sinning, whereas the translation allows for a one-time occurence. But biblical teaching brings us to the same place anyhow. For the Bible shows that once a person sins, he is no longer free to serve God, only sin. In fact, he is now compelled to sin, because sin is personified as a harsh, domineering master that has a stranglehold on us. Every sin only serves to bind us tighter in its lock. And once we are slaves to sin, we cannot free ourselves.

In addition, there is the plain teaching of Jesus about inherited sin. We don't have to wait until we commit the first sin to be bound in slavery to sin. We are born that way (Jn 3:6). Jesus certainly implies that truth here. By nature, then, we cannot do anything *but* sin. And if that is the case, then we really aren't children of God, but slaves, outside the family household. The meaning of Jesus' words is plain: "Don't think that by birth you are automatically children of God merely because of your being descendants of Abraham. There is your sin to consider! Because you are born sinful, you are slaves to sin, and not children." In effect, Jesus erases the distinction between Jew and Gentile which the Jews were quick to draw. At least when it comes to sin, there is no difference, "for all have sinned and fall short of the glory of God" (Ro 3:23).

There are, of course, other chains that follow once sin enters the picture, e.g. death, hell, Satan, etc. Jesus zeros in on the root of all our woes — sin. Augustine once said that of all the bondages that exist, sin is the worst because we take it with us wherever we go.

Jesus continues with a warning:

v. 35 — *"Now a slave has no permanent place in the family, but a son belongs to it forever."*

Slaves may enjoy their master's house for a while, but they may be sold or kicked out at any time. There is no inheritance either. The special privileges which the Jewish nation enjoyed under the Old Covenant were coming to an end. They were in the house by virtue of being Abraham's descendants, but that did not automatically make them Abraham's true spiritual children, as they mistakenly assumed. Only those who have the *faith* of Abraham are members of the household of God, and true children. Only they shall be allowed to remain (cf. Ro 9:6-8; Ga 4:21-31).

Only a son is free, and there is only one person who is by nature a Son, free, and who has the capacity to free those enslaved by sin:

v. 36 — *"So if the Son sets you free, you will be free indeed."*

Jesus truly is the Son who belongs to the house forever. His whole being remains in a lasting and special relationship of Sonship with the Father. That being the case, he has the ability to open up the possibility of being freed — in fact, he alone has that ability. If the Son frees us, we are really free, free from the compulsion and bondage of sin, free to serve God as he originally intended us to do and as Jesus did. So freedom is not just liberation from the slavery of Gentile ignorance; Jesus offers real freedom, freedom for Jew and Gentile alike, freedom from the slavery of sin.

What is more, the inference is that we are not just freed. We are adopted as God's children and therefore heirs of all the blessings and privileges that come with being part of the family (Ga 4:4). That is freedom plus, "free indeed."

All this is ours through faith, holding on to Jesus' word. Through faith we receive complete forgiveness of our sins and resurrection power to live as true disciples, serving only our Father. How important, therefore, is this fundamental truth of the Reformation, "**Sola Scriptura!**" God's Word alone contains the gospel, "the power of God for the salvation of everyone who believes" (Ro 1:16).

## Homiletical Suggestions

It is assumed that the preacher will insert pertinent illustrations and quotes from Reformation history at appropriate points in the sermon.

What forms the intellectual and emotional diet of our people today? The media. Television, movies, songs, magazines, newspapers, novels — these are the things which we absorb every day. They push the culture which produces them. Humanism — as evidenced in evolution, the feminist movement (in its negative aspects), popular morality, and a host of other things — is making inroads into the churches of today. The values of society have become the overriding influence in the lives of many. How important that the Word of God *alone* remains the basis of our faith and life. Only by sticking to the Word are we really disciples, do we know the truth, and are we freed. This sermon can reemphasize the current relevance of one of the Reformation's cardinal truths — **Sola Scriptura**:

**Sola Scriptura — Stick To The Word!**

1.  For true discipleship (v. 31)
2.  For genuine truth (vv. 31,32)
3.  For real freedom (vv. 33-36)

We are living in an age when Lutherans are taking their Reformation blessings for granted. No matter how much pastors plead with their congregations, only a small minority involve themselves in Bible study. Real discipleship means that studying the Word does not end at confirmation. It is a life-long pursuit. Neglecting the Word can easily lead to a hollow form of Christianity; the shell is there, but nothing of any substance is inside. Therefore:

**Use It — Don't Lost It!**

1.  Treasure Jesus' Word (v. 31)
2.  Treasure Jesus' blessings (vv. 31-36)

The cry from many quarters today is for freedom: freedom from political oppression, racial freedom, the freedom of sexual equality. Our own society pushes for the individual freedom of self-expression. People fight for the freedom to choose their sexual lifestyles, to print pornography, to set their own standards of right and wrong. Some of these freedoms may be worthwhile goals, others are merely license to sin. All such striving for "freedom" apart from God is really self-delusion. To be free to do what you want is no freedom at all. It is slavery! We are our own worst masters! Real freedom, the source of all other freedoms, comes from Jesus. In this sermon the preacher can nail down what freedom truly consists of.

**Free At Last!**

1.  Freed by the word (vv. 31,32)
2.  Freed from slavery (vv. 33-36)
3.  Freed for service (v. 36)

# FESTIVAL OF HARVEST

## The Scriptures

Old Testament — *Deuteronomy 26:1-11*
Epistle — *2 Corinthians 9:6-15*
Gospel — *Matthew 13:24-30*

## The Text — Matthew 13:24-30

This text is used for the Festival of Harvest for all three series of the ILCW Lectionary. It is also the Gospel text for ILCW-A, Pentecost 9, as well as the historic Gospel for Epiphany 5.

The Festival of Harvest is not observed as often as it once was, and in many churches it is combined with the Festival of Thanksgiving. The texts for the Festival of Harvest are also suitable for the Festival of Thanksgiving.

v. 24 — *Jesus told them another parable: "The kingdom of heaven is like a man who sowed good seed in his field."*

This parable was told to help us understand the kingdom of heaven. What is the kingdom of heaven? The kingdom of heaven is Christ's kingdom of grace here on earth, consisting of his gracious rule in the hearts of all true believers.

The subject of "the kingdom" was one of the main themes of Jesus' teaching. He spoke of himself as a king (Mt 25:34; Jn 18:37). Nearly all of his parables began with the words, "The kingdom of heaven is like...."

First-century Jews had false notions about the kingdom. They expected it to be an earthly kingdom. Even the twelve disciples shared these false expectations, and only the Holy Spirit could dispel them from their minds.

There are at least five terms for Christ's kingdom which are used in the Bible. It is called: "the kingdom" (Mt 13:19; 25:34; Jas 2:5; Ac 20:25), the "kingdom of God" (Lk 4:43; 8:1; 9:2,62; Ac 1:3; 8:12; 14:22; etc.), the "kingdom of heaven" (Mt 3:2; 4:17; 5:3), "the kingdom of Christ and of God" (Eph 5:5). Jesus refers to it as "my kingdom" (Jn 18:36; Lk 22:30; 23:42).

The kingdom of Christ differs from the kingdoms of this world. It is not physical, but unseen and spiritual (Lk 17:21; Jn 6:15; Jn 18:36,37; Ro 14:17).

It is not marked by pomp and splendor, but by meekness and humility (Mt 18:1-4; 8:20; 11:29; 21:1-9; Lk 2:7: Jn 13:4,5; Php 2:5-8).

Membership in it is not by birth but by spiritual rebirth and entrance into it is by repentance and faith (Mt 3:2; 4:17; Jn 3:3,5; Ac 2:29; 2 Co 5:17; Tit 3:5; 1 Jn 5:1).

It is not temporal, but eternal (Lk 1:33; Eph 1:20,21; Php 2:10,11; Col 1:16,17; Da 4:3,34; 7:14).

The kingdom of God is not only in the future, but right now (Col 1:13; Mt 4:17; Mk 1:15; Mt 16:28; 28:18).

Its realm is not confined, but embraces the entire universe (Eph 1:20,21; Ps 2:7-9; Mal 1:11).

It is not ruled by force, but by love (Mt 5:43-45; 26:52-54; Jn 18:36; 2 Co 10:4; Rev 12:11).

According to Jesus' own explanation of this parable, the sower of the good seed is "the Son of Man,'" a term Jesus frequently used when referring to himself (e.g. Mt 8:20; 16:13; 26:64; Jn 6:53). Jesus himself sowed the good seed and still does through his redeemed servants, both lay and clergy.

The good seed are "the sons of the kingdom" (Mt 13:38), the people in whose hearts Jesus is reigning as Lord and Savior. They are "good" (καλὸν) seed, that is, useful, profitable, productive. They are good, not because they are carefully bred, but because they have a righteousness from God which comes through faith in Christ.

By the power of the gospel which proclaims the life, death and resurrection of the Savior, Jesus plants "sons of the kingdom," the heirs of eternal life, into the world. He plants them in the world to testify to the glory of his saving grace and to bring forth the fruits of righteousness to his glory.

vv. 25,26 — *"But while everyone was sleeping, his enemy came and sowed weeds among the wheat, and went away. When the wheat sprouted and formed heads, then the weeds also appeared."*

The enemy of the Sower of the good seed is the devil, as Jesus explains in v. 39. Since the Garden of Eden there has been enmity between Satan and the "Seed of the Woman" (Ge 3:15). Here the great conflict between Christ and Satan for the hearts and souls of men is illustrated. We note that this enemy works in the darkness, in a stealthy fashion at night, so no one will know that he has been there. Satan is the prince of darkness, who seeks to undermine the kingdom of Christ and opposes all that Christ does.

This cunning enemy sowed "weeds" (ζιζάνια) everywhere in the wheat field. The Greek word ζιζάνια is translated as "tares, weeds, darnel, thistles." It was apparently a weed that was very difficult to distinguish from true wheat until it had begun to mature and form heads. Then its true nature was recognized. In his explanation of this parable (v. 38) Jesus says that the weeds are the "sons of the evil one." These are unbelievers who reject the gracious rule of Christ in their hearts. They are unfruitful and useless seeds of Satan.

However, these weeds are not always easy for us to recognize. They may be hypocrites with a Christian appearance. The "weeds" include people who lead outwardly decent lives, utter pious phrases and may even hold church membership. In their hearts, however, they do not trust in Christ as their Savior. Christ does not rule in their hearts, but Satan. These "weeds" have a "form of godliness" but deny its power (2 Ti 3:5).

Ananias (Ac 5:3) and Judas Iscariot (Jn 6:70,71; 13:2; 13:27) were among them. Judas appeared to be a disciple and even managed to disguise his wickedness so completely that, even after a clear revelation from Christ, the others still did not know or believe who the betrayer was (Jn 13:21-30).

It is a grim fact that Satan does his best to undermine the work of Christ in the church. The planting of hypocrites destroys unity within the church, hinders its mission in the world and harms its witness to the world. Luther once said, "Wherever God builds the church, the devil builds a chapel."

Everyone who hears these words of Jesus and takes them to heart must ask himself, "Am I a hypocrite? There are hypocrites among the believers — am I one of them?" Here is an opportunity to examine our hearts to see if we are "good seed" — seed that is useful, profitable and fruitful.

vv. 27,28 — *"The owner's servants came to him and said, 'Sir, didn't you sow good seed in your field? Where then did the weeds come from?' 'An enemy did this,' he replied. The servants asked him, 'Do you want us to go and pull them up?' "*

When they noticed the weeds among the wheat, the owner's servants were distressed. They could not understand how the weeds got into the field of wheat. Was the seed which the owner planted contaminated?

The owner, who knows all things, knew how the weeds got there. It was the work of his enemy, who opposed all that he was trying to do and who was attempting to ruin the whole field.

The servants were eager to correct the situation. If they had their way, they would have marched through the field and pulled up every weed right then and there. But the master knew that such a plan would not be wise.

v. 29,30 — " 'No', he answered, 'because while you are pulling the weeds, you may root up the wheat with them. Let both grow together until the harvest.' "

The Lord answers with an emphatic "NO!" It would be foolish to try to pull the weeds at that point, because the servants would also surely uproot the good wheat. The only solution would be to let both grow until the time of the harvest.

The servants longed to set things right, but the Lord's main concern was not to get rid of the weeds as soon as possible. He would take care of them in due time. Rather his main concern was preserving the wheat. All of the wheat was important and precious to him, and he would allow no rash action of the servants to harm a wheat plant.

Until the harvest, both the wheat and the weeds would grow side by side. The plants would, at times, appear to be very similar, but they were actually quite different. How about us? Is it easy to see that we are wheat, or is it difficult for people to tell?

Why did the Lord permit both to grow side by side? There was another reason beside preventing the harm of the wheat. As Augustine says, "Those who today are weeds may tomorrow be grain." The hypocrites and unbelievers might yet repent, and the Lord, who desires the repentance of all people, will give them every opportunity to do so. Judas Iscariot once again provides an example of this. Already a year before his crucifixion, Jesus spoke of Judas' hypocrisy (Jn 6:70,71). Yet, Jesus did not uproot him then and there but continued to reach out to him with words of truth and love.

v. 30 — " 'At that time I will tell the harvesters: 'First collect the weeds and tie them in bundles to be burned, then gather the wheat and bring it into my barn.' "

Though the enemy had done a disastrous deed, the Lord was still in complete control. It was still "his kingdom" (v. 41). At the right time he would set things right. The time of harvest would surely come. At the time God has appointed for the end of all things, he will give his command, the wheat and weeds will be separated, and the valuable wheat will be gathered safely into the barn.

The sower of the good seed will also be the reaper. His servants, the angels, will carry out his wishes at the right time and in such a way that all the good wheat is preserved. At the same time all of the weeds, the unrepentant, will be eternally destroyed.

**Homiletical Suggestions**

There will be those who hear the words of this parable who are frustrated by the impurities in the visible church. They will be able by hearing this parable better to appreciate the way the Savior is dealing with this problem, out of love and concern for the good seed, and the desire to see even the weeds become useful. This parable will also help those who are involved in church discipline to do so in an evangelical manner.

Many Christians, especially zealous pastors, would like to remove all the tares from the congregation and purify the church on earth. The danger in this zeal, however, is to condemn and uproot weak Christians and even some strong Christians who stumble at times. However, Jesus makes it clear that he and his angels will do the separating, not we. This does not discourage evangelical church discipline but rather helps us to see that there will be a need for it until the end of time.

Sometimes the unchurched complain about all the hypocrites in the church as a reason why they stay away. In accord with Jesus' words, we can acknowledge that there are indeed hypocrites within the visible church, but that the Lord will take care of them in his own time.

Hymn 574 in *The Lutheran Hymnal* follows the ideas of this text very closely and would be an excellent hymn to use in a sermon illustration or to accompany the sermon.

In the sermon outlines that follow, the text is treated analytically. In all three, thoughts of the earthly harvest may serve to illustrate the spiritual truths which Jesus reveals in the text.

A theme suggested by the August 12, 1984, edition of **Meditations** is:

### It All Comes Out In The Harvest

1. So be patient as the plants grow

Patience is required for the wheat to reach full fruition. God is patient with us, sowing, watering, and fertilizing with the gospel so that we will be fruitful unto him. Likewise he is patient even with the weeds, granting them every opportunity to repent.

2. So observe the ways of the wise farmer

The wise farmer takes care not to damage the good plants. His main concern is for an abundant harvest of the wheat. Congregations and pastors likewise will learn from Christ to exercise church discipline with care and love.

3. So rejoice at the harvest of the wheat

All will be made right when the harvest comes. The troublesome weeds will be taken away, and the righteous will shine like the sun.

The following outline is simpler. It provides an opportunity to analyze the origin, character, and destiny of both the believers and unbelievers.

**Weeds and Wheat**

1. The weeds (their origin, character and destiny)
2. The wheat (their origin, character and destiny)

Finally, this outline once again emphasizes the harvest:

**The Harvest And The Heavenly Kingdom**

1. The fields contain good and bad.
2. The final harvest will gather the good and destroy the bad.